W9-CZZ-461

DATE DUE

DEC 1

WITHDRAWN

WITHDRAWN

ARISTOTLE'S PHILOSOPHY OF ACTION

ARISTOTLE'S PHILOSOPHY OF ACTION

David Charles

Cornell University Press
Ithaca, New York

© 1984 David Charles

All rights reserved. Except for brief quotations in a review,
this book, or parts thereof, must not be reproduced in any
form without permission in writing from the publisher.
For information address Cornell University Press,
124 Roberts Place, Ithaca, New York 14850

First published 1984 by Cornell University Press

International Standard Book Number 0–8014–1708–2
Library of Congress Catalog Card Number 83–73068

Printed in Great Britain

138485

Contents

Contents

5. *Rationality, Practical Knowledge and the Explanation of Action*

Appendixes

To my parents

Maurice and Elizabeth Charles

Preface

In the philosophy of action, Aristotle occupies a central position analogous to that of Frege in the philosophy of language. He initiated the philosophical discussion of issues concerning the ontology, analysis and explanation of intentional action, and his questions, assumptions and arguments yield a framework within which much contemporary work can be located and better understood. Since the Second World War there has been a renaissance of interest in these problems; not since classical times have they received such sustained study as in the writings of Elizabeth Anscombe, Donald Davidson, Alvin Goldman, David Pears and Georg Henrik von Wright. My main aim is to bring Aristotle's pioneering contribution into direct and detailed contact with contemporary work of this type and in this way to assess its continuing philosophical value.

While I was working as a graduate on problems in the theory of action, I was influenced by specific insights in Aristotle's account and subsequently by his perception that discussions of ontology, intentional action, irrationality and mental states should form parts of a unified explanatory theory. At the same time, I came to realise that there was a vacuum between scholarly exegesis and modern work inspired by a reading of Aristotle, and that this could only be filled by a philosophical examination of his actual contribution to the issues which still concern us. Thus, it is my hope that both the study of Aristotle and modern action theory will gain by seeing his account of the nature and antecedents of action in the perspective which they share.

My approach may be characterised primarily as that of philosophical scholarship. This aims to represent Aristotle's discussion as focused, where appropriate, on questions which also interest contemporary theorists, and to assess the philosophical significance of his answers by comparing them with solutions put forward today. Philosophical scholarship is inseparable from contemporary philosophy, and differs from it only in taking as its starting point the examination of a previous philosopher's picture and in not developing in detail answers which are distinct from those which he himself put forward or presupposed. The latter limitation has proved useful in investigating the overall theory to which Aristotle committed himself; for if it is mistaken even in his outline account, little could be gained by attempting to make it more specific.

Philosophical scholarship, as I conceive it, differs in aim and method from traditional classical scholarship, since its goal is not to study an ancient philosopher in isolation from contemporary interests and questions, nor to give an interpretation of particular passages (or sets of passages) 'unblinkered' by modern philosophical concepts, nor to assess only their consistency (or lack of it) without regard to truth, falsity or philosophical significance. But philosophical scholarship differs also from original speculation inspired by a reading of Aristotle because of its attention to Aristotelian terminology, the detail of its interpretation of particular passages and its determination to place individual issues within the framework of Aristotle's own general theory. The philosophical scholar seeks to use scholarly techniques for philosophical purposes and should not turn his back either on scholarship or contemporary philosophy.

Philosophical scholarship, traditional classical scholarship and theorising inspired by a reading of an ancient philosopher have different aims, and are best conceived not as irreconcilable opponents but as non-competitive alternative methods. On occasion, I have employed the third of these in this book, but have tried to mark the transition from philosophical scholarship openly and to classify the results differently. While the first product of philosophical scholarship is an interpretation of Aristotle's views, that of historically based original speculation is the development of an *Aristotelian* account, which may be more detailed or more conceptually sophisticated than Aristotle's own. Thus my discussion of processes 'one in some sense' (Chapter 1, Section B) and of intentional basic action (Chapter 2, Section D) is classified as Aristotelian rather than as Aristotle's, because, although it builds on his suggestions, it goes beyond what he himself actually constructed. The boundary between philosophical scholarship and the contemporary development of Aristotelian themes is sometimes difficult to discern in detail. It may be that elsewhere I have been led mistakenly (and despite scholarly scruple) to attribute my own deployment of certain views to Aristotle. Any such paragraph or section would not contribute to philosophical scholarship but to contemporary theorising (assisted by a reading of Aristotle) about the problems to which Aristotle addressed himself.

Since my aim is philosophical and not traditional classical scholarship, I have relegated some of the necessary detailed discussion of particular texts to notes and appendices and also divided the chapters into more and less exegetical sections. I have sought (in general) to retain and assess the philosophical point and value of Aristotle's views in the main text, without becoming enmeshed there in fine points of exegesis, so as to make them more accessible to those whose interest is exclusively in the philosophy of action. Since it has not been possible to effect a complete division of this type between the main text and notes, those who wish to avoid the rigorous but necessary course of detailed exegesis involved in the scholarly study of Aristotle should read primarily Chapter 1, Sections A and C, Chapter 2, Sections A, B and D, Chapter 3, Sections A, D and E, Chapter 4, Sections A, B, D and E and Chapter 5.

I have been helped and encouraged in writing this book by the advice and criticism of friends, colleagues and students. Hugh Lloyd-Jones and Colin Haycraft first suggested that I should write a book on Aristotle's philosophy of action, and I am most grateful for their continuing support and enthusiasm for the project over the intervening years. On issues concerning the philosophical interpretation of Aristotle, I have benefited from discussions with Julia Annas, David Ball, Jonathan Barnes, Lesley Brown, Norman Dahl, Troels Engberg-Pedersen, Robert Gay, Paula Gottlieb, Tom Hurka, Edward Hussey, Christopher Megone, Richard Parry, Dory Scaltsas, Pantazis Tselemanis, Kathleen Wilkes and over a long period with Gavin Lawrence. I have gained from discussions in the philosophy of mind and action with Michael Bratman, Zafra Cooper, Christopher Peacocke, Michael Smith, Paul Snowdon, Fred Stoutland, Barry Taylor, Stephen Williams, and over many years with Kathleen Lennon. I am indebted to Christ Church and to Oriel College for giving me the opportunity to undertake and complete this project, and to ten years of sceptical undergraduates from both colleges who consistently and rationally resisted their tutor's account of parts of Aristotle's *Ethics* (now set out in Chapters 2 A and C, 3 and 4 and Appendixes 2–3). I have learned considerably from those whose exegetical views on Aristotle I have criticised, and in particular from Anthony Kenny's series of articles and books on *acrasia* and practical reasoning. Donald Davidson's essays on the philosophy of action (now reprinted in *Actions and Events*) have been a constant source of insight into the scope and significance of the issues Aristotle discussed, and have offered the most systematic and instructive point of comparison with Aristotle's own account of ontology, action and rationality. My greatest intellectual debts, however, are to John Ackrill and David Pears; they first introduced me to the study of Aristotle, and their scholarly standards, attention to what is exegetically and philosophically important, and sympathetic encouragement have sustained me throughout.

Oriel College, Oxford   D.C.

Introduction

The philosophy of action may be defined by its three major components: ontology, analysis, and explanation. Ontological issues concern the identity of actions, their location and their relation to events, processes and states. Analytical questions focus on what is to count as an 'action', an 'intentional action', and a 'rational action', and thus on the possibility of irrational but intentional action (*acrasia*). Problems in explanation centre on the type (is it causal?) and relevant antecedents (are they psychological or physiological?) of the preferred theory. In this book I consider only questions within the philosophy of action (thus defined) and do not discuss Aristotle's positive views on determinism, responsibility, or substantive moral theory. The study of his philosophy of action may prove a prolegomenon to a consideration of these topics; but they lie outside the scope of the present project.

The ontological aspects of Aristotle's theory are the least explored, partly because he does not discuss them directly in the *Ethics*, *de Motu* or *de Anima*, and one has to look to the *Physics* for his major discussion of the related topic of processes (*kinêseis*). In Chapter 1, after examining his account of the identity and nature of processes, we are in a position to identify what is distinctive in his treatment, and to use it as a basis for his discussion of causation and explanation and, in subsequent chapters, of action and the relation of the mental and the physical. Chapter 2 considers Aristotle's use of this ontology to discuss the identity and location of actions, and represents it as an essential ingredient in his partially causal analysis of intentional action. Chapter 3 investigates Aristotle's analysis of *acrasia* and rational choice, while Chapter 4 places Aristotle's account of *acrasia* within the framework of his desire-based psychological explanatory theory of the failure of the acratic and the achievement of the practically wise. Chapter 5 examines Aristotle's treatment of the explanation of action, the interconnexion of mental and physical processes and the nature of the relevant psychological states.

The themes discussed in these chapters are fundamentally interconnected. Aristotle's ontology of action, his analysis of intentional action, and his account of *acrasia* and rationality all rest on his view of the appropriate explanation of human behaviour. Thus the success of his discussion of the questions raised in Chapters 1–4 depends on the possibility of an explanatory theory of the type considered in Chapter 5.

On specific issues, Aristotle's thought contains insights which challenge, or suggest alternatives to, certain strands of modern orthodoxy. His characteristic method of sifting out what is correct in apparently conflicting or partial positions yields, on several major issues, an attractive mid-position between the alternatives canvassed in modern discussion. Thus his ontology of processes, states, activities and actions offers identity conditions intermediate between the highly intensionalist proposal of Goldman or Kim and Davidson's extensionalist theory. The analysis he gives of intentional action contains a causal component, but this is represented as complementary to agent's knowledge and teleological (or rational) explanation, and not as their rival. His discussion of *acrasia* and rationality is a desire-based one, but he seeks to incorporate many of the insights which motivate intellectualist theories. Aristotle is a materialist, who maintains that psychological states and processes are causally explanatory, although he is neither an identity theorist nor a reductionist.

Aristotle's thought is also illuminating at a more abstract level. His discussions of ontological and analytical issues manifest his aim of representing actions, rationality and mental states as elements in a unified explanatory account of the nature and antecedents of behaviour. In pursuit of this goal, he introduces a wider range of considerations to support particular proposals than is common in contemporary discussion, and seeks to provide the basis for an integrated causal theory of the connexions between psychological states and actions. In these two respects, Aristotle's distinctive method and general theory speak directly to those now engaged in the philosophy of action.

Since I have attempted to present Aristotle's account of action as a unified whole, I have offered interpretations of several topics: e.g. teleological explanation, efficient and material causal modalities, which require separate and extended scholarly discussion. While I hope to discuss these claims further elsewhere, I have included them because of their theoretical significance within Aristotle's account of the ontology and nature of action. In my search for Aristotle's overall theory, I have adopted a method different from that of some traditional classical scholars, whose aim has been to demonstrate from individual passages of the text (considered in isolation from other texts on similar themes) what Aristotle 'had in mind' when writing it. Repeated difficulties in applying this approach (whose roots lie in the tradition of the philosophical commentary) suggest that many particular key passages can be interpreted in more than one way and that the best interpretation emerges only through considering Aristotle's associated doctrines and attempting to form a unified account of them all. Thus I have proceeded with three exegetical principles in formulating, for example, Aristotle's account of the ontology of processes and actions in Chapters 1 and 2.

(*a*) *Principle of consistency*: If a philosopher uses conceptual appar-

atus $c_1 \ldots c_n$ at one place in treating a given topic, and returns to
that, or to a related topic elsewhere, without any specification of
conceptual apparatus, attribute $c_1 \ldots c_n$, if further apparatus is required to make the treatment coherent, there is no explicit change of
doctrine, and there is no textual evidence incompatible with $c_1 \ldots c_n$
in the second context.

(b) *Principle of explanatory adequacy*: If a philosopher uses conceptual apparatus $c_1 \ldots c_n$ at one place in treating a given topic, and
returns to that or a related topic elsewhere, without any further specification of conceptual apparatus, then attribute $c_1 \ldots c_n$, if it explains
why certain issues were problematical for him (if they were so), and
why certain issues were unproblematical (if they were so).

(c) *Principle of charity*: If a philosopher uses conceptual apparatus
$c_1 \ldots c_n$ at one place in treating a given topic, and returns to that or
a related topic elsewhere, without any further specification of conceptual apparatus, then attribute $c_1 \ldots c_n$, if it allows the second discussion to present plausible philosophical theories and avoid invalid
arguments or other forms of obvious philosophical error.

These principles are motivated by assumptions in the general theory
of meaning of the type advanced by Davidson and subsequently modified by others working in the Davidsonian tradition. A view of interpretation derived from Davidson's theory of meaning motivates my
specific method and provides the basis for my preference for philosophical over traditional classical scholarship. Although some classical
scholars proceed as if the nature of their general task were clear ('to
find out what Aristotle intends in a particular passage by deductive
argument using that piece of text alone as a premiss without introducing any of one's own philosophical concepts or beliefs') their method
rests on being able to maintain a rigorous distinction between what
Aristotle 'had in mind' in a given context and those of his beliefs we
hold constant from elsewhere, and demands that we are able to keep
in abeyance all our own relevant beliefs in interpreting the utterances
of another. Their reliance on these traditional (and much criticised)
semantical concepts itself stands in need of fundamental justification.

Use of the principles of interpretation I have employed depends on
one's view of the respective dates of Aristotle's writings. I have assumed that *Physics* II–VII may assist the interpretation of passages
in the *Ethics* and *de Anima*, and that the so-called 'Common Books'
fall within the provenance of the *Nicomachean* rather than the *Eudemian Ethics*. These assumptions are controversial and I have not
sought to support them here by detailed argument.[1] However, when

---

[1] For some of my reservations concerning Anthony Kenny's recent proposal that the
Common Books fall within the provenance of the *Eudemian* and not the *Nicomachean
Ethics*, see Charles, 1979, pp. 224f; 1980, pp. 220f. But the issues are interesting and
complex, and require further study. See also Cooper, 1981, and Rowe, 1983.

an exegetical claim depends on the latter assumption, I have sought to note this and (where possible) support it internally from (e.g.) the Common Books, if these form the immediate context. (See, for example, the discussion of intentionality and acrasia: Chapter 3, Section B; Appendix 2). The attempt to represent *NE* III. 1–5, *NE/EE* V.8 and *NE/EE* VII.3 as internally consistent, if successful, supports the traditional dating assumptions on which I have proceeded.

My hope is that these principles of interpretation and the underlying method of seeking a unified theory of action in Aristotle's discussion will be justified by their scholarly and philosophical results.

CHAPTER ONE

Ontology and Explanation

A. The theory of processes

In *Physics* III, V and VII, Aristotle undertakes his most systematic discussion of processes (*kinêseis*), and seeks to develop a theory of their nature and identity. There are (at least) three desiderata for such a theory: that it yield an account of the following factors:

(a) *The nature of processes.* What kind of entities are they? Are they reducible to simpler ontological categories: e.g. properties, objects and times, or do they constitute a separate and irreducible ontological category?

(b) *The identity conditions of processes.* Since there can be no entity without identity conditions, an adequate theory must provide a general filling for the schema '$x = y$ (where x and y are processes) iff . . .' in which the biconditional is completed by conditions necessary and sufficient for the truth of the identity claim. It should, therefore, give grounds for or against the claim that the sentences (i) 'The grey turned blue', (ii) 'The sea grew warmer', (iii) 'The sea turned to Socrates' favourite colour' and (iv) 'The reflector of the sky turned blue' describe, or contain expressions which refer to, one process, if the grey sea, which reflects the sky, at a given time grew warmer and turned blue, which is Socrates' favourite colour.

(c) *The individuation of processes.* We sometimes ask 'How many processes of a given type occurred in a certain place between given times?' and thus seem to require a procedure for counting those processes, which enables us to specify where and when one process ends and another begins, and to distinguish which processes have occurred or are occurring.

There may be theories which meet only some of these desiderata: but they will be less complete than one which meets all of them, unless our initial expectations are misplaced because at least one of these questions cannot be given a systematic answer.

This conception of a theory of the nature and identity of processes owes much to Donald Davidson's discussion of events, but differs from it in being concerned exclusively with processes, and in not considering either activities or states. It is a substantial question whether (and in what way) an account of processes can be extended to activities and states (Section C). Davidson has shown that a theory of events exercises a pervasive influence on the account of efficient casuality, explanation, action and the relation of the mental and the physical. In Section D, I investigate whether Aristotle's discussion of processes in the *Physics* provides a basis for his account of efficient casuality and explanation. In subsequent chapters I examine his use of this ontology in discussing actions (Chapter 2) and the mind/body relation (Chapter 5). Together with his account of causation, his ontology provides a basis for his analysis and explanation of intentional action.

In this chapter, Sections B–C concern Aristotle's account of the identity and nature of processes, and the motivations which led him to adopt it. Section D considers his use of this ontology in discussing efficient causality and explanation. Only with this basis will we be in a position to examine Aristotle's ontology of actions in the *Ethics*, *de Motu* and *de Anima*. While he does not discuss these topics in detail in those works, he relies implicitly, I will argue, on an account of the type advanced in the *Physics*.

B.   Aristotle's account of the identity of processes

Aristotle's central discussion of the identity conditions of processes is in *Physics* III 1–3 and *Physics* V4. He summarises his conclusions thus: 227b21–228a2.

> A process is one in an unqualified sense when it is one essentially and numerically. The following discussion makes clear what sort of process is one in this way. There are three types of thing in connection with which we speak of processes: that which undergoes the process, the 'that in which' and the time: ... for every process occurs in time. Of these three, being one in genus or species depends on the 'that in which' the process occurs, being consecutive depends on the time, being one without qualification depends on all of them; for the 'that in which' the process occurs must be one and indivisible (i.e. the species), the when (i.e. the time) must be one and unintermittent, and what is moved must be one as the white (in the sense of pale) that blackens is one or Koriskos who walks is one – not in the accidental way in which Koriskos and the white may be one, nor just as one universal may be common to more than one particular object (for then two men might undergo exactly the same cure at the same time from the same disease: e.g. inflammation of the eye; but this is not one process except in species).

This explication of processes being one in an unqualified sense involves three distinct categories: the object which is moved, the medium in which the movement occurs and the time at which it occurs. If the process is one in this sense, the object moved must be one non-accidentally, the species and the genus of the movement which determine in what medium the movement occurs (e.g. space or quality) must be one, the species must be incapable of further division, and the time must be one and without intermission. That is:

$x = y$ in the unqualified sense (where x and y are processes) iff
(1) x and y involve the same object, which is one non-accidentally, and a particular not a universal;
(2) x and y are one in species and genus, and the species is incapable of further division;
(3) x and y occur at the same time, and occur without intermission.

Within (1) and (2), 'one non-accidentally' requires further elucidation, as does the reference to 'genus' and 'species incapable of further division'. It proves initially difficult to spell out these conditions in more detail through exegesis of the immediate context in the *Physics*.

Aristotle begins V4 by saying that movements are generically one if they are assigned to one category of movement, and exemplifies this by distinguishing locomotion and quality-alteration; elsewhere he adds quantity change (e.g. 226a23–25, 227b5–6) as a third genus of process. Not all Aristotle's genera are so wide-ranging: 'apprehending' is classified as a genus in 227b14, learning appears to be a genus relative to learning geometry, but a species relative to apprehension. Since apprehension is a genus relative to learning but a species relative to quality change, the genus/species distinction appears relativised to the specific comparison at issue. Thus we require a criterion of identity for those genera that are also species of more abstract genera.

More generally, we need to know under what conditions two processes are one in species, and a species itself incapable of further division (227b6–7).

In V4 Aristotle's answers to these questions are elusive and incomplete.

(a) Since he holds that all cases of whitening are one in species (227b8–11), it seems that whitenings, which begin at one type of colour (e.g. black) will be the same in species as those which begin at another (e.g. red), provided that both end at white (cf. 224b7–8). But elsewhere Aristotle seems to require that all processes one in species share the same type of beginning as well as end points (cf. 242b36–37), and so tightens the conditions mentioned in 227b8–11.

One suggestion would be that two colour transitions from different starting points represent species incapable of further division, although both are members of one common (more general) species: whitening. There is, however, no direct evidence for this reconciliation in 227b4–20.[1] Indeed, on one reading, 227b8–11 takes whitening as an example of a species incapable of further division.

---

[1] In 227b14–16 Aristotle does assume identity of starting as well as finishing points in his discussion. It is not clear, however, whether this addition is part of possible sufficient conditions for one *indivisible species* of movement, or of possible identity conditions of *movements one in number*.

(b) It is not clear in V 4 which differences in starting and end points constitute differences in species. If a quality change always results in a metal being hot and red, is turning hot a different species of change from turning red? In 227b7–8, Aristotle concentrates on changes in colour, and this might suggest that changes in temperature have separate end points. But he does not actually assert this, nor does he consider cases where turning hot and turning red are both effects of a common cause.

(c) It is even less clear what differences in manner of movement constitute difference in species. Thus, in 227b19–20 he writes, 'Or has it been decided that if the "in which" is different in species, there is a difference in movement – and that the circular is different in species from the straight?'[2]

Even if Aristotle accepts that the circular and the straight are different in species, he does not elucidate what differences in general constitute a difference in species. His account, therefore, neither determines whether, for example, walking, running or strolling (unmodified processes) are the same in species nor which modifiers (such as circular and straight) produce difference in species. In 228b25–30 he rules that differences in speed do not yield differences in species as they are applicable to all species of processes; but he does not say *which* differences not applicable to all species of movement determine separate species of movements.

There is, therefore, a central gap in Aristotle's account in V4: he tells us that processes are one in number only if they are identical in species incapable of further division, but does not say either what can count as *a species* (incapable of further division) of process or under what conditions *two such species are distinct*. Thus, statements such as 'a process is not one in the unqualified sense – even if there is one temporal stretch – if there is not one species true of the whole process' (228b7–9) are left radically unclear within this chapter.

Aristotle addresses himself to similar problems in VII 4, but fails to arrive at a substantial conclusion (249b11–14):

So we must find out how many species of alteration there are and how many of locomotion. If the changing things to which the processes belong

---

[2] Ross translates 'in which' as 'difference in path'. Either 'path' includes 'manner of transit' or it does not. If it does not, since an object (e.g. a top) may traverse the same path (i.e. same space/time points) in different manners (e.g. spinning or not spinning), this criterion will not separate all cases of 'straight' and 'circular' journeying. If 'path' does include manner (as Ross accepts, loc. cit.) then it loses its clear intuitive sense as it is not determined by the space/time points crossed. If so, it cannot be used as the basis of an account of species-difference in movement. Hence Pacius is correct to interpret 'or has it been decided' as a reference back to 227b6–11, and to construe 227b19–20 as resting on the earlier unexplained account of 'indivisible species' (Commentary, 273). If so, 'in which' means (as in the parallel passage in 227b27f.) 'the respect in which the movement occurs' and thus embraces species and genus within it.

essentially and not accidentally differ specifically, then their respective processes will also differ specifically; if generically, generically; if numerically, numerically.

This seems unhelpful: for we wanted to know whether walking, running or rolling are the same in species, and are told only that they differ if the essential subject of change differs. So are the walker and the runner different (in species) as essential subjects of change? While Aristotle elsewhere appears to regard the walker and the musical as different essential subjects of change (224a22), he does not in VII 4 offer even the beginning of a general method for distinguishing species of process. He writes (as in 227b19–20) 249a16–17:

If the lines (traversed) are specifically distinct, the locomotions also differ specifically from one another: for locomotion is specifically differentiated according to the specific differentiation of that over which it takes place.

But he does not determine what differences in general constitute a full account of specific difference in locomotion; for he continues (249a17–18):

(It is also apparently specifically differentiated) if the instrument by which the locomotion occurs is different: if the feet, walking; if wings, flying. But perhaps we should say that it is not so, but rather that locomotion is differentiated by the shape (of the paths).

To this, he has no answer (249a21):

So that we need now to consider how motion is differentiated. (see 27–29).

So we still do not know either whether running, walking, flying, rolling constitute different species of process (as perhaps in *NE* 1174a29f. and 201a18–19), or what specific differences in types of route yield difference in species.

Aristotle notes in VII 4 that there is a problem as to how his account of locomotions applies to quality changes (249b7–11):

If on the other hand the affection is different: e.g. becoming white and becoming healthy, there is no sameness, equality or likeness since difference in affections makes alterations different; and there is no unity of alteration any more than there would be a unity of locomotion under like conditions. So now we must find out how many species of alteration and locomotion there are.

But this passage also fails to determine which affections are relevant to the identity of processes or under what conditions two such affections are distinct. While Aristotle appears to hold that if a man (e.g. in recovering from jaundice) turns white and becomes healthy he undergoes two distinct alterations, he does not outline what in general determines the answer to this type of question (e.g. if two processes are universally concomitant).

While neither V 4 nor VII 4 resolve those problems, both contain passages which together with III 1–3 allow us to determine under what conditions two processes are, in Aristotle's theory, *the same in species* (incapable of further division) and what counts as *a species of process.* Thus *Physics* III, V and VII, taken together, yield a unified account of the nature and identity of processes. In III 3 (202b8ff.) Aristotle writes:

> There is nothing to prevent there being one actualisation of two poten-tialities (not the same in being, but as what is potentially F is to what is actually F); nor is it necessary for the teacher to learn not even if to act and to be acted on are the same – not, that is, the same in definition of their essence (e.g. as 'raiment' and 'dress' are the same), but rather as the road from Athens to Thebes is the same as the road from Thebes to Athens . . . For not all the same predicates belong to things which are in a way the same, but only to those which are the same in being. But indeed not even if teaching and learning were identical, would to learn be the same as to teach – any more than it follows from the fact that there is one distance between two things that to stretch from here to there and from there to here are the same. But, to generalise, teaching is not the same in the primary sense as learning, nor is acting as suffer-ing, but what they (sc. the teaching, the acting) belong to: the process (sc. is the same in this sense as the learning or the suffering); for the actualisation of *x* in *y* and the actualisation of *y* through the agency of *x* differ in definition.

In this passage, Aristotle contrasts what is one in definition of essence with what is one in a looser sense, and identifies the former with oneness in the 'primary sense' and 'oneness in being'. He explicates 'oneness in definition' by reference to the example of raiment and dress, which elsewhere (185b20; 103a25–27) are used as examples of the primary sense of identity. Objects are identical in this sense only if the terms which designate them are the same in definition: either synonyms or terms which designate objects with the same essence. If processes are one in the primary sense they must have the same essence or be designated by synonymous terms. If the terms which designate them are not the same in definition, two processes cannot be identical.

In V 4, a process is one in number only if it is one in essence – where this is defined by its species and genus. But the essence of each thing is what is defined when one says what it is to be that thing (1017b21–23). If so, processes are one in number only if the definitions of what it is to be that thing are identical. If the processes are not given one essential definition, they cannot be numerically identical. But processes will be given one essential definition if and only if the terms which specify their essence are the same in definition. Thus, it appears that Aristotle is adopting the following criterion of identity for processes:[3]

$x = y$ iff

(1) If 'P' specifies the essence of x and 'Q' specifies the essence of y, 'P' and 'Q' are the same in definition;
(2) ($\forall t$) (x is at t iff y is at t);
(3) ($\forall s$) (x involves s iff y involves s);
(4) x and y begin and end at the same points.
(where t are times and s substances)

It follows that in III 3 teaching and learning must be numerically distinct processes since they differ in essence. Thus by taking III 1–3 together with V 4 we arrive at the basis for an interpretation of Aristotle's theory of the identity of processes.[4]

This account is supported by a more detailed exegesis of III 3. Aristotle begins this chapter by holding:

(1) Every change occurs in the subject of change (i.e. the patient) (202a13–14);
(2) The agent's functioning is the same as (not different from) the patient's functioning (202a15–20);
(3) But is different from it in description (202a20–21).

---

[3] In this argument the following premisses are basic: (1) It is not possible that x is one in number and two in *ousia* and (2) it is not possible that x is one in *ousia* and two in the *logos* of what it is to be x, where x is a process, and the relevant senses of *ousia* and the *logos* of what it is to be that thing are as defined in V 4 and III 3.

(1) is directly supported by 227b21–2 if the 'and' is taken as epexegetic, and the phrase understood as 'one essentially', i.e. numerically' (as Pacius, op. cit., 398). Oneness in *ousia* and oneness as a particular are identified elsewhere in the *Physics*: 191a11f., 214a12; see also 228a5–10 where 'number' and *ousia* appear to be used interchangeably. However, (1) does not require an *identity* of number and *ousia* in 227b21–2. If *ousia* is explicated rather by genus and species alone (*pace* 228b11–13), a process cannot be one in number and two in *ousia* (227b27–28). In the present context being one in *ousia* is clearly not taken as identical with being one in underlying matter (1017b22–26), as there is no reference to that concept in 227b21ff. If so, premisses (1) and (2) are not challenged by cases where an object is one in underlying matter but different 'in being' (e.g. 312a18–20, a32–b3; 319b2–6; 320b4–6, 14–16), or one in number and 'two in being' (217a24–27; 1018a6–8) since in these cases oneness in number is explicated by reference to oneness in matter.

(2) does not require (in general) that if x is one in *ousia* it cannot be two in *logoi* (description) – for some *logoi* will specify only contingent (and not essential) properties of the relevant objects. Thus in 262a21 and 263b13, Aristotle gives *logoi* which specify contingent properties of points, while holding on to the connexion in (2) between oneness in *ousia* and being (263b8–9; see also 202a20–21). That is, the *logoi* in question in (2), in giving what it is to be that thing, are ones which give the species of the object. Hence, provided that teaching and learning are distinct species of processes, these processes must be numerically distinct (227b21ff.).

[4] I have profited greatly from discussion of these passages with Edward Hussey; he construes them somewhat differently. See his commentary on *Physics* III and IV (also Appendix 1).

He uses as support for (2) and (3) the distance analogy: there is the same distance between 2 and 1 as between 1 and 2, although the distance may be described as 2:1 or 1:2. Distances are identical if they share the same end points irrespective of how they are looked at. If teaching and learning share the same end points in this way, and Aristotle adopts the distance analogy throughout the chapter, teaching and learning must be identical. However, Aristotle immediately expresses doubt as to whether teaching and learning are identical (202a21–27):

> Perhaps it is necessary that there should be one actualisation of the agent and one of the patient. The one is acting upon and the other being acted upon, and the outcome of one is the product of action, and of the other the modification through being acted on. Since they are both processes, if they are different, what do they occur in? Either both are in what is acted on *or* acting upon occurs in the agent, and being acted upon in the patient (if this is also to be called 'acting', that word will be used with two senses.)

Here, he sees it as an argument for treating teaching and learning as distinct changes that they have different results and are the functionings of different capacities – with the assumption (202a25) that there is more than one change occurring. This argument would be compatible with the distance analogy for processes only if teaching and learning were distinct because they did not possess the same end points (independent of how they are looked at).

Aristotle is faced with a general problem (202a21): should he say that there are two distinct processes or one in these cases? He presents two arguments on each side:

Arguments against there being two processes in the patient (202a28–36):
(a) If teaching and learning are both in the patient, the realisation of each capacity will not occur in the object whose capacity it is (202a31–34).
(b) It is not possible that there should be two quality changes which end at the same point within the same object (202a34–36).

Arguments against the view that there is only one process (202a36–b5):
(c) It is not 'logical' that there should be one process which is the actualisation of two distinct capacities (202a36–b4).
(d) If they are identical, then all predicates true of one will be true of the other (b4–5).

He then proceeds to outline his reply to them (202b5–22):

(1) 202b6–8: rejection of (a): there is nothing strange about the actualisation of teaching occurring in the learner.

(2) 202b8–14: rejection of (c): there may be *one* actualisation of two capacities – provided that this sense of oneness is explicated by the oneness of what is potentially F and actually F and the road to and from Thebes. This oneness is not oneness in essence but oneness in some other sense.

(3) 202b14–19: rejection of (d): this only applies to processes which are the same in essence, and not those which are the same in the looser sense in which teaching and learning are identical. However, not even if teaching and learning were identical in the strict sense would to teach be the same as to learn – any more than it follows from the fact that there is one distance that the stretch A:B is the same as the stretch B:A.

But what of (b)? Aristotle does not appear to reject (b) explicitly within this passage. However, if he accepts (b), does he apply it to show that teaching and learning are distinct because their results are distinct (as in 202a24–25), or that they are identical because their end points are identical (as suggested in 202a34–36)?

Aristotle's answer to (d) envisages two distinct ways in which this proposition might be rejected:

(1) 202b14–16: teaching and learning are not essentially identical but one in some other way, viz. in which the road from Athens to Thebes is one with the road from Thebes to Athens. (1) is taken to apply directly to the actual case.

(2) 202b16–19: teaching and learning might be essentially identical, but it still would not follow that all predicates true of one were true of the other. In this way, one distance might be the same but to stretch from A to B and B to A be different.

(2), however, is a possibility that is not utilised in this particular case as the antecedent is false: teaching and learning are not essentially identical (202b14–16, 19–21).[5]

In the context of III 3, (2) is important; for initially Aristotle had held that (e.g.) teaching and learning were numerically identical (202a18–20) on the basis of the analogy with distance. Hence if, in 202b16–19, he assumes that in fact teaching and learning are not like (non-directional) distances, he is rejecting his initial (non-directional) distance analogy for processes and so giving up his earlier grounds for treating teaching and learning as numerically identical. Earlier, he had taken the essential properties of processes to be, like those of distances (and not stretches: 202b18–19), their boundaries, irrespective of how one looks at them. If this was the basis on which he had previously concluded that (e.g.) teaching and learning were identical,

[5] These lines create a difficulty for the extensionalist reading of III 3, which represents Aristotle as holding that: (a) $x = y$ iff x and y occur in the same substances and have the same boundaries (202a18–20, 35–36); (b) teaching and learning are numerically

and he now rejects this analogy, he requires a distinct account of the essential properties of processes, and thus of their numerical identity, in 202b14–21.

202b14–16 shows his answer through his analogy with roads: the road from Athens to Thebes ends at a different point from the road to Thebes from Athens since roads – unlike distances – have as their essential properties not just their boundaries, but also which is the beginning and which the end: 'the whence and the whither' (their direction, cf. *NE* 1174b4f.). Since teaching and learning are one in the same way as the roads are one, these processes cannot share the same beginning and end points. If so, they may be numerically distinct compatible with (b) 202a34–36; for (b) assumed that teaching and learning had the same end point, and this turns out to be false on the basis of the analogy used in 202b14–16. However, if the end points of teaching and learning are distinct (in the way suggested in 202a21–24), and processes differ in number if they differ in end point (242b37–39; 227b16–18), it follows that teaching and learning must be numerically distinct in this chapter.

This account of 202b14–19 explains Aristotle's conclusion in b19–22:

> But teaching is not the same in the primary sense with learning, nor is acting (the same in the strict sense) with suffering, but that to which these (sc. the teaching and the acting) belong (cf. 202b9–10): the process, is the same (sc. in the primary sense with the learning and the suffering); for the actualisation of x in y (viz. the teaching) is different in definition (sc. of essence: 202b12–13) from the actualisation of y under the agency of x (viz. the learning).[6]

---

one; (c) 'numerical identity' is equivalent to 'being one in some sense' and not equivalent to 'being one in essence'. If 202b16–19 were concerned with a sense of essentially one which is not numerically one, it would be a confusion on Aristotle's part to use the same example here as he employed in 202a20–21 for numerical identity: distance. Conversely, if 202b16–19 were concerned with the accidentally one, it would be exceptionally misleading for Aristotle to begin this sentence with a connective 'Not but what . . .' which suggests a strong contrast with the case of accidental oneness mentioned in the previous sentence (b14–16), and to begin the next sentence (b19–21) with 'but . . . not' ('*But* to generalise, teaching is *not* the same in the primary sense as learning'), which appears to *deny* the implication, carried in b16–19, that teaching and learning are identical in the *primary* and not the *accidental* sense. Thus it appears that in 202b16–19 Aristotle is concerned with what he regards as the *false* supposition that teaching and learning are essentially and numerically one because like non-directional distances they share the same boundaries. It is this supposition that he rejects in 202b19–22 and b14–16.

[6] This sentence might be translated differently: '. . . but that to which these processes belong (viz. the teaching, learning, acting, suffering), the process: is the same in the primary sense (viz. as itself).' I reject this translation because (a) it gives up the essential connection on which Aristotle elsewhere insists between the process and the suffering (202a14–16, b25–27), (b) it postulates a process which is non-directional (and non-relational) and thus conflicts with Aristotle's general view of the essence of processes as the realisations of goal-directed capacities (201a16–18: see below), (c) the grammar of 202b19–22 seems to require that the clause 'the process is the same in the primary sense' takes over both the notion of sameness in the primary sense from b20, and also the grammatical object with which it is the same in this sense: viz. the learning, suffering.

Teaching and learning are numerically distinct, but are one in some sense because the teaching 'belongs to' the learning which 'underlies it'. Because Aristotle identifies the process strictly with the learning (the capacity of the patient: see also 202a14–16, b25–27), there is no non-directional process which underlies both teaching and learning. The underlying process is the learning, and not a non-directional (non-relational) phenomenon because for Aristotle all processes are directional (1174b4–5), relational (200b28ff.) and the exercise of a given subject's goal-directed capacity (see below). Thus, Aristotle has clear grounds for rejecting the distance analogy, which he had previously entertained (202a20–21, b16–18), as this might allow for the possibility of one and the same non-directional process possessing two distinct contingent descriptions when two capacities are actualised. Further, since in Aristotle's account there can be no non-relational or non-directional process underlying the teaching and the learning, he must also reject the possibility of one and the same non-directional process underlying two distinct and separate processes of teaching and learning. Rather, the learning is the underlying process which stands to the teaching in a relation akin to that of matter to form, because the latter 'imprints' on the learner the knowledge which he had possessed previously only potentially (202a9–12).

If this analysis of *Physics* III 3 is correct, the chapter as a whole[7] supports the original interpretation of Aristotle's criterion of numerical identity for processes derived by taking III 3 together with V 4:

$x = y$ iff
(1) if 'P' specifies the essence of x and 'Q' specifies the essence of y, 'P' and 'Q' are the same in definition;
(2) $(\forall t)$ (x is at t iff y is at t);
(3) $(\forall s)$ (x involves s iff y involves s);
(4) x and y begin and end at the same points.

This criterion rests on an account of what it is to be *a species of process* (an element which determines the essence); for it does not itself determine what counts as a *process species*. We require to know what the relevant essences of processes actually are. The criterion,

---

[7] III 3 creates difficulties for three other possible construals of the relation of teaching and learning: (a) One underlying substance-like process and two contingent descriptions of this as teaching and learning. Aristotle rejects this when he rejects the distance analogy for processes (202b14–21), and takes teaching and learning as essential properties of processes (b14–16: see below). (b) One underlying substance-like process with one essential description (e.g. learning) and one contingent description (e.g. teaching). Aristotle rejects this when he treats teaching as the essential property of a process (202b14–21; cf. 201a18, 202a22–29). (c) One underlying substance-like process with two numerically distinct substance-like processes belonging to it. Aristotle rejects this in 202b19–21 by emphasising the essential connexion of the underlying process with the suffering/learning in accordance with his general account (cf. 202a14) of the nature of processes as realisations of goal directed capacities (201a15ff.).

also, fails to specify which substances are involved in a given change. And this depends for its further elucidation on the notion of the 'subject of change' introduced in V 4. So although it spells out the basis of Aristotle's account of the identity of processes, it remains incomplete in these two exegetically important respects.

These two issues appear related. In 249b12–14 Aristotle notes: 'If what is moved differs in species (i.e. what is moved essentially and non-accidentally) the movements too differ in species', and so places the burden of his account of difference of species on a view of what is moved essentially. This latter notion is evoked but not clarified in 224a28–30:

> There is something which is in motion . . . in virtue of itself being directly in motion. Here we have a thing that is essentially moveable, and that which is so is a different thing according to the particular varieties of movement; for instance it may be a thing capable of alteration, and within the sphere of alteration it is again a different thing according as it is capable of being restored to health or heated.

However it seems clear in this passage that what is essentially moved is that which is in itself capable of a certain type of movement. That which is musical (224a21ff.) walks accidentally, while that which is capable of walking walks essentially. Thus, Aristotle's account of difference in species in movement rests on his theory of different types of capacity; there are as many distinct species of movements as there are distinct relevant capacities possessed non-accidentally by subjects of change. This provides a major indication of Aristotle's view of the nature of processes, and is confirmed by his discussion elsewhere. In III 3, he writes:

> The actualisation . . . of what is potentially alterable, *qua* alterable, is alteration . . . of what can be carried along, locomotion. If what is buildable, *qua* buildable, is realised there is building. Similarly with learning, doctoring, rolling, leaping, ripening, ageing. (201a10–19 with gaps)

What is essentially altered is that which is capable of being altered; so what is essentially being built with is that which is capable of being built with. Similarly, in all cases where one movement of one substance alone is specified, what is essentially moved is that in the substance which is itself capable of being moved in that way.

Substances are subjects of change only if they are that of which the actualisation is primarily predicated (249a3: cf. 224a27f. and 201b2–3). This is primarily predicated of that whose capacities are exercised in the process; hence the white (in the sense of the pale) is that whose capacities are involved in changing colour, while it is Koriskos whose capacities are primarily involved in walking (227b32). He is the subject of, and thus a constituent in, the change because he is self-moved (as an agent: 253a15f.), and it is *qua* an *agent* that his capacities are exercised. Since changing colour is not an action, the essential subject is not an agent, and hence is represented as the pale and not Koriskos (see Chapter 2, Section D). Since there are as many essential subjects of change as there are relevant possessors of capacities, Koriskos and the pale must be distinct subjects of change because Koriskos and the pale have different capacities. Thus, the phrase 'the white Koriskos' does not itself denote one subject of change, but two – as there is no one subject of change which possesses the two capacities for walking and turning brown, exercised if Koriskos walks from A to B and turns brown in the sun. There are, therefore, as many subjects of change as there are essentially distinct possessors of the relevant capacities.

In V 4 Aristotle is concerned exclusively with (intransitive) changes which involve one subject of change: walking, turning blue (227b32). But his account is extended to the transitive processes of teaching and learning discussed in III 3. Since Aristotle takes the subject of change to be that whose capacities are exercised, S's teaching T describes a process in which S is the subject of change, and T's learning from S describes a process in which T is the subject; for the former involves S's capacity for teaching and the latter T's capacity for learning.[8] In the full account of a quality change in a patient induced by an outside agency, there will be two distinct subjects of change: the agent of one change, and the patient of another. Since the subjects of change are different, the processes of teaching and learning must be distinct. This is why Aristotle concludes (202b21–22):

> They are not identical in essence because one is the actualisation of A's capacity in B and the other is the actualisation of B's capacity under the agency of A.

Since the capacities for teaching and learning are different, they are actualised in different processes.

This interpretation yields clearer insight into Aristotle's view of processes: they are essentially the realisations of given capacities of given subjects. If the capacities involved are different in type or if the (essential) subjects are numerically different, the processes will be numerically distinct processes as they are realisations of distinct types of capacities in distinct subjects of change. Since teaching and learning are the realisations of distinct capacities of distinct subjects of change, they must be numerically distinct – as must be all cases of S's producing T and T's being produced by S.

---

[8] In medicine the doctor is the doer (195b19; 224a32–34), and the patient the moved (224a30). Similar distinctions are clear in the case of building (195b19). Quality changes in the patient are essentially identical with the exercise of the patient's capacities and identical in the looser sense with the exercise of the agent's capacities (202b20–22). As such, any given quality change is 'the actualisation of what can produce a given type of change' and the 'actualisation of what can be thus changed, as such' (202b26–28: referring back to 20–22).

This suggests the following improved interpretation of Aristotle's criterion of identity for processes:

$x = y$ iff
(1) x and y are realisations of the same capacity (type) for change;
(2) $(\forall t)$ (x is at t iff y is at t);
(3) $(\forall s)$ (s is x's essential subject of change iff s is y's essential subject of change);
(4) x and y begin and end at the same end points.

Clause (3) does not entail that the subjects of change involved be specified intensionally so that 'Koriskos walks' and 'The white walks' describe different processes. For one subject of change can be described as 'the white' or 'the musical' or 'the walker', and need not be described by its essential properties. Thus the sentences cited earlier, (i) 'The grey turned blue', and (iv) 'The reflector of the sky turned blue', would describe the same process if the grey (viz. sea) is the reflector of the sky. Aristotle employs similar machinery in discussing the end point of a process (224b18–20): if the sea turns blue and blue is the subject we are discussing, then the sea changes to the subject we are discussing. If so, (v) 'The sea changes to the subject we are discussing' describes the process of the grey's turning blue and gives an accidental property of that process, whose appropriate goal, the blue, is not essentially the same as what is being discussed by us. Hence, the other sentence cited earlier, (iii) 'The sea turned to Socrates' favourite colour' will describe the same process as that described by (i) and (iv); but only (i) will describe the process by its relevant essential properties as only it specifies the subject of change to which the relevant capacity (turning blue) essentially belongs and the proper goal of the relevant capacity, the blue.[9] The sea's turning warm will be a different process from the sea's turning blue (even if processes of these types always co-occur) provided that the relevant capacities are different and possess different goals, the blue and the warm.

Aristotelian processes are essentially realisations of given capacities of given subjects: their essential properties include the subject of the change and the end point of the type of change (i.e. its goal).[10] They are distinct if they do not share all essential properties. They may also possess accidental properties which belong to the subject or the end point of the change, but are not themselves features which constitute essential properties of the change, or affect its identity conditions.

Aristotle's theory, however, remains incomplete. It requires supple-

[9] For a different account, see Hartman, 1977, 151. Aristotle's use of the essential/accidental property distinction allows A's owning a car to be identical with A's owning a white car.
[10] Difference in intensional end-point in general spells difference in process: see Appendix 1.

mentation by an account of (1) what makes something a capacity to be moved (*or* to change) rather than to be a state or an object, and (2) what determines how many different capacities for movement or change a given organism actually possesses. Since he regards processes as the actualisations of dispositions (or capacities), he requires an account of what counts as *a* capacity to change and as *one* capacity to change. Particular processes are identical only if they share the same process-species; process-species are identical only if they are the realisation of the same type of disposition for change. So what is *a* disposition for change, and what counts as *one* (type of) disposition for change? Only if he provides the basis for answers to these questions is his account sufficiently complete to withstand philosophical comparison with modern theories (Section C).

Aristotle's answers to these questions are again elusive; but his account provides the basis for a general theory.

(1)   What is distinctive of capacities for processes?

In III 1 Aristotle envisages a special type of capacity: a potentiality to become F which he distinguishes from a potentiality to be F; hence the potentiality of bricks which is relevant to building is the potentiality to become a house and not the potentiality to be a house. What Aristotle claims is distinctive of this type of potentiality is that a substance will still have the potentiality to become a house while it is actually becoming a house. This is distinct from the potentiality to be a house; for, in Aristotle's view, when x is a house, it no longer has the potentiality to become a house – for one cannot in the future become what one already is (while one still is that thing) (201b10–13, b28–29; 202a1). Thus Aristotle assumes that there are two distinct potentialities which bricks have: to become a house and to be a house, and analyses the process of being built as the actualisation of the first potential and not the second (201a27–b5). In general, Aristotle classifies change as the actualisation of what has the potentiality to be changed, as such (201a11ff.), and notes of this potentiality that the subject of change will still possess it while it is being changed.[11] Thus

---

[11] In this I follow Ross. A schema for definition of processes might run: For any φ, if φ'ing is a process, then φx iff x has the potentiality for φ'ing and x's potentiality for φ'ing is being actualised. That is, x will have the potentiality for φ'ing at the same time as that potentiality is being actualised. Since this schema of definition appears to yield truth even if φ'ing is a state and not a process, what is distinct about processes is the type of potentiality whose exercise they are. The account rests on there being a distinctive form of potentiality involved. Kosman (1969) suggests a different schema of definition here: For any φ, if φ'ing is a process, then φx iff x has the potentiality to be a potential φ (the product of φ'ing) and that potentiality is an actuality. In this, motion is defined as the actuality of an object with a certain potential as that potential. Thus the buildable has the potential to be a house; change occurs when what has the potential to be potentially a house actually has (at a given time) this earlier potentiality: is actually the buildable. But it is not clear that *being actually the buildable* involves

he seeks to mark out processes by reference to the actualisation of certain types of dispositional properties.

This account of processes as the actualisation of certain capacities has been the subject of criticism since Aquinas on at least two scores. Either all actualisations are processes (in which case one has not defined processes reductively in terms of actualisations) or they are not. But if they are not, the relevant capacities are defined as dispositions to change; and then one has not reductively defined process either. Is the basis of Aristotle's account therefore mistaken?

Aristotle attempts to meet the first horn of the dilemma explicitly: actualisations are not confined to processes, but apply in other categories as well (200b26–28; 1046a2–3). He employs this distinction in characterising the difference between 'being potentially F' (bone) and 'being actually F' (193b2–9) where the actualisation is a substance or a state of substance, and not a process. Actualisations themselves are not a category because they cut across all categories (1024b12–16; 1046a2–3). If so, the reduction of processes to actualisations, times, substances and certain capacities of substances is (for Aristotle) a genuine reduction which relies on his general distinction into capacity and actualisation which is not specific to processes.

It might appear that Aristotle only escapes from the first horn of the dilemma to fall victim to the second. If processes are not distinguished by being actualisations, they must differ from (e.g.) states because of the types of capacity which are actualised. But if these are characterised as dispositions for change, the definition of change in terms of them might appear circular. Aristotle, on occasion, notes that the actualisation is prior to the potentiality: the relevant potentiality is one for a given type of actualisation (1049b10–15). Such potentialities are defined by their goals, and their goals are activities or actualisations of the appropriate kind (1050a21–24): processes. Is this circular and uninformative?

It is not as it stands formally circular as it characterises change by reference to a capacity to be changed. However, Aristotle's account is actually more informative than this, since his characterisation of the relevant type of capacity, 'the actualisation of what is potentially alterable in that respect in which it is potentially alterable' (201a12–

---

actual building; for bricks are actually the buildable before they are built with, since they possess the capacity to be built with (as opposed to some earlier state before they had been made into bricks). By analogy, one could be actually a potential chess champion without at that specific time actually playing chess (e.g. at the lunch break in a competition). But if so, the type of 'actuality' or 'full manifestation' Kosman envisages is one which is of precisely the type which occurs only when there is change. Therefore, since he gives no further specification of this type of actuality apart from his reference to change, his account fails to capture what distinguishes those actualities which are changes from those which are states or objects (e.g.: being actually a visible object: 426a24–26).

13), leaves a gap (*qua* potentially alterable) for a positive characterisation of the basis and nature of the relevant capacity (see 202b23–
26). In this he draws on an analogy with certain natural kind predicates (201a30–32): the actualisation of bronze, as such, is being bronze.
This definition marked by 'as such' could be filled in a way which
clarifies the nature of bronze. Aristotle rests here upon the possibility
of specifying those (essential) properties of bronze (e.g. possessing a
certain atomic structure) which, when realised, make the object
bronze. Natural kind terms are sometimes characterised by phrases
such as 'whatever has the essential properties that this has' where
'this' refers to a particular example of that natural kind, and the gap
is to be filled by scientific investigation of what the essential properties
of this object are, which – when discovered – yield an informative real
definition of (e.g.) bronze. Aristotle's proposal for processes is analogous: one characterises processes as the realisation of a type of capacity, whatever it is, which when realised gives a process. This
proposal rests on the assumption that there is a distinctive type of
capacity which is actualised in all cases of change, and which can be
uncovered by further investigation of the organisms in question. As
such it might be called *the natural kind theory of processes*: within it
processes form a distinctive set of phenomena with their own essential
properties.

Aristotle, in pursuing this strategy, needed to substantiate his claim
that there is a distinct set of properties which when actualised yield
processes (rather than states or substances), and that the properties
involved can be characterised within his general theory in a way
which distinguishes *these* capacities for change from other types of
potentiality.

Aristotle seems to have no doubt that a positive theory of this type
can be developed. Thus, in general, he treats a capacity as an origin-
ative source (1049b6–7): as that in virtue of which there is a change.
In the *Categories* (9a14–16) capacities are those states of an object in
virtue of which it is a runner or a boxer or healthy – where one has
a physical capacity to run or box by means of which one can run or
box easily or a physical capacity to be healthy in virtue of which one
is not easily affected by what befalls one. Elsewhere, Aristotle specifies
the physical capacity to be healthy as a 'given balance of hot and cold'
(246b5–6) – as a bodily condition (9b17) of the object. Similarly the
capacity to run or box will be a certain physical condition of the object:
that physical structure of the body by which we are able to walk. The
ability to learn is common to all men because their matter is of a
certain type (417a26–28) which is brought to a developed stage by
learning (417b12ff.). But he would regard the development of a general
theory as dependent on the *a posteriori* discovery of the special kind
of essential property in virtue of which (e.g.) the buildable can be used
in building, distinct from the categorical property which grounds the

capacity to be a house (201b10–14). And that was not his task in the
Physics. Thus, while his account rests on broadly empirical considerations, it cannot be refuted directly by the dilemma traditionally used
against it.

(2)   The individuation of capacities for change

If process-species were determined solely by the different capacities
realised, the most direct extension of the account of processes to the
question of process individuation for a type of animal would run as
follows: there are as many distinct species of process as there are
distinct capacities for change; there are as many distinct capacities for
change as there are distinct essential properties of the appropriate
type in this type of animal. Thus, when asked 'Is running the same
species of movement as walking (for humans)?' the relevant question
is: are these different movements dependent on the same or different
essentially specified capacities of that type of animal? There would be
as many different types of capacities for change as in the preferred
theory of the animals in question. Thus, for example, difference in the
muscles used, or in their physical condition when used, might show a
difference in what is used essentially and hence in species of movement. In this account, there would be as many capacities for change
as there are distinct categorical bases in the preferred theory of the
species. But at its most abstract level, Aristotle's account depends only
on individuating processes by their essential properties, which he
takes as grounded within a preferred theory of the internal nature of
the substances which are capable of movement. They are essentially
exemplifications of certain types of constitutive properties of substances. At this level, he is not committed to any view as to what the
results of the preferred theory will be (for that will depend on the
number of the relevant capacities discovered *a posteriori*: 249b11–14)
or indeed as to the general form of the preferred theory. The former
constitutes the most specific level of his theory and lies outside the
range of *a priori* study. Thus (in his account) it is not possible to
answer through theoretical speculation alone the questions 'How
many processes occurred?' or 'Is this process identical with that?'. The
resolution of these depends on detailed *a posteriori* investigation of
the organisms' capacities.[12] The situation is analogous to that of substances; if there are as many substances as distinct essential properties
of a given kind, it remains a problem for the special sciences to determine how many substances there actually are; for that involves dis-
covering how many distinct essential properties of the relevant kind

---

[12] This is analogous to Aristotle's approach to biological species. His concern as a
philosopher of biology is not fully to classify all the separate species he encounters (that
is the task of the *biologist*), but to provide general guidelines for a systematic classification (e.g. *Part.An.* I.6; *Hist. An.* I.1–6).

there are – and that task cannot be completed *a priori*. At its most abstract, Aristotle's theory individuates capacities for change only by reference to the preferred theory of the species in question. And this seems defensible at the present high level of generality.

Aristotle, however, does have clear ideas about the nature of the results of the best theory of a given organism: growing white and being cured would be different (249b8–10), as would increases in size and temperature, since the former is a quantity and the latter a quality change. His confidence in these results depends on his intermediate level of theory, which separates capacities for change (as the relevant internal structure) by reference to differences in the goals (249b5–12) and categorical bases of the relevant capacities (their *oikeia hulê*: 414a25–27). For a given organism, there would be two supporting routes to determine species of process by difference in capacity; the first by separating relevant categorical bases, the second by distinguishing the goals of the organism to which the capacity is directed. Teleological theory makes demands on the account of categorical bases for the dispositions involved; within a given organism, there are as many relevant categorical differences as there are distinct goals to be achieved (within the preferred theory of the organism). Each capacity would be distinguished by (i) the goals of the organism at which it is directed, and (ii) its categorical basis in the organism. Two capacities are identical (for an organism) only if they have the same goal and the same categorical basis. In the simplest theory of this type for a given organism difference in goal spells difference in categorical basis (*Part. An.* 683a18–26).

Aristotle's theory however is more complex and applies across different organisms. Breathing is the same species of process in men and fish (645b5ff.) as the intake of air has a similar role (665a13–16) in the two organisms. Thus the same process-species may have different specific physical categorical bases (lungs, gills) in different organisms, although both bases must be of the appropriate type to ground capacities for processes and play the same functional role in the two cases. Aristotle may have believed that there was a more general level of physical description in which the categorical basis for breathing in men and fish was the same (see Chapter 5, Section B). But this is peripheral to his theory; for even if this were not so, breathing would still be the same process-type provided that the capacity to breathe plays the same structural role in the organisms (e.g. to maintain circulation). Thus, if there is to be identity of species of process in two organisms of this type, their goals must remain constant although their physico-chemical basis may vary within the (physical) type of basis appropriate for processes. There may be variable realisation of the capacity to breathe across different organisms in Aristotle's theory, provided that the capacity is realised by an appropriate categorical base with the same functional role in the differing organisms. For

Aristotle, some processes are *functional natural kinds*[13] with an underlying essence determined by the identity of goals for capacities in different organisms, although their respective categorical bases (which may vary) must be appropriate to ground capacities for processes. (Aristotle's preference for individuating some process-types functionally is at a more abstract level of theory than his particular teleological theory: see Section C).

Aristotle's detailed account of capacities and goals is complex. He distinguishes conditional and unconditional,[14] causal and non-causal capacities.[15] He also separates natural and non-natural realisations of capacities.[16] Not every process aims at a goal of the organism as then

---

[13] Aristotle's classification of natural kinds (192b22ff.) is not restricted to non-functional natural kinds provided that the relevant objects possess an internal origin of the appropriate type.

[14] An object's *unconditional capacities* are those which always belong to the subject of change, without addition, subtraction or change being required in the subject to allow their exercise, to which there are no internal obstacles in the subject and which can be exercised under all conditions. Its *conditional capacities* produce certain effects under given external conditions: (e.g.) in the absence of external hindrances. These capacities are conditional since the agent, constituted as he is, cannot exercise them except in certain circumstances: (e.g.) when an appropriate object is present and in a certain state (1048a16–21). Aristotle uses the conditions of exercise to specify the relevant capacity: a given object has the capacity to – if certain antecedent conditions obtain – produce certain results or be changed in certain ways (1048a16–21). Thus Aristotle unconditionally ascribes conditional capacities to the agent or patient in question. A subject has a conditional capacity only if no change is required in it for a given process to occur at a certain time, and nothing in it prevents the actualisation of such a process under those conditions. Thus any conditional capacity will have a categorical basis in the organism, which is actualised under given conditions. In such cases, there will be as many capacities as there are unimpeded actualisations; each such capacity will possess a distinct categorical base which grounds the ability to φ (if unimpeded) (see 1048a16–18). The other conditional capacities it possesses, e.g. to ψ if partially impeded, will be realisations of the same capacity under differing circumstances: if something impedes its ability to φ (see: on health, 1152b35–36; 1154b18–19). This explains why difference in speed will not constitute a different species of actualisations (228b25f.) precisely because there is only one type of categorical basis involved in such cases realised in different ways under different conditions (see 281a15–20). It also maintains the connexion between goal and categorical basis, while allowing that not all processes are directed towards the (unimpeded) goal of the capacity.

[15] Causal potentialities are a type of conditional capacity: the capacity to effect a given change in another object in certain conditions (1048a8–10, 15–20). If these potentialities too are defined by their categorical bases and goals, there will be as many causal capacities as there are distinct results produced under maximally favourable conditions and distinct categorical bases in the organisms which are agents (281a18–20). See Chapter 2, Section B for further discussion of causal potentialities.

[16] All Aristotelian processes involving x are *either* the exercise of x's capacities (either in x or in another object z) *or* the consequence of the exercise of another object (z's) capacities on x. The latter category is divided: some of x's processes under the influence of z will be actualisations of x's natural capacities under z's agency; others will be contrary to x's natural capacities if x – as properly constituted – obstructs the operation of z's causal capacities (1049a8–10). x's non-natural processes will be ones in which no goal of x's (as then constituted) is achieved – although some of these processes will achieve a goal of z's which influences x's development (255a24–29, b30ff.).

constituted. Some are changes induced in one organism by another contrary to its natural goals, others are the particular realisations of a capacity which in other (more favourable) circumstances aims at a given goal. Thus his theory of capacities and goals does not demand that each *particular* realisation of a capacity is goal-directed, provided that the capacity is itself goal-directed and, given optimal circumstances, leads to the relevant goal. Since goal-directness enters with type of capacity, all particular processes may be realisations of capacities without all being goal-directed. Thus, if a subject inadvertently kicks a stone sideways while walking, the particular process of kicking this stone will be the exercise of S's (general) goal-directed (causal) capacity for moving heavy objects with his foot; but this particular process need not itself (in this instance) aim at any goal of S's in causing this unnatural (upwards) movement of the stone.[17]

Two capacities are identical at this level of theory intra-species if and only if (1) they achieve the same goal for the organism under favourable conditions, and (2) the categorical basis (its *oikeia hulê*: cf. 414a25–27) in the organism when achieving that goal in those conditions is the same. Inter-species capacities are identical if and only if they achieve the same goal for the different organisms and possess the basis appropriate for processes. Within his preferred theory of capacities there are as many goals (in the sense specified) as there are categorical bases in a given organism with relevant antecedent causes.

Aristotle's proposal for the general form of the preferred scientific theory (for a given type of organism) is one in which the number of types of capacities is determined by the number of its teleological goals and relevant material bases. This constitutes the basis of the intermediate level of his theory: in it processes are essentially realisations of capacities with given goals and types of categorical bases. His theory at this level can be refuted neither by noting that not all particular processes are goal-directed nor by emphasising the possibility of variable realisation across different species of organism.

Since difference in capacity yields difference in species (249b11–14),

---

[17] Contrast Sarah Waterlow's treatment of such cases (1982(a), 127ff.). She assumes that (for Aristotle in III 1–3) each particular process realises a goal of the organism, and hence concludes that he cannot accommodate (within III 1–3) incomplete, inadvertent or non-natural processes. But in III 1–3 goal-directedness enters with capacities (202a22–26; cf. 201a10ff.), and does not require that *each* manifestation of each capacity itself be goal-directed, provided that the capacity itself is goal-directed (see 281a10–24: note 13). The unity of a process depends on the unity of the capacity realised, even though it fails to achieve (on a given occasion) its characteristic goals (compare Waterlow, op. cit., 136).

In general, I am sceptical as to the radical break Dr Waterlow discerns between *Physics* III, (V) and VII (or VIII), as the same concepts (subject of change, species of process, goal of change: 236a11–13) are employed with apparent cross-reference (242b35–42) and seem to form the unified theory indicated in V 4. But her account rests on further interesting arguments which I have not attempted to meet here.

there will be (at least) as many different species of process as there are different capacities. But are there also at most as many differences in species as there are differences in capacities exercised? Is walking in a circle different in species from walking in a straight line, because – although the subject of change is the same in type – the route is different in type (249a15–17)? Or is difference in type of route not a species of process but a contingent property of a species?

It appears that in the case of locomotion (at least) Aristotle envisages a further condition on species of process, namely that (249a16–17) 'the type of route followed be different in species', where this difference in species is determined by difference in types of route in the best theory of the subject matter. If so, his intermediate level of theory of species of process seems to have two ingredients required to answer the issues raised in V 4, identity of capacity and type of route. But what types of route are there? Are differences between species of route in walking straight and in a circle determined by the distinct geometry of the line (but if so, *which* geometric differences are relevant?) or because different capacities are exercised? If a tenor sings one piece of music low melodiously but high harshly, is there one type of route (one 'line' of notes) or two if there are two capacities exercised (in the higher and lower range)? Aristotle does not resolve these issues. It would be 'of a piece' with his reliance on capacity individuation to mark as relevant differences in route only those dependent on difference in capacity; but he does not explicitly embrace this option, and so does not determine fully his intermediate level of theory. There remains a lacuna as to how types of routes are to be individuated.

If species of process share type of capacity and route they will be given the same definition in Aristotle's theory; of these the former is the most important. If they share species, they will possess the same type of beginning and end point (242b35–37); so this condition may be included in identity of species, as the species will determine the relevant beginning and end points. It is an open empirical matter which species of processes are in fact identical in the preferred scientific theory of a given organism of this type (see Section C).

This account of the species of processes allows us to formulate Aristotle's criterion of numerical identity as follows:

$x = y$ iff
(1) x's and y's species of process are identical;
(2) $(\forall t)$ (x is at t iff y is at t);
(3) $(\forall s)$ (s is x's essential subject of change iff s is y's essential subject of change).

If there is one process (in number), it can be the realisation of no more than one capacity; for if the capacities had been distinct, the species and number of processes would also have differed (cf. 202b1–2). If more than one capacity is exercised at a given time, there must be (at least) two actualisations and, since processes are the actualisations of such capacities, (at least) two processes. Thus, since the capacities for teaching and learning are distinct both in goal and in material basis, particular cases of teaching and learning in III 3 must be distinct processes. Aristotle's insistence that there are two different capacities realised in this episode described in III 3 ensures that teaching and learning are distinct processes.[18] This criterion of identity provides the basis both for the philosophical appraisal of Aristotle's account and for his treatment of actions.

There are three further features relevant to Aristotle's ontology of processes: two of these are raised by III 3:

(1) If S teaches T, and T learns from S, where does the teaching occur: in S or in T?

(2) If S's teaching T and T's learning from S are not identical, what account is to be given of their relation?

(3) In 1174a29–34, Aristotle introduces the part-whole relation to account for certain relations between processes: what is this relation and does it apply to Aristotle's account of teaching and learning in the *Physics*?

(1) is discussed in the next Chapter; (2) and (3) are of more immediate significance.

(2)   What is the relation of S's teaching T to T's learning from S?

Aristotle in III 3 regards S's teaching T and T's learning from S as 'one in some sense or another' (202b15–16). T's learning from S is identical with the process (b20–21) and S's teaching T 'belongs' to the process. Hence S's teaching T 'belongs to' T's learning from S. But this is no advance until the appropriate sense of 'belonging' is characterised.

---

[18] This argument rests on the following premisses:

P   (1) Two processes are numerically identical only if they share essential properties.

P   (2) One essential property of teaching is that it is the exercise of the capacity to teach (see 202b5–7, 19–21).

P   (3) One essential property of learning is that it is the exercise of the capacity to learn (see 201a18).

2,3:   (4) The essential properties of teaching and learning are distinct (as they realise different capacities 201a10, 16–18; 202b23–25).

1,2,3:   (5) Teaching and learning are (numerically) distinct.

The *natural kind view of processes* expressed by premisses (1)–(3) supports the three independent exegetical arguments advanced above for the conclusion that teaching and learning are distinct processes in III 3; for it explains the significance of their difference in goal, capacity and subject of change (202b10–13, 16–21).

Within the chapter, however, Aristotle gives two significant indications as to how the relation is to be characterised. In 202b9–10 he writes: 'The actualisation of the capacities is one in the way that what is potentially F stands to (is one with) what is actually F.' But what is potentially F stands to what is actually F as matter to form, within Aristotle's framework (193a36–b2); what is potentially F is the matter from which what is actually F is constituted (193b6–8: 200b25–27). Since in 202b19–21 the underlying process is taken to be numerically identical with the learning, this stands to the teaching as 'matter to form'. Several distinct processes may be 'one in some sense', if there is one process which stands to these as 'matter to form'. Learning is identical with the (underlying) process, while teaching is not identical but belongs to it (202b19–21, 26–27).

Aristotle introduces the 'matter/form' analogy in the *Physics* by example: it is the relation of letters to syllables, material to manufactured items, parts to wholes, and hypotheses (premisses) to conclusions (195a16–19, 198b5f.). In the first of these examples the occurrence of certain letters,[19] in certain conditions, materially necessitates the occurrence of certain syllables. (The logical form of this type of explanation is further discussed in Section D.) The underlying process stands to the other processes as matter to form only if it is sufficient for their presence under certain conditions. In some cases (but not all: cf. 198b5) it will also be true that the occurrence of certain syllables necessitates the occurrence of certain letters, but this type of necessitation is not material causation; for it is part of the definition of these syllables that they are enmattered in these letters, but not part of the definition of these letters that they occur in these syllables.[20] While it is true that these letters could occur without being in these syllables, it is not true that these syllables could occur without these letters. The letters are the matter from which the syllables are comprised, but the syllables are not the matter from which the letters are composed. Thus, the letters are the material cause of the syllables in a way in which the syllables are not the material cause of the letters. The relation in question is asymmetric.

Let us define the notion of an Aristotelian underlying process as follows:

z is an underlying process relative to y iff
(1) ($\forall t$) (z is at t iff y is at t);
(2) ($\forall s$) (z is in s iff y is in s);
(3) z and y begin and end at the same extensionally specified points;

---

[19] *Post. An.* 94a24ff.: if ϕ obtains, then it is necessary that ψ obtains (see Barnes, Commentary, 215f.). A fuller examination of processes which are 'the same but different in essence' is given in Appendix 1. That these processes are numerically distinct provides a further argument for the theory of process-individuation here attributed to Aristotle.

[20] Aristotle in general requires that this mode of necessitation follows the direction of definition: 98b21–25 (see 78a26–b10).

(4) the occurrence of z in C materially necessitates the occurrence of y;

(where t are times and s substances)

This learning, with its causal antecedents (C), materially necessitates this teaching; given those conditions, this teaching could not occur without this learning. With this definition of an underlying process, we may define a relation 'R' which obtains between z and y:

zRy iff

(1) z and y share the same underlying process

provided that we allow z to possess itself as its underlying process.[21] 'R' thus defined, is transitive, reflexive and symmetrical, but it is not identity, since this teaching is not identical with this learning. All relations of this type are equivalence relations; hence 'R' defines an equivalence class whose members in this case are z and y. Thus Aristotle's notion of 'one in some sense or other' is, in fact, an equivalence relation other than – but close to – identity. If x and y stand in an equivalence relation, as Aristotle states, it is not in general true that:

xR$y \rightarrow (\forall F)\ (Fx$ iff $Fy)$

in contrast to his account of identity in which

$x = y \rightarrow (\forall F)\ (Fx$ iff $Fy)$

(202b14–16).

If so, using modern logical terminology, processes which are the 'same but different in essence' are non-identical members of one equivalence class: they are simultaneous, occur in the same substances and share one and the same underlying process.[22] This relation, therefore, is to be distinguished from a third item in Aristotle's ontological framework:

(3)   Unitariness

This obtains when consecutive and distinctive parts, which are themselves separate processes, together constitute one numerically

---

[21] If we allow z to possess itself as its own underlying process, processes which stand in the relation 'R' will at least be members of the same equivalence class. Some will also be numerically identical. This marks a departure from Aristotle's procedure if he construed numerical identity and oneness in some sense as mutually exclusive. However, it appears natural to regard processes which are numerically identical as also being one in some sense. Further, the equivalence class formulation gives a clear sense in which the looser sense of oneness approximates to identity; for identity is one type of transitive, reflexive and symmetrical relation. (z posseses itself as its own underlying process; self-possession requires neither a set of external conditions nor a distinct underlying process.)

[22] I will call the equivalence class formulation Aristotelian, rather than Aristotle's: see Introduction.

identical process. Within such a process the separate parts are distinct, and not the same (in any sense), although there is one process of which they are parts (1174a29–34). The parts are consecutive or successive, although they are parts of one continuous movement.[23]

Aristotle's account of processes has these three distinct elements. Together they form the basis of his ontology of actions and of the relation of mental and physical processes. But does his account withstand philosophical scrutiny?

C.   Aristotle's ontological theory: aims and levels

Aristotle's theory has several distinct levels. Some are more important and better motivated than others; the latter may be rejected without giving up the whole theory. His account (as a whole) offers an interesting alternative to those put forward in modern writings on the related topic of events. In comparing it with that proposed by Donald Davidson, on the one hand, and the alternative canvassed by Alvin Goldman (and held in a modified form by Jaegwom Kim, N. L. Wilson and Barry Taylor) we see some of its motivations, strengths and difficulties.

Aristotle's theory has two major aims:

(i) To give an explanation of what processes are in terms of their constituents: properties, substances, times and a property (actualisation,[24] which he employs in separate contexts), and thus to avoid introducing processes as a fundamental ontological category, which cannot be understood on the basis of separate and more basic ontological categories. Aristotle's metaphysics aims at providing an explanatory ontological theory in which derived categories are explained in terms of a world consisting of substances and properties.

(ii) To treat processes as seriously in his ontological theory as material objects by giving an account of their essential and contingent properties, where the essential properties are those described in the

---

[23] Since teaching and learning are simultaneous (and occur in the same place at the same time 202a6–7; 226b21–22), this part/whole relation cannot be used to clarify cases of 'same . . . but different in essence' (contrast F. D. Miller Jnr.'s suggestion: 1973). Three facets of Aristotle's ontology need to be separated: (1) numerical identity, (2) equivalence relation, (3) part-whole relation. If one assimilates (1) to (2), it appears that in *Physics* III 3 Aristotle has surrendered Leibniz's Law as a criterion of identity for processes (N. P. White, 1971, 194) and is confusing the two senses of oneness which he seeks carefully to separate in 202b5–22. If one assimilates (2) and (3) one allows Aristotle a clear sense of numerical identity, but construes teaching and learning as processes which are 'temporally distinct parts of one process' – in contradistinction to his treatment of processes which are *the same but different in essence* elsewhere (see Appendix 1).

[24] See 221b12; 232a12; 202a4–6. Remaining still is the privation of what is capable of movement: the non-actualisation of a capacity. Privation, like actualisation, cuts across categories and hence is not itself a category.

best theory of the nature of the relevant entities. Essential properties of this type allow him to give identity and individuation conditions for processes which are context-free, and depend on his account of the relevant dispositions in the substances concerned.

Discussion of the second aspect of Aristotle's theory leads to, and rests on, his account of the nature of processes.

Aristotle's treatment of the identity and individuation conditions for processes offers an intermediate position between that occupied by Davidson and Goldman. Aristotle took the identity conditions of processes to depend on those process–properties (e.g. running) which were part of the best theory of the organisms in question, and used his account of dispositions and goals to give what counted as the best theory. Thus, there will be as many processes as there are relevant properties in the best theory of the organism (Individuation condition). Two processes are identical only if the relevant properties are treated as identical in the best theory of the organism: if they are actualisations of the same capacity (with the same goals) along the same type of route (Identity condition).

Aristotle's account is, in this respect, closer to that developed by Goldman but differs from it in two important respects:

(1) Within the latter's formulation, there are as many different processes as there are non-synonymous process-predicates, but no detailed conditions are placed on what is to count as a process-property.[25] Hence 'Xenophon journeyed to the sea' will describe a different process from 'Xenophon marched to the sea', as 'journeying' and 'marching' are non-synonymous process-predicates. For Aristotle, by contrast, these sentences would describe the same process if there was only one relevant capacity realised on this occasion. Similarly if Xenophon's march was his strolling to the sea, Goldman would detect two different processes, but Aristotle only one (provided that there was only one disposition realised). In these cases, Aristotle's would yield the same result as the more ontologically parsimonious Davidsonian theory;

[25] Kim distinguishes as constitutive properties of events those properties which enter into lawlike regularities in a preferred scientific theory: 'the entities that enter into causal relations . . . and are the object of explanation' (1976, 169). But if so, Marching and Journeying will be distinct constitutive properties, as the explanation of why Xenophon journeyed to the sea (to escape the Great King) will be different from the explanation of why he marched to the sea (e.g. there were no other available means of transport). Kim would also distinguish Xenophon's march from his slow march (stroll) on similar grounds (op. cit., 169), and both from his march in the park (if the explanations differed). Aristotle's theory differs from Kim's in his conception of the preferred theory (involving goal and categorical basis) which discerns one process in these cases because there is one capacity realised with several descriptions true of it. (Compare the strategy rejected by Kim: 1976, 169–70. D. W. D. Owen contrasts these two accounts in an as yet unpublished paper, 'Kim's theory of events.')

and this seems to correspond to our commonsense reflection that there is only one occurrence in the case described.

(2) Within Goldman's formulation there are as many processes as there are predicates specifying processes in a language. The reference to language is ineliminable because states of affairs include intensions for primitive predicates of L. But this appears to have paradoxical consequences: if Xenophon marched and journeyed to the sea, he would do two actions relative to a language (e.g. English) where 'marching' and 'journeying' are distinct primitive predicates, but only one relative to a language in which there was only one primitive predicate relevant to what occurred. This degree of relativity to language does little to satisfy the intuition that events or processes are occurrences in the world, independent of the means we have for describing them in different languages. For Aristotle, by contrast, there are as many processes as there are realisations of relevant capacities, and these are distinguished not in terms of the expressive power of the language in which the object is described, but through the best explanatory theory of the organism in question. Hence, there will be the same number of processes actually occurring even if in one language (e.g. Welsh) there are more process-terms than in another (e.g. English). In Aristotle's view, processes are entities in the world not dependent for their identity on the range of predicates in a given language.

In this way Aristotle represents processes as particulars in the world independent of our linguistic resources by means of an account of which properties are, and which are not, process-properties (as specified by the best theory of the organism in question). Thus not all properties (apparently of the correct type) exemplified by an object at a time are process-properties since some (e.g. journeying) may be contingent properties of processes constituted by genuine process-properties marked out as realised dispositions in Aristotle's theory.

While Aristotle's account differs in these respects from that proposed by Goldman (and in a modified form by Kim) his disagreements with Davidson's proposal are more fundamental.

(1) Davidson gives as identity conditions for events:

$e_1 = e_2$ iff
($\forall f$) (f causes e_1 iff f causes e_2)
($\forall g$) (e_1 causes g iff e_2 causes g).

Davidson is not committed to any view of essential properties of events, and hence does not give an account of identity across possible worlds. But this seems a weakness in his account, for we seem to talk (in counterfactuals) of a particular event (this very event) possibly having different causes and effects. Thus we may say of the death of Kennedy: this very death could have been caused by a different bullet or bullets fired by a different assassin for different motives. Indeed, there is a possible world in which it was caused by the Mafia backed by the Cubans, and another in which it was caused by the CIA backed by the Mafia. If in all these situations we are concerned with the very same event, we require a criterion of identity that will carry across contexts of this type. For Aristotle, it is possible that Kennedy's death had different causes, since all that is necessary is that it was an actualisation of a given capacity of Kennedy's at a given time. This is because his particular processes have essential properties (subject of change, capacity actualised, time) which allow him to use them in modal and epistemic contexts where we may need to make sense of the very same process occurring in different counterfactual situations.[26]

But perhaps this use is mistaken. If causal connexions constitute event identity, perhaps it makes no sense to talk of this very event (but only of one much like it) occurring in different causal sequences. That is, it might be objected, the First World War (that very event) could not really have been caused by a different assassin slaying the Crown Prince at that place and time perhaps for a slightly different motive. Although the war would have been exactly like the war that actually occurred it would not have been *that* war if its causes were different.

This intuition is not one that Aristotle would share, since he sees a looser connexion between causation and event identity; for him the latter is determined by a different type of explanatory theory dependent on the realisation of a substance's dispositions. Hence he would see no conceptual difficulty in two distinct events (*a, b*) (i) having no cause and one shared effect, or (ii) one shared cause and no effects, or (iii) neither being caused nor having any effects, provided that *a* and *b* realise different capacities of different substances, or the same capacities at different times. The apparent possibility of these cases seems to support Aristotle's account of process identity, as it strengthens the modal intuition that the very same event (e.g. the First World War) could have had different causes and thus puts the burden of argument on those who seek to deny it. They also constitute examples where Aristotle's account of process-identity is more intensionalist than Davidson's because it sees different processes where there would be only one extensional event.

(2) Davidson regards events as an independent category of objects which is not reducible to other categories, but he is not optimistic about the possibility of giving ways of counting events in answer to questions such as 'How many changes/events occurred in the test-tube

[26] See (e.g.) 32a18–20, 1134b29–31, 1140a34ff. A full investigation of Aristotle's use of this ontology in modal, explanatory and epistemic contexts (e.g. *de Caelo* I.11–12; *de Interpretatione* 8–9) lies outside the present study. Some of these issues are discussed in Sarah Waterlow: 1982(b).

after the liquid was inserted?', except relative to descriptions we employ of the events that occur. Indeed since he offers no essential descriptions true of processes, answers to these questions can only be relative to the descriptions chosen: there is no absolute answer. Aristotle's position is different: processess, for him, are essentially realisations of different dispositions with distinct categorical bases and goals, as marked out in the preferred theory. This conception determines answers to questions such as 'When did a given process begin and end?' in terms of when a given disposition (thus individuated) began and finished being actualised. It may be difficult in practice to find answers to such questions; but there are absolute answers which follow from Aristotle's conception of processes, e.g. as many occur as there are relevant dispositions realised (perhaps, by relevant types of route).

These distinctive features of Aristotle's theory of the identity of processes arise because he represents processes essentially as the actualisations of certain capacities of given substances. In this Aristotle – in common with Kim and Goldman – is seeking to explain the nature of processes in terms of simpler ontological categories and is not introducing events as a separate irreducible and unexplained ontological category to stand alongside substances.

Is this aspect of his theory well motivated or are there grounds for preferring to treat processes or events as an irreducible ontological category in Davidson's style? There is no incompatibility between seeing sentences such as (i) 'Xenophon's march to the sea in 400 was successful' as containing a referring expression denoting an event (or process) and seeing that process itself as being a complex which consists of Xenophon's realisation of his capacity to walk at a given time. That is, (i) may be represented as

(i) $(\exists \eta)$ $(\eta$ is an event & $(\exists ! t)$ $((t$ is in 400 B.C.) & $(\eta$ is $<$INT MARCH-TO (Xenophon, the sea, $t) >$ & successful $(\eta))))$

in which the event is represented as the complex described by the sentence:

(ii) 'Xenophon marched to the sea exactly once in 400 B.C.'

But perhaps it is better to treat processes as irreducible because the alternatives are objectionable in detail: they involve too much set theory, or introduce unanalysed primitive motions. Or perhaps any attempt to explain the nature of processes in Aristotle's way is unmotivated. Let us take these points separately, as they constitute a challenge to the most abstract level of his theory. If it were to fail at this point, little could be salvaged from the intermediate or lower levels of his account.

Aristotle is not committed to the use of set theory to characterise processes (unlike Goldman). While Aristotle's processes may be identified or referred to by means of sets of the type specified, they are not themselves sets. They are (at the intermediate level) actualisations of given dispositions, which when actualised yield the process-properties which are members of the sets described by Goldman. Aristotle is not content to allow processes to be specified in terms of certain special types of property: process-properties, exemplified by certain substances; from his viewpoint, it would seem uninformative to characterise processes in this way. Thus he does not define processes as ordered triples of the set-theoretic type suggested by Goldman, Kim and Taylor, but rather represents them essentially as properties being exemplified by given substances, and characterises the relevant properties as those exemplified only when the substance's dispositions of a given type are realised. He shares (at the abstract level of his theory) the motivations which led Goldman and Kim to explain processes in terms of simpler categories; but at the intermediate level he differs from them by seeking to say what the relevant properties are, and how they are exemplified, by reference to the actualisation of a substance's dispositions. Thus his theory cannot be attacked on the grounds that it involves essentially too much set theory in defining processes; for it involves none. It is (at this level) as defensible as the notion of realised disposition (see below).

But why should we seek to represent processes at the most abstract level (as within Aristotle's metaphysics) as substances exemplifying given properties, and thus to explain their nature in terms of simpler categories? Is it well motivated to aim at a theory of the nature of processes which explains what type of entity they are, and how they differ from other entities.[27]

Aristotle's discussion of the differences between activities, processes and states provides a partial answer to this question and distinguishes it further from Davidson's account of events as an irreducible category.

Davidson's proposal does not distinguish (categorially) between processes and activities. If these are separated, it is because they are different descriptions which may be true of the same events; as such, Davidson's proposal does not reflect a difference in entity between them.

Aristotle's discussion of processes and activities is quite distinct: they form mutually exclusive classes of entity, since there is a test which all activities pass and all processes fail. This test may be represented grammatically as follows:

(1) For all activity verbs, every period within the period of application of that activity verb is itself a period of application of that verb.

---

[27] P. F. Strawson has emphasised the need for an explanatory metaphysical account of the nature of processes in terms of simpler categories: see 1959, 45ff.; 1974, 204ff.

Taking 'A(s,t)' as 't is the period of S's A'ing', then
A(s,t) → (∀t') (t' is a period included within t → A(s,t'))

(2) For all process verbs, no period within the period of application of that verb is itself a period of application of that verb.

Reading 'Pr(s,t)' as 't is the period of S's Pr'ing,' then
Pr(s,t) → (∀t') (t' is a period included within t→ *not* Pr (s,t'))[28]

Thus, in the case of a process, 'S has φ'ed' is applicable only when S has ceased φ'ing; conversely, in the case of activities 'S has ψ'ed' may be true at a given moment and Sψ at that moment and continue to do so thereafter. Hence each process is 'incomplete', while no activity is 'incomplete'.

That activities and processes form distinct classes follows directly from the framework Aristotle advanced. Activities and processes have different goals as revealed by the tense-test: the goal of an activity is present in the activity throughout, while that of the process is at the end of the process (1048b20–24). Since difference in goal of this type necessitates difference in actualisation and capacity, there can be no process which is identical with an activity.

A process is essentially 'from *a* to *b*' – where *b* refers to the goal for the sake of which the process occurs. Activities, by contrast, are not essentially directed toward the attainment of a further goal; hence, while they may occur from *a* to *b*, this is a contingent and not essential property of them. Since difference in essence compels difference in number, no activity can be identical in number with any process.

This difference will apply even when activities and processes co-occur. Take the case of a spectator who enjoys listening to a symphony which consists in four movements. It is plausible to say of him that 'he cannot have enjoyed listening to the symphony' until the symphony is completed, and hence to conclude that it is not possible that he may *have* enjoyed listening to the symphony and continue thereafter listening to it. But if enjoying is the same occurrence as listening, it appears that 'enjoying' cannot be (after all) an activity-verb, as it does not pass (in this case) the tense-test as set out in the *Metaphysics*: and

---

[28] In this analysis of activity and process, I follow J. L. Ackrill (1965, 123). However, the present argument requires only that activities and processes form distinct classes and does not depend on the exact analysis of these terms. My formulation owes much to Taylor's work on tense (1974, 1977). He notes that state-verbs can be distinguished from both activity and process verbs as they lack continuous tenses in standard English. Thus state-verbs may be represented (roughly) as, 'S(s,t) → (Per(t) iff (∀t') (Moments (t') t' is included in t → S(s,t'))'. For further details see Taylor 1977. The implied distinction between state and activity verbs rests on the Aristotelian distinction between moments and periods on which he relies in analysing Zeno's paradoxes. The full development of Aristotle's account of states lies outside the present project.

so Aristotle's paradigm example of an activity fails his favoured test for being an activity.[29] But within Aristotle's ontology, this case would be interpreted differently so that there are two distinct occurrences: enjoying (hearing music) and listening to the symphony, since the former is an activity and the latter a process with distinct essential properties. In this way his account of the activity/process distinction depends on (and is saved from incoherence by) his ontological theory.[30]

Terry Penner (1971) has employed extensional events of Davidson's style to provide an analysis of activities and processes; thus, he argues the logical form of 'I am walking from Oxford to London' is

$(\exists x)$ (I am doing x and x is a walking and x is from Oxford to London
and x is between t_1 and t_2)

where x ranges over extensional events. He then argues as follows:

(1) Activities do not contain reference to their beginning and end points in the specification of their type (p. 422).
(2) Hence, activities and processes do not have the same predicates true of them (p. 424).
(3) Hence, activities and processes are non-identical (p. 424).

If so, 'I enjoy listening to the symphony' should be construed as:

$(\exists x)\,(\exists y)$ (x is an enjoying and I enjoy x and y is a listening and I listen
y and y is from t_1 to t_2 and y is of the symphony and x does
not equal y).

But, Penner notes, the derivation of (3) will 'involve a suspect use of Leibniz's Law if activity-verbs introduce intensional contexts; for if an activity verb is false of an event under one description, it may be true of it under another' (p. 424). This, Penner concludes, constitutes an objection which Aristotle cannot meet, and which shows that Aristotle's account of activities and processes is invalidated by his lack of awareness of the problems of intensional contexts.

Penner is correct to this extent: one cannot consistently introduce extensional events of Davidson's style and then separate processes and activities by Leibniz's Law. If there were events of this kind in

---

[29] J. L. Ackrill raised this problem: 1965, 131–5.

[30] Since Aristotle could only have held (1) that activities and processes form distinct classes (see 1048b28), and (2) that some activities and processes may co-occur, consistently if he adopted identity conditions of the type indicated in Section B, we should construe him – given the Principle of Consistency mentioned in the Introduction – as employing these identity conditions in these contexts. That these identity conditions make sense of the activity/process distinction is a further argument to favour their attribution to Aristotle (see Appendix 1).

Aristotle, activities and processes would not always be distinct entities but (merely) on occasion different descriptions true of one event. Hence, any predicate which was true on one occasion of an activity and not a process would be true of the event only 'under a description', and so could not be used to distinguish two entities: a process and an activity. Hence, either Aristotle operated with Davidsonian events or he took processes and activities to be distinct entities. He could not, consistently, do both. Since he did the latter (1048b28), he must have employed the account of identity developed in the *Physics* (see Section B) to represent listening and enjoying (or hearing) as distinct entities in discussing pleasure.

Aristotle seeks to explain the differing inferential powers of sentences concerning processes and activities in terms of differing ontological classes. Since places are essential features of processes, there is no point during a process of ϕ'ing before the end at which one can be said to have ϕ'ed. Since 'the whither and whence' are not essential properties of activities, one may have ψ'ed (where ψ'ing is an activity) at a given time and still continue that activity after that time. Thus, if Alf contemplated from t_1 to t_2, it is possible that Alf continued that contemplating after t_2; if he ran home from t_1 to t_2, it is not possible that he continued that running home after he had run home: i.e. after t_2. This difference in inferential power may be represented, as above, by the differing grammatical features of the types of verbs in questions and their distinct tense-postulates;[31] but for Aristotle the syntactical distinction rests on a categorial difference between distinct types of entity: processes and activities (in terms of their essence, differing goals and differing connexions with time and place) which allows him to represent logical differences of this type in a systematic way as generally, or categorially, valid.

In Davidson's account, by contrast, there is an antecedently given and undifferentiated characterisation of an event, and tense is seen as a relation between such events.[32] The differing inferential powers of process and activity-verbs will be represented as different relations between events which are neither logically nor categorially valid, and will depend (it seems) on special features of the different descriptions of the events involved (in this case on a set of special postulates for individual predicates such as 'kick' and 'contemplate'). What appears lost is Aristotle's explanatory connexion between type of entity and tense-inference which shows why certain verbs behave in a given way, and others not. (I assume that for Davidson processes and activities would both be events. If only processes were treated in his theory as events, he would still need to show the connexion between the antecedently given nature of an event and the particular inferential powers of process-predicates.)

---

[31] See, for example, Taylor, 1977.
[32] Davidson, 1980, 154.

It may be that this loss of explanatory power would not trouble a proponent of Davidsonian events. Failure to explain tense-inferences in a systematic way would not be a significant loss if one seeks only to represent as logically valid those inferences which rest on a favoured number of logical constants of predicate and propositional calculus; for all other inferences will rest only on special pragmatic features of differing predicates, and hence require no general 'categorial' distinction to explain them. Aristotle did not share this conception of the undertaking nor (I suspect) the view of logical validity which underlies it: his prime concern was rather to develop an explanatory semantical theory in which generally truth-preserving inferences were explained in terms of his favoured metaphysical and epistemological theory, and hence did not distinguish (fundamentally) between those inferences which rest on the logical constants and those which rest on other aspects of his metaphysical system. If one is concerned to capture the most general forms of truth-preserving connection, both types of inference will play a role in a common theory which locates both 'logical' and the 'metaphysical' inferences within one integrated picture.

Aristotle's theory requires support from his account of categorially valid inference if his distinction (as he draws it) between activities and processes is to be preferred to Davidson's more austere conception of logical form. Detailed consideration of these issues would require an assessment of their differing approaches to issues in the philosophy of language.[33] Thus one of Aristotle's major motivations for seeking to explain derived categories (such as processes) in terms of simpler categories (substances and properties) depends on his conception of categorially valid inferences and lies beyond the philosophy of action and within his metaphysical and logical theory. Thus the first defence of Aristotle's abstract level of theory is, at this point, inconclusive.

There is a second, related, motivation for Aristotle's account of processes, activities and states: his use of them in discussing causation and explanation, which is closer to our present concerns. State-verbs are unlike process-verbs in respect of their inferential powers; for if Alf is bald through a period of time, it will be the case that there is a moment within that period such that he was bald before that moment and continued being bald after it. If so, states and processes will be

---

[33] What is required is a treatment of Aristotle's account of validity which shows its connexion with his metaphysical and epistemological categories, and its differences from post-Fregean metalogic. (For a differing view see Jonathan Lear, 1980: also my review, 1981.) Gareth Evans' idea of 'structurally valid inferences' seems to approximate more closely to Aristotle's view of his project: to give a semantic theory for a natural language whose domain is divided into the fundamental categories of object required for a full understanding of reality – which categories validate certain general truth preserving connexions (see Evans, 1976). For Aristotle the required explanations of the differing theoretically significant inferences would rest on his favoured metaphysical/ explanatory theory and not be internal to the philosophy of language.

distinguished within Aristotle's ontology, as they form mutually exclusive classes of entity whose distinct essential qualities explain the differing inferential properties of sentences which describe them. Thus his account will recognise three distinct types of entity: processes, states and activities, with differing essential properties, which explain the distinctive grammatical and semantical features of the sentences that describe them.[34] States are especially significant since they are required for causal statements and appear (intuitively) distinct from events (processes or activities). In Aristotle's theory, they will be marked as distinct ontologically, but will also be realisations of a substance's dispositions and hence capable of being represented as complexes of similar structure to processes. Thus both states and processes may play within Aristotle's account a comparable role in his (conditionalist) account of efficient causation (see Section D). Aristotle's theory is thus able to represent both the similarities and differences between processes and states in a unified (and firmly based) way.

Davidson's theory is not (explicitly) extended to states. By parity with his treatment of action sentences, one would expect him to treat sentences containing phrases such as 'Alf was handsomely bald' as

$(\exists s)$ (Being Bald (Alf,s) & Handsome s)

as specifying properties of states. But he does not do this, and elsewhere comments that his theory of events 'is silent about processes (and) states if they differ from individual events'.[35] Nor is this silence difficult to understand: if his theory of states distinguished them from events, and he allowed states to be causes, he could no longer accept that causes are (always) individual events, or that causal relations hold only between events. Rather, he would require two causal relations (distinct from causal explanation): one obtaining between events and the other involving states. And this would render his account of causation less simple and attractive. There is an apparent dilemma at this point.[36] Either states are entities separate from events (in which case the account of 'cause' becomes more complex), or they are not (in which case there is a lacuna as to how to treat certain adverbs which appear to modify state-verbs). Aristotle's theory escapes this dilemma by giving a unified account of causation (see Section D) while treating

[34] Contrast Amélie Rorty's account of these inferences as 'purely grammatical' (1974).

[35] Davidson, 1980, 210.

[36] The dilemma could be avoided if one held: (a) that there were no states at all; or (b) that states were never causes; or (c) that 'causes' relates entities which are not divided into processes and states. (a) and (b) are problematical as states seem needed for certain adverbs, and also as causes in sentences such as 'John's baldness caused the sun-rash to spread', or 'John's desire to ψ caused his ψ'ing'. If states are required to account for (e.g.) adverbial modifications, they are an integral part of the ontology which should be used for causal sentences (contra (c)).

states and processes as distinct types of entity. In this case (irrespective of considerations of categorially valid inferences) Aristotle's distinction (as he draws it) between states and processes constitutes an important, if partial, defence of his theory. For it gives a motivation for seeking to explain the nature of processes in such a way as to distinguish them from states (and activities) in terms of their intrinsic character; and this *seems* difficult to achieve when events are treated as an irreducible category not related in an explanatory way either to distinct capacities or simpler categories.

A full defence of Aristotle's account of the state/process/activity distinction would require a discussion of its ability to treat adverbs, variable polyadicity and the other basic syntactic and semantic features of sentences containing verbs describing processes and states. Such a task lies outside the present project. However, the sustained work of N. L. Wilson and Barry Taylor on a theory which – in salient respects – resembles Aristotle's suggests that theories of his type are defensible in detail. It would be mistaken to conclude that the Davidsonian theory alone is capable of handling these syntactical and semantical features in a systematic way. What is required (at this point) is further motivation not for Aristotle's account but for one which like Davidson's does not contain the resources to distinguish states, processes and activities in an analogous way.

This claim can only be substantiated if Aristotle's theory can meet the following requirements: (i) it should be a part of an account of causality and causal explanation (and other modes of explanation) (see Section D); (ii) it should show how it can be applied to an account of actions and agency (see Chapter 2, Sections B and D); and (iii) it should show how it articulates the relation of the mental and the physical (see Chapter 5, Sections B, C). Aristotle (I will argue) himself used his ontological framework for these purposes, and hence his account of processes, activities and states provides the basis for his treatment of these difficult topics. If such contexts can be understood without using irreducible extensional events, examination of Aristotle's account will constitute a reply to those who claim that such contexts require events of this type,[37] and hence provide a challenge to produce a deeper defence of Davidson's ontological theory.

But is Aristotle's theory of processes defensible at its more specific levels? At the intermediate level, it offers a general account of what is distinctive of constitutive process-properties by representing them as realised (or actualised) dispositions of substances of a given kind. This forms his attempt to state what is distinctive of the exemplification of a process-property by a substance. Failure at this point would leave his reduction of processes as only partial; for they would be the exemplifications by substances of certain constitutive properties, but their distinctive nature would be left undefined. Aristotle's theory is

---

[37] Davidson, 1980, 164–5.

ambitious because it aims to characterise all processes as realisations of a particular type of disposition, and to construe the realisation non-set-theoretically. But is it over-ambitious?

It may be objected that Aristotle's account (at even the abstract level) cannot apply to all processes, since some do not appear to be realised dispositions of substances as they do not involve substances at all. Thus, while the sentence 'It is raining at t_1p_1' describes a process, it does not (it appears) involve any substance whose property is exemplified. Other processes (e.g. the stone's moving upwards when kicked by S) may be better described as the causal consequences of a substance's realised disposition, and not as themselves realised dispositions (contrary to the intermediate level of his theory).

Aristotle has two strategies for replying to these criticisms. He might represent sentences (such as 'It is raining') as describing the contingent properties of a genuine realisation of a substance's disposition (water's falling at a given time.) Thus he characterises sentences such as 'There was an eclipse' as describing the process of the earth standing between sun and moon (e.g. 88a1; 90a17). In other cases, he would see what occurred either as the realisation of a substance's causal capacity (e.g. S's moving a stone upwards) or as the exemplification by the stone of the property of moving. Aristotle is attracted by the idea of causal dispositions which produce changes in other objects. If he is correct to accept this variety of capacities into his ontology, it will be difficult to find a clear case to which his intermediate level of theory fails to apply. But if his account were rejected at this point, causal consequences would be represented (at the abstract level of theory) as property-exemplifications of the affected object, even though they were not realised dispositions of a subject of change.

The intermediate level of Aristotle's theory views processes as essentially *realised dispositions* of a substance with given goals and categorical bases. In this chapter, his account has been defended against the charge of circularity, and the nature and variety of the relevant capacities has been sketched (in Section B). However, a full defence would require consideration of his use of these capacities in a range of contexts involving causality and modality to propound his anti-Humean causal realist theory. It would also require further assessment of his use of teleology and categorical basis to individuate these dispositions. Some of the difficulties and advantages of this account will emerge in discussing agency (see Chapter 2, Section B); but a full discussion lies outside the scope of the present project within a general account of Aristotle's metaphysics of capacity and actualisation.

Assume, however, that Aristotle's theory proved untenable at the intermediate level. This would leave his theory at the most abstract level incomplete rather than overthrown, and capable of further independent development. For processes could be constituted by distinctive property-exemplifications picked out in the best theory of the organism and its internal structure, and explained in terms of simpler ontological categories, even if the best theory was not one which took Aristotle's realised dispositions as its basis. If the account was to approximate to his, some of the properties constitutive of processes would be those which sustained the tense-inferences distinctive of process-verbs (see above) and were required in an explanatory theory of a functional kind of the relevant organisms. These process-properties would be identical only if they played the same functional role in the account of the organisms, as breathing may do in fish and men (see Section B). Other process-properties would be those which (as well as sustaining the requisite tense-inferences) were required in an explanatory theory of the interactions characteristic of the organism's fundamental (non-functional) constituents: movement, combination etc. (e.g. heating). Thus, some processes would be functionally individuated, and others non-functional natural kinds (individuated by means of the types of process required in a theory of the fundamental physical level). In both cases, species of process would be individuated, in Aristotle's style, by reference to tense-inference and the appropriate (functional or physico-chemical) basic level of explanatory theory. As within Aristotle's own account there would be no separating the issues of ontology and explanation.

It lies outside the present project to develop and test an Aristotelian theory of this type. But, in outline, it would – like Aristotle's – yield an alternative method of selecting those properties which constitute processes, different from either Goldman's or Kim's highly intentionalist theories; for in it journeying, marching and walking would not be different process-types if only one of them (e.g. walking) was required within the preferred functional theory of the organism. Processes would be the exemplifications by substances of such properties and need not themselves be set-theoretic entities. In this way, Aristotle's theory would be philosophically interesting even if his own intermediate level (realised dispositions) were mistaken. Thus, at its most abstract, it points to the considerable middle ground left unoccupied by the opposed modern theories of Davidson and Goldman (or Kim) and introduces a wider range of motivation than is common in modern discussions:

   (i) *metaphysical*: to represent derived categories as explained by simpler categories (substances, properties, times);

   (ii) *logico-semantical*: to represent structurally valid inferences (e.g. involving activity-, process-, state-verbs) as ontologically based;

   (iii) *explanatory*: to represent processes as an element in a preferred theory of the organisms involved, and as part of his account of causation and explanation. (see Section D).

For Aristotle, logico-semantical proposals (concerning adverbial modification and variable polyadicity) need to be vindicated by support within a more general explanatory and metaphysical theory, and are incomplete if defended only by considerations internal to the philosophy of language. It is the range of motivation that Aristotle adduces which leads him (at the abstract level) to a distinctive and promising mid-position on the nature and identity of process, activities and states, which is independent of the difficulties which arise for his intermediate or more specific level of theory.

This account (as a whole) provides the basis for his discussion of central issues in the philosophy of action. But before considering those, we need to examine one further aspect of his ontological theory: the interaction of ontology with efficient causation and explanation. This will prove central in subsequent chapters, and gives further insight into his account of processes and states.

D.   Ontology, efficient causality and causal explanation

Ontology is interconnected with efficient causality in several ways:

(a) Are causes processes, activities, states or objects? If they are the former, what account is to be given of them?

(b) If 'A causes B' is to be analysed so that the occurrence of A is a condition for the occurrence of B, 'cause' itself is a connective which stands between distinct sentences, since sentences express conditions for the truth of other sentences. If so, the cause is something that corresponds, and is described by, a sentence: that complex of substances, properties and times which together comprise one event. Conversely, if 'A causes B' is to be analysed using Davidsonian events, 'cause' cannot be analysed conditionally since non-complex entities denoted by singular terms cannot be the conditions for one another.[38]

(c) If 'A causes B' is true, and A is 'The French President's resigning', is it also true that M. Mitterand's resigning causes B? Are causal contexts intensional or extensional?

Processes play a central role in Aristotle's account of efficient causation (in the *Physics*) as his activating causes are frequently objects undergoing processes. He takes as examples of particular activating causes: the builder building (195b6), this man exercising his medical skill (195b19), this man exercising his building skill (195b19–20), things which are in activity (195b17, 28). These are objects actually exercising their relevant capacities, and not merely possessing those capacities unexercised (see 195b17–18). Indeed what distinguishes activating from potential causes is that they are the relevant objects in activity as F's, and not merely potentially F's. Hence actual causes in

---

[38] See Davidson, 1980, 151.

these contexts are for Aristotle objects in certain conditions,[39] and not just objects, because reference to the conditions is necessary to account for the production of the effect at one time and not another (195b16–20). Elsewhere (in the *Posterior Analytics*) it is the condition of the object that proves basic for his account of efficient causes: it is because the Athenians were the first to attack that they were warred upon (94a36ff.), and because water completely lacks heat (95a16–21) that it freezes. Reference to the state of the object is fundamental, since it is because the object is in this state that it produces the effect.

Not all Aristotelian causes are processes; others are states of the agent, and still others are his absences or failures to act. Aristotle treats all these as causes indifferently: in *Physics* 195b22–24; 196b26 and *Metaphysics* 1013b6–7 he speaks of the 'art of building' or the 'art of sculpture' as the cause, where the possessing of such arts is a state of the agent, and not a process which he undergoes. Elsewhere (1013b15–16) absence, (87b8ff.) deprivations or failures to act are held to be causes in the same way as actualisations of capacities.

Aristotle's causes are phenomena in the world, and not sentences describing such phenomena, since they are activating (195b19, 26–28) and may effect changes in the world by physical interaction with other substances (243b16–17). Since entities and not sentences pull and push, Aristotle's causes must be elements in his ontological theory of the fabric of reality.

Substances and their actualisations (whether processes, activities, states or privations) admit of different descriptions. If a substance's actualisation causes an effect when described in one way, it will do so when described in another. Causes may be described in several different ways: for example, if Polykleitos, the sculptor, makes a sculpture, this may be variously described as (195b4–6, 10, 12):

Polykleitos makes the sculpture.
The musician makes a sculpture.
The sculptor makes a representation.

For the particular process is the realisation of one capacity of a simple substance and this may be described in different ways; hence, if Polykleitos is a musician, and his sculpture is a representation of Athena, it is true to say that a musician made a representation of Athena.

[39] It is well known that Aristotle speaks not only of events as causes, but also of objects or agents (e.g. *Physics* 195a21, 30: the doctor; 195b5, 21, 23, 197a14: the builder; 195b1, 10f., 27: the sculptor; 195b1, 10f.: Polykleitos). Several of these cases actually refer to potential causes, and not actual ones – but this is not true of them all (e.g. 197a14). However, given his distinction between actual and potential causes, the latter cases must be examples of shorthand presentation. Indeed Hume – who originated the modern view that causality is a relation between events – talks frequently of causation as being 'in the objects' (see Julia Annas, 1978, fn. 17). For a contrasting view see Wieland, 1975, 150–1.

Similarly with all other (potentially infinite) predicates true of Polykleitos and the sculpture (196b27–29). If the sculpture is a source of joy to the city but a source of envy to the Spartans, Polykleitos made something which is a source of joy to one group and a source of envy to another (1026b6–10). In *Physics* 195b4ff., Aristotle makes it clear by his use of the terminology of predication (195b4, 6, 10, 14, 21–22: cf. 1044b1ff.) that there is one cause which is differently described. For Aristotle, there is one entity (substance's actualisation) which is the cause (in the world) under all relevant redescriptions.

This account of the entities which are causes follows from Aristotle's identity conditions for processes (as generalised to activities and states). One distinct subject of change can be described by its contingent properties (e.g. as 'the white' or 'the musical', if Koriskos, the white musician, walks), and need not be described by reference to those features of the substance which are essential for the change. That is, because the sentences 'Koriskos walks' and 'The white walks' describe the same process (since both describe one subject of change undergoing one actualisation), processes can be causes and be described differently. Aristotle's ontology of processes in *Physics* III 1–3 and V 4 (as outlined in Section B) permits the type of description and redescription required by his discussion of causality in *Physics* II 3. Together they form the basis of a unified theory.

Aristotle introduces two modes of describing the entities which are causes: as essential and as accidental causes, where these modes of description introduce intensional contexts. In giving the essential cause, one is seeking that description of the subject which is most specifically connected with the relevant actualisation. It is not as Polykleitos that the subject of the change sculpts, but as a sculptor – or better – as possessing the required disposition (skill) of sculpting. Similarly, elsewhere (224a21–29) Aristotle insists that the essential specification of the subject of change is by that description (224a24; cf. 195b22ff.) which specifies the feature of the subject in virtue of which he changes; hence, it is *qua* walker that Koriskos walks, and not *qua* musician or even *qua* Koriskos. He is an agent *qua* possessing this capacity to walk.

In giving 'the essential cause', Aristotle aims at giving that description of the substance involved which is most specifically or directly connected with the actualisation which is causally efficacious. By contrast, 'the accidental cause' will be given using a description of the substance which is not connected in this way with the relevant actualisation. Hence, 'the white building' gives an accidental specification of the cause, if it is not *qua* white but *qua* builder that the builder builds. Similarly there may be an accidental specification of the effect: the builder's activity may accidentally cause a given effect under a given description, if that description is not one which specifies the effect in such a way as to relate it appropriately to the cause. Thus, if the house is a source of joy to Z, 'a source of joy to Z being built' describes the effect accidentally, because when described thus (and not as 'this house being built') the effect is not appropriately related to the cause: the builder's building.[40]

Aristotle's causes, therefore, are substances in a given condition, and thus are complex entities described by sentences.[41] The required account of 'cause' is as a sentential connective:

CAUSE (Fat$_1$, Gbt$_2$)

where the truth of the first sentence is what makes the second sentence true. The causal sentence cited is true if the complex described by 'Fat$_1$' obtains and is a condition for the distinct complex entity described by 'Gbt$_2$'.[42] Thus in logical grammar, 'cause' is a non-truth-functional sentential connective, and causal contexts are

---

[40] See Ross, *Physics*, 518–19. Both types of case are concerned with accidental properties of the substances involved. Aristotle treats a further case as analogous (196a3–5, b33–197a5, 197a15–18): S came to the square in order to look for W, but meets T and thereby regains his debt; thus it happened that S, who was in the square for a different purpose, met T and regained his debt. In such a case, it was *qua* seeker of W that S was in the square, and hence under the description 'seeker of W', S's being in the square was the accidental cause of S's seeing T. This description is relevant in such cases, as is the one which states S's purpose in coming to the square (197a1–7). But this is compatible with S's seeing T being essentially caused by S's being in the square, *qua* 'looker round of the square at the time when T was present': using a different description of S. As Ross remarks (ad loc.) these cases are compatible with the processes in question being necessitated, *qua* determined under some description. *Qua* seeker of W, S comes to the square then (thinking that W is there then); *qua* looking round the square, S sees T; *qua* seeker of T's debt, S accosts T, etc. Indeed Aristotle introduces such cases to show that where there is apparently chance, there is in fact necessitation. Thus it is only *qua* seeker of W, that S's meeting T is not determined. If all that is required for the determinist thesis is that there is *some* description of the relevant processes under which the effect is determined, such cases are compatible with determinism (see for a different view Sorabji, 1980, Ch. 1; also my review, 1981, 269ff.).

[41] In recent years it has been generally accepted that Aristotle's four causes represent distinct kinds of 'explanation' (e.g. Hocutt, 1974; Moravcsik, 1974, 1975). However, if explanation is linguistic, it relates sentences and not entities in the world. If so, what account is to be given of 'efficient causality' which, at least, appears to be a relation between entities in the world? Talk of 'explanatory factors' cuts no ice until we know whether explanations relate sentences or entities. Most classical sholars who have discussed efficient causality seem unaware of any difficulty, but Julia Annas' recent papers (1978, 1983) raise the issue in an acute form. Its resolution depends on discerning Aristotle's ontological basis; without that the debate (e.g.) between Moravcsik and Bogen (1974) is inconclusive.

[42] In the *Physics*, Aristotle uses conditional vocabulary in discussing particular causes in 198b11–14, 19–21 to explain the sense in which the effect is necessitated (198b5–6; 195b19–21). He also employs conditional vocabulary elsewhere (1032b18–20; 1065a16ff.) in discussing efficient causality. While I favour attributing a conditionalist analysis of 'cause' to Aristotle, detailed discussion of this issue lies outside the present project.

extensional.[43] This account will represent processes, activities and states as causes, in sentences such as:

'John's run from the base-line caused the crowd to complain',
'John's anger at the net-call caused the crowd to complain',
'John's contemplation of the net caused the crowd to complain',

in a unified way as

CAUSE (Fat$_1$, Gbt$_2$);

it does not require a distinct causal relation for processes and states (see Section C). The types of entity will differ in Aristotle's theory, but his account of 'cause' will be the same. Further, his account of causation seems well-suited to states (as well as processes); for 'John's anger at the net-call caused the crowd to complain' appears to describe the condition of John's being angry as what brought about the crowd's complaint – in line with the conditionalist account of causation which Aristotle adopted. At this point Aristotle's ontology and his account of efficient causation fit together into one unified (and satisfying) theory.

His account, however, requires supplementation in two respects which bear on the relation of cause and causal explanation. We need to know (a) which descriptions of the cause are the appropriate ones for essential causation; and (b) the relation between the account of 'causes' derived from the *Physics*, and Aristotle's analysis of efficient causality in the *Analytics*. For while in the *Physics* causes are objects in the world, in the *Analytics* Aristotle is concerned with the relation between terms, premisses and conclusion in a syllogism of a given type, and so seems to be analysing a connexion between sentences and not objects in the world. These questions are related; Aristotle holds that in cases of essential causation, the cause and effect are described in such a way that the effect follows necessarily or generally (1065a1–3, 5–8: cf. a24–27). When in the *Analytics*, Aristotle represents a conclusion describing the effect as necessitated by certain premisses, which include a term referring to the cause, he gives those descriptions of cause and effect which are relevant in the case of essential causality. Therefore his conditions for the appropriate specification of the cause and effect in the *Analytics* may serve to pick out those descriptions of the cause relevant for essential causation.

In the *Analytics*, Aristotle proposes to represent the efficient cause by the middle term of a syllogism (94a36–b8; 95a19–20; b15–16). Thus in 94a36ff., taking 'A' to represent war, 'B' to represent the first attack,

---

[43] If Aristotle is committed to the possibility of non-truth-functional but extensional contexts, his account is challenged by the so-called 'Frege argument' which is taken to prove that there can be no contexts of this type. Davidson has used this argument extensively (see 1980, 117–18; for critical comments see Cummins and Gottlieb 1972, 151–2, Lycan, 1974, and Taylor, 1976. Further discussion of this argument cannot be attempted here.

and 'C' to represent the Athenians, he holds that 'A φ B, B φ C → A φ C'. In this 'φ' represents 'belongs to', 'B' (the middle term) introduces the cause and the premisses entail the conclusion syllogistically and represent the necessitation of the effect by its cause. Aristotle's understanding of these premisses appears to be as follows: the minor premiss is a sentence in which a term specifying a property is predicated *per se* of the relevant subject,[44] the initial premiss is a sentence which states that having that property makes it the case that one possesses a further property, and the conclusion states that the subject of change has that further property. 'Being the first to attack' is predicated *per se* of the Athenians. The first premiss states that being the first to attack makes it the case that one is warred upon, and the conclusion states that the Athenians are warred upon – where this follows of necessity from the earlier premisses.

The predication is *per se* if the term predicated belongs to the object itself in virtue of its nature; that is, if the predicate belongs to the object as such, and not in virtue of the object co-occuring with another to which the predicate belongs as such. In the immediate context of causation, this requires that the object be the one to which the relevant disposition belongs, and be specified in such a way as to pick out that object under a non-accidental description. The property is the actualisation (or non-actualisation) of the substance's disposition which 'brings with it' the property specified in the conclusion.[45] The descriptions relevant to essential causation are of those realisations of the substance's dispositions which are mentioned in the major premiss where they are represented as generally or necessarily connected with the resultant property. That is, the descriptions relevant to essential causation are those in which (a) a disposition or state is described in such a way that another property follows (either necessarily or generally), (b) the disposition is described as belonging to the substance to which it belongs *per se*.

This interpretation allows us to see the general connexion between

---

[44] The properties belong *per se* to the subject of change (*Post. An.* 73b16ff.) if and only if they belong to the subject 'in itself and of necessity'. They belong to the subject in itself, if it is in virtue of the 'nature of that subject (so specified) that they belong to it (73b10–15). This definition does not require that the property belong to the essence of the substance (in contrast with 73a34ff.). Since the point of introducing the weaker notion (73b10f.) is to allow 'in itself incidentals' to play a role in deduction (73b31–33), it is not necessary that the relevant major and minor premisses state necessities; all that is required is that the predicates used belong to what they are predicated of in themselves. (e.g. 94a36ff.). For a contrasting view, see Barnes, Commentary, 114ff. In the *Analytics*, Aristotle allows the essential subject to be described in this way as (e.g.) *the Athenians*, while, in the *Physics*, he insists that the required description pick out that feature they possess (e.g. being *the aggressors*) in virtue of which they are the essential subject. While the latter is the more stringent instrument, in both accounts Aristotle's conception of the essential subject with its relevant capacities plays the determining role.

[45] That is, the property belongs to the original property in itself and not vice versa (78a35–38).

Aristotle's treatment (in the *Physics*) of efficient causes as processes in the world and his account (in the *Analytics*) in terms of the syllogism. The latter is concerned with explanation in which a description of the substance and property involved is placed within his favoured deductive scheme of explanation; the former is concerned with the entities in the world which interact with one another when one causes the other. The latter may be represented by sentences of a conditional structure:

'CAUSE (Fat$_1$, Gbt$_2$)'

in which the object a being in condition F at t$_1$ makes it the case that b is (e.g.) in a state G at t$_2$. This connective will truly connect sentences describing the two processes if and only if there is a description of a realised disposition of a, which is predicated *per se* of a, which is connected appropriately (see below) in the major premisses of the syllogism with a description of a state of b, which is predicated *per se* of b. The first process causes the second if and only if there is a pattern of explanation in which *per se* predicates of a and b appear in the way specified above and in which a statement describing the effect is the conclusion.[46]

The restriction imposed in this pattern of derivation is significant; for the only permissible predicates and terms are those which designate either realised dispositions which belong *per se* to the substances, or the substances to which they *per se* belong. Other contingent or accidental predicates of the processes cannot be used within this pattern of explanation, as they would not describe either the relevant disposition itself or the substance of change. 'Cause' itself relates processes, states and activities in the world which are objects exemplifying given properties; but there are true causal sentences of this type only when the objects and properties involved appear, non-accidentally described, in an 'essential causal' explanation. Aristotle's causes (complexes of objects and properties) are closely related to his account of causal explanation, as he requires that *per se* descriptions of the objects and properties that constitute his causes should appear in the causal explanatory story. If there is no causal explanation involving only *per se* descriptions of (e.g.) processes a and b, a cannot cause b.

In this account, essential causes necessitate because they (unlike accidental causes) give descriptions of cause and effect under which they may be placed within the favoured deductive model. Although accidental causes may necessitate derivatively *qua* descriptions of a process which described differently necessitates non-derivatively, the mode of necessitation in the cases is distinct. Essential causes are explanatory because only thus described can they appear in proposi-

---

[46] See (e.g.) 195b24–25. Aristotle occasionally uses 'cause' for 'essential cause'; but this should not disguise the clear distinction in ontological status between them.

tions describing cause and effect which are deductively related.[47] Attention to Aristotle's ontology allows us to see the connections between his account of causality and explanation, where the latter is linguistic, and concerns descriptions of processes which may be placed within Aristotle's favoured explanatory model (which, at least in the *Analytics*,[48] involves the deduction of a conclusion describing the effect from premises one of which describes the cause). Thus his account of processes forces a clear distinction between efficient causes, which are entities in the world, and the way in which they are described in causal explanation. The latter form relates propositions such that (e.g.) P and Q and R necessitate S, where P . . . S are propositions of a given form; the former relates entities in the world construed as the actualisations of given substances' dispositions.

This result is of more general application: teleological and material explanation will also relate propositions in an analogous way. What is distinctive of teleological explanation is not that it is linguistic, but that it involves as premises propositions concerned with the object's goal at a given time. If there is necessitation in the case of teleological explanation, this is real enough provided that Aristotle can show how the conclusion can be validly entailed by its premises. There is no need to regard it as merely 'as if' necessitation on the grounds that it does not involve a special force pulling objects towards a future goal.[49]

In cases of material causation, the occurrence of a given physical process and of certain conditions necessitates the occurrence of the non-underlying process which belongs to it. Explanation of this kind, too, involves propositions (94a23ff.); as such it may be represented as follows:

O(w) and O(C) materially necessitate O(z)

where 'O(w)' is the proposition that w, the underlying process, occurs, 'O(z)' the proposition that the non-underlying process occurs, and 'O(C)' the proposition that the required conditions obtain. Thus w is an underlying process relative to z iff

[47] Thus Aristotle may hold consistently: (1) that coincidences lack essential causes, and (2) that coincidences may be (obliquely) necessitated in the situation *qua* descriptions of processes which are, under different descriptions, necessitated in the appropriate explanatory form; without concluding (3) that essential causation does not involve necessitation. (3) is a paradoxical conclusion to attribute to Aristotle, as in *Metaphysics* V 3 he emphasises that causation and necessitation go together. It could only be derived if one held – in place of (2) – that coincidences are necessitated in *precisely the same way* as essential effects. For a contrasting view, see Sorabji, 1980, Ch. 1.

[48] Aristotle does not explicitly adopt this model in the *Physics*, nor show how it can be extended to deal with the cases he discusses there (II 6–8). One suggestion might be: This house is a house that the builder's building has caused to exist/A house that this builder's building has caused to exist is a house that has been built (by this builder)./ This house is a house that has been built (by this builder). These syllogisms are not exactly of the form of the *Posterior Analytics*; but both types are deductive.

[49] Compare Wieland (1975, 152). The issue of whether teleological explanation is defensible is raised in Chapter 5, Sections A, E.

(1) w and z occur at the same time and in the same substance(s);
(2) w and z begin and end at the same points (extensionally specified);
(3) O(w) and O(C) materially necessitate O(z),

(Compare the earlier account given in Section B.)

Since there is a clear break between causation and explanation within Aristotle's theory, his account resembles that given by Davidson, and differs from Kim's.[50] However, there is also a difference between them. Since Aristotle's causes are the realisations of substances' dispositions, he limits permissible redescriptions of the cause (for explanatory purposes) to those which specify non-accidentally either the actualisation of a disposition which belongs *per se* to the substance, or the substance to which it *per se* belongs. No redescription is permissible which specifies (even accidentally) the actualisation of a disposition which belongs (*per se*) to another subject, or a different actualisation of another or the same subject. The objects and properties which constitute Aristotle's causes appear under non-accidental descriptions in the sentences which exemplify his theory of causal explanation. Thus Aristotle avoids (because of his conception of processes as reducible to objects and properties) the radical difference between irreducible events and descriptions true of them which arises in Davidson's theory, while still maintaining a distinction between cause and causal explanation.

Aristotle's account shows that there is no need to employ extensional irreducible events to effect a clear separation between cause and causal explanation. Indeed his own method has an advantage in comparison with Davidson's, as the latter runs into difficulty at precisely this point. For, as he notes, if there is no limitation on the contingent descriptions of a process we can introduce, we can show that there are causal relations between causally unconnected processes. Consider the description of an event $(\imath x) Fx$ which is sufficient for b to exist and is itself a description of a, where a causes b. Take a further event c which is causally unconnected with a and b, and rig up a description as follows:

$$(\imath y) (y = c \; \& \; (\exists! x) \, Fx)$$

which is a description of c such that the existence of c is now sufficient for the existence of b. Hence we can show that any arbitrary event is sufficient for b. Clearly added restriction on the range of permissible substitution is required to block this consequence, but Davidson con-

---

[50] Aristotle agrees with Kim (1971) and Taylor (1976) in favouring a conditionalist account of causation, but differs from Kim in not accepting that 'events ... are the entities that enter into causal relations and can be the objects of explanation' (1976, 169), since he regards processes as causes, and descriptions of them as explanatory within his favoured syllogistic theory.

cedes that 'it is unlikely that any simple and natural restrictions on the range of allowable descriptions would meet this difficulty'.[51] What seems required is a method of limiting the relevant events or processes to those that are themselves conditions for the effect, and thus a way of restricting permissible descriptions to those that describe the constituents of those events or processes. But this is difficult to do within Davidson's account as his events cannot themselves be conditions and are irreducible to their constituents. Without a basis of this type the restrictions on the range of allowable descriptions required within Davidson's account may seem unmotivated. That Aristotle's account meets this requirement in a motivated way is an advantage of his ontological theory.

Aristotle's account of essential causal explanation requires (1) that a realised disposition be described in such a way that another property follows either necessarily or in general, and (2) that the realised disposition is described as belonging to the substance (or substances) *per se*. Aristotle takes this necessity as basic and does not seek to locate it within a framework of generalisations and laws (in contrast to Humean notions of explanation), or to give a reductive account of its nature or origins. It lies outside the present task to discuss this aspect of his account further. Aristotle's notion of the 'in general' will be important later,[52] however, and requires some further comment. He notes that certain cases of causal explanation involve statements which hold 'for the most part' and not always,[53] and here all that can be deduced (it appears) is that a given effect is probable, and not that the effect must happen.[54] If so, in these cases, efficient causal explanation may not involve necessitation at all. However, elsewhere (198b5–6) Aristotle writes: 'In each case, one must state the cause, e.g. this is necessary from that (where this results from that either without qualification or for the most part).' Nor is his representing 'for the most part' statements as necessitating an aberration; he distinguishes between universal and for the most part statements on the one hand, and cases of accident or chance on the other, and locates the former as essential and the latter as accidental causes. If essential causes necessitate (1065a25–26) 'for the most part' causes must also necessitate their effects.

Aristotle suggests in two difficult passages in the *Analytics* a partial route through this problem (75b33–35; 98b29ff.):

There are demonstrations of what occurs often – e.g. the eclipse of the moon; it is clear that, in so far as they are demonstrations of a given type of occurrence as such, they apply universally; but when they are not

---

[51] See Davidson, 1980, 158, 160.
[52] See Chapter 5, Sections A, E; also Chapter 3, Section C (and Appendix 3).
[53] 198b6, 11; 79a21; 1094b21; 1027a21; 1064b35.
[54] *Posterior Analytics* A 30:

universal, they are partial (i.e. are concerned with only one type of the universal class mentioned).

Shedding leaves may apply (in a conclusion) to a whole (e.g. being a tree) even though it applies universally to a subset of trees (and, by implication, does not apply to others.)

That is, 'A's are deciduous' will hold for the most part, even though 'A's which are B's and C's are deciduous' will apply universally, while 'A's which are B's and D's are deciduous' will be false. Within a given class of occurrences which are for the most part F there will be a sub-class which are universally F; with reference to the latter class, the conclusion may be deduced by a logically valid argument form.

In the case of trees it may be possible to break down the 'in general' statement into distinct universal statements; but Aristotle is clear that not all 'in general' statements can be converted by us into complete universal generalisations (1027a24–28), because we cannot state in full those in which exceptions occur. Cases where we cannot formulate non-question-begging exceptionless generalisations might be called 'law-allusive'.[55]

Take the case of a prospective generalisation 'A's which are B's are Z'. If one is confronted with an A which is a B and has no further relevant property, one may conclude that it is/will be a Z. However, an A which is a B *and* a C may not have this property, as being a C may make all the relevant difference. Further, one may not be able to state all the range of possible factors affecting A's which are B's that prevent them from being Z's. Thus we are confronted with an open and extending range of generalisations of the form 'A's which are B's are Z', 'A's which are B's and C's are not Z', 'A's which are B's and C's and D's are Z'. . . However, if one selects the most specific antecedent which is satisfied by a particular case before one (A's which are B's and C's . . .) and judges that there is no feature of this case (e.g. being D) which prevents the object being Z, one can represent the relevant conclusion as necessitated. For the specification of the object *as such* in the major and minor premiss limits these premisses to specifications of all and only those features of the object which are judged relevant, even if one cannot (in principle) specify all those properties now absent whose presence would upset the conclusion. Thus, in effect, one compares the immediate case with others judged relevantly similar and on the basis of the total evidence one possesses deduces the conclusion, while acknowledging that the relevant generalisations are not complete. If one selects correctly the most specific antecedent satisfied by the particular case one can represent the conclusion as necessitated, provided that the relevant generalisation is one concerned with precisely those features (even though one cannot oneself fill it out into a

---

[55] Grice, 1975. This classification appears to be at work in 75b33–35 with its reference to 'as such'. See also Mignucci, 1981.

complete universal conditional). There may, of course, be types of cause which are objectively indeterministic; but they will not be causes which (in Aristotle's account) hold 'for the most part', but cases of 'accidental' causes (1027a24–28).[56] Objective indeterminacy seems difficult to reconcile with Aristotle's account of essential causal explanation involving 'in general' statements.

Aristotle's account of 'in general' statements will become important later in assessing his views on action-explanation (see Chapter 5); it suggests that there may be genuine causal explanation involving psychological states in areas where we are not ourselves able to formulate the relevant universal conditionals in a precise or complete form. However, a full defence of the interpretation offered here of this and other causal modalities lies outside the present project. In the immediate context, it is sufficient to show that Aristotle's ontology of processes and states provides a basis for his account of efficient causality and causal explanation (whatever the correct analysis of the modalities involved in the latter). For this gives us a clearer understanding of his account of processes, and shows one of his motivations for adopting it as a central component in his explanatory theory.

E. Ontology, action and action explanation

Aristotle uses his account of processes and states in his biological works, his general discussion of explanation and his account of physical change. A systematic examination of his ontological views would require an analysis of several areas of his philosophy. But action-theory provides a central case both for his ontology and for his account of causal and teleological explanation. Indeed Aristotle frequently seems to begin his discussion by taking action as the paradigm case and then to extend it to a wider range of physical and biological phenomena. Thus examination of his account of action (Chapter 2), psychological theory (Chapters 3–4) and action-explanation (Chapter 5) provides a testing ground for and allows for the further development of the ontological and explanatory doctrines considered in this chapter. If his discussion of action and its explanation is shown to rest on the ontological theory discussed in the *Physics*, this will strengthen the

---

[56] In 1027a24–28, Aristotle emphasises the *epistemic difficulty* of completing the relevant generalisation. In contrast with accidental causes which may be 'objectively indeterministic' (1027b10–15; 1065a25, although in fact different descriptions of processes which – differently described – are essential causes), the cases specified in 1027a24–28 need not be objectively indeterministic. It falls outside the present study to consider further whether Aristotle elsewhere held that there were any indeterministic causes (which were not descriptions of (e.g.) processes, which are under different descriptions, essential causes: see Sorabji, 1980, chs. 1, 2, 3; also my review, 1981). A full account should also consider whether determinism requires that *all* our laws actually terminate (in our theory) in properly universal and exceptionless generalisations (see note 40).

exegetical claims made in this chapter. And if this account is successful as the basis for his theory of action, it constitutes a partial defence
of the abstract and intermediate levels of his ontological theory. In
particular, it will vindicate his attempt to view ontological issues
within the perspective of explanatory concerns, which has already
manifested itself in his explication of processes in terms of more basic
categories, his preference for explanatorily fundamental properties as
constituents of processes, and his unified account of cause and
explanation.

CHAPTER TWO

Intentional Action

A. Outline of Aristotle's account

We see Nefeli walking across the square towards us; she scans the faces of the tourists sitting outside the café and, intent on this, she – inadvertently – jostles some of the people standing nearby. When she sees us, she shouts a greeting and holds up a letter to signal that there is post for us today. In doing this, she is – as she realises – attracting the attention of all the people in the square, but this is not part of her aim; also, she is (although she is unaware of this) annoying the Orthodox priest who is walking behind her because he disapproves of all barbarian visitors to this holy island.

How many actions did Nefeli perform when she held up the letter to signal that there was post? Was there one, as there was one bodily movement, or *several* – as there are several specifications of what she did? If there are several, which (if any) is basic? These questions concerning the ontology of action prove central for the analysis of intentional action and agency.

In this chapter, I shall discuss Aristotle's pioneering discussion of 'voluntary' action (to follow Ross's translation)[1] in the *Nicomachean Ethics*, *de Motu* and *de Anima* using as a basis the ontological theory presented in the *Physics*, and thus seek to assess his ontology and analysis of action.

Aristotle summarises his discussion of 'voluntary' action in *NE* III 1 thus (1111a22–24):

> The voluntary would seem to be that of which the causal principle is within the man, and he knows the particular features in which the action falls.

Elsewhere Aristotle notes that the causal principle in question is constituted by desire (*de Anima* 433a31–32):

---

[1] For the moment; see below. In what follows, the values of the variables x, y and z will be what is done (the deed), and the predicate letters 'ϕ', 'ψ' and 'χ' will represent doing the deed (i.e. doing x, doing y, doing z). Aristotle does not clearly separate specific types and individuals as (e.g.) objects of desire (see Appendix 3), and on occasion I have preserved the same indeterminacy.

It is clear then that desire is the capacity of the soul which causes movement.

Desire produces action and is itself produced by an antecedent psychological state: imagination, perception or thought.[2]

The connexion between desire or preferential choice and action involves efficient causation (*NE/EE* 1139a31–33):

> The causal principle governing action is choice – that is its efficient cause and not its final cause.

Thus preferential choice (a species of desire: 1139a23) is characterised as the immediate efficient cause which sets the body in movement, and not as the goal. My desire to drink a glass of water is the efficient cause of my reaching out my arm to take the glass, while the final goal may be to quench my thirst or to drink a toast. Other passages confirm this account: in *de Anima* 433b19ff. Aristotle writes:

> The means by which desire produces movement is physical – and so must be considered in discussing the functions common to body soul. (Cf. also 701a35–37)

He then proceeds to analyse these means in terms of pulling and pushing, which elsewhere are two basic components in his account of efficient causation (*Physics* 243b16–18). The connexion between desire and the relevant bodily movement in these cases is that of efficient causation.

A first attempt at Aristotle's account of voluntary action in 1111a22ff. might run:

z is a voluntary action of S's at t_1 iff
(1) z is a bodily movement of S's at t_1;
(2) S knows the relevant particulars involved in doing z (what he is doing at t_1; to whom; with what: 1110b33); and
(3) z is caused efficiently by one of S's desires at t_1.

However this requires supplementation in a number of crucial respects:

(a) Are all actions, for Aristotle, bodily movements? What are bodily movements? Where do actions occur?
(b) What are the identity conditions for actions?
(c) What type of knowledge is specified in condition (2) as the type of knowlege characteristic of the agent?

---

[2] Examples of this account are given at *de Anima* 433b11–12, 27–29; *de Motu* 701a4–6, 36–38; 701b33f.; *Meta* 1048a10–12. I take 'preferential choice' at this point as a type of desire; but see *EE* 1223a26–28, 1224a24–26.

(d) What analysis does Aristotle give of 'desire' in condition (3)?

(e) Is the only explanatory connexion between S's desires or (more generally) psychological states and action that of efficient causation?

These issues will be discussed in the remainder of this chapter. It seems clear, at the outset, that Aristotle analysed voluntary action in terms of efficient causality *and* knowledge, and regarded the presence of teleological factors (if any) as compatible with desires being efficient causes of action. These two elements are central to Aristotle's account: neither causation nor knowledge alone is sufficient to analyse the concept; both causal and teleological considerations may play a role in it without inconsistency. Most recent work[3] has sought to analyse voluntary action in terms either of causation *or* of knowlege and teleology (but not both). Aristotle's theory (if it proves defensible) may avoid those difficulties which undermine contemporary accounts which take one of these features alone as the analysans; for it would yield a (partially) causal account of intentional action and the basis for a (partially) causal analysis of freedom to act (see Section D).

One less significant feature should be tackled at the outset: which of S's desires is the efficient cause of S's doing z? The obvious answer is: S's desire to do a z-type action. But this is not unproblematic (as Aristotle himself notes), since one may do z 'voluntarily' without wanting to do it. This issue is raised in the discussion of 'mixed acts' in 1110a9–19:

> Things we do through fear of greater evil or for a further noble end – for example, if a tyrant who had control of your parents or children were to tell you to commit a terrible crime or else he would kill them – such cases give rise to a dispute as to whether actions are voluntary or involuntary. A similar example occurs when a man discharges cargoes in a storm. For no one throws cargo overboard for its own sake (i.e. no one wants to do this), but everyone with sense does it to ensure his own safety and that of the rest of the crew. Such cases are mixed actions, although they resemble most voluntary actions.

Aristotle then notes their similarity to voluntary actions:

(1) they are chosen when they are done (1110a12–13) – so the man acts voluntarily (1110b4–6), and

(2) the governing principle of action lies in the man himself, and so he is able to either do or not do it (1110a16–18) – hence his act is voluntary,

---

[3] Anscombe (1957), Von Wright (1971) and Stoutland (1970, 1976) have urged exclusive reliance on knowledge and teleological considerations. Davidson (1980) has shown the limitations of purely causal analysis, but has been sceptical of the use of knowledge considerations, and – in this – he has been followed by Peacocke (1979). Pears (1975b) has experimented with one form of the 'joint approach' considered here, but his account differs both in detail and in general conception from Aristotle's. See Section D.

and so concludes (1110b5–7):

> These actions resemble more voluntary actions; for the actions are in the class of particulars, and the particulars in such cases (viz. the actions) are voluntary.

However, Aristotle also notes their similarity to involuntary actions (1110a18–19):

> Such acts therefore are voluntary, although taken by themselves they are perhaps involuntary; for no one would choose any such act for its own sake.

In this context, the meaning of 'by themselves' and 'for their own sake' may be clarified by 1151b1–2:

> If someone chooses or desires to do x for the sake of y, he chooses and desires to do y for its own sake but x only derivatively; if a man chooses something for its own sake, he chooses it taken by itself.

If so, mixed actions are 'mixed' precisely because two conditions conflict in their case: (a) they are chosen in certain conditions as means to a further goal, and (b) they are not wanted (for their own sake).[4] Given this clash, Aristotle distinguishes between acts that are done 'voluntarily' – which he identifies with (a) – and those that are wanted for their own sake, and rules that mixed acts are 'voluntary' provided that they are chosen for the sake of a goal which is desired for itself (e.g. safety: the release of your parents or children).[5] Hence 'voluntary' actions are caused either by a desire to do the action itself non-derivatively or by a desire to do the action as a means to a further goal; thus the relevant desire in the third condition may be expressed thus:

---

[4] Aristotle appears here to counter an argument he deployed in *EE*: (e.g.) 1223a31–34; 'that which is contrary to desire is painful, and therefore is forced and unintentional'. For in the present context something can be painful and still be intentional. Thus in the *NE* (unlike the *EE*) he separates what is painful (against one's will) and what is unintentional.

[5] Contrast this with Siegler's interpretation (1968). He regards what is done as intentional under the description 'throwing the cargo overboard to save the crew', but unintentional under the description 'causing or permitting harm'. But the latter is not to be found in the relevant text; in 1110b2–7 (cf. 1110a9–11, a5) the act in question is (e.g.) this throwing of the goods overboard, which is chosen for the goal of safety. Nor is it clear that it would be unintentional under this description since the captain chooses to cause harm in a specific way and at a specific time (e.g. 1114b16–18), and it is particulars which are intentional or unintentional (1110b2–7). Aristotle's problem seems to arise because, influenced by his own ontology, he focuses only on the basic action of throwing the goods overboard (which he sees as distinct from the non-basic action of saving the crew: see Section B), and asks of it (intrinsically described) 'Is it intentional?' Had Aristotle employed Siegler's ontology of extensional events without intrinsic descriptions, he would have avoided this difficulty, since under the description 'throwing the goods overboard for safety' the action is obviously intentional.

(3)′ z is caused by S's desire to do a z-type action *either* for its own sake *or* as the means to achieving a further goal which he desires for its own sake.

This distinction is important and influences the translation of *hekousion*. Only some acts which are *hekousion* are wanted for their own sake; others are chosen as a means to a further goal. Within the latter category fall some acts (including at least one of Aristotle's cases of mixed acts (1110a4–8)) which we would class as coerced, and not 'voluntary'. Since Aristotle in *NE* III places them in the same category as non-coerced actions, his classification there is not of 'voluntary' but rather of 'intentional' actions. For of the latter (but not the former) we may ask: 'Given that the action was intentional, was it freely or willingly choosen?' Since he classifies mixed (including coerced) acts as *hekousion* in III 1, I will take 'intentional' to be the correct translation of this term when applied to actions and not Ross' 'voluntary'.[6]

(3)′, however, is incomplete. An act may be caused knowingly and hence be intentional (1111a22–24) even if it is neither desired for its own sake nor as the means to a further end. For example, the sea captain, when throwing the cargo overboard to save the crew, may know that he is ruining his employer, which he neither wants for itself nor derivatively for a further end. Indeed it is because he is ruining his employer that he does not want to throw the cargo overboard for the safety of the crew. But such an act is taken as *hekousion*. Thus (3)′ should be amended to capture Aristotle's requirement:

(3)″ z is an action which is caused either by S's desire to do a z-type action (for itself or derivatively) *or* by his desire to do a y-type action (for itself or derivatively), when S knows that in doing y he is also doing z.

If z is an action which is caused by S's desire to do a y-type action, but S does not know that in doing y he is also doing z, it will be unintentional in Aristotle's account (cf. 1111a15–17).

Does the addition of (3)″ challenge the translation of *hekousion* as 'intentional', if (as might be claimed) the captain does not intend to ruin his employer and hence does not ruin him intentionally? Perhaps the latter case is neither intentional nor unintentional. Or is his ruining his employer an intentional (but undesired) aspect of the captain's plan, because he then prefers to do it rather than lose the lives of his crew etc. This philosopical issue is complex but lies outside

---

[6] The assumption that Aristotle is concerned with intentional action in *NE* III 1–5 and *NE/EE* V 8 is highly contentious and would, apparently, be rejected by the majority of modern commentators who see Aristotle as concerned wholly or partly with acts for which the agent is responsible, and distinguish these from acts which are intentional. On this, see Appendix 2.

our present project. For present purposes I will adopt the second alternative, and accept that 'ruining his employer' is intentional in a *derived sense*, while throwing the goods overboard is intentional in an underived sense. If this is mistaken, *hekousion* should be translated as 'intentional *plus* (this special category of) non-intentional', but not (for the reasons given above) as 'voluntary'. In what follows, I take *hekousion*, when predicated of actions, as *intentional*.

Clauses (1), (2) and (3)″ raise problems about the ontology of actions, (Section B), the nature of desire (Section C) and the interconnexion of desire and knowledge (Section D) in Aristotle's theory. Appropriately supplemented, they yield Aristotle's distinctive account of intentional action and agency.

B.   The identity of actions; basic and non-basic actions

Aristotle's discussion of intentional action requires an ontological basis which determines (a) the identity conditions for actions, and (b) the location of actions. Without this his account is seriously incomplete and fails to say what counts as *one* action or as *an* action. In this section I will argue that (even if not fully developed in every detail) it is sufficient to provide the ontological basis for his theory of agency and intentional action. It is also central for his discussion of moral action and practical reasoning, but consideration of these topics lies (mainly) outside the present project.

1.   The identity of actions

Aristotle writes as if he possesses an account of the identity of actions:

- (i) *EE* 1223b17–18: It is not possible that one and the same man does the same thing intentionally and unintentionally;
- (ii) *EE* 1223b25–26: If then it is impossible for the same man to act at the same time intentionally and unintentionally in respect of the same aspect of what is done . . .
- (iii) *NE* 1111a2: The man who is ignorant of any of these things acts unintentionally.

Nor is the appearance misleading; there is further evidence that Aristotle had developed the basis of such an account which, although not completed, underlies his discussion of actions.

Since actions in his account are either activities (1176b1–4; 1094a4–6) or processes (1220b28–30; 701a4–6, 34–6), they should have the identity conditions described in Chapter 1, Sections A–C: two sentences describe the same action only if they describe the realisation of the same capacity of the same agent at the same time. Actions may be intentional under one aspect or description, but unintentional un-

der another (cf. *EE* 1223b25f.), although the substances involved in
the action itself are specified extensionally.

In the *Physics*, the account of processes is applied explicitly to actions: teaching, learning (III 3), walking (V 4), building, doctoring,
jumping (III 1). Aristotle himself assumes that in giving an account
of processes he has provided an ontology of actions. The only issue
therefore is whether he consistently employed his *Physics*-based
account of actions in the *Ethics*.

Aristotle, on occasion, appears to regard actions in the *Ethics* more
intensionally than this: in 1111a15–17, it might seem that there is a
different action corresponding to different descriptions of one process,
since corresponding to each piece of ignorance there seems to be a
distinct action which is done unintentionally. Thus, if Merope kills
her son unintentionally and yet kills a man intentionally, she would
perform two actions: one intentional, the other unintentional
(1135a24–26, 28–29). What she does, what is intentional, what is
known, and what is noble would be the same. There would be as many
actions as there are intensional differences between different ways of
explaining what she did. The sentences 'Merope killed her son' and
'Merope killed the man who approached' would describe different actions contrary to the ontology set out in the *Physics*.

It would be misleading, however, to conclude that Aristotle discerned more than one action in these cases. In 1135a26–28 he employs
his favoured mode for introducing intensional contexts to describe a
similar incident: a person strikes the man who approaches, but only
incidentally strikes her father (if she is unaware that she is striking
her father: 1135a28–30). In the case of efficient causation, this terminology introduces different descriptions of the same process (Chapter 1, Section D). Consistency of use suggests that there is one thing
done which can be variously described (cf. 1223b25–26) – and that
this is the action. That is, although talk of intentional actions induces
intensional differences, what is done (a process construed as the action)
can be variously described as intentional or unintentional.[7]

If Aristotle had (like Kim) discerned more than one action in these
cases, he would not have distinguished the features 'in which' the
action occurs and its goal from the circumstances 'which surround
it' (manner, situation and instrument: 1111a14–16; a18). Each
relevant difference in the circumstance described by the sentences
'Merope killed the man who approached with a spear' and 'Merope
killed the man who approached in the park' would generate a different
action with a different explanation. However, in 1111a14–18, he

---

[7] J. L. Ackrill (1978) is rightly sceptical of construing *NE* 1111a10ff. as committing
Aristotle to a highly intensionalist view of actions; for although there is some description
of each process which can be picked apart as that under which what is done is intentional
or unintentional, the latter is itself extensional (in the substance place). He suggests a
different construal of this passage.

distinguishes the action from its surrounding circumstances, and characterises the former by answers to the questions 'Who?' and 'What?' as opposed to situation, manner and goal.[8] And this is precisely what one would expect if – as in the *Physics* – actions are essentially the realisations of the agent's capacities, and as such capable of being differently described (contingently) depending on circumstance and manner of execution. Thus Merope's killing could be described as being done with a spear, in the park etc. without these descriptions generating distinct actions. And in this his ontology of actions is less intensionalist than that proposed by Kim (see Chapter 1, Section C).

But is Aristotle's ontology of actions in the *Ethics* consistent with his account in the *Physics*? If his view is distinct from Kim's – does he also discern distinct actions when Davidson's theory would see only one? Aristotle's treatment of basic and non-basic actions and *praxeis* and productions appears to show that he does.

In the discussion of mixed acts in *NE* III. 1. 4–11, one example is this throwing of the goods overboard (which is distinguished from the goal of safety), and the relevant class is specified as actions which involve movement of the agent's limbs (1110a15–17). Thus the action in question meets two conditions: (a) it is a means to achieving the agent's goal, and (b) it involves a movement of the agent's limbs. Elsewhere (a) is restricted even further to the first stage in the agent's plan for achieving his goal (cf. 1112b16–24, b27, 32), which he can effect without further deliberation to means. In 1032b6–9 the last specific item which he deliberates represents the first action to be performed in his plan.[9] In *de Motu* 701a20–24, the action (cf. 701a23–24) is chosen as the means to make the cloak (e.g. the washing of the wool); and this is distinguished from the making of the cloak (701a21) which is the subject matter of the conclusion of the first syllogism; for the latter is described as '*an* action', but not '*the* action'. Thus there are two distinct acts (the washing of the wool and the making of the cloak), where the agent does the latter by doing the former and the former is *the* action. It is these distinct particulars that are indicated by the separate 'this'es' in 1032b6–9.

We might initially formulate Aristotle's conception of basic acts as follows:

z is a basic act token for S at t_1 iff
(1) z is the first specific means to be essayed in S's plan at t_1;
(2) S is able to do z at t_1 without further deliberation about means;
(3) z involves a movement of the agent's limbs (see *NE* 1110a15–17);

---

[8] If one takes 'in which features' as those which define which act occurred.
[9] See also *de Anima* 433a16–18 and *EE* 1227b33–34. The issue of specificity is discussed in Appendix 3.

and regard Aristotelian basic acts as teleologically basic acts (see below). Basic acts of this type are treated by Aristotle as distinct from non-basic acts in several contexts. Aristotle distinguished two types of goal: (a) one in which the goal of an action is the activity itself (1094a16–18; 1050a24–26, 34–b2): in such cases, the goal is not 'over and above' the action in question and occurs in the agent (1050a34–35); (b) another one in which the goal is over and above the action, a result produced by the action, e.g. a house produced by building (1050a30–32); in such cases, the result occurs not in the agent but in what is being built. In the first category, the goal will be a *praxis* if it is an activity which is chosen for its own sake; in the second, the goal will be a production (if the action itself is specified). But in both cases the non-basic act will be distinct from the basic act (non-basic actions are also discussed in more detail below).

Basic acts are spatial movements, and therefore processes; *praxeis* by contrast are those activities that are chosen for themselves (1140b6–7; 1094a4; 1176b2–10). Since activities and processes form distinct classes of occurrence (see Chapter 1, Section C), no *praxis* can be a basic act, and no basic act can be a *praxis*. Hence if basic acts are chosen for the sake of a *praxis*, that *praxis* will be a distinct act apart from the basic act, even though both occur at the same time, are executed by the same agent and would be treated within the Davidsonian account as the same act (under different descriptions). Thus if S pulls the trigger and thereby acts courageously, he will perform two distinct Aristotelian actions (if acting courageously is his praxis).

One value of this account of Aristotle's ontology of actions is that it shows coherence in exegesis where others have found confusion. Thus in their commentary on *NE* 1112b32–33, Gauthier and Jolif write 'il arrive ici à se contradire formellement, en déniant à l'action (*praxis*) l'immanence dans laquelle il avait reconnu sa caractéristique propre, et en lui attribuant une fin extérieure à elle-même, ce qui partout ailleurs est la caractéristique propre de la production (*poiêsis*)'. They can only obtain 'a formal contradiction' by assuming that there is only one *praxis* – the basic action – which is (contrary to Aristotle's thesis about virtuous action) chosen for the sake of something else. But since the basic act is a process, and the virtuous act is an activity, these must be distinct acts. If, therefore, there is no *one* action which is both the virtuous act and chosen for an exterior end, there is no contradiction in Aristotle's account.

Ackrill[10] also sees an 'incoherence' in these passages: (a) Mending the fence is the just act. (b) One chooses to mend the fence not as mending the fence, but as the just act. (c) There are not two things done, mending the fence and acting justly. Therefore (d) there is one thing only done (mending the fence = acting justly). But (e) Aristotle still says that mending the fence is not done for itself but for its

[10] 1978.

justice, and the just act is done for itself. The tension between (d) and
(e) arises because Aristotle (in Ackrill's view) lacks an adequate ontology of actions. However, if the interpretation given above is correct,
mending the fence and acting justly must be distinct acts, as one is a
process and the other an activity and they are categorically distinct.
But if Ackrill's premiss (c) is rejected, mending the fence may be
chosen as a condition for acting justly without contradiction. And this
supports the line of interpretation of Aristotle's ontology which has
been offered here.

Productions are distinct both from basic acts and from *praxeis*:
house-building occurs in the bricks and not in the builder (1050a24–
26), as teaching occurs in the taught and not the teacher (202b5–8).
Basic actions occur in the agent. Since actions are identical only if
they are in the same substances, basic actions cannot be identical with
productions. For the latter occur outside the agent's body (and his
instruments: 'detached limbs', cf. below). Aristotle also argues that
praxeis and productions are distinct classes of entities; for they are
different genera (1140b2–4).[11] Hence, no *praxis* can be a production
and no production a *praxis* (1140a3–6); even if they co-occurred, they
must be distinct. One may formulate the following general structure
for non-basic acts. (i) If they are activities, they are distinct from the
basic act but related to it as they occur in the same substance at the
same time.[12] (ii) If they are processes which operate on different substances than those involved in the basic act, they must also be distinct
from the basic act. Aristotle's basic acts may co-occur with both types
of non-basic acts, but cannot be identical with them as in Davidsonian
theory. Aristotle's account of their identity conditions must be different; for even if *praxeis*, productions and basic acts co-occurred in the
same substances at the same time they would not be treated by Aristotle as identical.

Thus Aristotle's discussion of basic, non-basic acts, *praxeis* and productions confirm that he is employing a general ontology of actions in

---

[11] And hence as distinct as quality and quantity changes, which form distinct classes
of phenomena (see Chapter 1, Section B). This is supported by Aristotle's argument in
this passage, which runs: (a) *praxeis* and productions are distinct genera; (b) skill is
concerned (exclusively) with production; (c) skill is (entirely) different from practical
wisdom; therefore, (d) practical wisdom is concerned (exclusively) with *praxeis*. For this
rests on the assumption that there is nothing which is both a praxis and a production
(see also 1140a3–4); for, if there were, even granted (a)–(c), practical wisdom might
have as its object something which was both a praxis and a production, and hence would
not be concerned exclusively with *praxeis*. Hence, unless there is nothing which is both
a praxis and a production, this argument is invalid. This strongly supports the contention that Aristotle is not operating with Davidsonian events: for if he were, there could
be one event which a praxis under one description and a production under another. For
a contrasting view see Ebert (1976).

[12] Thus, in the case of enjoyment, the activity may co-occur with (indeed be a member
of the same equivalence class as) the process (e.g. bodily sensing: 1173b6–10), but the
two be distinct entities with distinct properties.

the *Ethics* of the type suggested in the *Physics*; for he requires an account which is thus more fine-grained than Davidson's but less intensionalist than Goldman's or Kim's. But does he develop it in sufficient detail to form a complete theory?

The general ontological structure is sufficient for some of his purposes: Nefeli holds up a letter, attracts the attention of the people in the square and annoys the priest. These actions occur in different places: the priest's being annoyed by Nefeli occurs where the priest is, as the people's attention being attracted occurs where the people are, and thus both are distinct from Nefeli's holding up the letter (which occurs where the letter is). Further, if Nefeli thereby does a generous action, that will be a separate activity distinct from the basic act of holding up the letter.

Considerable unclarity remains: in some cases, an agent might be taken to perform two or more distinct actions which are both processes at the same place. Thus S in holding out his arm may signal that he is turning left, or in jumping six foot break his previous record, or in asserting *p* tell a lie and break a promise. In these cases (in which the actions occur in the same place) is the further action identical with the basic action or not?

Aristotle provides no direct answer. Indeed he may have thought it unimportant; for whether these actions are distinct or merely separate descriptions of one action, they will be intentional or unintentional depending on the factors mentioned in Section A. Since his ontological framework can accommodate such cases *either* as distinct acts *or* as contingent descriptions of one act, he may not have considered it essential to determine which examples fall into which category. To this extent, his account of actions is incomplete; but can it be completed using the conception of identity devised in the *Physics*?

Aristotle has two distinct elements in his intermediate theory for process identity which he can apply to this issue:

(i) *The categorical basis test*: this may yield clear answers to some of these questions: the categorical basis for jumping six feet may be the capacity to break one's previous record (as both involve the same physical capacity), while the categorical basis for putting out one's hand may be distinct from that for signalling – as the latter is an acquired skill (as part of the art of driving) which requires technical knowledge separate from that required to put out one's arm. But is the categorical basis for asserting *p* the same or different from that for telling a lie or for breaking a promise? It is not clear that there is a definite Aristotelian answer to this question. Aristotle might have argued that vices, like virtues, are acquired. If the man is a liar, the categorical basis for telling a lie will differ from that for asserting *p*; if he lacks this categorical basis, he will say something which is a lie but not actually realise a separate disposition. He will do something that is unjust, but not act unjustly. But is breaking a promise the realisation of the same capacity as that required for telling a lie? Aristotle's difficulty is that the categorical-basis test lacks a clear application in this case. While basic acts are those which the agent is able to do without deliberation and thus are connected to his specific abilities, non-basic actions which result from basic actions need not (it appears) be tied to the agent's categorically based abilities. The difficulty is not just that Aristotle fails to work out in detail the different species of non-basic actions; it is rather that since the nature of their required categorical basis is obscure, his theory lacks the resources for giving a definite answer.

(ii) *The goal test*: If there are as many actions as there are capacity goals (202a24–26) and these are established by the agent's own aims, then if S asserts that p with the goal of breaking his promise there will be two distinct actions in this case as well. But what if S asserts p, and thereby breaks his promise without knowing that he is doing so: i.e. without having this as a goal? Is this a separate action or not? Is Aristotle depending on potential goals and not actual goals? It seems paradoxical that whether there are two or three actions in this case should depend on whether S actually has breaking a promise as a goal. But if Aristotle uses potential goals, there will be as many non-basic actions as there are possible intensional differences between properties constitutive of processes. Thus if S jumps six feet with the goal of breaking his record, these will be distinct acts. More generally (at least) non-synonymous action types will be distinct. This may afford a successful way of individuating actions; but it appears to snap the connection between process-types and categorically-based dispositions on which Aristotle's treatment of processes relied. For unless there is a real distinction between different dispositional bases for these distinct action types, one cannot explain the essence of a given process, except in terms of the goals of the process themselves. One has no grasp on what counts as one action apart from the specification of the agent's aim in doing the action.[13]

The source of Aristotle's problem is clear: in the *Physics* the categorical-basis and goal test were taken to march together; in the case of non-basic actions, they do not always do so. On the categorical-basis test, S's jumping six feet in order to break his record will be one action; on the goal test (thus interpreted) they will be different. In the case of non-basic intentional actions there can be more goals than there are relevant categorical bases (even in those cases where the categorical bases are not themselves obscure).

---

[13] It might be suggested that (in this case) one should take the goal of the capacity as the relevant feature and not the agent's intentional goal in doing particular actions (see Chapter 1, Sections B, C). The difficulty is that – relative to the teleological explanation of what occurs – the agent's goal seems the more important. Indeed, in some cases (e.g. breaking promises, telling the truth, lying) it is not clear what counts as the goal of *one* capacity apart from the agent's intentional goals.

One response to the problem would be to surrender one of the two criteria for species of actions: if one holds to the categorical-basis test, there will (on occasion) be one action with different descriptions for different goals. If one maintains the goal test, non-synonymous action-species will typically describe different actions – even though they are the realisations of only one categorical basis. Alternatively, Aristotle could argue that all actions must *both* be realisations of a categorical basis of the type appropriate *and* possess an appropriate intentional goal. If there is no separate categorical basis, there can be no separate action even if there is more than one intentional goal (e.g. lying and breaking a promise). Difference in intentional goal will only lead to difference in action if there is a non-obscure categorical basis for the realisation of that goal. If there is no categorical basis of this type there will be no separate action; nor will there be a separate action if one (non-obscure) categorical basis is used for these different goals. What will determine non-obscurity of the basis and the relevant goal of the ability will depend on the best theory of the organism (and lies outside Aristotle's *a priori* study).

These options yield different results: if Aristotle holds that different goals separate action-types (irrespective of relevant categorical bases), his theory would resemble Goldman's: there would be as many different actions as there are distinct intensional differences (non-synonymous action-types). If he maintains that goal differences are only relevant for individuation if they are achieved by the realisations of different categorical bases, his theory will be more parsimonious: he would only accept as distinct non-basic actions those which manifested a capacity with a categorical base distinct from that of the basic action (and other non-basic actions). There may be distinct non-basic actions of this type (e.g. realisations of non-basic skills), but many (apparent) non-basic actions would in fact only be descriptions of basic actions (e.g. if there was no basis for breaking the window apart from that for throwing a stone.) This latter option seems the more Aristotelian, as it requires a separate basis for each relevant goal-directed capacity (in line with the discussion in the *Physics*); but it would be idle to suggest that Aristotle explicitly adopted it in the case of non-basic actions. The most that can be claimed is that this option is closer to the intermediate level of account given in the *Physics* and (perhaps) is more consistent with his theory of the organism (cf. Chapter 5).

Aristotle's macro-theory requires us to discern as many different action-types as are required in the best theory of the organism in question. If that theory concerns only extensional physical changes (efficient causality) we shall require only as many action-types as stand in genuine causal relations. This would require further changes in Aristotle's general theory, and might under certain assumptions yield a result with strong analogies to Davidson's account. If the theory has a teleological component, there may be more distinct action-types than are required to account solely for efficient (extensional) physical changes (although there will be differences, depending on whether a distinct physical basis is also required). The question of action-individuation (in these cases) cannot be decided except by determining which of these constitutes the best general theory of the organism. The general issue of action-individuation cannot be separated from the underlying issues of which is the best theory to explain the organism, its internal structure, and its goals.

The Aristotelian approach has merits at the macro-level, despite the incompleteness of Aristotle's own theory at the micro-level in the case of non-basic actions. What remains unclear in modern discussions of action-individuation is the basis for preferring one theory over another; considerations internal to the philosophy of language (Chapter 1, Section C) do not by themselves determine (e.g.) whether telling a lie and asserting *p* are the same or different actions. What is required (in Aristotle's view) to settle the issue is attention to the entities required in the preferred explanatory theory of the organism (i.e. whether the theory is teleological or causal, and how it introduces the categorical basis in considering human action). Aristotle's mistake was not to tackle in sufficient detail the question of how these considerations apply to non-basic actions,[14] although his preference for an account with a teleological component is clear (see Chapter 5).

2. *The location of basic and non-basic acts*

(a) *Basic acts*. The account given of teleologically basic acts requires supplementation in two respects. Thus far, it runs:

z is a basic act token for S at t_1 iff
(1) z is the first means to be essayed in S's plan at t_1
(2) S is able to do a z-type action at t_1 without further deliberation about means
(3) z involves a movement of the agent's limbs.

Aristotle held that the basic act is typically a spatial movement of the agent's limbs, and occurs where the limb's moving occurs. If the basic act is S's moving his hand, this occurs where S's hand is moved (by S) but is distinct from it. The latter process occurs where S's hand is, and is the result of the action but not itself the action. The two distinct processes are members of one equivalence class, but are distinct as they exemplify the agent/patient structure. Aristotle holds that in such cases there are two processes only: S's moving his hand, and S's

---

[14] This indeterminacy in Aristotle's *actual* theory partially supports Ackrill's contention (1978) that Aristotle had not fully developed his account of the identity conditions of actions. It should be noted, however, that in this account Aristotle's ontology of action is less indeterminate than Ackrill suggests (at least in the case of basic actions, *praxeis* and productions).

hand being moved by S. There is no third distinct process: S's hand being moved, or S's hand moving, or S's hand being in motion. Sentences apparently referring to an intransitive process are to be analysed as referring to one or other of the two transitive processes. Of these only the former is S's action, the latter is the product of S's action. Thus the third clause of the definition of a basic act requires modification: it should read:

(3) z is S's moving his limbs at t_1,

and this can be understood to refer to a process which occurs where S's limbs are moved by S, but to be distinct from S's limbs being moved by S.[15] In the case of S's moving his hand, this occurs at the periphery of S's body (where S's hand is).

These basic actions are teleologically basic as they are the first means in S's plan at t_1. Aristotle treats them as distinct from the causal antecedents of S's moving his hand. In 701a1–6, he writes:

> It is not necessary for the last stage in what is moved to move anything. Thus it is clear (as is plausible) that spatial movement is the last thing to occur in things that are moved. For a living animal moves (i.e. spatially) through desire or preferential choice, when something has changed through perception or imagination.

The previous stages before S's moving his limbs are quality changes or quantity changes (703a10–22, b20–22: cf. 701b13–16) which are the physical basis for S's relevant desire or the physical processes in between the movement of the hand and S's desire, the movement of the wrist, elbow etc. (702b8–11).

If so, the causally basic process is S's desire or preferential choice, or the physical movement of the innate spirit which embeds it (703a10–22, b20–22). In Aristotle's picture:

$$x \quad x \quad x \quad x \quad x \quad x \quad x \quad x$$
$$O \quad a1 \quad a2 \quad a3 \quad a4 \quad a5 \quad a6 \quad a7$$

O is the causally basic process and is a mental (or neural) event such as desire; $a1$–$a6$ are S's intermediate actions (if they are actions and not merely processes): moving his shoulder, elbow, wrist, knuckle,

---

[15] The relation between these is that between teaching and learning: they are members of one equivalence class. The action is S's moving his hand (*poiêsis*) which is distinguished from S's hand being moved by S (*pathêsis*). Both distinct processes involve distinct relations between S and his hand, and have different subjects of change. For Aristotle there is no further process described by 'S's hand being moved (intransitive)'; all such cases are either processes of S's hand being moved (transitive) by S or S's (transitive) moving S's hand. Aristotle's emphasis on processes being relations (200b30) leads him to analyse such cases as active/passive examples of one transitive verb; for him (in this example) there is no additional (intransitive) movement. See also Section D.

finger joints etc., and $a7$: S's moving his finger is S's teleologically basic action (if S's plan is to move his finger, and thereby attract attention). Teleologically basic actions are thus distinct from the causally more basic actions which precede them.

In Aristotle's account, teleologically basic actions are not always the agent's moving his body. In 702b3–6, he notes that there is no relevant difference between the movement of the wrist and of the stick it moves; 'for the stick becomes like a detached limb'. Thus, basic acts may extend beyond bodily movements to include movements with implements (extended limbs). But this is characteristic of teleologically basic acts; for in the case of an acquired skill, the expert (e.g. the skilled typist or tennis player) will not deliberate as to how to move his hand in such a way as to type a letter or play a certain stroke (cf. *Physics* 199b28: 'Skill does not deliberate').

This passage compels us to modify the earlier account of teleologically basic actions. Aristotle insists on the first two clauses:

z is a basic act token for S at t_1 iff
(1) z is the first specific means to be essayed in S's plan at t_1; and
(2) S is able to do a z-type action at t_1 without further deliberation about means.

This therefore must lead him to reject the third clause (proposed on the basis of 1110a15–17)

(3) z is S's moving his limbs,

and to include cases where the first stage in the agent's plan involves reference to implements (e.g. a stick, a cricket bat), which the agent is able to manipulate without further deliberation and which Aristotle describes as 'detached limbs' in *de Motu* 702b5–6. Hence (3) should be replaced with (3)':

(3)' z is S's movement of his limbs, or his 'detached' limbs.

This modification is characteristic of teleologically basic acts, but is not reconcilable with causally basic acts; for S's movement of his wrist is causally basic to the movement of his stick.

Teleologically basic acts, thus conceived, are relative to an agent's plan and abilities at a time; one act-type may be basic at a time for one agent and non-basic for another at that time (or, for himself at another time). Thus, for example, an agent may normally signal by putting his hand out of the window; but, on occasion – if, for example he is directed to find a reason for putting his hand out of the window, he will put his hand out of the window *by* signalling. Other examples of this kind will count against any attempt to fix 'basic acts' by determining 'basic acts types' independently of the agent's plan and abilities; for the direction of his plan or the increase or decrease in his abilities will, on occasion, upset such an approach. Hence it seems a merit of Aristotle's account that it makes teleologically 'basic acts' dependent on the direction of the agent's particular plan at the time of action.[16]

Aristotle's teleologically basic actions have two salient features: (a) they involve no further deliberation about means to effect them, and (b) the agent specifically intends (or plans) to do them, as they are the first specific stage in the agent's plan. Such actions are objects of agent's knowledge in that the agent is non-inferentially aware that he is about to do this action. Thus, to revert to the sequence of processes (O to $a7$) represented above, $a1$–$a6$ will yield S agent's knowledge that he is about to ($a7$), where $a1$ is the causally basic action and $a7$ the teleologically basic action. Agent's knowledge, thus, rests on what the agent does ($a1$–$a6$) and gives information about what he is about to do ($a7$) (see Section D).

Aristotle's separation of teleological and causal basic acts has strong intuitive appeal. We tend to think of actions such as moving one's hand as occurring at the periphery of the body, and not at the prior stage ($a1$) which is causally basic. Two arguments support this intuitive conclusion. We think that it is true that 'I am moving my hand' only when (and where) my hand is being moved. At previous stages ($a1$–$a6$) we hold that it is true that 'I am about to move my hand' but not (during the micro-seconds before my hand is being moved) that I am now moving my hand or that I am now about to do something which will make it true that I am now moving my hand. During the time in which $a1$–$a6$ occur, it seems that one looks forward to a future state of which it will be true to say that 'I am moving my hand' as one is about to enter a state of which the continuous tense will be true. 'Being about to ϕ' appears both to exclude present ϕ'ing and to point to a future state of ϕ'ing – which occurs at $a7$, and not at either $a1$, or $a1$–$a6$.

Aristotle is concerned both with animate and inanimate movements, and aims to give a general account to cover both cases. When the wind moves my hand, that occurs where my hand is moved, and not at some antecedent point.[17] If both animate and inanimate movings of my

---

[16] Contrast with Goldman's account of the basic act-token (1970, 42–43), which he treats as sufficient for the non-basic action. Thus if S signals by putting his arm out of the window, his putting out his arm is sufficient for signalling. But if the only way of signalling then is putting out one's arm then it is true that: (a) if S signals, S puts his arm out, (b) if S did not signal, he did not put out his arm, and (c) if conditions for signalling were different, then S could have signalled without putting out his arm (which Goldman claims applies only to basic actions). Thus, if the conditions are necessary and sufficient, basic and non-basic acts are reversible and there is no basic act. Hence, we require (as Aristotle provides) a further clause dependent on the agent's actual plan at t: to put out his arm and thereby signal, to determine the basic action.

[17] The parallel with inanimate action is implicit in Aristotle's account as he applies the *poiêsis/pathêsis* analysis of processes to both animate and inanimate processes: cf. *de Gen. Corr.* 324a5–8, 15–24, b1–3; *Phys.* 194b31–32; 201a16–22; *Meta.* 1050a30–34. I am indebted to Stephen Williams for alerting me to the importance of these passages.

hand occur at the same place, *my* moving my hand should occur at the same point as the *wind's* moving my hand: where my hand is moved. If there is no such general account, the sentence 'Someone or something is moving that hand' would refer to two distinctly located events, depending on whether the agent or an added electrical discharge caused the hand to be moved. But the sentence appears to identify one definitely located event (someone/something moving that hand) and to suggest a question about its antecedents, 'Who or what moved it?', rather than to raise the question of *where* the moving of the hand occurred. And this is what is to be expected within a general theory of animate and inanimate movings of the hand (see also Section D).

Aristotle's account separates S's doing something which causes his moving his hand and his moving his hand, as the latter occurs where S's hand is and not where the cause of its moving is. S's moving his hand might be described as 'S's producing the effect that his hand is moved by him', and thus be distinguished from S's doing something which causes his hand to be moved. In the sequence of processes sketched above,[18] $a1$–$a7$ are all actions of S's, moving his finger, hand, wrist, elbow etc., and this sequence extends back to the original causally basic action which is caused by S's psychological states, is a process inside S, and causes S's hand to be moved (O).

So is Aristotle correct to adopt the apparently intuitive view that teleological and causal basic actions are distinct, and thus to locate S's moving his hand at the same point as S's hand being moved by S? What objections may be brought against his positioning of the teleologically basic act? Several suggest themselves:

(1) In Aristotle's account, not all 'by' relations will be univocal. In certain cases 'by' will point to a causal connexion, in others to a teleological connexion. Hence if it is a requirement of an adequate

---

[18] See *de Gen. Corr.* 324a26–b4, 9–16 for a sequence of stages in a causal chain which are treated as discrete events ($a1$–$a6$). $a7$ is the bringing about of the effect as in the case of teaching (202b16–18) or building (195b19–21). Aristotle analyses 'S moves T' as 'S brings it about that T is moved by S', and not as 'S causes it to be the case that T is moved by S', if the latter is taken to designate an event antecedent to T's being moved by S. The latter sentence, however, may be taken to refer *not* to the earlier event of 'S's doing something which causes T to be moved' *but* to 'S's effectively causing T to be moved', which occurs when S actually brings about the effect that T is moved: when T is moved. This ambiguity explains how S's φ'ing may be identified with S's causing it to be the case that φ, without being identified with an event antecedent to φ. Thus one cannot proceed directly from identifying 'S's φ'ing' with 'S's causing it to be the case that φ' to the conclusion that the action occurs at a stage prior to the bodily movement. Since linguists do not (in general) separate these or other explanatory uses of 'cause', their evidence for the *causative hypothesis* cannot by itself establish the identity of the action with an event antecedent to the movement (intransitive) of the body (see Fodor, 1976, 130f.; McCawley, 1968; Chomsky, 1970; Hornsby, 1980, p. 13ff.).

theory that all cases of 'by' are analysed univocally, his account is mistaken. But why should this be so? Take the following examples: (i) S contracted his muscles by clenching his fist, and (ii) S clenched his fist by contracting his muscles. Both may be true: (i) represents S's plan for contracting the muscles of his forearm; (ii) represents the causal route by which S clenched his fist. However, if the causal 'by' is asymmetrical, then there must be two distinct relations implied in those cases. If so, not all 'by' relations can be the same (however any particular 'by' relation is to be analysed). Hence Aristotle's rejection of the univocality thesis seems justified.

If Aristotle rejects the univocality thesis, he will also reject the following argument.[19] (i) By S's clenching (transitive) his fist, his muscles contract (intransitive) (or are contracted (transitive) by him). (ii) By his muscles contracting (intransitive), his fist is clenched (intransitive). (iii) 'By' is univocal and causal. Therefore (iv) S clenching (transitive) his fist precedes and causes S's muscles to contract (intransitive) and S's fist to clench (intransitive). This assumes that in (i) and (ii) 'by' denotes a causal relation; for unless this is so, there is no reason to assume that S's clenching (transitive) his fist causes and precedes S's fist clenching (intransitive) or S's muscles contracting (intransitive). But if (as above) 'by' in (i) represents the teleological relation involved in S's plan to achieve the goal of his muscles contracting (intransitive), it must differ in sense (or applicaton) from the causal 'by' in (ii). If so, this mode of argument (by itself) gives no reason to reject Aristotle's claim that S's clenching his fist occurs at the place where his fist is clenched.

(2) A second argument against Aristotle's location of S's moving his hand might run as follows:[20] (i) We try to do everything we do intentionally. (ii) If we try to do *x* and succeed in doing it, our trying is our succeeding. (iii) Unsuccesful acts of trying are internal events which fail to produce the desired result. (iv) Successful acts of trying differ from unsuccessful ones only in that they produce the desired result. Therefore (v) Tryings that are actions are internal events. If this argument is correct, S's moving his hand occurs at some stage previous to the movement of S's hand, and so cannot be located at the periphery of the body. Aristotle does not himself use the notion of 'trying'. However, if the argument was valid it would show that Aristotle's theory was not adequate for any language which contained that concept. Hence it is instructive to see whether an Aristotelian theory could reply to this line of reflexion.

[19] Contrast Hornsby, 1980, 20ff. In this formulation, I follow Hornsby in talking of movement (intransitive) as well as movement (transitive). See note 15 for Aristotle's scepticism about movement (intransitive). This section owes much to Jennifer Hornsby's illuminating discussion of these issues.

[20] Distinct forms of this argument are proposed in Armstrong (1973), O'Shaughnessy (1973), Hornsby (1980, 38).

In the sequence of actions that lead to the teleologically basic act of moving one's hand, $a1$–$a7$ may represent S's trying to move his hand, but only $a7$ is S's moving his hand. Thus, at any stage of $a1$–$a6$, it would be true that S is trying to move his hand, but not true that S is moving his hand. Trying would be construed as doing what one can to achieve a goal one has set oneself, and may include achieving the goal. But trying to do $a7$ and doing $a7$ will not be identical since the former will extend from $a1$ to $a7$, while the latter only occurs at the end of the sequence. Acts of trying to do non-basic actions will typically include basic actions, if (as in Aristotle's view) the non-basic action ($a8$) occurs after the basic action ($a7$). But, while doing $a7$ may be identical with (or part of) trying to do $a8$, it does not follow that doing $a7$ is identical with trying to do $a7$. So Aristotle would reject premiss (ii).

But Aristotle could also reject premiss (iv), if he accepted the view of trying sketched above. Certain cases of trying will fail to produce the desired result because of breakdown at various stages pre-$a7$ing, e.g. immediately after $a5$ or $a1$, depending on the position of the obstacle. In the latter case, S will only do the causally basic action, and this will constitute his trying. In the former case, he will do $a1$–$a5$ in trying to do $a7$, and his trying to do $a7$ will include his moving his elbow and wrist (located where they are). $a1$ will also be part of his act of trying, but will not be all of it. Actions of this type ($a1$'s type) may always be elements in the trying to do $a7$. Indeed, in cases of successfully doing $a7$, the trying will include $a1$–$a7$. It does not follow, however, from the fact that all trying to do a7 involves actions of $a1$ type that trying in all cases consists in just doing $a1$. Thus Aristotle could also reject premiss (iv): successful acts of trying differ from unsuccessful ones in the constituent action-types involved.

But could that very token action ($a1$) have occurred and not been S's trying to do $a7$? One reply runs as follows: that very $a1$ (in the other cases considered) would have been an element in S's trying to do $a7$, but would not have been all of it. When trying to do $a7$ is construed (essentially) as doing what one can to achieve a goal one has set oneself, one would not expect all parts of a particular trying to be essential parts of it. For it could have been that very trying and proceeded further than (or not got as far as) it did; it would have been the same trying if it had stopped at $a4$ rather than $a5$. (Thus Evans's first try (attempt) at climbing Everest would have succeeded if it had continued for a further four hundred feet.) In this way, that very act of trying could have lacked one particular event stage ($a5$). If so, Aristotle could reject premiss (iv) for particular tryings also: that very trying might differ in the successful and unsuccessful cases because it ends at a different place, but still be that very trying. A particular trying to do $a7$ may include *both* a given neural event ($a1$) *and* subsequent straining of the muscles of the hand and arm ($a4$ to $a6$). And this seems correct, as what is frequently meant by saying (e.g.) 'Try to raise the weight on your hand' involves an injunction to tense the muscles of the forearm and wrist, etc., after the initial neural event.[21]

(3) Aristotle's teleologically basic acts can extend beyond the body to include 'detached limbs' which the agent is able to move without further deliberation about means. Thus S's playing a forehand drive may be a basic act for S at t_1, if S is able to do this without further deliberation about means. Doing an action which one is able to do without further deliberation about means is (for Aristotle) the first specific means to be attempted in an action plan at t, and is thus the teleologically basic action. Abilities are characteristically specified by specific action types ('playing a stroke' and not 'doing whatever is involved in playing a stroke'), and thus the first stage in one's plan will be a specific stage.

It is often held, however, that basic actions are always S's moving of his body and do not extend beyond its periphery. In this view, S's basic action if S plays a forehand drive would be: S's moving his body in just the way required to play the stroke. This view does not use the resources of specific intention and specific ability on which the teleologically basic act (sketched above) depends. So what is its basis? One argument runs as follows: when S moves his body in a given way, then he knows not only that he is trying to move his hand but also (because of the appropriate feedback mechanisms) that he is succeeding in doing so. If the basic action extends beyond the body, one will not know in the same way whether one is succeeding – as there is no feedback mechanism from (e.g.) the stick one is moving. If basic actions require that one knows while doing them that one is *succeeding*, and one only knows this in the case of S's movements of his body, then Aristotle must be mistaken in locating teleologically basic acts (on occasion) beyond the body.

Why should non-inferential knowledge be an essential feature in the correct characterisation of basic action? Knowledge of this type is useful because it enables the agent to monitor his action while acting and readjust immediately if he is failing to act as he intended. In

---

[21] I am indebted to Michael Smith for several discussions of this argument. In his paper (1983) he gives several examples in which the principle that 'A particular event has all its parts essentially' seems false. This principle seems plausible only in cases (like *successfully* drawing with a *specified* pencil at a *specified* place an equiangular triangle of a *specified* size) where the event cannot occur without (i) reaching a specific goal and finishing at that point, (ii) following a precisely specified route (see Aristotle's remarks: *de Gen. Corr.* 321a2–10). 'Trying to φ' (like growing bigger) seems to fulfil neither of these conditions, and hence not to have its parts essentially. Assume, however, that this principle turned out to be universally valid (*argumenti causa*). If this trying is understood as the very event brought about in furtherance of a goal, the trying would be a different token event in the successful and unsuccessful cases, and premiss (iv) in the original argument would be false. The major issue (which still awaits a resolution) is that of giving a rigorous criterion to mark out those events which do have their parts essentially. Trying (as construed in the main text) exemplifies unitariness: see Chapter 1, Section B.

certain cases this type of non-inferential knowledge may be essential
for the agent, and he may insist on selecting as the teleologically basic
action one for which he has immediate feedback of success/failure. But
it remains unclear why for all cases the theoretician should take as
the basic action only those with immediate feedback mechanisms.
Teleologically basic actions will be actions which the agent (if successful) knows he is about to perform, and of a type which he knows
how (is able) to do (without further deliberation); indeed it is for this
reason that they are chosen as the first means in his plan. Hence they
too will allow rapid adjustment if his intention is not fulfilled, and he
comes to believe that he is not about to do x. So why insist that all
basic acts be ones which the agent (if successful) knows he is doing,
rather than ones he knows he is about to do?

There may indeed be further theoretical purposes for which actions
which are causally basic or have immediate feedback mechanisms are
required. But within Aristotle's theory, teleologically basic actions are
connected with (i) the agent's specific abilities (as they enter into his
deliberation), (ii) knowledge of what one is about to do, and (iii) teleological explanation in his own explanatory account of intentional action (see Sections C, D and Chapter 5, Section A). Indeed one might
doubt whether there is a theoretically neutral conception of basic
action; for some theoretical purposes, causally basic actions may be
preferable, for others teleologically basic actions. Different theoretical
purposes will require distinct types of basic actions from Aristotle's;
the only test for acceptance will be the explanatory value of the theory
within which they are placed. It remains to be seen whether Aristotle's
preference for teleologically basic actions located at or beyond the
periphery of the body is well-motivated within his own theory of
intentional action (see Sections C and D).

(b) *Non-basic acts.* Aristotle separates productions and *praxeis*. The
latter occur where the agent does the basic act. The production, however, occurs in the object affected and not in the agent:

> It is not absurd that the actualisation of one thing be in another. Teaching
> is the activity of a person who can teach but it occurs in someone and is
> not cut adrift from the subject, but rather is an activity of S in T. (202b6–
> 8: see also 202a34; 426a11)

In *Metaphysics* 1050a28–32 Aristotle writes:

> The act of building is in the thing being built . . . In all cases where the
> result is distinct from activity – in some the activity occurs in what is
> being produced (i.e. the act of building in the thing built, the act of
> weaving in the thing woven) and in a similar way with other cases (i.e.
> not productions) and in general, movement occurs in the thing moved.

And he contrasts this with cases in which there is no separate result beyond the activity, which occurs in the agent himself (e.g. seeing occurs in the person who sees, speculation in the speculator and life – and happiness – in the soul: 1050a32–b1).

The position appears general. In those cases where a basic act causes an effect in another object (e.g. the smashing of a window), Aristotle locates the non-basic act of S's smashing the window where the smashing of the window occurs: in the window. This parallels his location of basic acts (moving my hand) at the point where the relevant spatial movement (my hand's moving) occurs. In both cases, the causally efficacious act occurs where its effect occurs.

Aristotle's positioning of basic and non-basic acts runs contrary to one strand in contemporary philosophy, in which the non-basic act is located at the point where the basic act occurs, and not where its effect is.[22] Thus, if the non-basic act is my smashing the window, this occurs where my hand is (if I throw a stone) and not where the window is smashed, if the former is what causes the window to be smashed. In the case of basic actions with a causal component (e.g. moving my hand) the analogy suggests that one should locate them at the point where the cause of the moving hand occurs: at some antecedent stage which causes the moving of the hand, and not where the effect occurs. Let us call this the 'regressive' tendency.

Aristotle resists this 'regressive' line of thought in the case of basic action by locating the basic action at the periphery of the body (or beyond). In the relevant sequences of processes $a1$ to $a7$, Aristotle locates both the basic and non-basic act ('progressively') at the final stage and not the first.[23] In these cases he separates the agent's doing something which causes the window to be smashed ($a1$), and his causing the window to be smashed (or his bringing it about that the window is smashed ($a7$)) in a way parallel to his discussion of basic actions. In this way Aristotle, in effect, maintains the following co-location: the window being smashed by me occurs where my smashing of the window occurs; since the former occurs where the window is smashed (in the window pane), so does the latter.

An example may clarify Aristotle's position: if S sends a letter to T with a vial of poison, knowing that T will take the poison and die, S does not begin to poison T or to kill T before the poison begins to have effect on T (within his account). Thus while the letter is still in the post (even when it is certain that T will take the poison), S is not then poisoning T (or killing him); he is doing something which will lead to T's being poisoned but is not yet actually poisoning him. It is not true that S *is* poisoning T (and will never be true that S *was* poisoning T)

---

[22] As in Davidson's proposal, 1980, 52ff.

[23] The regressive view identifies the action in both cases at $a1$, the first stage. If basic and non-basic actions occur at the same place, $a1$ will be (in both cases) a neural event. The third alternative identifies the action with the set of events ($a1 \ldots a7$). See Thalberg, 1977a, 85ff.; Miller attributes this view to Aristotle (1975).

before T takes the poison and it begins to affect him. When S has posted the letter and while the letter is still in the post, S is not yet poisoning T although he has done something which will result in T's being poisoned. Thus, Aristotle identifies S's poisoning T neither with the initial action ($a1$) nor with the series ($a1 \ldots a7$), although these may constitute S's trying to poison T.

How defensible is Aristotle's account of the location of non-basic actions of this type? Is he compelled to adopt it? Several objections may be raised:

(1) It is sometimes argued that while the smashing of the window by me occurs where the window is, *my* smashing of the window does not. After I have thrown the stone there is nothing else for me to do; the rest is up to nature,[24] and does not rest with me. This objection is in danger of begging the question: if it asserts that there is nothing which *I* do after I throw the stone, then it assumes that my smashing the window does not occur after my throwing the stone. Of course, there are *no more bodily movements* of mine which I am required to do in order to bring this result about; but this only shows that the resultant actions (if there are any) are not my movements of my body – and does not prove that no further actions of mine occur. Nor is it clear why all actions of mine should be confined to those of which I am the *sole controller*. Why so stringent a requirement? While it may be necessary that all actions of mine result from an action of which I am sole controller, why should all *my* acts be ones of which I am sole controller? Of course, if one defines '*my* action' by reference to *my* causally basic acts, then there will be no possibility of my smashing the window occurring where the window is smashed. But it remains to be shown that this definition would be well-founded.

(2) It may be objected that if non-basic actions occur after the basic action (and are located where the effect is), an agent may be correctly described as acting after his death. Suppose that Padraig plants a bomb at t, which will explode at $t + 5$. On his escape-route, he is shot dead by the security police at $t + 3$; at $t + 5$, the bomb explodes and blows up the Woolwich Arsenal. Does Aristotle then have to say that Padraig blew up the Woolwich Arsenal at $t + 5$, when he was already dead and buried? If death is the end of action, this might seem a paradoxical consequence of Aristotle's theory.

Death, however, may be the end only of *basic* actions. Padraig's non-basic actions may continue after him, even if his basic actions die with him. I do not myself find this reply paradoxical. However, if we were reluctant to *assert* that Padraig acts once dead, this could be because we are *interested* in attributing actions only to those we can regard (for the purposes of moral assessment) as being happy or sad at the success or failure of their action-plan at the time when the action occurs. Thus we could explain why it may seem (to some)

[24] Davidson argues in this way: 1980, 59.

paradoxical to *assert* that the dead perform non-basic actions (even if they can, in fact, do so), without limiting all the actions (of the living) to basic actions.

Aristotle's location of non-basic acts may still *seem* mistaken because we frequently reserve the term 'action' for the basic action, and use other locutions for the bringing about of more distinct effects ('this action resulted in . . .'). Perhaps this is because we are typically most interested as agents in whether or not to do a basic action now. But to prove that this element of *immediacy* is essential to the concept of action requires further argument, which would show (if successful) what is paradoxical about Aristotle's location of non-basic actions.

But it is not clear that Aristotle is forced to adopt a 'progressive' view of *both* basic *and* non-basic actions. His own theory of actions and processes provides grounds for doubting his location of non-basic actions in cases in which there is no separate categorical basis of the required type in the agent (e.g. if the non-basic action is the result of the basic capacity *plus* circumstances). Here (if he requires a separate categorical basis for action – individuation) there would be no non-basic action at all, but only a further (non-basic) description of the basic action, and so the action would not fall outside the agent. If Aristotle adopted this requirement (see above), there might seem to be an internal tension in his theory: not all non-basic (causal) actions *could* occur where the effect is, but some (e.g. inadvertently smashing the window) would occur where the basic action is (e.g. kicking the stone).

If there is an internal tension of this type in Aristotle's account, it should be best resolved (within his theory) through a study of the preferred theory of the organism's dispositions to determine whether there are actions (appropriately individuated) beyond the agent. In this way Aristotle's macro-theory of processes may provide stronger grounds for doubting his own (micro-level) location of all causally non-basic actions beyond the agent than the two narrowly analytical arguments so far considered. Indeed there would be no causally non-basic action located beyond the agent, if there were no separate categorical bases of the kind appropriate for non-basic causal dispositions within the agent. The legitimacy of this, or the more limited claim that some causally non-basic actions occur beyond the agent, would depend not on linguistic intuition but on the securer foundation of the demands of the preferred explanatory theory of the internal structure of the organism. For Aristotle there can be no settling of these issues apart from consideration of the requirements of explanation. And his account provides one way of achieving this.

There is one further (exegetically important) addition to Aristotle's account of non-basic actions. We separate two superficially similar but radically distinct locutions: if I push the door and thereby open it, my pushing and my opening the door are distinct acts. However, in a different idiom, my action of pushing the door results in the door being open, which is a state brought about by my action. These distinct locutions require differences in ontology: in the first case (for Aristotle) the act of 'my opening the door' immediately follows 'my pushing the door' and ends when the door is opened; in the latter the door being open begins just at the point when the door is opened, and endures for as long as the door remains open. Hence, if I push the door and it is opened by the momentum of my push, the state of the door being open will outlast my act of opening it.

These differences may be formulated thus:[25]

Model I	*Model II*
The act/act model	*The act/result model*
(1) ϕ'ing is an action;	(1) ϕ is a state, and not an action;
(2) If ϕ'ing is a process, it finishes when the state is produced;	(2) the state produced will continue after b'ing is completed;

where ϕ'ing is (e.g.) my opening the door and b is the door being open. The door being open is the final result of my action: the state that has to be achieved if my action is to be successful. The action ϕ'ing can only occur if the end-state b is achieved; it is the state that has to be brought about if the action is to occur. ϕ'ing is the bringing about of the state b; b is what is brought about by ϕ'ing. ϕ'ing results in the obtaining of b.

Aristotle used Model II in analysing the results of production in cases where the goal of a basic action is a house (200a24–27), health (1111a31; 1032b6–9), money (1227a13–15; 1112b25), droughts and rains (1112a26–27) and safety (1110a10; 1111a14). In such cases, Aristotle could have used the act/act model and taken the goal to be 'producing a house' or 'making health' (the non-basic act) but prefers to operate with the act/result locution. Nor is this surprising, since in these cases what is sought is a state which endures after the action has been completed.

But can Model II also apply where what is done is a *praxis*, and not a production? In such cases the result will *not* (typically) continue existing after the action: for example, if S contemplates a proof, what is brought about by S is that he is in (or continues to be in) a state of contemplation – which will not continue after S has finished contem-

---

[25] In what follows, Model I is, on occasion, specified as the 'Act/Act Model' (or the 'Two Act Model') and Model II as the 'Act/Result Model'. The former is employed (*mutatis mutandis*) by Goldman in his writings (1970, 21ff.). The latter is favoured by Von Wright, 1971, 66f., 75., 87f., 92), although he has reservations about applying it to activities (1963, 41ff.; 1972, 38ff.). Miller (1975) suggests a modified account of Model II in certain contexts, but does not consider how moral *praxeis* can be accommodated within it.

plating. If S is to contemplate, it is necessary that he bring about that he is in this state, which is the result of S's action and has to occur if S is to contemplate. In such cases 'what is done' is ambiguous: it may refer either to S's bringing about of the state, or to the state (e.g.) of contemplation which S brings about. The former is S's action; the latter is the state in which S's action results. If so, Model II requires a more general formulation to cover both *praxeis* and productions:

Model II
The act/result model

(1) *b* is a state brought about by S's action, and not S's action of bringing that state about;
(2) the state brought about is the result of S's action.

The result, in the case of a production, will outlive the producing; in the case of *praxis*, it will not typically do so. Thus, contemplation (the state produced by contemplating) may be conceived as an internal state (immanent state) which results from the action of contemplating, as health is the immanent state which results from being healthy (1174b31–32).[26]

Contemplation (the state) is a part of virtue (*NE/EE* 1144a2, 5) and is the internal result of contemplating. Can Model II be applied to other virtuous actions? Do actions of this type have results (e.g. being generous or noble) which result from acting generously or nobly? If they do, there will be an intrinsic state: nobility or courage (1115b20–24) conceived of as the logically necessary internal result of acting nobly or courageously. Aristotle appears confident that this is so, for elsewhere he emphasises that activities as well as processes have results of this type (1050a21–22):

> The result is the end, the activity is the result, and this is why the term 'activity' is predicated of the result (*ergon*) and extended to refer to the actualisation.

In this passage, 'activity' is said to designate either the actualisation of a capacity or its result (or goal) (viz. its actuality). If this is correct, in all cases where the non-basic action is an activity, there will be an internal result which is brought about by doing it. Thus the result of courageous action would be (e.g.) the actuality of courage which is the goal of the courageous man, who would aim to make courage actual by his action of acting courageously. If so, Model II will apply to both productions and *praxeis*; in the former case what is brought about (or

---

[26] In this interpretation of 1174b31–32, I follow Ramsauer, Burnet and Festugière. Immanent states and supervenient ends may both be formal causes, although of different types (contrast Stewart, Gauthier/Jolif).

preserved) is the product, in the latter the actuality of (e.g.) a virtue itself.

If there are logically necessary internal results of activities of this kind, Model II may be applied in all cases where Model I is employed.[27] Although Aristotle may have used Model I in arguing that *praxeis* were the non-basic acts chosen by the virtuous agent, he could exchange this for Model II when he analyses the structure of moral reasoning without contradiction. For whenever there is a *praxis*, there will be a corresponding internal result as required by Model II. Further since the result is a logically necessary condition of there being that *praxis*, if the agent chooses the act as his goal he thereby chooses to bring about the result, and if he chooses to bring about that result himself he chooses to do the *praxis*.

If this is defensible, Aristotle had two distinct modes of representing actions. In one (act/act model) both basic and non-basic act were taken as actions, while in the other (act/result model) there is no non-basic act, but a result produced by a basic act. If Model II applies to *praxeis* as well as productions, its use does not betoken a difference in the structure of practical reasoning from that required for Model I. On the contrary, what would be shown is a difference only in ontology as Aristotle moves freely from act/act to act/result models without inconsistency. Thus attention to Aristotle's ontology would illuminate his account of practical reasoning and virtuous action.[28]

Aristotle's ontology of actions is used as the basis for his account of agency and intentional action in Section D. His discussion of these topics provides further evidence of his aim of discussing ontological questions within an explanatory context. Before turning to those issues we should examine Aristotle's account of desire and the practical syllogism; for these constitute two other bases for his analysis of intentional action.

C. Desire, acceptance and the practical syllogism

Desire is, for Aristotle, the cause of the basic action. He offers two routes to characterise it: in the first he compares it with assertion (or

[27] It is not claimed that Model I applies in all cases where Model II applies. Indeed Model II may be used when the result is not an action of the agent of the basic act at all, but is done by someone else on his orders. Model I, by contrast, can only be used if the agent of both acts is the same (see 1112b26–27).

[28] Aristotle comments on the relevant ambiguity between process and product (*EE* 1217a35–41) when he remarks that 'what is done' is ambiguous between the states achieved by action (e.g. money, well-being) and the actions done to bring them about (making money, doing what constitutes well-being). This distinction might enable Aristotle to allow that certain activities may constitute well-being, be virtuous or pleasurable and yet be done for the sake of the state of well-being, virtue or pleasure conceived of as the logically necessary internal result (without being done for the sake of a further independent goal). It lies outside the scope of the present project to examine this proposal from either an exegetical or a philosophical standpoint (see Charles, 'Ontology and moral reasoning in Aristotle', forthcoming).

belief); in the second he links it with action. His account appears composite; and this raises the question of how the components are related, and which, if either, is fundamental.

The connexion with assertion is made in several contexts. Thus in *de Anima* 431a8–14:

> Perception then is like merely saying; when the object (s.c. perceived) is pleasant or painful, the soul pursues or avoids it – as it were affirming or denying a proposition. Indeed to feel pleasure or pain is to be active with the perceptive mean towards good or bad, as such. This is what avoidance and desire (when actual) are, and the faculties of desire and avoidance are not different either from each other or from that which can perceive, though their essence is different.[29]

Aristotle contrasts desiring an object with perceiving it by contrasting saying and affirming a proposition. Since affirmation is a mode of accepting a proposition, desire (given the analogy) is represented *either* as a mode of accepting a proposition (although a different mode from asserting) *or* as in some other way analogous to a mode of accepting a proposition which characterises assertion, but not itself a mode of accepting a proposition.

Aristotle employs a similar analogy elsewhere (1139a21–26):

> What in the case of intellect [cf. 1139a1, 11–13] is affirming or denying, that in the case of desire is desiring or being averse. So, since ethical virtue is a disposition to make choices, and choice is a desire to do what is deliberated, the argument must be true and the desire correct, if the choice is to be excellent: i.e. what the argument asserts must be exactly what the desire pursues.

Since, in this passage, what the argument asserts is exactly what is desired (what desire pursues), and what is asserted is a proposition (1147a27), the object of desire must also be a proposition. That is, desire is represented as a mode of accepting the conclusion which reason has asserted to be true (e.g. φ is good).

This interpretation of desire gives clear point to the analogy in the

---

[29] I follow Rodier and Hicks in taking 'pleasant and painful' as neuter nominatives complementing a noun (e.g. the perceived object) which needs to be understood. I favour construing perceiving as also propositional, on the basis of Aristotle's use of saying in 430b26–27 and 431a16, and thus take the distinction to be between saying and affirming. In the parallel case of the thinking soul (431a14ff.), the soul says that φ is good, and desire (as the affirmer) affirms this by pursuing it (see also 431b8–10). Saying is sometimes used in a more technical sense (1051b24–25; cf. *de Int.* 17a17ff.; 16b27), which is equivalent to referring to *x* and distinct from asserting a proposition. If this were present in 431a9, it would not challenge the claim that desiring is a mode of asserting a proposition (like affirmation); it would be contrasted, however, not with saying a proposition (430 b26ff; 431b8–10) but with saying 'apple' or 'pleasant'.

two passages.[30] If it is a mode of accepting a proposition (in these contexts), it might be represented as

DES. (φ'ing is good)

on the basis of an analogy with assertion (see 17a25–26)

AS. (x is an apple)

where the former is appropriate if what is sought is the good or the bad (431a12; see below).

The second ingredient in Aristotle's account of desire in 431a8–14 is that it is an *activity* of the soul in respect of objects conceived of as pleasant and painful or good and bad. Elsewhere, he writes that if one desires to φ and certain conditions obtain (1048a10ff., i.e. absence of external obstacle: 1048a16, presence of the appropriate object: 1048a10–14, the absence of any opposed desire which has not been defeated: 1048a21–22), then one will φ. Desiring is that type of activity which – if certain conditions obtain – will by itself produce the relevant action. Thus it is the mode of accepting a proposition which under certain conditions will by itself lead to action; it is distinct from belief (or affirmation), which does not, by itself, produce a relevant action under any conditions (in Aristotle's theory; see below).

Why then does an agent on occasion accept a proposition in the way that is characteristic of desire? *De Anima* 431a8–14 provides the beginning of a solution: to desire is to be active towards the good. If one desires to φ one accepts a proposition about φ'ing in the way which is appropriate given this aim. The relevant proposition will be one in which some feature of φ'ing is characterised in a way appropriate for acceptance in this mode: as good in some way. Thus we desire φ because φ'ing seems good to us (1072a29: 'we desire because it seems good to us, rather than it seems good to us because we desire it').

These passages suggest the following characterisation of desire:

S desires to φ iff
(1) S accepts the proposition that φ is good in the way appropriate if S's aim is to do what is good, &
(2) S is in a state which causes φ'ing if nothing intervenes.

This is neutral as between decisive and non-decisive desires; the former may produce actions in the absence of external obstacle and the presence of the object – i.e. will only be prevented by the presence of

---

[30] One alternative would be to say that aversion and pursuit are analogues of affirmation and denial as these are the final stages in the case of desire and thought. But this gives less clear sense to the claim that the objects of assertion and desire are identical (1139a25–26) as well as to the contrast between saying and affirming in 431a9–12. The major exegetical argument for this 'mode of acceptance' account of desire, however, lies in the unified picture it gives of the role of desire in practical reasoning, *acrasia* and practical wisdom. See this section and Chapter 4, Sections C, D, E.

external obstacle or the absence of the object; the latter, by contrast, may be prevented by the presence of other opposed desires from issuing in relevant action (1048a21–22). However, the passages do not themselves require that (1) and (2) give Aristotle's definition of desire; for they leave unresolved the question whether the causal role of desire is an element in the definition of desire or a property which desires possess.[31] Further, while they suggest that in certain instances the object of desire is itself actually propositional (i.e. involving a proposition which the agent accepts), they do not require that this is so in all cases. The definition, therefore, is a characterisation of at least one type of desire. The issue of the generality of this account is discussed below.

To accept a proposition in the mode characteristic of desire is to be in a state which leads (in appropriate conditions) to the action. If S accepts in this mode that φ'ing is good, S must desire to φ, as in the analogous case of belief, if S accepts that *p* is true, S must believe it. If he is not in this state, he does not desire to φ, and so rejects the proposition that φ seems good or pleasant, if this is suggested by perception (431a8–10).

This account of desire has several important features:

(1) it treats both components in the propositional act

DES. [φ'ing is pleasant]

as having equal importance. φ'ing cannot seem pleasant or good to S without his desiring it, and S cannot desire to φ (in these cases) without φ'ing seeming to him to have a good-making feature. Further it does this without reducing φ'ing seeming good to S to S's desiring it (1072a29ff.). For just as assertion may be characterised as a mode of accepting a true proposition without reducing the notion of truth to that of assertion, so desiring may be the mode of accepting that φ'ing is good without reducing the notion of good to that of desire. This account also explains why φ'ing seems good to S if and only if he desires to do it without building this connexion into the meaning of 'good'. Thus it is possible that both 'good' and 'true' have descriptive meaning compatible with it being the case that accepting in this mode that φ'ing is good is action-guiding; for it is the mode of accepting the judgment that leads to action, and this does not demand that the proposition be non-indicative.

(2) It does not require that what is desired is judged pleasant. Thus Aristotle is able to define one subset of desires (i.e. sensual desires) as having pleasure as their goal (414b5–6; 1111a32,b17) while characterising a distinct set of desires as not focused on to pleasure: (rational desires are: for the good and not the pleasant: 1369a2–3; 1111b26). This is because all that is required for the presence of desire is that

---

[31] See Chapter 5, Section C.

S sees some good-making characteristic in the object; since there are good-making features (e.g. nobility, advantage) other than the pleasant, Aristotle's account of desire does not focus desire on the pleasant.[32]

The application of 'good' is thus extremely wide, and applies in Aristotle's account to any object of desire. Thus Aristotle represents premisses which are gerundive in form:

Let me drink

as containing tacit reference to the good (701a24); for him the basic form of such syllogisms is indicative and involves expressions of goodness. Thus Aristotle's strategy is to seek to reduce all other moods to the indicative to fit in with his truth-based semantics for the practical syllogism.[33]

The range of cases to which 'good' applies in this account is large; it may apply to any object if S thinks that it will satisfy his desire, or which he considers noble or obligatory. If so, in every case in which S acts intentionally on a desire, he will accept a judgment that a given object is good. This wide-ranging use of 'good' will become important later: for it raises issues central to Aristotle's account of *acrasia* and practical wisdom.

(3) This account of desire requires only that if S desires to φ, φ seems good to S (and vice versa). It does not require that S desires to φ as strongly as he judges φ to be good. Thus an object may be perceived by S as highly valuable but not be strongly desired by him or (conversely) perceived as of little value but be strongly desired. While desire is open to cognitive factors (via the content of the proposition it accepts) it may also be influenced by other (possibly) non-cognitive elements which determine (e.g.) the strength of the desire the agent experiences for a given object. This will also prove significant later in discussing the acratic case.

(4) The account of 'desire' does not require that all desires are for instrumental means to an independently specifiable goal sought whenever one accepts a proposition in this way. That is, there may be certain desires so constitutive of the agent's conception of the good that he accepts them (non-hypothetically) without having any further independent goal.

However, the neutrality of the account does not render it unconten-

---

[32] Thus, Aristotle's use of 'desire' covers both what (e.g.) Nagel (1975) describes as 'desire' and his other motivational states. Since Nagel does not define desire explicitly (see also Irwin, 1976), it is not clear whether there is an actual debate on this issue between Aristotle and those who reject his inclusive conception of desire. For even if – in English – 'desire' (or even 'wanting') were tied to one subset of motivational states (e.g. directed towards pleasure) Aristotle's concept is designed to fill an essential explanatory role (see his discussion of the psychological explanation of *acrasia* in Chapter 4).

[33] See Appendix 3.

tious. Some may object that the further appetitive element is not required, since the propositional content alone suffices for explanation of action. Others may suggest that the propositional content is dispensable because the appetitive element alone is required to explain action.

Aristotle firmly rejects the first objection by noting that 'thought by itself moves nothing' (1139a35), and by insisting that desire itself is required as a causal feature motivating action (1139a17–18; 701a30–36; 433a21ff.). His essential claim is that a separable desire component is required fully to explain behaviour. If so, his reply must depend on his analysis of those cases in which he argues that desire is required to explain behaviour; in accounting for acrasia and separating the virtuous and the self-controlled man (see Chapter 4).

But does the desire to φ require that φ seems good? Aristotle sees this as essential for intentional action. 'The living creature is not capable of appetite without imagination' (433b28); 'the object of desire is either *the* good or the apparent good' (433a28–30). So desire (assisted by imagination) needs to grasp that φ'ing is good, if the agent acts intentionally (433b16–19). It is not sufficient that there is some internal state which produces that movement and the agent knows what he is doing. For this will apply to breathing, coughing and sneezing. What distinguishes the internal state which produces intentional action (for Aristotle) is that it is based on perceptual or calculative imagination, and accepts the proposition that φ'ing is good (or pleasant) in such a way as to produce the bodily movement. Desire differs from other states which produce non-intentional bodily movements in that it accepts (or may be represented as accepting) a proposition of this type. The qualification is important. Aristotle does not demand that all desirers actually formulate to themselves the judgment that φ seems good; the salient feature is that to desire is always *like* judging that φ seems good, and hence can be represented as accepting the judgment that φ is good.

Aristotle's discussion of the practical syllogism in *de Motu* 6–8 provides a test case for this account of his theory of desire and its propositional content. The general theory in these passages seems to run as follows: if an action is preceded by a practical syllogism, the agent possesses a desire which accepts the major premiss, and a belief which asserts a minor premiss. These propositions support a further proposition, which is the conclusion of the syllogism. If the agent appropriately accepts this conclusion, he desires to do the action which is the subject matter of the conclusion and acts accordingly. If he does not desire to do the action specified in the conclusion, he must consequently reject either one of the premisses or the inference from the premisses to the conclusion.

Propositional content plays two roles in this account. It rationally explains why one action was relevant given the agent's antecedent desires and beliefs, as it was the action which was specified as the one to be done in a conclusion supported by premises which express the agent's reasons for acting. It has a second, derivative, role: the conclusion will not be accepted unless the agent actually desires to do the action specified, and thus will act appropriately, if nothing prevents him. Thus, the premisses of the syllogism may explain action (but only derivatively) by yielding a propositional conclusion about the action to be done; if they are appropriately accepted by desire and nothing intervenes, action will result.

Within *de Motu* (if this account is correct) Aristotle is making two distinct claims: (a) intentional actions preceded by the syllogism are rationally explainable by a syllogism whose conclusion specifies the action in question, and (b) if there is a syllogism of this form and the agent accepts the premises and conclusion in the appropriate way, he will act. This line of interpretation rests on two essential exegetical claims: (i) that the conclusion of the practical syllogism is a proposition and not an action, and (ii) (at least) some action is explained by the acceptance of a conclusion of a practical syllogism in appropriate conditions, and not by the propositions which constitute the syllogism itself. Desire is required to produce action from the syllogism in these cases; but the actions thus produced will only be rationally explained if there is a syllogism whose conclusion specifies an action of that type.

The second claim rules out the possibility that the propositions of the syllogism alone may explain action. But it also pinpoints the role of desire: one has to accept the relevant proposition in the specified mode if one is to act on it. Thus in 701a28ff. Aristotle writes:

When an agent acts for the object which he has in view from either perception or imagination, he immediately does what he desires: instead of inquiring (as in dialectical reasoning) or thought (as in demonstrative reasoning), the activity of desire occurs. For example, Let me drink (desire says). This is a drink (imagination or perception or thought says). Immediately he drinks. In this manner animals are impelled to move and act, and the final cause of movement is desire; and this comes about through either sensation or imagination or thought.

Desiring to do what is suggested by imagination and a general desire is the cause of action, and is the surrogate of assertion in theoretical reasoning or asking a question in dialectical reasoning. Thought is a mode of accepting the proposition characteristic of theoretical reasoning. When desire 'takes its place', the agent accepts the conclusion in such a way as to lead to action (if nothing intervenes). Thus it is not the *conclusion* but the *activity of desire* which accepts it which explains the action (as its efficient cause). This reflects the distinctive role of desire in rendering the syllogism valid (see Chapter 4, Sections D, E).

The first exegetical claim: that the conclusion of the syllogism is a proposition, rests on several pieces of evidence but faces at least one textual difficulty. The evidence may be tabulated as follows:

The conclusion of the syllogism is a proposition and not the action

(a) 701a13–16: 'If you conceive that on a particular occasion no man ought to walk, and that you are a man, you immediately remain at rest. In this, action follows unless there is hindrance or compulsion'. Thus, if there is hindrance or compulsion, the action will not follow, although the conclusion may be drawn (701a12). Hence the conclusion is not the action.

(b) 1147a26–31: 'When one proposition emerges from these two (major and minor premisses), it is necessary then for the soul to assert it immediately, and in cases productive of action to do it immediately. For example, if the major premiss is "Taste all sweet things" and the minor is "This is sweet", it is necessary for the man who is able and not prevented straightaway *also* to do the action.' Here Aristotle envisages two separate activities: drawing the conclusion and *also* acting, which occur in favourable conditions at the same time. If so, the conclusion of the syllogism cannot be identical with the action (see Chapter 3, Section B)

(c) 701a19–21: 'The cloak is to be made' is a conclusion which predates action as there is further reasoning between it and the action: 'If there is this, then this etc.' If the conclusion predates the action, they cannot be identical.

The conclusion of the syllogism is an action and not a proposition

(a) In 701a21–22, Aristotle categorically states: 'That the action is the conclusion is clear'. If the action is identical with his acting, the conclusion is his acting.

(b) In 701a11–13, Aristotle may be taken as saying: 'The conclusion which results from the two premisses is an action', and not 'The conclusion which is drawn from the two premisses becomes an action'.

(c) In 701a8–25, Aristotle is attempting to answer the question: 'Why does thought sometimes result in action, and sometimes not?' (701a8–10). He does this by giving an explanation of how action occurs and not (merely) an account of how propositions hang together. But if the conclusion is merely a proposition, we have not advanced towards explaining action at all.

The conclusion of the syllogism is a proposition and not the action	*The conclusion of the syllogism is an action and not a proposition*
	For there still remains the basic question unanswered: how does the conclusion of the syllogism produce an action? Since any view which does not take the conclusion to be the action leaves this problem unresolved, Aristotle must take the conclusion to be the action.
(d) 702a16–21: 'A man thinks that he should go, and goes virtually at once, unless something prevents him ... the relation is simultaneous, i.e. quick'. Here Aristotle appears to be considering the state immediately prior to action and not (e.g.) entertaining the major premiss (cf. 701a15–16), as the major premiss may predate the action by a considerable time. If so, drawing the conclusion which is the state immediately prior to action, cannot be identical with the action.	(d) In 701a14–16, 33 and 434a16–20 Aristotle refers to an action (e.g. walking, keeping still) which results from the premisses. But if the action is the conclusion of the premisses, Aristotle must, in this passage, assimilate the action and the conclusion.

There is, therefore, an apparent conflict of evidence.[34] On occasion, Aristotle appears to consider the conclusion to be a proposition distinct from the action, and to take the conclusion as supported by premisses in an argument form. But elsewhere he appears to take the action itself as the conclusion and not a proposition which is distinct from the action. One explanation of this would be that Aristotle is concerned with distinct issues in these passages: in the first, he is examining practical reasoning as a mode of reasoning distinct from, but analogous to, theoretical reasoning, and thus naturally considers it in terms taken from his discussion of theoretical reasoning: premisses and conclusion; in the second his primary interest is in the explanation of action, and desires and beliefs, represented by relevant propositions, which are the relevant explanatory antecedents. Thus one account of this conflict would be that Aristotle is conflating answers to distinct

---

[34] See, for contrasting view, Nussbaum, 1978, ch. 4. She follows in outline the interpretation of these passages adopted by Von Wright, 1971. See for some later reservations Von Wright, 1978.

questions: 'What is the nature of practical reasoning?' and 'What is the appropriate explanation of intentional action?' under the ambiguous heading: 'Thinking in what way does a man sometimes act, and sometimes not?' (701a8–9).

The appearance of confusion, however, proves illusory if we employ Aristotle's concept of desire as a mode of acceptance in considering *de Motu* 7.

Consider the third argument in favour of taking the conclusion as an action. If the appropriate mode of accepting a conclusion is to desire to do the act specified, then there will be an answer to the question 'How does the conclusion of the syllogism produce an action?' which does not rest on taking the action to be the conclusion. For if the conclusion is appropriately accepted, and nothing intervenes, S will act accordingly, because he would not accept it if he did not desire to act on it. Thus it is not the *conclusion* that by itself explains the action by being identical with it; rather, *accepting* the conclusion explains the action – with the added proviso that if the conclusion were not accepted, the agent would not possess it, but would reject one or other of the premisses.

The first two arguments in favour of the view that the action is the conclusion depend on the interpretation of 701a19–22 and 11–13: the former passage runs as follows:

> The conclusion: I ought to make a cloak is an action. The agent acts from a desired goal: if there is to be this, then something else; and this one immediately does. That the action is the conclusion is clear.

This passage is problematic for any interpretation: in 701a19, the conclusion specified as a proposition 'I ought to make a cloak' is said to be an action, while in 701a22 the conclusion is again identified with the action. If Aristotle had intended the conclusion to be an action, he should not consistently have used a proposition to express it in 701a19. Alternatively, if he had intended the conclusion to be a proposition it seems that he cannot consistently say that it is an action in 701a19 and 22. Either way, Aristotle's position in this passage seems radically confused: in 701a18–19 he appears to hold *both* that the conclusion is a proposition *and* that it is an action.

There is one way of resolving these difficulties which is compatible with Aristotle's usage elsewhere (*Pr. An.* 53a17: 30a29; see *Post. An.* 94b1–8). 'The conclusion', as he uses it, may mean either the proposition which is the conclusion *or* the subject matter of the conclusion. Thus in 53a17–21, 'the conclusion' is used to specify things in the world – what is spoken of – and not the proposition used to speak about them. When these things are said to be placed in 'the conclusion', this is either literally false or 'the conclusion' means the subject matter of the conclusion. Since the latter is preferable (see Liddell & Scott on '*sumperasma*'), Aristotle is guilty in this passage of a use/mention confusion, and takes 'conclusion' to mean not proposition but rather the objects referred to in the proposition.

This yields a consistent reading of 701a18–23 – 'The subject matter of the conclusion: "I ought to make a cloak" is an action . . . That the action is the subject matter of the conclusion is clear' – which is compatible with the conclusion not itself being an *action*, but a *proposition* about an action. The subject matter (a somewhat vague notion) of the proposition may either be the objects described (here, an action), or what is said of the objects thus described (that the action ought to be done). If so, the subject matter of the first proposition will be the action of making a cloak, which is said to be required in 701a19–20, and is what is done in 701a24. If by contrast 'conclusion' does not refer to its subject matter in 701a18–23, it is difficult to give an interpretation which is not radically inconsistent because it takes 'conclusion' to mean 'proposition' *and* 'action' within the same sentence. Hence we should conclude that this passage does not support the contention that the conclusion is the action; rather, it favours the view that, for Aristotle, the conclusion is a statement about an action which is to be done.

There remains 701a11–13, which is sometimes translated as 'The conclusion which results from the premises is an action' (i.e. conclusion is identical with action), and sometimes as 'The conclusion drawn from these premises becomes the action' (i.e. conclusion is not identical with action). The second alternative has grammatical merit: it takes 'become' as the main verb connecting the conclusion and the premises. It would be (at least) unusual for Aristotle to delete the main verb, place the subordinate verb outside the immediate grammatical scope of the subordinate clause and take it as the only verb in the sentence. However, there is a countervailing reason put forward in favour of the first alternative: if Aristotle's concern is to contrast theoretical and practical reasoning, it would be odd to find a contrast between the conclusion of the theoretical syllogism and the *result* of the conclusion of the practical syllogism. We would expect rather a contrast between their two conclusions: the one being a proposition and the other being an action.

This line of thought forces one to locate more precisely Aristotle's perception of the difference between theoretical and practical reasoning (701a9). In one, to accept the conclusion is to believe it (701a31; 701a11); in the other, it is to desire to do the action specified. As Aristotle notes (701a31–32), here 'the activity of desire takes the place of thought and inquiry'. Thus what is distinctive of practical as opposed to theoretical reasoning is (at least) the distinct mode of acceptance in each of the premises and conclusion. Desire, unlike belief, is characterised as that mode of accepting the conclusion of a syllogism which explains action under given circumstances.

This account of the *role* of the practical syllogism sees its primary function as articulating Aristotle's conception of practical reasoning;

but this conception is closely tied to the explanation of (at least) some actions as appropriate acceptance of the conclusion will, under the right conditions, produce the relevant action. Thus, given Aristotle's account of the role of desire as a mode of acceptance of the conclusion, he was able both to distinguish practical from theoretical reasoning (701a10–12, 30–32) and to explain why under certain conditions action follows. The success of this interpretation in yielding a coherent reading of these passages provides further support for its attribution to Aristotle. Thus in *de Motu* Aristotle should be interpreted as holding: (a) that some intentional actions are preceded by a syllogism accepted by the agent whose conclusion is a statement about the action, and (b) that if the conclusion is of this form, and the agent accepts it, he will act on it if appropriate conditions obtain.

This account of the connexion between desire and propositional content in *de Motu* sees them as combined in a unified account of the practical syllogism. But it raises two central questions: (a) What is the basis of Aristotle's analogy between theoretical and practical reasoning? What are its implications? (b) What range of actions is explained by a syllogism of this form? Are all or only some intentional actions preceded by a syllogism?

Aristotle's account of desire shows both an analogy and a disanalogy between theoretical and practical syllogism in distinguishing separate modes of acceptance in the two cases (701a11–12; 701a30–32). We will return to these later in discussing *acrasia* and wisdom in Chapter 4, and the role of the syllogism in the explanation of action in Chapter 5. These will serve further to distinguish desire and belief in Aristotle's account.

There remains the second question: is the practical syllogism taken by Aristotle to be present in all cases of intentional action?[35] Or is it present only when the agent actually reasons, and draws the conclusion as a consequence of his reasoning?

It is sometimes held that Aristotle attributed the practical syllogism to an agent in all cases of intentional action. This exegetical view, however, is problematical on several grounds.

Animals (for Aristotle) act intentionally (1111a26) although they do not perform higher-order *praxeis* (1139a19f.). If they act intentionally only if they possess a practical syllogism, they must also possess the cognitive states which Aristotle sees as necessary for the use of such a syllogism: thought (701a7) and inference (701a27). However, elsewhere Aristotle makes it clear that (in his view) animals lack both the thought and calculative ability required (cf. 433a10–12; 415a7f., 11–12, 434a6–8). Indeed, more generally, Aristotle appears unwilling to attribute to animals conceptual machinery which outruns their actual ability (1147b4–6; 433b5–7). If so, it is in his account not necessary that all intentional agents act on a practical syllogism.

[35] See, for example, Nussbaum, 1978, 207, 205–6.

There is further evidence for this conclusion; elsewhere Aristotle regards reasoning as a process: (969b1), which takes place over time (1142b2–5) and which may stop and consider individual premises (701a26–27). Processes of this type are psychologically real processes which actively engage with the premises in the argument. Indeed in one of the paradigm cases of *acrasia*, the agent fails in reasoning precisely because he fails to see a connexion between the premises (1147a7, 26–27; see Chapter 3, Section B). Reasoning of this type can only be attributed when the agent is psychologically active in himself working through a practical argument.

In several contexts, Aristotle's agents act intentionally but without practical reasoning or 'syllogising'. In discussing types of *acrasia* (1149a32ff.) Aristotle distinguishes the acratic through anger from the acratic of sensual desire. In the former case the acratic 'as it were syllogises that he should fight this type of enemy, and immediately strikes back'. In the latter, 'desire, if reason or perception says that it is pleasant, leaps to enjoy it'; here, as opposed to the former case, there is no syllogising. This is why 'anger follows reasoning in a way, but sensual desire does not' (1149b1–3). Such a case would be one in which an agent acts on perceptual rather than logistic imagination (434a5ff.); all that is required is that he sees that a given course is pleasant (or good) and acts. There is no necessity to attribute to such agents calculation or practical reasoning. In their case, there is a sequence involving perception and desire (see 431a8–12; 701a35–37, b14–18) in which 'the final desire arises through perception' (701a35–36) without the agent reasoning about what to do. For Aristotle, there can be intentional action without the agent reasoning or going through a practical syllogism. There is no Aristotelian ground to attribute a practical syllogism to explain all intentional action.

Desire, therefore, may lead to intentional action without the agent's reasoning practically (in Aristotle's account). When the agent does reason practically, action will only result if he accepts the conclusion appropriately in the desire-based mode. This account of desire and reasoning will provide the basis for Aristotle's discussion of *acrasia*; it both allows an explanation of why the *acratês* fails to act on his good conclusion, and points to the limitations of rational explanation of intentional action (see Chapter 3, Section D; Chapter 5, Section A). For some intentional action is not rationally explained by a syllogism of this type; and when a syllogism is present this only explains action if the agent's mode of acceptance of its conclusion is appropriate, and leads him to perform the teleologically basic action it describes. In these cases the teleologically basic action is explanatorily significant, since it is this which is explained in this way. Aristotle's preference for teleologically basic actions (see Section B) reflects his use of the syllogism as an element in teleological explanation (see Chapter 5, Section A). Thus his ontological preference depends on his explanatory interests.

D. Basic intentional action and agency

Aristotle analyses intentional action in terms of causality and knowledge (Section A). In this section, we will consider his account of intentional basic action (Section B) and of the wider category of actions. This will enable us to combine some elements of his ontology with his (partially) causal account of action and intentional action, and see his approach to ontological issues at work in a difficult area.

An intentional basic action (z) is caused by S's desire to do a z-type action where z is the first specific means in S's plan (if he possesses one), and is S's movement of his body or 'detached limb'. If S is ignorant of what he is doing, he does not do z intentionally.

The ignorance in question is of a special kind. Aristotle envisages a case where a speaker becomes confused and 'does not know what he is saying' (1111a8–9).[36] This type of ignorance is compatible with (and generally co-occurs with) the agent hearing what he says and hence learning what he is doing. The relevant type of ignorance, therefore, is *agent's ignorance* of his action, since the only knowledge he possesses is based on *observing* what he is doing rather than on *doing* it.

Agent's knowledge (in the case of the basic action), by contrast, is dependent on the fact that one is an agent, and may be expressed in terms of the agent's non-inferential beliefs concerning what he is about to do, which arise from his activity *qua* agent. Thus, in the sequence of occurrences (see Section B) between his final desire to do $a7$ to his doing $a7$, $a1$–$a6$ must afford the agent knowledge that he is about to do $a7$. If this does not happen and S has no knowledge of what he is doing or about to do (e.g. if S 'blacks out') z will not be intentional. In the case of basic actions, this suggests an added clause in the account of intentional action, which I will classify as 'Aristotelian' (see Introduction).

z is a basic intentional action of S's at t_1 iff
(1) z is S's movement of his body or one of S's 'detached limbs';[37]
(2) z is the first means to be essayed in S's plan at t_1;[38]
(3) S knows the relevant particulars involved in doing z;
(4) z is caused by S's desire to do a z-type action by a route which gives S non-inferential and non-observational knowledge that he is about to do z.

---

[36] The text is in dispute here; but the difference in readings does not affect the sense. The case in point is a basic action: e. g. saying.

[37] Roughly, z is a detached limb for S at t_i iff (1) S is able to use z without deliberation about means at t_i, (2) S has non-observational (agent's) knowledge of what he is about to do when using z. The full account of 'detached limbs' depends on a more detailed spelling out of this Aristotelian condition and on discerning its connexion with S's unconditional capacities; (to show how (if at all) 'detached limbs' can become like parts of S's body).

[38] If S has a plan to do z for a further goal. If he has no goal beyond doing z, (in my use) his plan is one-stage: to do z. One-stage plans are described as 'plans' only for convenience of formulation.

The fourth requirement allows one to count certain actions as un-intentional where the latter are caused 'deviantly'. If an agent acts unintentionally out of nervousness (even if he does what he intended), there may be a stage in the chain (a type of nervousness, Nz, for example) which prevents him from knowing that he is about to do z. This will be so even if Nz reflects[39] (e.g.) S's desire to fidget sufficiently to produce an action of that type. Nervousness, by contrast, will be an 'action-aid' to an intentional action if the type of nervousness in ques-tion (Nw) both leads to fidgeting and does not prevent S from knowing that he is about to fidget.

Agent's knowledge (thus characterised) distinguishes the Aristote-lian account from those which analyse intentional action solely in terms of knowledge, and from those which – leaving knowledge out of the picture – describe the appropriate dependency of the action on agent's desire in purely causal, counterfactual or functional terms. Unlike the former[40] it uses the causal connection between S's desire to do z and his doing z as the basis for agent's knowledge of what he is about to do.[41] Unlike the latter, it employs agent's knowledge to determine which are the relevant functional dependencies between desire and action. It is an attempt, therefore, to specify the types of function required for intentional action in terms of a general account of knowledge.

The Aristotelian account promises several advantages over purely functional theories. It seeks to isolate those functional dependencies which convey sufficiently specific and determinate information be-tween $a1$ and $a6$ to yield agent's knowledge that one is about to do $a7$, and to discount as irrelevant to intentional action those which do not. Thus it aims to specify *which* functional dependencies lead to inten-tional action in terms of a theory we can apply as agents, without an understanding of underlying functional or neurophysiological theory. Its goal is to employ the requirement that knowledge be *discriminating* to capture which dependencies are of the appropriate type for the resultant action to be intentional. It has a second aim: to use the demand that knowledge be '*non-accidental*' to capture which types of functional dependencies, in differing organisms, connect intention and

[39] In a way which met Christopher Peacocke's conditions of differential explanation and stepwise recoverability: see Peacocke, 1979, 66–8, 80–1. I am considerably indebted to Peacocke's rigorous discussion in this section.

[40] Compare Anscombe 1957, 14, 50–1. Her account differs from Aristotle's also in requiring agent's knowledge not only of what is being done (1111a8–9) but also of to whom, with what, etc., and in (apparently) applying this to both basic and non-basic actions. In what follows I take Pears's criticism of her view that the presence of agent's knowledge is sufficient for the action being intentional as decisive (1975b, p. 57).

[41] And knowledge of what one is trying to do. Agent's knowledge, thus conceived, is concerned only with what is relevant to what the agent is about to do in implementing his intention. (For further discussion see Parry, 1974, 44ff.) In the present context, agent's knowledge is confined to knowledge that one is about to do a basic action, and is not extended to non-basic actions.

intentional action. Thus, if two types of organism conveyed information from intention to action in different functionally specified ways (e.g. one like a camera, the other like a hologram), both could be intentional agents provided that their different functional connexions sustain agent's knowledge.[42] If there are animals who act intentionally without agent's knowledge, clause (4) should be amended to read

(4)' *z* is caused by S's desire to do a *z*-type action by a route which gives S *the* possibility of non-inferential and non-observational knowledge that he is about to do *z*.

But can the promise of the Aristotelian account be made good?

An account of the appropriate causation of basic intentional action should specify both (a) the types of functional dependency which are relevant if the action is to be intentional, and (b) the elements which can figure as stages in a chain. The Aristotelian knowledge condition: (4) is the basis for an answer (a); Aristotle himself provides an answer to (b), which can be used to make clause (4) more precise.

Elements in a correct chain should be ones which S – as then constituted – is able to make occur at will. Since intentional action has its 'starting point in the agent' (1110a15–16), it is up to the agent to do or not to do (1110a16–18), and is within his power to do (1140a31) as the *originator* of the action (1113b18–19). Thus the basic action and the intermediate steps between it and S's relevant desire must be processes which the agent is able to effect as their originator. In the sequence of occurrences described in Section B, S must be able to bring about $a1$–$a6$ without further deliberation, since he knows how to do $a7$ without further deliberation. Further, since the basic action is S's movement of his body or 'detached limbs' (which are *as* parts of his body), S must be able to bring about $a1 \ldots a7$, when he intends to $a7$, without 'external' assistance. For if he received that, he would not be exercising his own unconditional capacity as their originator (without change in or addition to himself as subject of change) nor stand to the

---

[42] Compare Peacocke's account, 1979, 78ff. There are cases in which Aristotle's account yields different results. It seems conceivable that complex physiological study may reveal certain functional dependencies of Peacocke's type, in which the resultant action is unintentional because no *determinate* information or information of the *wrong type* is conveyed: e.g. if S intends to type a given letter, this may always lead him only to twitch his wrist or raise his knee (if severely paralysed) and nothing else could have this effect in the circumstances. If one knew the covering laws for the organism one could recover the intention from the twitch or knee-raising, but this would not appear sufficient to make his action intentional, since the distinctive nature of his intention is obliterated. Secondly, there could be cases in which, for a given organism, the message was conveyed dispersed through the organism (e.g. for certain types of memory) in a way analogous to that represented by one of Peacocke's camera examples (1979, 80–1). This would seem permissible provided that the route (even if abnormal for this mechanism) was capable of conveying the possibility of knowledge (Martin Davies discusses the second type of difficulty in detail: Davies, 1983; he alerted me to its existence.)

parts moved as to parts of his body. Permissible stages in a non-deviant chain, therefore, are of a type which S (a) can make occur without deliberation about means, and (b) can make occur *by himself*, as constituted at t_o, without change in or addition to himself as the subject of change.

This account has the following consequences. Since S, as constituted at t_o, lacks the ability to make (e.g.) lightning of a given type occur (without additional assistance from processes which he cannot, un-aided, make occur), such lightning would not count as a stage in a non-deviant chain even if it manifested the appropriate functional dependencies.[43] Conversely, S (as constituted at t_o) will have the power to make $a1$–$a6$ occur if he has the relevant causal power at t_o, without further external assistance from features he cannot at t_o make occur. And this will be so even if S has before t_o given himself unusual powers (e.g.) by taking an enabling drug or by fitting a prosthetic device; provided that the latter may also be counted as part of himself *qua* agent (either as a 'detached limb' or as a functionally equivalent replacement for a part of his body). And these consequences seem intuitively attractive in distinguishing cases where the surroundings contribute *too much* assistance for the result to be an intentional basic action.

The ability condition takes a time-slice of S *by himself* at the moment of intention, and asks: is S, as now constituted (without external addition or subtraction or change in the subject of change, see Chapter 1, note 14) able to φ (where φ refers to each stage in the chain between S's desire to do $a7$ and his doing $a7$)? S, as then constituted, cannot *by himself* make a given stage (M) occur if (i) there can be no causal connexion between $a1$ and M, or (ii) there can be a causal connexion between $a1$ and M, but one which requires the occurrence, indepen-dently of S's desire to do z, of conditions which are external to S (as constituted at t_o), and which he does not then by himself have the capacity to make occur.

An Aristotelian *basic action-producing mechanism* consists of stages which S (as constituted at the time of intention) can make occur without the assistance of external circumstances, which he himself cannot make occur (at the time of the intention). These Aristotelian conditions depend on an intuitive distinction between S (and S's un-conditional capacities) and S's surroundings, which needs to be cap-tured in any account of non-deviance of the type characterised. And this will need to be sharpened if the conservative notion of 'an origin-ator' is to prove useful for all types of case; so too will the degree of independence (within (ii)) from S's intention of the occurrence of M if

---

[43] In certain cases he may know how to direct the lightning flash so that it strikes at a particular point or in a certain way. In such cases, S's directing the lightning will be a non-teleologically basic action which S does by doing something else. Our present concern is exclusively with teleologically basic actions. For a differing account, see Peacocke, 1979, 93ff.

the action is to be unintentional (e.g. if M is another agent who seeing S's desire decides to enable him to do z: e.g. by turning on a support machine). Borderline cases may survive, but the proposal seems to locate them at the correct place. (Further investigation lies outside the present project in a study of Aristotle's views on the *person*, as this will define the boundaries of the agent as essential subject of change. See Chapter 1, n. 14).)

An Aristotelian action-producing mechanism (for basic actions) should meet two separate conditions. (a) It should consist of elements within the range of S's unconditional abilities as an action-originator at t_0 (as specified above), and (b) it should yield (the possibility of) agent's knowledge of what S is about to do. This characterisation permits a fuller specification of agent's knowledge. S has agent's knowledge (on one account) only if:

there is no stage R in the action-producing mechanism (of which S may be unaware) such that if S (who desires to ϕ) had been aware only of R (and R's relation to stages in the action-producing mechanism prior to R), S would have good reason (in the best theory) for not believing on balance that he was about to ϕ.

If a stage of type R occurred, S would be aware of cases exactly like this one in respect of the action-producing mechanism up until R and with an R-type stage, which failed to lead to a ϕ-type action. The occurrence of such cases would undermine S's agent's knowledge[44] and show the particular case to be a deviant chain, which leads to an unintentional action (even if the intended action actually occurred).

This suggests a general strategy for problems of deviant causal connexions: regard the relevant chains as parts of knowledge-producing mechanisms, and allow one's general account of knowledge to determine (within the subject's relevant ability range) the appropriate type of dependency. Aristotle himself did not specify the general account of knowledge in such a way as to carry through this strategy nor seek to apply it to the related problems of memory and perception. Hence its detailed deployment and examination lies outside our present project. In the case of action, the Aristotelian requirement is in some ways a stringent one. Not all chains which are discriminating in the actual situation will meet these conditions; certain of them will fail because they contain elements which are not essential components in S's abilities as an originator at t_0 – as they are features of the surrounding circumstances and not intrinsic to the action-producing mechanism (e.g. lightning in the case specified); others will fail because they are not sufficiently discriminating to meet the agent's knowledge condition (although they meet other functional specifications). The knowledge condition 'swallows up' and aims to make more

---

[44] For an account of knowledge which allows for this, see Goldman, 1976.

precise the functional dependency theory (see Peacocke 1979, 105ff.). It will prove successful in this only if the type of 'non-accidentality' characteristic of knowledge is the correct one to employ to capture non-deviance.

This Aristotelian account is, in a certain sense, a generalisation of a proposal recently canvassed by David Pears (1975b) as both rely on knowledge and causation, but unlike Pears's, it does not require the agent to hold any theory of the internal chain between his intention and the bodily movement, or presuppose that non-deviant chains run through a given essential initiating event. Aristotle's account in fact does not depend at any point on the findings of physiological science, and does not specify any particular physiological mechanism or concept as intrinsic to the action-producing mechanism. Although both proposals aim to use knowledge *and* causation in their account of basic intentional action, their theories differ in detail and in principle.

Within this account of basic intentional action, teleological basicness is important as it permits the agent knowledge that he is about to do z before he does z. Thus, in the sequence of actions ($a1$ to $a7$) described above, $a1$–$a6$ yield agent's knowledge that one is about to do z, where this knowledge is required to fix the relevant functional dependencies between the desire and action if the chain is non-deviant. Causally basic acts ($a1$) do not yield this type of non-inferential knowledge, since if the action ($a1$) is immediate, there is no knowledge that one is about to do it. Further, teleologically basic acts are connected directly with the relevant account of unconditional ability (doing $a7$); for our interest in ability is in successful performance, and not in the stages antecedent to this. Thus we deliberate until we reach an action-type we are able to do without further assistance or deliberation. In these ways Aristotle's preference for teleologically basic actions depends on his being able to use them within his account of the agent's behaviour which uses both causal and teleological terms. It is because they (situated at or beyond the periphery of the body) appear in his theory of intentional action that he has good grounds for employing them in his ontology. Since his account is one which seeks to explain action causally and teleologically, his characteristic concern with explanation leads him to employ basic actions of this type within his ontological account.[45]

Aristotle's discussions of action, self-movement and the intentional

---

[45] Intentional non-basic actions will be brought about by intentional basic actions caused appropriately. In some such cases one may now know that one is about to do the non-basic action. Thus, if you fire at a distant target, you may know that you are such a bad shot that you think it very unlikely that you will hit it, and hence (even if you hit it intentionally) will not know that you are about to do it. In some cases the most one knows is that (in doing a basic action) one is *trying* to hit the target (even if one does not believe that there is greater probability of hitting the target by firing than by not). If Aristotle applied his knowledge condition to non-basic actions, and required more than this, he was mistaken.

also exemplify this general approach by giving further reason to locate basic actions at (or beyond) the periphery of the body, as well as showing the power of his ontological theory. Within it the intentional is not confined to actions. Refraining from action (1226b33–4) remaining where one is (1115b12, 23) and being at rest (406b22–25) are also treated as intentional, but are distinguished from actions (1226b34, 1115b23). If John remains silent under torture or remains at his post while the enemy advance, he refrains from action intentionally but does not act at all. Not everything which is intentional is an action; for deprivation of action is not itself an action. Aristotle's ontology of states and processes allows certain phenomena to be intentional, but not be actions (e.g. standing fast). He is not compelled to treat the latter as bodily movements, as he would have been if his ontology consisted only of substances and processes.[46]

Self-movers (259b1–3) are subjects of change with distinctive causal antecedents (caused by the agent: 252b12–13). In 253a10–21, Aristotle classifies as processes not caused by the subject those not caused by the following route:

perception → desire or thought → process

Falling asleep, waking up and dreaming are not classified as actions because, although they may involve desire or thought, they do not depend on the agent's original perception (at the time) (a15–21). Thus Aristotle appears to hold that if S is to act *qua* self-mover, he must have an appropriate desire, and this desire arise either from S's perception or S's imagination and S's thought (701a32–36). His desire, thus caused, must make some difference to what occurs (1110a2–3) by causally altering the course of events. The occurrence of a self-moved process necessitates the previous occurrence of a desire of this type.

The absence of this structure shows why increase in size, decay and breathing are not cases of self-movement (259b8–10). The same applies to growing old and death (1135b1–2). Aristotle notes (259b5ff.) that certain cases of self-movement

> suggest the opinion that motion cannot come to be in a thing without having previously existed (for it seems that they are unmoved at one time and subsequently moved), and that we should accept that things only move by locomotion, and that it is not strictly originated by them. For the cause is not the agent himself, but there are present certain natural motions in animals, in which they are not moved by themselves: e.g. increase, decrease, and respiration – which movements occur when the animal is not self-moved. In such cases the cause is the environment and things that enter the animal such as food . . . And this is why animals are not *always* moved by their own agency; for there is something else that moves them, itself being in motion and changing as it comes into relation with each thing that moves itself.

---

[46] Contrast Davidson's account: 1980, 49.

But he cannot accept the initial opinion that *all* locomotion of self-movers is not strictly originated by them; for he continues (b14–21) to assert that there are cases of self-movement without qualification. Rather, he sets out the opinion with its ground (259b4–11), and then notes that the latter in fact gives only one isolated type of example in which the environment (and not the agent) is the cause (b11–14) and hence can only be used to explain why the agent is not *always* (continually) self-moved. Thus he (implicitly) concludes that the opinion (in its universal form) is false, and that there is a range of cases in which the subject of change is self-moved: those in which the causal sequence runs through the agent's appropriate psychological states of desire, imagination, perception or thought.[47]

If the subject is not self-moved, the resultant movements are (typically) non-voluntary (703b8–11; 1135b1–2); for neither imagination nor desire is strictly responsible for them. There is, however, an intermediate case: movements which occur through perception and desire, but are unintentional because 'they are not commanded by thought' (703b5–7), although they are self-caused (253a12–15; 259b5ff.) by the agent's psychological states. Thus perception and desire may cause one to be sexually aroused (703b5–7), frown, blush, sigh, bite one's lip in anxiety, raise one's eyebrows or raise one's heartbeat (703b5–7); yet these self-caused processes are not intentional (under any description) either because one is unaware that one is acting in this way or because one's action is not based on the thought that it is good or best to do an action of this type at the time. Such cases (e.g. frowning) seem to be self-caused processes on three Aristotelian grounds: (a) they are caused by the relevant psychological states; (b) they are realisations of one of S's abilities; and (c) the realisation of these abilities depends on the presence of the relevant psychological states. They constitute 'sub-intentional' occurrences, which may be classified as actions even though they are not intentional under any relevant description, and do not accord with the agent's thought (or desire) that it is good to do them.[48]

Aristotle discerns a variety of cases which he treats separately: (a) non-self-moved processes, e.g. growing old, breathing; (b) sub-intentional processes which are self-moved, e.g. frowning, being sexually aroused; (c) intentional processes, not supported by practical reasoning (see Section C); (d) intentional processes supported by reasoning (see

---

[47] Contrast Furley, 1978, 168–9, 176–7, who offers a different reading of 259bff. and 253a10ff. and hence sees tension between these passages and Aristotle's discussion of self-movement elsewhere.

[48] A basic action (S's ϕ'ing) *accords with* a proposition *p* (which expresses one of S's desires) if and only if: (i) *p* states that an action of that type is good (*or* better *or* best); (ii) *p* states that an action of that type is to be essayed as the first stage in S's plan at t_1; and (iii) actions of the type described in (i) and (ii) are ones which S can do without further deliberation about means (cf. fn. 37.) This account can be modified in an obvious way for non-basic acts.

Section C); and (e) intentional states: remaining at one's post. For (a)–
(e) involve difference either in explanation or ontology. Aristotle is
prepared to treat (a)–(d) as actions (*prattein*: 1135b1) even though (a)
and (b) need not be intentional under any description. His concern is
not to answer the narrowly analytical question 'Is ɸ'ing an action?',
since this may be given different answers depending on the relevant
point of comparison (with non-self-moved processes, with processes not
involving our capacities, with processes which are not intentional
under some description), but to draw distinctions within the hetero-
geneous class which may be called actions. His interest in explanation
and ontology leads him to emphasise the variety of the phenomena
and not to seek to force all actions and relevant inactions into one
procrustean framework of processes which are intentional under some
description and capable of being rationally explained by the attribution of a practical syllogism.[49]

This account serves to lend further support to Aristotle's location of
teleologically basic actions at the periphery of the body. Frowning
may be either sub-intentional or intentional, as breathing (in a certain
way) may be within category (a), (b) or (c) on different occasions. But
when these actions exemplify (a) or (b) there is no internal act of
trying (or will) which leads to the frowning or breathing, and the
actions must be located at the periphery of the body. If so, the causal
explanation of these types of phenomena will locate them at the surface of, and not inside, the body. Hence, if there is to be uniformity in
what is explained in all cases of frowning, this should also occur at
the surface of and not within the body in cases exemplifying (c) or (d);
otherwise, 'frowning' will be a homonym, as Aristotle himself insists
(202a26–28), and lack a single meaning. His interest in giving a
uniform explanation of the cases (a)–(d) supports construing what is
done (frowning) as having the same point of application in all these
cases: to an occurrence (at least) at the periphery of the body. Thus
Aristotle's location of teleologically basic actions at or beyond the
surface of the body reflects his aim of giving an explanation of the
agent's behaviour in cases (a)–(d), which emphasises both their relevant uniformity and difference. At this point, preference in ontology
rests on interest in explanation and not on the weaker ground of
non-theoretical intuition (see also Section B).

But is Aristotle's account defensible in the central cases of agency:
(c) and (d)? Within his theory S's raising his hand is not identical with
his hand being raised by S (or S's hand rising). They are distinct
members of one equivalence class (see Chapter 1, Section B; Appendix
1). S is a constituent of the action (subject of change) only if it is his
capacity for hand-raising that is realised. As an agent, he does not
stand in an external relation to a distinct intransitive event, but is a
constituent in the action itself. The bodily movement of S's hand being

---

[49] Contrast Davidson's account of agency: 1980, 46–9.

raised by S is caused by S in a given condition, and exemplifies only process or state causation.

To be an Aristotelian agent in category (c) is to be the subject of a transitive change (S's raising his hand) with distinctive antecedents (S's abilities and psychological states as characterised above). S can be a constituent of changes other than actions of this type (e.g. growing old, breathing) provided that they realise his capacities. Thus Aristotle separates two questions in accounting for agency: (a) What is S's relation to S's moving his hand? and (b) Under which condition is S the subject of a process which is an action of his in categories (c) and (d)? The answer to the second question does not depend on a special external relation between S and the change of which he is the subject (or constituent), but on the types of antecedent the process must have if S is to be an intrinsic constituent of the relevant type to be an agent in these categories. Thus he avoids the necessity of characterising an objective (extensional) relation between S and an intransitive process (or event), if S is to be its agent. Aristotle could capture sentences of the form 'S did it' within his account as:

$$(\exists \eta_1)\ (\eta_1 \text{ is } < \text{INT VERB (S, object, } t_o) > \& \text{ S did } \eta_1)$$

but the fundamental explanation of agency would be given by the relation between S and (e.g.) his hand when he exemplifies the property of (e.g.) moving it, and thus realises one of his causal powers. It would not involve, in contrast with Davidson's theory, a relation between S and an intransitive event: S's hand rising.

But is Aristotle's account itself misleading? If one operates with transitive events of which the agent is an essential constituent, one neither requires a separate mode of causation (agent-causation) linking S and his act nor (more generally) sees 'S did it' as representing a causal relation between S and the act. Since S, *qua* agent, is a constituent of the action and not its cause, Aristotle can maintain his general account of causation (see Chapter 1, Section D) as involving states and processes, and has no need of a special causal connexion between S and the intransitive event of S's hand rising to capture agency.[50] For the same reason, S's raising his hand will not itself be analysed by representing S as a participant in an antecedent mental event (e.g. trying) which is the cause of S's hand rising. This would capture *not* S's relation to his action, *but* the conditions under which S is the subject of a process which is an action (and so would answer question (b) not (a)). This would be a disadvantage of Aristotle's theory only if S's distinctive relation to the antecedent mental event (e.g. trying) was itself illuminating of agency in a way not captured by S's relation to his raising his hand. However, if trying itself is an action,[51]

---

[50] Contrast Chisholm, 1966, 21ff.; for reservations (with respect to Aristotle) see Thalberg 1977(b), 237, fn. 1.

[51] Given Aristotle's account of self-movement and agency, the steps between S's desire to do z and his z'ing will themselves be actions (*qua* self-moved).

it also will be analysed in such a way that S must participate in an antecedent event which is the cause of his trying. There is no antecedent (intransitive) event in which S can appear essentially in a way which differentiates his role from that in moving his hand. Thus S's relation to trying (or any event which is an action) is of the same type as his relation to the event of his moving his hand. Examination of S's relation to his action (under question (a)) does not illuminate, within this ontology, the nature of agency; for that one requires an answer to question (b) which specifies under what conditions the process is an action and S an agent in the relevant category. Thus S can be treated as a subject of change (when he moves his hand) without loss of explanatory power. While Davidson's formulation will not be false when S acts, it does not seem to capture in a perspicuous form the relation between the agent and his act. Aristotle, therefore, appears to lose nothing by not using it to give an account of the fundamental relation of agency.

Transitive events of Aristotle's type represent the agent as an essential constituent of his actions and reflect his agency by representing him in this way as a distinctive type of subject of change and not, *qua* agent, as the cause of his action. In this way, Aristotle's ontology seems to yield an acceptable account of agency (within the relevant categories) which is no less explanatory than the alternative Davidsonian formulation. And this, combined with the plausibility of Aristotle's treatment of the individuation of actions (Section B) and of basic actions (Sections B, D), strongly suggests that his ontological theory offers, at least, as successful an account of action as the Davidsonian one. If this is correct, there is no need to introduce a separate category of irreducible events to analyse action or agency (see Chapter 1, Section C).

E.   Action and explanation

In Aristotle's account of action and intentional action, ontology has intersected with teleological and causal explanation. His analysis of intentional action and of self-movement embeds causal components, and his preference for teleologically basic actions located at the periphery of the body reflects his goal of using such actions in both of his favoured types of explanation at the psychological level. Hence for Aristotle the fundamental issue is to articulate an explanatory theory at this level which integrates his account of self-movement and intentional action with an account of mental states (and events) which precede action, and to use both causal and teleological elements within that theory. Because his ontological theory rests upon explanatory requirements of this kind, it can only be assessed fully within the context of his explanation of intentional action. Aristotle's treatment of *acrasia* and rational action shows further parts of his explanatory theory, which we shall consider as a whole in Chapter 5.

The issues, however, are clear. Since his account of intentional action embeds a causal component, Aristotle needs to specify the causal conditions under which (e.g.) S's desire to do x leads him to do x. On occasion, he uses an 'and nothing prevents' clause to point in the direction of the relevant conditions (701a16–17; 702a15–16). But this cannot be the complete account; for that requires a full specification of the causal conditions under which (e.g.) prevention occurs. To meet this challenge, Aristotle must give an empirical theory of the causal antecedents of action (see Chapters 4 and 5, Section A), but one which is compatible both with teleological explanation and with the apparently *a priori* connexion between desire and action, implicit in his definition of desire (see Section C of this chapter, and Chapter 5, Section C).[52] Thus he needs to show the interconnexions between empirical generalisation and analysis in his theory of the antecedents of action.[53] His attempt to do this is illustrated by his discussion of the *acratês* (Chapter 3) and the fully rational agent (Chapter 4). Together with his account of intentional action, they form the basis for his explanation of action.

[52] Aristotle's account of intentional action and of action more generally provides the basis for his account of free action as involving the realisation of one of the agent's causal powers under conditions in which he desires to realise it (1048a15–21). But consideration of this topic lies outside the present project.

[53] For a survey of Aristotle's general views on the close relation of analysis and explanation, see Sorabji, 1969.

CHAPTER THREE

The Possibility of Acrasia

A. The problems of acrasia

A person is confronted by two courses of action (x, y), believes that he will do x or y but not both, decides that it would be better to do x rather than y and is able to do x and y (but not both). There is no change of mind, and no further reasoning as to which is the better course. It seems reasonable to expect the agent to do x, if he acts intentionally and freely. The self-controlled person will certainly do x, if he does either intentionally and freely; the acratês, however, will – on occasion – do y freely and intentionally.

So far there is no problem: the acratês has simply not acted as we expected. Perhaps if he never acted in the way which he decided was best, we would have reason to doubt that he had in fact decided that it was better to do x than y. But this is not the case imagined. So where is the problem? Or is it that a mistake has already been made in thinking that there is a problem?

The difficulties in allowing for the possibility of acrasia and explaining its occurrence may be the consequence of philosophical theories; but the theories themselves, when exposed, exercise so natural and pervasive an influence over such a large range of issues in the philosophy of action that attempts to modify or replace them can appear sufficiently implausible to lend credence to Socrates' famous conclusion: there can be no cases of free and intentional acratic action.

The problems of acrasia may be divided initially into two main areas: those which concern its very possibility, and those which bear on its appropriate explanation.

These problems are, however, related even at the present level of generality. An account of the possibility of acrasia requires a theory of free and intentional action, of intending, of practical reasoning and rational choice, for acrasia is free and intentional (and apparently intended) action against the conclusion of one's practical reasoning and against one's rational choice. This circle of problems (the first circle) might be called the Socratic puzzles; Aristotle's attempts to meet them will be the principal focus of this chapter.

Attempts to resolve the Socratic puzzles, therefore, require an account of practical reasoning and rational choice, and thus place constraints on the form of the psychological theory needed to explain the occurrence of *acrasia*. But any adequate theory of this type will require further ingredients: a more general account of rationality (for *acrasia* is irrational action), of practical wisdom (since – for Aristotle – the practically wise man is never acratic: 1146a6-7; 1152a5–8) and of the emotions (for *acrasia* is frequently, and, for Aristotle, paradigmatically, action on an emotion against one's better judgment: 1145b12–13; 1150b19–21). More generally, any such psychological theory may need to show how the acratic's valuation of the options can come apart from what he actually desires to do; for *acrasia* appears to occur when the *acratês* acts against his preferred evaluation of what should be done. And this raises further questions about the nature and origin of his valuational structure, and the nature of his failure when acratic (see Chapter 4).

The second circle, then, is concerned with the general form of psychological theory required to explain the occurrence of *acrasia*. But this second circle points to more general problems still. Is the mode of explanation at the psychological level of rationality and irrationality a species of (efficient) causal explanation, or does it exemplify a distinct (and possibly incompatible) form of explanation: rational or teleological explanation? Are the distinctions required in the favoured psychological theory ones which may be employed within a satisfying and empirically testable theory of the explanation of action? What relation is there between the explanation of behaviour at the psychological level and the alternative explanation which may be given in terms of purely physical processes and states? Hence the third circle of puzzles raised by consideration of *acrasia* concerns the nature and level of the preferred explanation of behaviour and, more generally, the relation of psychological and physical theory. These issues are central to the final chapter, where Aristotle's psychological theory is located within his general account of explanation and the mind/body relation.

In this way, the discussion of the possibility and explanation of *acrasia* places in sharp focus many issues which are central to Aristotle's – and, I suspect, any – general theory of the explanation of action. For any systematic account will need to answer the difficulties in all three circles within an integrated picture of the mind.

The possibility of *acrasia* appears to be threatened if one holds a certain picture of practical reasoning and of the rational explanation of intentional action. I will first trace this picture, and then in this and the following sections attempt to see which parts of it (if any) Aristotle rejects.

(a) Practical reasoning

If an agent reasons practically and successfully compares the alternatives, he must be able to assess the options in terms of some one common value which both share. This requires that the opposed courses are first assessed in terms of their contribution to achieving this shared value, and then compared against one another on this one scale. When he weighs them, he aims to find which of the options has the greatest amount of the common value, and his conclusion (if he reaches one) will be as to which option is the more valuable on his present scale: this I will call his better judgment. This conception of practical reasoning has three distinct ingredients:

1. *A weak commensurability thesis.* For all pieces of practical reasoning involving the successful comparison of alternatives there is a common factor shared by the alternatives in terms of which they may be compared. This is a weak commensurability thesis, and states only that for any piece of practical reasoning of this type there will be a common scale in terms of which the options can then be compared; it does not entail the stronger thesis that there will be one common scale shared by all pieces of practical reasoning in terms of which any option can be compared against any other option.[1]

If there is no (weak) commensurability, it seems difficult to make sense of rational choice between distinct alternatives resulting in a best judgment. For if there are alternatives which cannot be compared in this way, it is not clear on what basis one can be rationally preferred to another. At least (weak) commensurability is part of our metaphors for rational choice: we speak of weighing alternatives, deliberating between them, comparing their merits and disadvantages, etc.

2. *A valuational thesis.* The common factor in terms of which the alternatives are to be compared in practical reasoning is a value which the agent accepts. If so, in any piece of practical reasoning involving alternatives, the premises are to be represented in terms of the common value by which they are to be compared.

This thesis attempts to capture one aspect of practical reasoning which distinguishes it from merely predicting what one will do. For one's aim in practical reasoning is not merely to work out what one will in fact do, but also to determine what one should do (or what is best to do) given the alternatives. Here what one should do (or what is best to do) expresses one's valuation of the alternatives.

3. *A transference of value thesis.* Practical reasoning transfers value (or the truth about value) from premises to conclusion as deductive theoretical reasoning transfers truth from premises to conclusion. Hence, if the shared value in terms of which the premises are expressed is, for example, pleasure, the conclusion will represent one particular course of action as pleasant (or most pleasant). If so, the

[1] Compare Socrates' pattern of argument (*Protagoras* 355B2–C1) and contrast Wiggins (1978/9, 271ff.).

conclusion of practical reasoning will be expressed in terms of the same value as at least one of the premisses.

The aim of practical reasoning is to discover which of the alternatives open to the agent has the most of the common value in terms of which the alternatives are to be compared. If the alternatives are compared in terms of pleasure, his aim is to find the most pleasant, if in terms of goodness, the best. The conclusion at which practical reasoning aims is one stating which of the alternatives is (in the sense explained) most valuable.

These three theses articulate a common sense picture of practical reasoning which is as old as Plato's *Protagoras*.[2] They do not by themselves render *acrasia* problematic: for the *acratês* may still reason in the way indicated but not act on his conclusion. In this case his practical reasoning will be (in a certain sense) useless or idle as he does not put into practice its conclusion. But this appears to be a redescription of the phenomenon of *acrasia* rather than a challenge of its possibility.[3]

The situation is altered, however, when one adds to this conception of practical reasoning a certain picture of the rational explanation of intentional action.

(b)   Rational explanation

If an agent acts intentionally in doing x, his doing x is to be explained by means of the premisses of an argument which we attribute to the agent in which the conclusion *either* is his doing x, *or* is sufficient for his doing x (in a sense to be explained) *or* has as its one unique conclusion a judgment favouring doing x above all other options.

If the agent has not reached any such conclusion, or has reached one to do y and not x or (if this is possible) has reached a conclusion to do x and a conclusion to do y, one cannot rationally explain his doing x. Hence, if all intentional action is rationally explainable, his doing x – in such a case – would not be intentional. Within this picture the agent's intentionally doing x can be explained by means of premisses and an argument form in the same way as what is concluded from a theoretical argument can be explained by means of its premisses and a valid argument form. If there are alternative courses of

---

[2] See *Protagoras* 355D5–357B7. Such premisses are also to be found in modern writing on *acrasia*: see Davidson, 1980, 31ff.

[3] This gap could be filled by stipulating that unless the *acratês* acts on his conclusion he has not reasoned practically – where practical reasoning would be described as finding out what is best to do so as to do it. But this would have little value: for the *acratês* would be very much like the practical reasoner – and his reasoning, even if dubbed 'theoretical', would be unlike other theoretical reasoning in that the *acratês* would consider himself to be honestly working out what he *should* do.

action open to the agent, his doing x rather than y will be explained in the same way.

It seems (at least) plausible that the argument to be attributed to the *acratês* to explain his action *rationally* should be, or include, the valuational argument which he consciously goes through in practical reasoning, and whose conclusion is a valuational judgment about which of the options is more valuable: his better or best judgment. Since in conflict cases we have evidence to believe that the deliberator actually goes through such an argument, it would be perplexing if the argument and conclusion which rationally explained his action were different from the one which he would give to explain his action.

This combination of theses gives rise to (what I shall call) the four major Socratic puzzles to be analysed in this chapter:

(1) *The identity thesis.* If the conclusion of practical reasoning is his best judgment and is identical with the action,[4] a man who reaches his best judgment acts on it – for his reaching that judgment *is* his acting on it. Consider the purported case of the *acratês*: *either* he does not reach his best judgment *or* he does and acts on it. But either way *acrasia* appears impossible: if the man does not reach a best judgment, he cannot act against it and the case described is not *acrasia*. If the man does reach a best *judgment* and acts on it, he is not acratic either – since he now acts on his best *judgment* and not against it. Hence, in neither case can the man act acratically. If so, *acrasia* seems impossible.

(2) *The sufficiency thesis.* If the conclusion of practical reasoning is the agent's best judgment, and that conclusion is always sufficient for action, if the agent acts intentionally, a man who reaches his best judgment must act on it, if he acts intentionally. More formally,

(ꓱJ) (p is the conclusion of S's practical reasoning & Accords (p, S's doing x) & $pJ \rightarrow$ S does x, if he acts intentionally).[5]

Consider the possibility of *acrasia*: if the agent reaches his best judgment he either acts intentionally on it, or he does not act intentionally at all. But in neither case does he act acratically, since that requires that he acts intentionally against the conclusion of his practical reasoning (i.e. his best judgment). Hence, *acrasia* appears impossible.

(3) *The uniqueness thesis.* If for one piece of practical reasoning there is one unique type of judgment which is its conclusion (and this

---

[4] This interpretation of Aristotle has been developed by Von Wright, 1971, ch. 3 and Nussbaum, 1978. See Chapter 2, Section C for reasons for rejecting it.

[5] The formalisations of the Sufficiency and Uniqueness theses offered here follow the outline proposed by Michael Bratman (1974). In this version of the Sufficiency thesis, 'Accords' denotes the relation thus described in Chapter 2, Section D (fn. 48). In other versions the agent is required to act 'freely' as well as intentionally; but consideration of free action lies outside our present project.

is the agent's best judgment) and the agent acts intentionally on a conclusion of this type, *acrasia* also appears problematic. More formally, if for any piece of practical reasoning,

∃!J) (*p* is the conclusion of S's practical reasoning & S acts intentionally on *p* in doing *x* & Accords (*p*, S's doing *x*) → *p* J)

in which J is a better judgment, *acrasia* appears impossible. If the agent does *x* intentionally, there must be (at least cases where reasoning conflicts) a judgment stating that doing *x* is better than the other options. The *acratês* is supposed to do *y* intentionally against his better judgment that (e.g.) *x* is better than *y*. But, under the uniqueness thesis, if he does *y* in such cases intentionally, he must have concluded that doing *y* is better than *x* immediately before acting. Since we assume that the *acratês* does not self-consciously hold formally inconsistent beliefs, he cannot also hold that *x* is better than *y*. Thus, if he previously held that *x* is better than *y*, and now does *y*, either he does not do *y* intentionally or has changed his mind and now holds that doing *y* is better than *x*. But either way he is not acratic. Hence, if one accepts the Uniqueness thesis, *acrasia* appears impossible.

These three arguments against the possibility of *acrasia* rest on two main assumptions about the relation of the agent's best judgment and his action. Either these are so closely connected that the agent cannot arrive at his best judgment and not act on it if he acts intentionally (Identity or Sufficiency thesis), *or* whenever the agent acts intentionally (in a conflict case) he acts on his best judgment (Uniqueness thesis). *Acrasia* would appear problematic if one held either of these views of the connexion between best judgment and action.

These three arguments are special cases of a more general conception of intentional action as rationally explained action. They – as it were – spell out the machinery for the schema of rational explanation. This conception of rational explanation itself, however, when allied to the picture of practical reasoning generates a fourth (more general) Socratic problem.

(4) *The rationality thesis.* If any action is intentional, it is rationally explainable. In conflict cases, this means that it is explainable by a pattern of argument that culminates in the conclusion that one course of action is the best of the available alternatives. Since it is rational to do the action which is the best of the available alternatives, in such cases if the action is rationally explainable, it is rational. Hence, if an action is intentional in a conflict case, it appears that it cannot be rational. For if it were, it could not be rationally explained, and so could not be intentional. If so, given the following two premises:

(a) if an action is intentional, it is rationally explainable, and
(b) if an action (in a conflict case) is rationally explainable, it is rational,

one can show, using only modus tollens, that there cannot be intentional irrational action. Hence, from two premises, Socrates' implausible conclusion follows – that there are no cases of intentional irrational action.[6]

The Rationality thesis resembles the Uniqueness thesis, but is distinct from it since, provided that the conclusion of the agent's practical reasoning is rationally explained (via an acceptable argument form) by the premises he accepts, the specific form of the conclusion is of little importance. Thus to deny the Rationality thesis requires either that one shows that not all intentional action is rationally explainable or that not all rationally explainable action is rational; by contrast, the sting of the Uniqueness thesis could be drawn by showing merely that the specific form of the agent's conclusion need not be identical with (or entailed by) his better judgment.

Consideration of Aristotle's responses to these four Socratic arguments will uncover fundamental aspects of his own positive theory.

Aristotle's approach (as I interpret it) is to reject the basic elements of the conception of rational explanation which make *acrasia* problematical while holding a version of the picture of practical reasoning outlined above. That is, Aristotle (I will argue) rejects the Identity, Sufficiency and Uniqueness theses in forms which exclude the possibility of *acrasia*, and discards the Rationality thesis, although he accepts that certain acratic intentional action is rationally explainable, that the *acratês*' acratic conclusion is valuational and that the *acratês* acts intentionally against another valuational judgment (i.e. best) which represents his rational choice. My argument will be based on a detailed analysis of *NE* VII 3 (Section B) and of Aristotle's account of preferential choice and practical reasoning (Sections C and D).

This approach stands in marked contrast to three other theories which seek to allow for the possibility of *acrasia* – each of which has been urged to be Aristotle's. These are:

(a) To deny one certain central aspect of the picture of practical reasoning by denying that all values are commensurable (in the required sense). Thus the *acratês*' action may be rationally explained

---

[6] Davidson raised this issue (1980 and 1982). In Chapter 2, Section C, I argued that Aristotle did not hold that all intentional action is rationally explainable by a syllogism: some actions are not rationally explainable as they result from only the perception that 'This is pleasant'. However, in conflict cases involving practical syllogisms on both sides, there will be rational explanation (of a type) of both the *acratês*' and the *encratês*' action. Hence the rationality objection to the possibility of *acrasia* will apply in at least those cases. See Section D.

by reference to a scale of value distinct from – and non-commensurable with – the scale on which his better judgment is registered. Within this picture, *acrasia* occurs only when there is a conflict between values which the agent cannot compare.[7]

(b) To accept the general outline of practical reasoning traced above and to accept the Identity or Sufficiency and Uniqueness theses in the form stated (i.e. with the relevant conclusion as valuational), but to allow for *acrasia* by giving an account of practical reasoning in which the final evaluation conflicts with but does not overthrow an earlier judgment which represents his own better judgment. *Acrasia* is now represented as a species of failure of reasoning in which the *acratês* arrives at the wrong conclusion given his own better judgment, although the failure is not so gross as to involve him in failing to draw an entailed conclusion. In Davidson's recent sophisticated development of this conception of *acrasia*, the better judgment against which the *acratês* rebels is represented as an All Things Considered judgment (ATC) that it is better to do x than y (xBTy), which does not entail (although it supports inductively) the non-relativised conclusion that xBTy. Hence the *acratês* can without inconsistency hold (it is contended) ATC xBTy and yBTx, and act acratically in doing y without inconsistency. However, the *acratês*' failure to draw the appropriate conclusion (xBTy) makes his subsequent action irrational. Further, if the feature which explains why he held yBTx and not xBTy after having held ATC xBTy cannot itself be a reason (for if it were it would overthrow his initial ATC judgment by introducing a new reason not previously considered), his forming the intention represented by yBTx and his doing y cannot be rationally explained. Hence, if acratic action is intentional and irrational, not all intentional action can be rationally explained. If so, one aspect of the Rationality thesis alone is discarded. (See Sections D and E.)

(c) While the second proposal represents the *acratês*' intention as a non-relativised evaluation and hence treats *acrasia* as a failure in valuational reasoning, an alternative is to accept both the conception of practical reasoning and either the Identity or Sufficiency thesis or the Uniqueness thesis, but to deny that his conclusion is a valuational judgment at all. That is, *either* his conclusion just is his acratic action (Identity thesis), in which case there appears no failure of reasoning at all and the irrationality occurs only in the action, *or* it is an antecedent stage as in, e.g., the Sufficiency thesis which either is non-judgmental or, if judgmental, is non-valuational (e.g. a belief that one will do b, or perhaps a self-addressed command to do b).[8] Since

---

[7] Versions of this view have been developed by Wiggins (1978/9) and Burnyeat (1981). See Section C.

[8] Peacocke (1981) argues that the state is non-judgmental and suggests a comparison with the 'Aristotelian' view that the conclusion is an action (but see Chapter 2, Section C). Pears (1981) takes the intention to be non-valuational. See Section E.

there is no step in argument between the agent's best judgment and his intention (thus construed), pure *acrasia* is not a failure of argument, but is rather a weakness on the *acratês'* part to will (or intend) or do what he has judged best. Hence his irrationality is not an intellectual failure, but consists just in his not intending or doing what he knows is best.

Aristotle's strategy (as it is presented below) has certain affinities with each of these alternatives, but differs from them both in detail and general conception, and so is at least a competitor to the three 'going' types of theory mentioned here. Throughout the subsequent discussion it is important to keep vividly in mind the appeal of the Socratic arguments against the possibility of *acrasia*, and the widespread conviction that Aristotle succumbed to them.

B. Aristotle's approach to acrasia. Does one type of acratês hold the good conclusion and not act on it?

If Aristotle accepted either the Identity or Sufficiency thesis (in the form in which the relevant conclusion is a valuational best judgment), the acratic cannot reach the conclusion that e.g. doing x is best, and do y intentionally. If he maintained the Uniqueness thesis (in a similar form), the acratic could not hold the conclusion that e.g. x is best while doing y intentionally. Hence, if he accepted any of these theses, it is not possible for any Aristotelian *acratês* to hold the good conclusion while acting against it. If so, the breakdown must occur either before the final step of reaching the conclusion (Identity or Sufficiency) or be a change of mind about what is best after reaching the good conclusion (Uniqueness).

It has been generally accepted[9] that Aristotle adopted (at least) one of these theses, and hence that his *acratês* cannot hold the good conclusion and act against it. Rather there is a breakdown in his reasoning at an earlier stage where the *acratês* is (in some sense) ignorant of the minor premiss of the good syllogism. If so, Aristotle would have accepted a version of the Socratic position – there are no cases of intentional acratic action against a best judgment one then holds. Either the *acratês* never gets to the good conclusion, or does, and forgets it because of his ignorance of the minor premiss.

The discussion of ontology and intentional action in Chapters 1 and 2, however, (together with two further Aristotelian assumptions) creates a difficulty for this position, and raises a severe exegetical

[9] By most recent commentators: Robinson, Hardie, Cooper, Santas, Owen, Walsh, Anscombe, Sorabji, Wiggins, Nussbaum. But not, however, universally: Kenny has argued against it (1966a, 163ff.), although – for reasons to be given below – I do not accept either his main argument or several central aspects of his exegesis of the disputed texts.

dilemma, whose resolution will uncover one part of Aristotle's strategy for allowing for the possibility of *acrasia*. In this section, it is argued that Aristotle must have held (in the light of his treatment of intentional action) that some acratic agents reach the good conclusion and do not act on it, and that his discussion of *acrasia* in *NE* VII 3 confirms that this was his view.

Aristotle appears to have held the following thesis:

(1) It is possible that S acts intentionally acratically, where what S does intentionally is the same as what he does acratically: cf. 1152a15–16; 1136a32–35.

That is, it is possible that there is some one thing that the *acratês* does which is (under some one description) both intentional and acratic: i.e. it is, as such, an act judged either less good by him than another, or simply bad. Such a case will be described in what follows as intentional acratic action.

This thesis needs to be distinguished sharply from another – stronger – thesis, which it is less clear that Aristotle accepted:

(2) It is possible that S acts acratically intentionally: cf. 1145b12–13; 1146a7.

In (2), as opposed to (1), it is necessary that S knows at the time of action that he should not do the action he is doing; that is, in (2), S knows that it would be better to do x rather than y, while doing y, but this is not demanded by (1), since (1) requires only that y is – in fact – an action of a type which he should not do. In what follows, only (1) is used as a premiss. ((2) entails (1)).

If the *acratês* judges that he should not do y, or that xBTy, his doing y is the acratic action since it is this action (under this description) which violates a principle or judgment that he holds (1136b4–10; 1146a7; 1223b8–10). That is:

(3) The acratic action is the action under a description under which it should not be done given the man's principles.

In Chapter 2, Section A (and Appendix 2) it is argued that:

(4) S does y intentionally $\rightarrow$ S knows that he is doing y, and knows the relevant descriptions true of his action (e.g. that it is a cake which he is eating).

Suppose we take (1), (3) and (4) together with:

(5) S's knowledge of the relevant descriptions is expressed (in part) by the minor premiss of the good syllogism.

It follows that if the *acratês* acts intentionally acratically, he must know the minor premiss of the good syllogism. For if he does not know, e.g., that this is a cake, he cannot eat this cake intentionally. If so, there will be no one action which is under one description both intentional and acratic, and (1) – contrary to Aristotle's dicta – would be false.[10]

This argument will be clearer if we take two distinct cases:

(a) *The simple case.* In such cases, there is only one minor premiss shared by two opposed major premisses:

x-type actions are bad	x-type actions are pleasant
This is an x-type action	

If S does the x-type action intentionally because it is pleasant, he must know that it is an x-type action. Further, since in this case, the acratic action is doing an x-type action (for they are bad, in S's estimation), and he acts intentionally and acratically, the agent must know that it is an x-type action. Hence, in the simple case, the *acratês* must know the minor premiss of the good syllogism.

(b) *The complex case.* In complex cases, the relevant syllogisms are as follows:

syllogism of temperance	*syllogism of pleasure*
x-type actions are bad	y-type actions are pleasant
[This is an x-type action]	This is a y-type action
[This is bad]	This is pleasant

For example, S is presented with the alternative principles: 'Eating sweet cakes is bad', and 'Eating whatever Aunt Matilda makes is pleasant', where Aunt Matilda has in fact baked a sweet cake, and S is faced with the possibility of eating it.

If S is ignorant that the cake is sweet, he does not eat the sweet cake intentionally, although he does eat what Aunt Matilda has baked intentionally. But the acratic action under the relevant description is eating the sweet cake, and this is distinct from the action description of eating something baked by Aunt Matilda. For Aristotle held that one could not do one and the same action intentionally and unintentionally under the same description at the same time (1223b10–11, 17–18; 1111a1–5), and developed an ontology of actions and descriptions in which there is a separate action description corresponding to

[10] This argument from the possible intentionality of the acratic act is the first of the arguments I will employ to support the conclusion that at least one Aristotelian *acratês* reaches the good conclusion. Another argument is developed in Section C and rests on Aristotle's account of preferential choice. The third support for this thesis comes from the analysis of VII 3 given below.

the relevant knowledge and ignorance of the agent.[11] Hence, although he may do the *y*-type action intentionally and in doing *y* do *x*, he will not do *x* intentionally. If so, there will be no one thing which S does intentionally and acratically (against Aristotle's dictum (1)), if he is ignorant of the minor premiss of the good syllogism. For that ignorance would make the acratic action not intentional (at least) under the relevant description.

It is not possible, therefore, that the *acratês* acts intentionally acratically and is ignorant of the minor premiss of the good syllogism in either the simple or complex case. If complete ignorance of one proposition in the syllogism is common to all types (intentional/unintentional; simple/complex) of *acrasia*, that proposition cannot be the minor premiss of the good syllogism. Since Aristotle describes the *acratês* as either ignorant or 'quasi-ignorant' of the same thing (1147b9–12), he cannot be quasi-ignorant of the minor premiss of the good syllogism either. Since the *acratês* cannot be completely ignorant of the major premiss of the good syllogism,[12] the object of acratic ignorance (common to all types of *acrasia*) must be the *conclusion* of the good syllogism. If one type of *acratês* is 'quasi-ignorant' of the conclusion of the good syllogism, he reaches the good conclusion but holds it in an 'off-colour' fashion. Hence at least one type of *acratês* must reach the good conclusion, and thus will hold it (in this 'off-colour' way) while acting against it.

If this is correct, in those passages of *NE* VII 3 where Aristotle considers directly the case of *acrasia*, the focus of acratic ignorance and quasi-ignorance (common to all cases) must be the good conclusion. One type of *acratês* fails to reach the good conclusion (although he will have the relevant premisses if he acts intentionally acratically); the other actually reaches the good conclusion but holds it in an 'off-colour' way. In particular, in 1147b9 the *final proposition* is the good conclusion and not the minor premiss. If so, the concluding lines of VII 3 should be translated thus (1147b9–18):

Since the last proposition[13] is a belief about a perceptible and is what determines our action, either a man does not have this when he is in a

---

[11] See Chapter 2, Section B.

[12] If so, he would be a bad man with corrupted general principles and not an acratic one; see 1110b31–33; 1151a5–7. The *acratês* is only 'half-bad' (1152a17), and does bad acts without being a bad man (1151a9–10).

[13] *Protasis* is introduced as Aristotle's technical term for proposition in *Pr. A.* 24a16–17 (cf. Ross, p. 288), *Post. An.* 72a7 (cf. Barnes, 101f.), *de Int.* 20b24; so 'last *protasis*' should mean 'last proposition' and not 'last premiss'. However, earlier in the chapter (1147a1–4) Aristotle appears first to use *protasis* to refer to major and minor premisses and then to use a distinct term (1147a27) to designate the conclusion. If so, it might be thought that in the context of this chapter, 'last *protasis*' must mean the minor premiss and not the conclusion. Neither of these arguments is conclusive: (a) In 1147a1–4 Aristotle is restricting his attention to premisses since he conjoins with *protasis* his favoured terms (universal:specific) for referring to major and minor premisses in a

state of passion or he has it in the sense in which having knowledge is not knowing but merely saying something – as a drunken man may be said to have knowledge of the verses of Empedocles. And because the last term is not universal nor an object of knowledge equally with a universal term, what Socrates was seeking to show seems to turn out to be correct; for it is not in the presence of what is thought to be proper knowledge that the affection of incontinence arises nor is it that which is dragged about as a result of a state of passion but it is in the presence rather of perceptual knowledge.[14]

Thus, *acrasia* occurs when the *acratês* either does not have the conclusion or – in the case more central for our purposes – reaches the conclusion, but holds it in an 'off-colour' fashion and acts against it intentionally under the influence of passion.

The exegetical dilemma arises precisely because 1147b9–18 (together with 1147a5–10) is held to require that one *acratês* is completely ignorant of the minor premiss of the good syllogism, while 1147a25–31 (and other passages elsewhere) are taken to show that no *acratês* can arrive at the conclusion of the good syllogism and not act on it. If so, one of three things follows: Aristotle rejected one of the assumptions used above to argue that the *acratês* must know the minor premiss of the good syllogism if he acts acratically and intentionally,[15] *or* the passages in VII 3 are consistent with (or support) the

syllogism. Hence, when used with these terms, *protaseis* are restricted in extension to propositions serving as premisses. However, when conjoined with 'final' (a term not used to designate a type of premiss), '*protasis*' can refer – without change in sense – to a final proposition. In this way, the reference of '*protasis*' can alter in these two contexts while its sense (as defined in 24a16–17, etc.) remains constant. (b) In 1147a25–26, Aristotle appears to argue: 'The one proposition (*protasis*) is a universal opinion, the other proposition is concerned with particulars . . . When one proposition (*protasis*) emerges from these, it is necessary for the soul then to assert the conclusion . . .' This reading takes 'the other' as assuming *protasis*, and not *doxa*, in line with Aristotle's general word of reference to the minor premiss. (The 'other *doxa*' would be an extremely unusual way of referring to the minor premiss.) The *protasis* which emerges from these two will be the third and final *protasis* (1147b9), and be identical with the conclusion, which the soul asserts at the stage when the final *protasis* emerges. See below.

[14] Accepting Bywater's text at 1147b16 (with the MSS) and not the emendation suggested by Stewart and Robinson (1969).

[15] Those who have been aware of this argument and have been attracted to the view that Aristotle's *acratês* is (in general) ignorant of the minor premiss of the good syllogism have held (or might hold): *either* (a) that actions done in ignorance through passion are voluntary/intentional for Aristotle (Robinson/Hardie); *or* (b) that the description under which the action is acratic is the same as that under which it is intentional because Aristotle either had no ontology of actions or else regarded (confusedly) doing *x* and doing *y* (in the complex case) as *one* action (under *one* description); *or* (c) that the description under which the action is acratic is not the same as that under which it is intentional, and is (in the complex case) doing *y* and not doing *x*; *or* (d) that the minor premiss of the good syllogism does not express the information which is essential if the acratic act is to be intentional. Chapters 1 and 2 (and Appendix 2) attempt to answer (a) and (b). (c) has been discussed above (cf. 1152a15–16; 1136a32–35). Aristotle does not in 1147a31ff. clearly distinguish the simple and complex cases, but appears to offer an analysis which – unlike (c) – applies to both (see below). (d) also

acratês' knowing this minor premiss, *or* Aristotle's position is inconsistent in the *NE* (regarded as including Common Books).[16] In the
remainder of the section it is argued that VII 3 (as a whole) is consistent with certain types of acratic agents knowing the minor premiss
of a good syllogism, and that parts of it strongly support this interpretation. I will analyse the problematical passages in the following order:
(a) 1147b9–18; (b) 1147a1–24 and the structure of the chapter; (c)
1147a24–b9.

(a)   1147b9–18: the illusion of a Socratic account

In 1147b10, the 'final proposition' is a judgment about a perceptible,
and in 1147b16–18 'perceptual knowledge' is said to be present and
'dragged about' by passion when *acrasia* occurs. This passage creates
an exegetical difficulty for both interpretations: if perception is concerned exclusively with factual and never with valuational judgments[17] or perceptual knowledge is never reached by reasoning from
more general premisses (see 1143b1–4) the object of perception cannot
be the valuational conclusion of the good syllogism, but must be its
minor premiss. However, if perceptual knowledge is of this minor
premiss, and is present when *acrasia* occurs, the *acratês* must know
this premiss while acting against it. Hence it appears that this passage
is difficult to reconcile with the view that the *acratês* is ignorant
either of the conclusion or of the minor premiss.

Attention to Aristotle's use of 'last term' and perceptual vocabulary
elsewhere suggests a solution. In the syllogisms

All A's are B's	*or*	A belongs to B
C is an A		B belongs to C
C is a B		A belongs to C

C is the last term which will designate (in the practical case) either
an action or a particular object to be acted on. C will not be grasped

---

is difficult to reconcile with the examples of minor premisses discussed in VII 3 (1147a6–
8, 29, 33). The argument employed in this section does not rely on the premisses that
if S is blamed for doing φ, he does φ intentionally or knows that he is φ'ing. See 1136a5–
8 (and Appendix 2) for evidence that Aristotle did not accept this premiss: for a contrasting view, see Kenny 1966a, 164, 167, 173.

[16] In this chapter and Appendix 2 my concern is with the Common Books in the
context of the *NE*. There is a difficulty, however, in the context of *EE* also: that in
1225b10–17 a man who *has* but does not *exercise* knowledge acts unintentionally –
unlike the acratic who acts intentionally (see note 15 above). My argument could
proceed only on the basis of the Common Books (cf. 1135a24–27; 1136a5–8).

[17] See Cooper, 1975, 49ff. This argument cannot rest on the extremely strong assumption that Aristotle never speaks of evaluative judgments as the domain of perception – see 1113a1–2; 1126b3–6; 1109b14ff. The issue is: what is his use in 1147b10–18?

by reasoning but by perception, and will not itself designate a value. Hence perceptual knowledge may be (in part) knowledge of C without being (thus far) an evaluative judgment or a judgment derived from reasoning. Further, the final proposition may be a judgment about a perceptible (i.e. C), without perception, in this context, being concerned to give a valuational judgment about C.

Elsewhere (1143a35–b5) perception is said to be concerned with the last term and the minor premiss,[18, 19] and is sharply distinguished from what is derived by reasoning. Perceptual knowledge, therefore, is concerned (in a three-term syllogism) with C and with the judgment that 'C is an A' (or that 'B belongs to C') and so with the minor premiss and C when it appears in the conclusion, and not the judgment that 'C is a B' or 'A belongs to C', when these constitute the conclusion.

Acrasia occurs in the presence of perceptual knowledge and it is this that is dragged around when *acrasia* occurs. If so, the *acratês* must know at least the relevant minor premiss since this introduces the final term and the relevant perceptual predicate. For if he does not grasp the minor premiss, *acrasia* cannot occur in the presence of perceptual knowledge since such knowledge is completely absent. By contrast, if the final proposition is the conclusion, perceptual knowledge may be present but under attack and dragged about in two ways: either the *acratês* does not come to a conclusion about the perceptible (proceeds no further than the minor premiss) or he draws the conclusion in an 'off-colour' way. Since this interpretation gives clear sense to the text as it stands and draws on Aristotle's favoured terminology, it favours the conclusion that both acratic agents know the minor premiss. (This is why opponents of this interpretation have to emend the text in 1147b15–16.)

This interpretation allows one to explain why Aristotle can congratulate Socrates on being correct in thinking that proper knowledge is not attacked by *acrasia*, and is not immediately present when it

---

[18] Taking 'last' and 'contingent' to assume 'term' from 1143a36. In this passage, 'the last' cannot be the subject matter of the whole of the conclusion CφB because this could be reached by reasoning from major and minor premisses of the form 'AφB, CφA → CφB'. Rather Aristotle is emphasising that one feature of practical reasoning is to grasp which specific course of action (C, e.g. resisting the enemy) is the one which represents the agent's goals (expressed in the major premiss) in this situation: see Appendix 3.

[19] 'Last terms', so construed, may appear in both minor premiss and conclusion. This allows one to resolve a textual dilemma which arises if one insists that *ta eschata* be the subject matter of *either* the whole minor premiss *or* the conclusion *but* not both. For in 1141b25–28 they appear to be the subject matter of the conclusion – the decree that φ should be done – but in 1143a36 they cannot be the subject matter of the conclusion, while 1142a21–30 refers back to 1141b25–28, but is phrased in terms similar to 1143b1–5. For the 'final term' in 1143a36, 1142a21–30 and 1141b25–28 may designate a specific action (C) without taking 'what is to be done' in 1141b27 as the subject matter of the whole conclusion. Thus, since the final term may occur in *both* minor premiss *and* conclusion and specify the action, knowledge of the final term is knowledge of the action (type) whether the term occurs in premiss or conclusion.

occurs. Socrates had held (in Aristotelian vocabulary) the following premisses: (1) proper knowledge involves knowledge of particulars (perceptual knowledge), and (2) proper knowledge is sufficient for action, and concluded both that (3) proper knowledge cannot be overcome or dragged about like a slave (1145b24), and that (4) *acrasia* cannot exist (1145b25–26). Aristotle, in reply, rejects (1) by separating proper knowledge from perceptual knowledge i.e. perception of particulars (1142b25–28), since proper knowledge is concerned exclusively with universal terms. However, (3) remains correct: for it is perceptual knowledge of particulars and the last term that is the subject of attack from *acrasia* and not proper knowledge. Since Socrates arrived by chance (*sumbainein*) at the correct interim conclusion (3) by means of two mistaken but self-cancelling premisses: (1) and (2),[20] Aristotle can congratulate Socrates on this one success with mild irony; for the truth of (3) in Aristotle's view leaves open the possibility of *acrasia* (contra 4).

If so, 1147b9–18, so far from supporting Aristotle's adoption of the Socratic position, actually shows him rejecting it. Both acratic agents described here possess the minor premiss of the good syllogism and at least one reaches the good conclusion. Since 1147b9–18 appears to summarise the argument of *NE* VII 3 one would naturally expect to find these two cases discussed previously when Aristotle specifically discusses *acrasia* earlier in the chapter.

There is, however, an earlier passage (1147a5–10) which threatens to undermine this interpretation of the chapter as a whole.

(b)   *1147a1–24, and the structure of the remainder of the chapter*

The immediate context is set by a distinction between two types of possession of knowledge: having and exercising knowledge (1146b31–35). Aristotle notes that it seems difficult to act against knowledge one is exercising, but not difficult to act against knowledge one merely possesses. He then separates in effect two types of premiss, major and minor, and says that there is nothing to prevent a man possessing both but acting against his knowledge, provided that he exercises the major premiss but only possesses the minor (1147a1–4). He continues:

> There are two kinds of universal term: one applies to the agent and the other to the object. For example: 'Dry food is good for every man', and 'I am a man' or 'A given type of food is dry'. But if this food is of such a type, this the man (acting against knowledge) *either* does not have *or*

[20] Since proper knowledge is not concerned with particulars it cannot be sufficient for action, since actions are particulars (cf. 1110b5–7). As such it requires supplementation from other psychological states (e.g. perceptual knowledge) which fail when *acrasia* strikes. Perception is of the final term and of the minor premiss (1143b2–4; 1147a26); so this seems the range of perceptual knowledge. Proper knowledge is actually present in the acratic case if the *acratês* grasps the good major premiss (1147a32; cf. 1146a13–15) as he must, if his soul says the good conclusion (1147a34).

does not exercise.[21] There will be a great difference between these ways of knowing so that to know in one way (and act against it) is not paradoxical, but to know in the other (and act against it) is extraordinary.

So it appears that in 1147a7 one man who acts against his knowledge is completely ignorant of the minor premiss; he does not possess it all. If this man is acratic at least one *acratês* is ignorant of the minor premiss of the good syllogism and acts unintentionally acratically. (If he were not an *acratês* this passage would create no difficulty for the interpretation I have sketched.) Since the general context, introduced by 1146b24–26, appears to be one in which Aristotle considers which epistemic state (belief, knowledge of a given kind) it is against which the *acratês* rebels, it seems best to assume that the man described in 1147a7 either is an *acratês* or one who exemplifies a type of failure to which an *acratês* is also prone (viz. ignorance of a minor premiss). In what follows I accept this assumption, and the attendant assumption that 1147a10–24 is focused in one of these ways on to the acratic cases, both for this reason and also because it appears least favourable to my analysis of this section and most favourable to my opponents'.

1147a6–8 would constitute a counter-example to my original argument only if the latter had assumed that *all* acratic actions were intentional (under the relevant description). In fact that argument rests on a weaker claim: it is possible that there are intentional acratic actions. This allows that there may be unintentional acratic actions but denies that all acratic actions can be of this type. It is, therefore, compatible with the existence of cases in which the *acratês* does not possess the minor premiss at all. If 1147a5–10 contains an example of this, Aristotle is citing in this passage two ways in which the *acratês* may fail to reach the good conclusion: either by not knowing the minor premiss or by not exercising it. In both cases the *acratês* will be ignorant of the good conclusion, and this will still be the one common focus of ignorance in the whole range of acratic cases (intentional/unintentional; simple/complex; minor premiss had but not exercised/minor premiss not had). If so, this passage is not a counter-example to the original argument; it introduces (if the text is unemended) two ways in which the *acratês* may fail to come to know the good conclusion.

This passage (1147a1–10), however, is more problematical than it appears. Aristotle sums it up (a8–10) with a reference to (a1–4): 'if a man has knowledge but does not exercise it, he may act against his knowledge without paradox, but otherwise it is extraordinary'. Since 'not possessing knowledge at all' that *p* is *not* a way of knowing that *p*, either Aristotle's distinctions in (a8–10) between different ways in which a man may act against his knowledge are not exemplified by the previous sentence (which is thus beside the point) or, if they are

---

[21] Accepting for the moment Bywater's text; but cf. below.

(as Aristotle appears to take them to be), that sentence (a7) cannot contain a reference to complete ignorance that p.[22]

The latter alternative appears the more attractive, and is supported by the texts of the best manuscript[23] which may be translated 'This he does not possess, or rather does not exercise' where the 'or rather' is added to qualify the sense in which he does not possess it – where this distinction is clarified further in the next sentence by separating (once again) knowing and not exercising from knowing and exercising. That is, if (a7) is to be relevant in the immediate context to a man acting against knowledge he then possesses, the only case considered must be that of a man who has but does not exercise the minor premiss. If so, it would introduce (if the text is emended) only one way in which the *acratês* may fail to know the good conclusion: by not exercising the minor premiss he possesses.

Failure to exercise the minor premiss may be diagnosed (in the light of 67a35ff.) as failure to survey together major and minor premisses with reference to the particular case before him. Thus in a non-practical case a man may know 'All mules are sterile' and 'This is a mule', but not conclude 'This is sterile'. Rather he may believe 'This mule is in foal' because he does not put his knowledge that this is a mule into operation to draw the relevant conclusion. His failure to exercise the minor premiss is a failure to use (*suntheôrein*, 67a37; b5–10)[24] the

---

[22] In 1147a1–4 Aristotle is concerned with a syllogism with only two premisses; in 1147a4–6 he considers a more complex case with more than two premisses:

Dry food is good for a man
Chicken is dry food. I am a man

Chicken is good for me
This is chicken

This is good for me

which he seeks to accommodate within his earlier distinction between possessing and using knowledge (1147a8–10). This he should do in the obvious way: there is nothing to prevent a man with all the premisses acting against them provided that there is at least one minor premiss that he has but does not exercise. For if, in the more complex case, he had considered the further possibility of breakdown beyond those in the simple case (e.g. complete ignorance of one of the additional minor premisses, 1147a6–8) he would no longer have been analysing the case of the man who acts against knowledge he then has (1147a2–4); for the latter must have the relevant premisses (1147a8–10; cf. 2–4), but not exercise one of them.

[23] K^b. M^b also deletes the first (*ê*). For this rectificatory use of *ê*, see for example 1135a31ff.

[24] Joachim adopts this view (Commentary, 228) of *Pr. An.* 67a33–b3. In this passage Aristotle distinguishes knowledge of universal and of particular propositions (a18, 20, 23, 27). The latter may be divided into active awareness that (e.g.) 'The mule is sterile', which arises when one contemplates together the major and minor premisses (67a36f.), and potential (or dispositional) awareness of this particular proposition which may be present when one does not. Thus, if one knows 'All mules are sterile' and 'This is a mule', one knows (dispositionally) that 'This is sterile', even when one asserts 'The mule is in foal'. For although one has not joined together the premisses, one has the conclusion dispositionally. However, in a different sense, the *acratês*, who fails to put together the premisses, does not have the conclusion (1147b10–11).

major and minor premisses he possesses to draw the relevant conclusion. If so, in the practical case, the *acratês* will know the relevant major and minor premisses but fail to draw the good conclusion because he does not activate the minor premiss.

Both readings of 1147a5–10 yield a coherent interpretation of the chapter as a whole. One type of Aristotelian *acratês* introduced in this passage does not reach (or possess) the good conclusion because he fails to activate (or possibly possess) the minor premiss. His non-possession of the conclusion (1147b9–11) is explained by non-activation (or non-possession) of the minor premiss (1147a5–10). In the case on which Aristotle concentrates, *acrasia* occurs when no good conclusion results from major and minor premisses (1147a26–27), because the minor premiss is not active (contrast 1147a33). Such a case (which is used after 1147a24) is characterisable in the terms of Section A as a failure of valuational reasoning. (The other case – not having the minor premiss – is not to the fore in VII 3 after 1147a24; it may however be exemplified elsewhere (e.g.) by the impetuous: 1150b19–21; see 1152a19).

There is, however, a second type of *acratês* who arrives at the conclusion but possesses it only in an 'off-colour' way (1147b11–12). That is, he has the conclusion in such a way as 'not to know it but only to say it'. His state is clarified by some of Aristotle's examples in 1147a11–24: (1) people asleep, or drunk or mad; (2) those 'in passion' repeating proofs and poems of Empedocles; (3) students who have first learned something and 'put together'[25] arguments, but lack knowledge of the subject; for that requires the knowledge to become part of their character, which needs time; (4) actors. In this sense (or senses) one *acratês* possesses the conclusion in a 'deviant way' either because he undergoes an intellectual failure of one of these types or because he undergoes an analogous failure of practical knowledge (see Chapter 4, Section A). His failure, like all acratic failures, results from the impact of passion (a14–18), but it allows him, unlike other *acratês*, to *say* what is best (a23–24).

The second type of *acrasia* arises when a conclusion is drawn from the good major and minor premisses, but the *acratês* is 'quasi-ignorant of it' and is prevented from acting by the presence of sensual desire. He says the good conclusion (1147b10; cf. 1147a34) that he should abstain from this, but does not act on it, since he takes what is pleasant under the influence of sensual desire. Thus one type of *acratês* appears to reach the good conclusion, but does not act on it. As such, his *acrasia* is not apparently a failure of valuational reasoning, but rather failure to grasp the good conclusion he draws appropriately (i.e. so as

---

[25] Ross translates *suneirein* as 'string together', but its sense is not always pejorative: *Soph. El.* 175a30; *Meta.* 986a7, 1093b27; *de Gen. Corr.* 316a8, 336b33; *de Gen. Anim.* 716a4, 741b9 (see Burnyeat, 1981, 89ff.; also Bonitz). The young students may 'put together' arguments perfectly, but lack knowledge because they have not made them 'part of themselves'.

to act on it). This case will be that of the weak *acratês* (1150b19–21; see 1152a18ff.), if the latter is characterised correctly as one who fails to grasp the conclusion fully.

Hence both types of *acrasia* in 1147b10ff. occur in the presence of the minor premiss and final term, but in different ways: one *acratês* does not reach the good conclusion (1147a1–10, 25–27, a33, b10) because he does not put together his premisses and arrive at a conclusion; the other does reach the conclusion but possesses it in an 'off-colour way' (1147a34; a17–24). Hence both failures relate in their different ways to the conclusion (1147b10), as is required if the *acratês* is to be able to act intentionally acratically.

If this account of the chapter's structure is correct, there is one type of *acratês* who actually reaches the good conclusion (in an off-colour way) but does not act on it. If so, Aristotle cannot have held either that the good conclusion was identical with the action (Identity thesis)[26] or the strongest form of the Sufficiency thesis, in which it is sufficient for action. However, in 1147a25–31, Aristotle appears to adopt this Sufficiency thesis in precisely such a form. To this passage we must now turn, for it threatens the line of interpretation of *NE* VII 3 which we have so far advanced.

(c) *1147a24–b9, and Aristotle's more specific discussion of acrasia*

Aristotle begins as follows (1147a24–31).

> Let us now consider the case of *acrasia* more specifically.[27] The one proposition is a general opinion, the other proposition is about particulars, with which perception is concerned. When one proposition arises from them, it is necessary for the soul here to assert the conclusion, and in the case of propositions that are productive to act immediately.[28] For

---

[26] See also Chapter 2, Section C.

[27] Translating '*physikôs*' as referring to problems or arguments specific to a given subject matter; '*logikôs*' features, by contrast, are of a general kind not based on principles particular to a given science or subject matter: cf. 316a11, 280a32, 283b17; see Barnes ad 82b24. After 1147a24 Aristotle applies some of the distinctions drawn earlier in the chapter to the specific case of *acrasia*, without now considering whether these may apply more generally to other cases as well as that of *acrasia* (contrast a10–14, 18–22 and perhaps a5–9). This passage is not more physiological in character than 1147a16–24 (contrast Robinson, Hardie ad loc.).

[28] Of 1147a25–28, Robinson writes: 'What a paradoxical thesis! And what a very Socratic thesis! I think that it is the most Socratic sentence in this fundamentally Socratic chapter.' He does not, however, discuss how far this sentence is modified by the introduction of the qualifications involving prevention in the next sentence. In this translation of 1147a27, I understand 'here' as referring to the particular stage of asserting a conclusion (cf. 1139a25–26) of the form: 'ɸ' or 'ψ is good' (a judgment about a perceptible: 1147b9). It seems extremely difficult to construe 'here' as referring to a theoretical syllogism in this context, as none are present in the passage. The next phrase should read 'in the case of propositions that are productive of action' (cf. 701a23–24: also note 13 above) and refer to propositions which are productive of actions as efficient cause of actions (430a12, 729b13). The following sentence exemplifies this

example, if one should taste all sweet things, and this particular thing is sweet, it is necessary for the man who is able and not prevented immediately also to do this action.

Thus it might appear that no agent can reach the conclusion of the good syllogism and fail to act accordingly, if he acts intentionally. But if Aristotle accepts the strongest form of the Sufficiency thesis, the breakdown in all cases of *acrasia* must predate the conclusion and occur at the stage of the minor premiss.

This interpretation might be supported by passages where practical wisdom is described as 'prescriptive' (1143a8–10), and the practically wise man as 'practical' as he always does what he judges should be done (1146a8: 1152a8–10). If so, *acrasia* might appear strongly to resemble epilepsy (1150b33–34) – a disease which incapacitates and renders (free) intentional action impossible.

There is, however, no compelling ground to attribute to Aristotle so strong a form of the Sufficiency thesis, and some evidence against doing so.

(1) 'Prevention', in Aristotle's usage, need not be limited to external prevention which stops the agent putting into practice his decision. The term itself is used of a range of factors: logical reasons against a proposition (340b33; 1101a14), of legal prohibition (1130b24; 1113b26; 1304b28; 1309a17), and of moral qualities which exclude their opposites (1096b9–12). Hence 'there being nothing to prevent S's φ'ing' rules out the presence of internal factors which prohibit (1147a31–32) or impede his action as well as the special case of external physical prevention emphasised by the use of 'outside' (1048b16–17 (see a21–24); 417a28). If so, one cannot conclude from 1147a24–31 that only external prevention is intended in this context; if Aristotle had intended that, he would have restricted the extension of 'prevention' here as he does elsewhere.

(2) In *de Motu* 701a16 Aristotle uses a similar phrase, but elsewhere spells out the factors that can impede e.g. the conclusion in favour of walking[29] from producing the appropriate action (702a15–20): revolt on the part of the passions which stand between the final desire and the action (701a31–36; 702a3–5). If so, it is Aristotle's view that the

---

structure: the agent reaches the conclusion and acts immediately if there is nothing which prevents him (a30–1: cf. Chapter 2, Section C). The conclusion is the productive proposition in this case, as it is the one proposition which results from the previous two (a26–27); as such, it may be specified subsequently as what is responsible for action (b10) – as was to be expected given that the 'final proposition' is the conclusion. 'Productive' propositions may be contrasted with those which are not immediate causes of action (as action is not then appropriate as in deliberation about future actions) and with critical conclusions which are reached by similar reasoning to productive ones but for different purposes (1143a8–16; a30–b5). 'Productive' propositions will embrace both technical and practical reasoning (as in *de Motu* 7). For a different view, see Kenny, 1979, 157 n. 2.

[29] See Chapter 2, Section C.

presence of an opposed affection (e.g. sensual desire: cf. 1147a33) may prevent the conclusion from producing the appropriate action. Hence, in *de Motu* Aristotle explicitly allows that the agent may reach the conclusion and not act accordingly. If so, he cannot have held a version of the Sufficiency thesis which renders such a case impossible.

The structure of the present context (1147a26–35) suggests a similar account of *acrasia* incompatible with a strong Sufficiency thesis. Aristotle continues (a31–35)

> When, therefore, there is, on the one hand, a universal proposition present forbidding us from tasting, and, on the other, another proposition that everything sweet is pleasant, and this is sweet (the proposition that says that is active), and sensual desire is also present, the soul then on the one hand says that we should avoid this, but sensual desire leads one towards it; for each of the parts of the soul can move the body.[30]

The first part of this sentence seems to resume with elements from the immediately preceding sentence (1147a29–31) although it points back also to 1147a26–28 (which a29–31 exemplifies). Thus, the most natural major premiss seems to be 'Do not taste sweet things' to match 'Taste all sweet things' in a29. Further, the previous sentence allows a minor premiss to be introduced by its content, 'This is sweet' (1147a33), without a separate premiss being mentioned (before the brackets) as in a29. If so, the phrase 'Sensual desire happens to be present' should exemplify the role designated by the phrase with the same grammatical role in the previous sentence, 'The agent not being prevented', to show that sensual desire is present as an intervening factor in the case of *acrasia* to explain why the good syllogism fails to issue in action. Aristotle then expands on this with a reference back to 1147a26–28:

> The soul says that we should avoid this, but sensual desire leads towards it.

One *acratês* says the good conclusion, but his syllogism is not productive of action as sensual desire leads him to act against it. This *acratês* gets as far as saying (with his whole soul) the good conclusion, but part of the soul (sensual desire) revolts and prevents him from

---

[30] In 1147a34 it is the *conclusion* which the soul says because (i) the relevant proposition contains a 'this' and 'flee'; (ii) the relevant proposition should be identified with the 'final proposition' said (but not known) in 1147b10–12, and this has been argued above to be the conclusion; (iii) the structure of a26–35 suggests this: the 'therefore' in a34 picks up the 'therefore' of a31 and points back to a26–28 (beyond the example of 28–31), in which the contrast is between asserting the conclusion *and* (in productive cases) acting (as well). Thus in 1147a26 Aristotle gives an example of a productive case in which the agent asserts the conclusion and acts also at the same time (see Chapter 2, Section C). He then sets out the syllogistic machinery for the acratic case and notes the presence of sensual desire as a preventive factor before returning to his basic structure: the soul says the conclusion *and* sensual desire leads to action.

acting on it by dragging him to the acratic action. The presence of sensual desire as a preventive factor is what stops the syllogism from being productive of action, but does not stop this *acratês* from reaching the good conclusion – for his minor premiss 'This is sweet' is active (in contrast with the case considered in 1147a7) in yielding the conclusion 'Avoid this' which this *acratês* says. Therefore one *acratês* arrives at the good conclusion but does not act on it. If so Aristotle does not hold the strongest version of the Sufficiency thesis which excludes this possibility in this passage (see also Chapter 4, Section A). Thus detailed consideration of the key passages in VII 3 supports the view that one of Aristotle's acratic agents arrives at the good conclusion but acts against it.

In the translation offered of 1147a31–33 no specific account was given of the role of the proposition:

(2) All sweet things are pleasant

and to this we should now turn. If the first proposition in this sentence is (to match a29)

(1) Do not taste sweet things

(2) cannot be a minor premiss, since it plays no role in deriving

(4) Do not taste this

and should rather be an opposed major premiss. Thus if (2) were to be construed as a minor premiss, the relevant syllogism would have to be of the form:

(1)′ Do not taste pleasant things
(2) All sweet things are pleasant
(3) This is sweet
(4) Do not taste this

However, if this were correct, there would be strong grounds for attributing to the *acratês* also the proposition:

(5) This is pleasant

as this is the appropriate focus for sensual desire (1149b2) when it leads to action, is entailed by two propositions he already accepts (67b5ff.), and is needed to derive (4) from (1)′ in the standard Rule-case form as the relevant minor premiss for (1)′. (5) is not explicitly stated because Aristotle is concerned to contrast *saying* the conclusion with *acting* on it (a28), although he notes (a30–1) that acting on the conclusion also involves asserting it. However, its assumed presence gives clear sense to the incidental opposition of the *acratês*' reasoning and opinions to his right rule (b2–3), since it commends a course of action which (as it happens) conflicts with 'This is to be avoided', although the two propositions can both be true (contrast non-incidental opposition: 13a37ff.; 72a17ff., b17f., where one judgment always excludes another; for degrees of opposition see 1108b26ff.; 1225b4–7). If (5) is absent, (3) 'This is sweet' and (1)' 'Do not taste pleasant things' are themselves in no way opposed (not even incidentally), as they do not commend alternative courses of action, and so the *acratês*' judgments themselves are in no way opposed (contra b2–3).

However, if (5) is present, the *acratês* has (in effect) two distinct if overlapping pieces of reasoning:

Do not taste pleasant things!	All sweets are pleasant
All sweet things are pleasant	This is sweet
This is pleasant	This is pleasant
Do not taste this!	

as he has two distinct conclusions drawn from distinct premisses. Since the *acratês* has (in effect) two syllogisms even if the minor premiss is treated as composite, Aristotle cannot be relying (in his account of *acrasia*) on the view that the *acratês* has only one non-standard syllogism. Nothing would be altered therefore by introducing as a major premiss (1)' 'Do not taste pleasant things' rather than (1) 'Do not taste sweet things'. In both cases there will be two syllogisms[31] and the *acratês* will get to the conclusion of the good one and act against it. Since this will be so whether (2) 'All sweets are pleasant' represents a desire (but not a sensual one) or an opinion which prompts a subsequent desire (1370a20ff.), there is no need to decide between these options. In both cases, the *acratês* in 1147a31–35 is the weak one who gets to the good conclusion but does not act on it because of sensual desire (1150b19–21). This interpretation of VII 3 confirms the result of the earlier argument based on intentionality: one type of Aristotelian *acratês* (described in *NE* VII 3) gets to the good conclusion, but does not act on it. It remains to explain how this case, which is central to the study of *acrasia*, can occur.

C. Best judgment and practical reasoning: Aristotle's rejection of the Uniqueness thesis

The *acratês* acts on his sensual desire, and not on his preferential desire;

---

[31] For a contrasting view of this passage, see Kenny, 1966a, 179–81. I am uncertain whether 'All sweet things are pleasant' could be a minor premiss as it is as universal in form (containing 'All') as the major premiss, in contrast to 'Sweet things are pleasant', which appears indefinite (26a29; 29a7f.; cf. 1141b19–21), or 'Particular sweet things are pleasant' (see Lukasiewicz, 1951, 5). Kenny's own examples seem to be particular or indefinite.

the *encratês*, by contrast, acts on his preferential desire and not his sensual desire. (1111b13–14)[32]

That *acrasia* is not a vice is clear (except perhaps in a way); for *acrasia* is action against preferential desire, while vice is in accordance with the agent's preferential desire. (1151a6–7)

Aristotle's rejection of the Identity thesis and the strongest form of Sufficiency thesis does not (as yet) show how an *acratês* can act intentionally against a best judgment that he then holds. If Aristotle had accepted the Uniqueness thesis and taken the relevant type of judgment as a valuational better judgment, such a case would still have been impossible. For if S does x intentionally, and has previously judged yBTx, he must have subsequently changed his mind and now hold xBTy. In this way no agent can act intentionally against a better judgment that he holds at the time of acting (see Section A).

The Uniqueness thesis in this form gains support from two sources: a conception of practical reasoning and a view of rational explanation (see Section A). In this section and the next, I argue that Aristotle holds this conception of practical reasoning, but rejects the relevant strong view of rational explanation. One type of Aristotelian *acratês* reasons practically to a best judgment that xBTy which is accepted by his preferential desire, but acts on a distinct judgment that y is good which is the conclusion of a syllogism expressing his sensual appetite, and which he can hold while judging xBTy without inconsistency.

The defence and development of this interpretation requires us to consider in detail Aristotle's account of practical reasoning and preferential desire; for the *acratês* (on Aristotle's account) acts against his preferential desire under the influence of passion. Thus we need to see how Aristotle's theory of practical reasoning, when integrated with his account of preferential choice, allows for the possibility of *acrasia*.

(a) Aristotle's general conception of practical reasoning

1. *Weak commensurability thesis.* Aristotle insists that what is preferred is what has previously been deliberated (1112a15–17; 1113a4–6, 9–12). Deliberation is concerned to discover what is better and worse (1226b14ff.), and involves 'calculation' (1139a12–13) and the inquiring intellect (1112a15–17; 1142b12ff.). Calculation is clarified by Aristotle in his discussion of the calculative imagination (434a6–10):

---

[32] The *encratês* is defined as one who has strong sensual desires which he restrains (1146a9–11; 1152a1–3). Hence to describe him as acting 'choosing not sensually desiring' must mean that he acts *on* his choice and not *on* his sensual desires. By contrast, the *acratês* must act *on* his sensual desire and not *on* his choice; this is compatible with the claim elsewhere that he has a preferential desire although it does not issue in action (1151a6–7, 1152a14–16).

Whether to do this or that is the appropriate function of calculation; one
must measure by a single standard; for one pursues what is greater.

This presupposes comparison of opposed courses on a single scale – or
in the light of a common standard – where the aim is to determine
which course achieves a higher score on the relevant scale. The activity of the inquiring intellect has as its goal finding out what is best
for a man to do (1141b12f.); and this too presupposes the possibility of
assessing the alternatives by calculation of this type. Thus Aristotle's
account of deliberation appears to rest on his acceptance of (at least)
the Weak Commensurability Thesis.

This interpretative claim might be resisted as follows: Aristotle on
occasion separates as distinct forms of valuational factor which may
lead to action: the noble, the advantageous and the pleasant (1104b30–
33, 1155b18–23), and represents them as in conflict (e.g. 1166b8–10).
Sensual desire is concerned with the pleasant and the painful, but
preferential desire is not (1111b16–18). It might appear, therefore,
that pleasure and nobility are distinct values, which lack a common
scale in terms of which they can be compared when they conflict. If
preferential desire is for the better course (1112a6–8), and sensual
desire is for the pleasant, there may be no common denominator by
which to assess them. *Acrasia* occurs (in this view) when the agent
acts to gain the pleasant against his better judgment which aims at
the noble or the advantageous.[33]

---

[33] Other evidence has been adduced (see Burnyeat, 1981, 91, fn. 29) for an Aristotelian
denial of weak commensurability:

(a) *Pol.* 1283a5–10. In this passage, Aristotle appears to deny that *all* good qualities
can be compared with specific reference to political office, and to insist that *only* those
relevant to political office can be thus compared. He relies on the following assumptions:
(i) weighing is always relative to some end (1283a13–14), (ii) there is no general (i.e.
end-independent) scale for comparing health and height and free birth, (iii) only certain
goods are relevant to given ends, and concludes from these first that not all things can
be weighed together in assessing fitness for political office, as some are irrelevant, and
second that nothing has a set general value apart from particular ends in view. But
this is compatible with all relevant goods being comparable for a given agent given
some particular end (e.g. political office) as the non-relevant goods will be 'zero rated'
relative to this end, and with all goods being comparable relative to some more general goal
(e.g. well-being). Either would allow for the relevant sense of weak commensurability.

(b) 1243a22–23. Aristotle speaks of different ways of assessing what is just employed
by different people, and the difficulties of deciding such disputes (1243b5–10) without
a third person who will judge on a common scale both sets of considerations (1243b28–
32). However, since for each person involved the values will be commensurable, and
the third party can compare the other two men's comparison, all the cases exemplify
(rather than undermine) weak commensurability.

(c) 1164b2–6. Writing on those with whom one has studied philosophy, Aristotle
argues that no honour can equal their services, and that money is not relevant to the
assessment of their worth. But this seems to be *either* because their worth far outstrips
the value of money (as with parents or the gods) *or* because one's relations with them
are not based on money as the single common value (1164a1–3, b1–3, 6–8). Both are
compatible with there being a single value on which one's return can be assessed as
'enough' (as Aristotle says in 1164b5); indeed Aristotle here and elsewhere takes the view
that such assessments are difficult but should be made (1164b27–28; cf. 1164a34–35).

This objection rests on the assumption that if φ'ing seems pleasant to S, φ'ing does not also seem good to him. For if it did, and ψ'ing (the noble action) also seemed good, they could be compared in terms of this shared value: what is good to do.

Aristotle, however, insists in a wide variety of contexts that if a course of action seems pleasant, it will also seem good. Thus in (*de An.* 433b5–10) a case of conflict of desires, sensual desire bids us pursue present pleasures – which seem good without qualification to the agent. Similarly, in 1227a39–41, Aristotle writes that the pleasant seems good to the spirit, and the more pleasant better, and in 1113a32 regrets that people pursue the pleasant as good and avoid the painful as bad. Further, in the *Rhetoric* (1378a3–4; see 1362b5–7), Aristotle notes that although sensual desire is for the pleasant, what is desired will seem good, and hence that both the pleasant and the noble may be classified as good (see Chapter 2, Section C for the general account of desire). Deliberation (it appears) may always be for the better and the worse (1226b14ff.), as all alternatives may be calibrated against one another in terms of their respective goodness. If so, pleasure, nobility and advantage appear to be sub-divisions within one common valuational dimension (1104b30–33), and sensual desire aims at the pleasant *qua* good (1113b1–2, see *de An.* 433a22–30). Thus the distinction between preferential and sensual desire adumbrated in 1111b16–18 and 1112a8 cannot be one between two incommensurable systems of value, as (when they conflict) there may be a rational choice of the type indicated between them as to which is better. If so, Aristotle held the Weak Commensurability thesis.

2. *Value and transfer of value theses.* It is a consequence of the form in which Aristotle accepted the Commensurability thesis that the common factor in terms of which the alternatives are compared is a value (e.g. goodness) which the agent accepts. If so, one would expect the premisses representing the desirability of each alternative to be expressed in terms of that value or a sub-division of that value – pleasure, nobility, advantage.

Aristotle appears to accept this conclusion in *de Motu* (701a22–25):

> The premisses which stand in practical reasoning are of two kinds: expressed through the good or the possible.

The premisses which are expressed using the good are the major premisses which express the agent's rational or sensual desire (701a10–16, 32). Some of Aristotle's practical syllogisms are explicitly stated by him using major premisses which are overtly valuational (434a18–20; 1144a32–34; 1147a5–7, 29, 33–34), but not all are (701a12–18, 19–21, 32–34). However, Aristotle's note on the syllogisms in *de Motu* shows that major premisses expressed in such a form as 'Walking is to be done by everyone', or 'Drinking is to be done by me' are to be understood as expressing (at least) a judgment of value: 'Walking is good for everyone', 'Drinking is good for me'.

Since these practical syllogisms represent one part of Aristotle's account of practical reasoning and their conclusions are propositions about what is to be done (see Chapter 2, Section C), practical reasoning conveys the shared value from premisses to conclusion. If so, the conclusion of a given piece of practical reasoning will be either that a particular course of action is good, or pleasant (and therefore good) or best. If theoretical reasoning conveys truth from premisses to conclusion, practical reasoning conveys the stated value (whatever it may be) from premisses to conclusion; if the conclusion is accepted appropriately, action follows (see Appendix 3).

In this account I dissent from J. M. Cooper (1975, pp. 24ff.) who suggests that the only role of the syllogism is to explain how a deliberated decision (the major premiss) issues in action by means of a psychological process in which perception is the additional causal factor. Thus for Cooper the practical syllogism does not represent any part of the agent's practical reasoning.[34] The exegetical evidence against his view is substantial:

(i) Aristotle uses the same vocabulary in discussing the practical syllogism in *de Motu* (thought: 701a8; thinking, syllogism: 701a8–10, 26, 28, 30) and deliberation elsewhere (1112a15–16; 1139a34–35; 1032b5–10). But if the practical syllogism involves calculation and the inquiring intellect, it involves deliberation.

(ii) In 1032b5–10, a process of deliberation is characterised as follows: 'If there is to be health, there must first be this . . . if this, then heating . . .' Such a process is described in *Physics* 200a20–24 as an example of calculation. But a similar process is described in 701a22–23 as part of a syllogism leading to action. If so, *de Motu* must also be concerned with deliberation prior to action (and leading to it in a way explained in Chapter 2, Section C) in those passages which analyse the practical syllogism.

(iii) In 1142b27–28, Aristotle characterises 'good deliberation' as 'correctness in respect of what is useful for the right end in the right way at the right time'. The reference to time is important since in *de Anima* 434a18ff. Aristotle's practical syllogism contains a minor premiss which says that now is the time to act, while the major premiss lacks time reference. If good deliberation requires consideration of temporal factors, and these may enter (as late as) the minor premiss of the syllogism, the syllogism must be part of the deliberation.

(iv) In 1142b21–30 Aristotle uses the terminology of the syllogism to express the stages of deliberation (1142b23: syllogism; b24: middle

---

[34] Cooper holds this view for two reasons: (a) in *de Motu*, he takes the conclusion of the syllogism to be an action and not a proposition about an action (already discussed in Chapter 2, Section C); (b) he sees the major premisses as making sense only if they are the expressions of an agent's decisions in a specific situation, and not of his very general goals (see below).

term), and so suggests that the syllogism may be used with appropriate major premises to represent deliberation. Nor is this surprising since for Aristotle a syllogism 'is an argument in which – certain things having been posited – something else follows of necessity' (24b18–20), and all his practical syllogisms (see Appendix 3) fall into this pattern. If so, practical syllogisms will be suitable components of deliberation. (i)–(iv) appear strongly to support the view that the practical syllogism represents a part of deliberation.

It appears therefore that Aristotle's general conception of practical reasoning includes the practical syllogism within it and is precisely the one which – together with certain premises about rational explanation – makes *acrasia* problematic. Thus it seems that Aristotle is attracted towards the Uniqueness thesis, which (by itself) threatens the possibility of *acrasia*.

(b)   Aristotle's account of preferential choice

In this sub-section, two exegetical claims are defended:

(1) preferential choice is a desire to do what is judged best of the alternatives open to the agent in deliberation;

(2) preferential choice is the unique state which characteristically immediately precedes action, and is the acceptance of the conclusion of the agent's completed deliberation.

These claims, if true, bear directly on Aristotle's treatment of *acrasia*. If the *acratês* acts against his preferential choice, and this is the state which accepts the conclusion of his practical reasoning, at least one *acratês* must reach the good conclusion and act against it. If preferential choice is the acceptance of an appropriate better judgment, and if the *acratês* has no such better judgment which favours his acratic course, he will act acratically because he does what seems to him to be good and not what seems to him to be better. If so, he may consistently hold '*x*BT*y*' and '*y* is good' (even as 'conclusions') and do *y* acratically without contradiction, even though the two courses share a common value. And this would mark the basis of Aristotle's rejection of the Uniqueness thesis.

That preferential choice is the desire to act on a better judgment may be supported by several exegetical arguments:

(i) What is chosen preferentially is what is judged as a result of deliberation as preferable to other alternatives (1112a15–17; 1113a4–6, 9–12). What is preferred to other alternatives in deliberation is what is better (1226b14ff.), where what is better is determined by calculation (1139a12–13; 434a6–10; 1112b14ff.) and the inquiring intellect (1112a15–17; 1139a33; 1142b12). Since the latter aim to establish which is the better or best alternative, preferential choice will be a desire to do what is judged best. If desire is a certain mode of accepting a valuational proposition (see Chapter 2, Section C) the agent in making a preferential choice accepts that one alternative is better or the best of those on which he has deliberated: in other words, he accepts a best judgment.

(ii) The *acratês*, by contrast, does not act on a preferential choice because he does not desire to do what is judged best. Indeed he acts against such a judgment (1151a1–8, 32; 1152a17) and thereby against his inquiring intellect (1148a9ff.) and calculation (1119b10, 1146a32f., 1150b24). The judgment on which he acts cannot be a better judgment founded on logistic imagination; rather he acts under the influence of passion, which Aristotle describes as a non-rational desire. But the appropriate expression of such a passion is a non-comparative judgment: y is pleasant (or good), which is founded on perceptual and not logistic imagination. If so, the *acratês* does not have a comparative judgment in favour of his acratic course, but only a non-comparative judgment (y is good). Hence that he lacks a preferential choice is explained by his not having an appropriate comparative judgment in favour of his acratic course, given that preferential choice is exclusively the acceptance of a comparative judgment.

While the *acratês* may go through reasoning about the best way to satisfy his passion (1142b18–20) such reasoning cannot result in the conclusion either that he should do the acratic action (for he would then be self-indulgent and not acratic) or that it is best to do it (for he would then not act against his inquiring intellect which aims at what is best for man: 1136b8–10; 1152a6–8). His reasoning does not result in a preferential desire in favour of doing it because he cannot derive from it that it is best to do x, or that he should do x.

This account shows a principled way of rendering the following three propositions consistent: (a) what is judged on the basis of deliberation is chosen preferentially (1113a4), (b) the *acratês* acts on desire, not on preferential choice (1111b14), and (c) the *acratês* . . . reasons (deliberates) correctly (1142b18–20). This is because (a) involves a better judgment, while the *acratês'* acratic line of reasoning in (c) does not. That is, in 1113a4 preferential choice is for what is judged best of all options open to him – using the inquiring intellect which aims at the best and a comparison of the opposed courses on a single scale. The *acratês* may reason as to how to satisfy a desire (or implement a non-comparative major premiss: 1147a31–32) but does not reach a comparative judgment of this sort in favour of his acratic course.[35]

[35] This account is compatible with the view that preferential choice occurs after deliberation is completed (see below). Anscombe (1965) has suggested an alternative solution in which (a) there is a preferential choice antecedent to the final executive decision in certain cases, (b) the final executive decision is only a preferential choice if it is based on an antecedent preferential choice, and (c) the antecedent preferential choice (which the *acratês* lacks for his acratic action) is based on 'moral' reasoning derived from one's conception of the good life. There is a degree of similarity between the view proposed here and Miss Anscombe's; but in this section I will reject (a), and hence (b), of her proposal, and in the next section dispute (c).

Given that the acratic's major premiss is the expression of a passion, and that passions issue in non-comparative judgments that a certain type of act is good (or pleasant), the most that can be inferred from his reasoning is that *y* is the best way to secure *z*, which is good (or pleasant) given that he has compared alternative ways of achieving *z*. This allows us to deduce only that '*y* is good'. But it is compatible with this that another course (e.g.) *x* is better (either in an unqualified way, or relative to another goal which seems best, or relative to all of S's goals). If so, since the *acratês*' acratic conclusion is not a preferential choice, he does not act on a judgment that *x* is better (in one of these senses). Hence what is required at this point is (1) a more detailed account of the preferential judgment reached by the *acratês*, against which he rebels (i.e. what form of best judgment is it, when does it occur, how is it related to practical reasoning), and (2) an account of rational choice which explains under what conditions one may reach a preferential (better) judgment of this form, and how they are distinguished from the irrational choice of the *acratês* (see Section D). Only when these topics are resolved can we see in what way one Aristotelian *acratês* accepts one course as the better course through deliberation and acts against it.

The relevant preferential desire appears to be the final desire which (at least in certain cases) immediately precedes action, and accepts the conclusion of practical reasoning. This is supported by three exegetical arguments.

(i) Practical reasoning aims at finding *a* (or *the* best) means to reach a given goal, and to trace such means back to what can be done by the agent immediately. Hence its conclusion (in such cases) is that an action of a given type is to be performed here and now (1112b22–24; 434a16f.; 701a21ff.). Preferential choice is subsequent to the final stage of deliberation and is for what has been judged preferable by deliberation. Since what has been judged preferable in such cases is an action (type) that can be performed now, preferential choice must be at least in part for this action-type as executive means to be done to achieve a given goal. Hence in such cases it is not exclusively for a general goal chosen antecedently to the executive means. Nor could there be a preferential choice exclusively for a policy decision (in such cases): for since there can be a preferential choice only when there is no more deliberation to be done, there cannot be a general preferential choice which precedes further deliberation (given the relevant definitions in *NE* III 3).

(ii) Preferential choice is described as a proximate cause of *praxis* (1139a31) and of action more generally (701a4–5, cf. a34–36). Since the proximate efficient cause is simultaneous with the effect – in the sense that nothing intervenes between them (243a33–34), there can be no further stages of deliberation which intervene between the preferential choice and the *praxis*. Hence preferential choice cannot be for a general policy antecedent to action which requires technical deliberation to implement. Rather it must be directed at, and occur after, the final stage of deliberation (at least) in cases where action follows it. In such cases preferential choice immediately precedes action and is (at least in part) for the specific means to be done to achieve the goal.

(iii) Preferential choice is not for what is impossible – but rather is for actions which the agent thinks he can do (1111b30). Indeed, deliberation consists, in part, in finding out whether one can implement steps to reach a goal; if one cannot do so, one gives up the project (1112b24–25). If preferential choice could be (exclusively) for a policy decision which the agent had not as yet discovered means to implement, it might be for something which was not in his power or which he had no reasons for thinking he could effect. Since this cannot be the case, there can be no preferential choice exclusively for a policy decision; for, since it is always an open question whether – in the circumstances – a policy can be effected, no policy decision can be – without further deliberation – something which one can have the appropriate grounds for believing that one will implement.

The first and third exegetical arguments show that deliberation is concerned (at least) in part with means to execute a policy decision, and that there can be no preferential choice which is exclusively for a policy decision. If preferential choice always succeeds deliberation about means to achieve the goal, in cases where action is required immediately, preferential choice will be for (at least in part) the basic action. In such cases, if the preferential choice causes the action, there is no further internal stage between cause and effect – and, in particular, no further deliberation.

There is, however, some evidence which appears to run contrary to this conclusion. In 1144a20ff. Aristotle writes:

> Virtue makes preferential desire correct, but what has to be done for the sake of preferential desire does not belong to virtue but to another potentiality . . . which they call cleverness: this is what makes one able to do those things which lead to the goal one has set oneself and so reach it. If the goal is noble, it is praised; if ignoble, it is a form of villainy. This is why both the practically wise and villains are clever.

Subsequently he describes cleverness as an excellence of reasoning (1144b15). Hence it appears that, in opposition to my account, cleverness aims to implement a preferential judgment fixed by virtue, and is used at a stage after there has been a preferential judgment, but before the final executive decision.

This passage is itself problematical since it suggests that cleverness is the reasoning faculty which comes into operation only after the earlier moral decision has been reached. However, if virtue supplies only the goal (1144a8), and cleverness is what is required for subsequent deliberation (a30–35), cleverness should operate throughout all stages of deliberation. If so, cleverness is not involved *only* in one final stage of reasoning but in *all* those shared by the clever *acratês* and the practically wise (1152a11–14; 1227b39ff.), and the restricted use of cleverness in 1144a20ff. appears atypical.

However, a closer examination of 1144a21 and 25 suggests a solution to this problem: cleverness is focused in this passage on the *doing* of the actions which lead to the goal and *getting* to the goal (*doing* a25; a21). That is, it represents the practical executive ability which enables one to put into effect one's completed plan and reach the goal one has set oneself. Thus cleverness (like practical wisdom: 1140b5–7, 1141b9–10, 1146a6–8) will have two points of application as (i) the ability to deliberate means to a goal, and (ii) the ability to effect the means once deliberated. While (i) is required to devise a way to one's goal (1144b14), (ii) is essential at the next stage if one is to carry it through. This solution has a further advantage: it shows there is no paradox (or ambiguity) in holding both that cleverness operates after preferential choice (and hence after deliberation) as an executive ability and also that it is a deliberative ability which characterises the reasoning of the clever *acratês*. Thus preferential choice may occur after deliberation is completed and immediately prior to action in this passage as in the others considered above.[36]

There may, however, be cases of deliberation about future actions which one cannot then do. In such examples, there could be preferential choice only if the deliberation terminates in the selection of a specific action (type) sufficiently determinate that if the present were the time for action, the agent would act immediately without further deliberation about means. Only thus would deliberation yield a determinate answer to the question 'How shall I act?' which is its goal; if

---

[36] In 1151a6–7, *acrasia* is described as 'action against preferential choice, while vice is action in line with the preferential choice'. If *acrasia* covers (here) both weakness and impetuosity but involve action against preferential choice. But since the impetuous agent does not deliberate (1150b21–22), he cannot act against an executive decision that φ is best, but at most against a general policy decision which he previously reached by deliberation. If so (it will be objected), preferential choice in this context is not an executive decision to do a specific action-type.

An alternative analysis runs as follows. Since the impetuous *acratês* does not deliberate when acting, his preferential choice may either have been reached in previous completed deliberation in a relevantly similar case *or* is the one he would have reached in the present case had he deliberated. It need not be a previous general policy decision against which the impetuous *acratês* rebels here. The alternative analysis, which allows all preferential choice to occur after the completion of the type of deliberation characterised in III 3, has the advantage of explaining why the *acratês* is described in 1151a6–7 as acting against '*a*' preferential choice, not '*the*' preferential choice. For the impetuous, unlike the weak, *acratês* acts against, not his immediate preferential choice, but a preferential choice he has previously made (or would have made, if he had deliberated).

further deliberation about means were required after t, there would be no complete deliberation or preferential choice at t.[37]

The exegetical arguments of this sub-section yield the following picture: preferential choice in the case of a present action is the acceptance of a judgment that an immediate action is the best executive means to reach the goal that the agent has set himself. This is why Aristotle speaks of preferential choice as a choice to do something for the sake of a given goal (1225a10–14; 1226a12–14; 1228a1–4) and as the acceptance that a given means is best to achieve that goal (1111b25–27), but not as focused on to the goal itself which is the object of rational desire. Within this account, there may be ignorance within a preferential choice of the relevant major premiss (1110b32–34) or of the appropriate goals of the good man (1228a1–10), and so, even though preferential choice itself does not select the goal, vice may make the preferential choice incorrect, and virtue be required to make it correct (1144a19–22).

If preferential choice is of the form 'x is the best means to reach the goal G' (*the* goal is used in 1112b26ff.; 1112b15–16; 1142b31–33), it must be distinguished from the *acratês*' desire by difference in attitude to the goal. The former requires that the deliberator regard G as the goal, i.e. the best (1144a32) of the goals open to him and not as a goal (one of the goals open to him). If the agent accepts that a given goal is best, and judges that a given means is the best way to achieve that goal, he can conclude 'x is the best means to achieve the best goal' and infer 'x is best', while from his acratic syllogism, he can only infer 'y is good' from 'y is the best means to achieve a goal (pleasure).' Thus the conclusion of the agent's valuational reasoning accepted by his preferential desire will be a comparative or superlative judgment that x is best while the *acratês* acts on a rival conclusion that y is good, which he can hold without inconsistency (1147b1–4).

If one type of *acratês* acts against his preferential choice, he acts against the conclusion of his valuational reasoning in a conflict case (as represented by the conclusion of his good syllogism that x is best). If so, as argued in Section B, at least one type of *acratês* acts against the conclusion of his good syllogism (which he then accepts) that x is best, when he does y intentionally.

In this sub-section, it has been argued that preferential choice is the desire to do what is judged *best* (i.e. the good conclusion of the agent's

---

[37] It is not clear that Aristotle explicitly rules on such cases, as he seems to consider only the case in which action immediately follows. However, his conditions for preferential choice are (a) that it comes after deliberation about 'How shall I act?' which is concerned with finding means to a goal, where the last means is the first stage in execution; and (b) that it is for a determinate (specific) action-type (see Appendix 3). These allow for future directed preferential choices provided that they are sufficiently specific for immediate action (if the time for action were the present). There could be no preferential choice if S's completed deliberation did not yield a specific action-type of the kind required.

reasoning) and is what precedes such action as proximate cause. It remains to be seen how this account of preferential choice meshes with Aristotle's picture of practical reasoning and rational choice. If these connexions can be made precise, the present account shows Aristotle rejecting the Uniqueness thesis by allowing the weak *acratês* to act on '*y* is good' against his best judgment that *x* is best.

(c) Specific conception of practical reasoning and preferential choice
(see also Appendix 3 for further detailed textual support)

In the general picture of practical reasoning the major premisses are part of deliberation, and hence some of them must state general considerations in favour of one course of action. But taken as major premisses as they stand, some could only command assent from the insane. That is, if premisses such as 'Taste all sweet things' or 'Every man is to walk' are taken as universal conditionals and as action-guiding, one who assents to them should (it appears) always be tasting sweet things or walking. But there will be situations in which one would not want to taste (another) sweet thing or walk – e.g. if walking meant death!

Aristotle's picture of practical reasoning introduces two features which serve to resolve these difficulties: the concept of 'in general' and the distinction between premisses which concern the good and the best.

Deliberation is concerned with matters which hold 'for the most part', in which 'the issue is obscure and in which things are indeterminate' (1112b9). Practical generalisations hold 'for the most part' because 'one cannot give a complete specification due to the endless possible cases . . . for a lifetime would be too short to give an adequate account here' (1374a30–34). In such cases one may say 'ϕ'ing is in general good (or bad)' (1137b16–18; 1027a22–25) although one cannot complete the conditions under which ϕ'ing is not good (or bad). For example, a certain medical treatment 'is in general useful for a man in fever – except under certain conditions in which it is not, e.g. at full moon' (1027a22–25); in such a case the relevant major premiss cannot be a (non-trivial) universal conditional. Rather, it should be construed (see Appendix 3) as 'In general, *x*'s are good', or 'In general, *y*'s are to be avoided (bad)'. Thus Aristotle states certain laws in this form (1374a32–34; 1137b12–14), but his treatment should be extended to all cases where the major premiss concerns a certain phenomenon (e.g. dry food, sweet things) which is not always good (e.g. if the food although dry is maggot-ridden).

It would be possible to extend this treatment to all cases where the major premiss is non-comparative. If so, 'Walking is to be done by every man', 'Staying still is to be done by all men', would express judgments of the form 'Walking is good – in general – for every man', 'Staying still is good – in general – for every man', etc.

Major premisses of this form require that, before deciding to (e.g.) walk, the reasoner considers:

(a) whether in this case there is anything that *undermines* the goodness of walking;
(b) whether in this case there is anything that *detracts* from the goodness of walking;
(c) whether in this case there is anything *better* than walking;

These three stages appear distinct. Consider the following example:

(a) Buying silk ties is good – unless they are brash or gaudy.

Here being brash undermines the goodness of buying them, since, if brash, they are not pleasant to wear. Contrast:

(b) Buying silk ties is good – unless they are expensive.

Here their being expensive does not *undermine* (they are still pleasant to wear), but does *detract* from, the value of buying them: it is less good to buy them than it would have been had they been less expensive.

(a) and (b) differ from:

(c) Buying silk ties is best

as it may be good to buy a silk tie (the ones on offer are neither brash nor expensive) but I may have something better to do with my money. So, while it is good to buy a silk tie, it is not the good (or best) thing to do.

Corresponding to these three distinct stages, there are distinctive types of de-relativisation. In the first it is necessary to see whether there is anything about this case which undermines the beneficial aspect of doing x; e.g. it is now full moon (1027a24–26). In the second, one is required to check whether there is anything which, while not undermining the beneficial aspect of doing x, makes it less good to do x considered as an isolated option in the light of one's valued goals. In the third, the issue is: is doing x the good (best) option (overall – or without qualification)? In the first, one sees whether doing x now has a good quality; in the second whether doing x now is good (considered as a package by itself); in the third whether doing x now is the good thing to do (considered as against all other options), even though nothing undermines or detracts from its goodness.

The distinction might be drawn thus: in the first case, the conclusion expresses a judgment relevant to the specific good feature of doing x, which is based on all the evidence relevant to the presence or absence of that feature. Thus it may end with a categorical judgment 'x has one good feature', or 'There is something good about x'. In the second, the judge considers all the evidence for and against doing x as one option taken by itself, and concludes 'x is good', or 'It is good to do x'. In the third, the judge considers all the evidence for and against x as one against all other options open to him, and concludes 'x is the good', *or* 'It is best to do x'. In the second case (unlike the first) the judgment is based on the total evidence relevant to the question: is x good to do? In the third, it rests on the total evidence for and against doing x as opposed to all relevant options. In both, we must assess the total relevant evidential support for the distinct judgments reached, and so must seek to see what in the situation bears on the relevant assessment of doing x.

Major premisses which are non-comparative will lead rationally to action only if (e.g.) the particular case of walking has a good feature *and* it is good to walk *and* (typically) if there is nothing better than walking. Such premisses, therefore, could be assented to by all: sane and insane alike. But what of major premisses which are comparative or superlative? Can these be accepted by the sane also?

The account of practical reasoning given above explains how premisses of this type may arise. In the third case, the reasoner judges not only that doing x is good, but *the* good in the present situation. Such cases may be formulated using overtly comparative or superlative terms:

'In this situation x is the best' (434a15–20; 1144a32; 1147a29), even though the agent cannot complete the list of factors which, when added to – or subtracted from – this situation, would render this false. These major premisses are grasped quasi-perceptually (1144a30ff.) in conflict cases where the agent realises that there is more than one distinct course which is good.

The conclusion of such syllogisms will be an unqualified judgment: 'x seems best without qualification.' But not all conclusions will have this form: the best means to a good goal need not themselves be classified as *the* good or *the* best, as there may be (a) features which undermine its goodness, (b) features of this alternative which detract from its goodness, or (c) other better alternatives. In the first case the reasoner could not arrive at a non-relativised conclusion in favour of doing x; the most, he could say, is 'x is the best way to achieve goal *g*', or 'x is (or seems) best, if one seeks goal *g*'. In the second, the conclusion arrived at would be 'x has a good feature (non-relativised)', while in the third case the appropriate conclusion would be 'x is (or seems) good (non-relativised)'. Since there is a definite step from these judgments to 'x seems best', the *acratês* may hold either 'y is good' or 'y has a good feature', while holding 'x seems best'. The *acratês* accepts one of the former pair decisively, while also reaching the latter.

But which conclusion is characteristic of the *acratês*? It seems that one *acratês* arrives at 'y is good (by itself)' and 'x seems best' (433b10) because in coming to this judgment he ignores the future bad consequences of doing y, which he had taken into account in his better judgment. From his reasoning he should have concluded only 'y has a good feature' and not 'y is good (by itself)'; for he was aware of certain features which would undermine the latter judgment.

Not every *acratês* needs to reach the conclusion that '*y* is good (by itself)', since reaching this conclusion will typically involve turning one's back on evidence one possesses and has used in reaching the best judgment that (e.g.) *y* will produce bad consequences. Since in 1147b2 Aristotle notes that the reasoning and opinions of the *acratês* are not essentially opposed to right reasoning, this reasoning should not involve a judgment of the form '*y* is good (by itself)', but only '*y* has a good quality', as (in this case) his acratic conclusion is not essentially opposed either to the better judgment or its supporting evidence.

There are thus three types of conclusion on which an Aristotelian agent may act: '*x* seems best', or '*x* is good (by itself)', or '*x* has a good feature'. All three are non-relativised, as they are distinct from '*x* is best if one is seeking goal *g*'. There are, however, significant differences between them. '*x* seems best' is a conclusion because no further reasoning is required after it. By contrast '*x* is (or seems) good (by itself)' or '*x* has a good feature' may be conclusions because the agent himself reasons no further after them.

There is (it seems) no general ground for demanding that all these three conclusions have precisely the same form; for they are conclusions of different types of different pieces of reasoning, which represent different stages in the agent's thought. An agent may (in Aristotle's theory) act intentionally on any of them.

Aristotle thus rejects the Uniqueness thesis by denying that all conclusions of practical reasoning are of the same form (e.g. '*x* seems best') and by allowing, consonant with his general valuational picture of practical reasoning, that '*x* seems best' and '*y* is good (by itself)' and '*y* has a good feature' are all conclusions on which one may act. The *acratês* acts irrationally on one of the latter against the former, and thus against a best judgment which he then holds. In acting contrary to his preferential choice, at least one of Aristotle's *acratês* reaches the good conclusion and does not act on it.

This account shows the basis of Aristotle's theory of practical reasoning, and how it is integrated with his picture of preferential choice. The specific and general accounts of practical reasoning presented in this section have direct consequences for Aristotle's account of the rational explanation of acratic intentional action in conflict cases. In the next section we will assess these in considering his discussion of the Rationality thesis.

D. Rational choice, rational explanation and intentional action

Aristotle rejected the Sufficiency, Identity and Uniqueness theses, and held that the *acratês* judged, at one and the same time, that *y* is good and *x* is best, and acted acratically but intentionally on the former conclusion against the latter (see Section A). At the same time he maintained the three theses which comprise the original conception of practical reasoning. Did he accept the Rationality thesis? This states that

(i) if an action is intentional, it is rationally explainable;

(ii) if an action is rationally explainable, it is explainable by means of an argument that culminates in a conclusion that one action is the best available;

where (ii) entails

(iii) if an action is rationally explainable (in a conflict case), it is rational.

It seems clear that – given the account of *acrasia* in Sections B and C – Aristotle must have rejected either (i) or (ii) even in the cases of explicit conflict of reasons. (For Aristotle's rejection of (i) in certain cases which do not involve conflict of reasons, see Chapter 2, Section C.) But which? This issue will become clearer if we consider initially a question raised, but not answered, in the previous section: under what conditions does an agent rationally choose one course and not another, and hence reach a preferential judgment xBTy? Or alternatively why does not the *acratês* reach a preferential conclusion yBTx in favour of doing the acratic course? Until we have resolved this issue, the formal account of practical reasoning given in Section C lacks a foundation.

These two issues, rational choice and rational explanation, appear connected. The *acratês*, let us assume, acts acratically against his better judgment because he has a strong desire to do the acratic action or an image of himself doing the acratic action which is sufficiently attractive to lead him to do it. If the added desire or the image constitute a reason for acting as powerful as their motivational force, then the *acratês*' 'acratic action' will be rationally explainable and rationally chosen; for the added desire or image will now tip the balance in favour of the purportedly acratic action. Hence *acrasia* appears impossible. However, if one seeks to avoid this dilemma by denying that the added desire or image is a reason and by postulating a sequence of explanation in which there is a motivational factor F which is not a reason, one needs to show why F (if a psychological feature of this type) is not a reason. For, if F is an image or added desire, it may be represented as the agent's seeing something desirable in an action of a given type; further, given that the *acratês* believes that doing an action of that type is a way of satisfying his desire or imagination, he will have the relevant desire and belief required to rationalise his action.[38] But if F is a reason, and its rational power is the same as its motivational power, the agent's action will once again be rationally explainable and rational – and, as a consequence, *acrasia* will prove impossible. Hence, while the introduction of a feature F of

---

[38] Within at least Davidson's liberal conditions for 'being a reason': 1980, 4–8.

this type appears to allow for *acrasia*, this appearance is illusory if one is given no ground for rejecting F''s claim to be a reason.

On both sides of this dilemma it is accepted that if (in cases of conflict of reasons) an action is rationally explainable, it is rationally chosen. But the existence of this dilemma casts doubt on the assumption. Aristotle, I will argue, in effect rejected it by developing a distinctive account of rational choice and expecting less of rational explanation.

(a) *Rational choice.* Aristotle's general account of rational choice is clearest in *NE* III 3. If there is one goal at issue (e.g. health) the rational choice is for what is best as a means to that goal (1112b15–18); in a case where no further issues are relevant, the best means is the one which contributes most to the goal.[39] In such a case, the value of the alternative means depends on how much they contribute to the goal which the agent has set himself.

If there is more than one possible goal (e.g. health and pleasure), the deliberator asks himself 'What general goal should I promote here?', postulates a goal and then asks himself which of the alternatives contributes most to the goal he has set (or is the best way of achieving it). Hence the comparative value of each course resides only in its value as a means to the goal which the agent has set himself; for the contribution to this goal allows a common dimension in terms of which the alternatives can be assessed rationally against each other (434a8–10).

The rational deliberator, therefore, evaluates his opposed desires comparatively in one given perspective: how far do they contribute to my favoured goal? The relevant comparative value of each course is not fixed by the support they receive from their grounds (e.g. pleasure) or from strength of desire, firmness of belief or conception of subjective probabilities – except insofar as these are relevant to the goal he has set himself. Thus, for example, that the agent has a strong desire to φ (or an image of himself contentedly φ'ing) will not be relevant to his comparative evaluation of the alternatives given that *g* is the goal, or will be relevant only insofar as the strength of his desire contributes to achieving the goal. If its strength (or the potency of the image) does not contribute at all (or greatly) to the goal, it will not play any (or a large) role in his calculations of the comparative value of the alternatives. Such features would have a greater comparative valuational impact if their comparative value were dependent on their strength or motivational power. Given the goal-directed conception of rational choice, strong desires will only be (equally) strong comparative valuational reasons if they contribute equally strongly to the goal. Hence

---

[39] In taking *NE* III 3 as a general pattern of rational choice and using 'contribute' as a term which covers both causal means-ends and rule-case reasoning, I follow Wiggins (1975/6, 34ff.); see Appendix 3.

Aristotle's picture of rational choice allows him to distinguish between the motivational and valuational impact of (e.g.) different desires, as the latter – but not the former – is determined by their contribution to the goal the agent has set himself.

It is now clear why the *acratês'* acratic decision is not his best judgment. He has not abandoned his assessment either of the goal or of the course preferred in the light of that goal. While his strong desire to act differently may provide a reason for his acratic action it is not one which changes his comparative valuational assessment of the alternatives; for the latter is fixed not by the strength of his desires, but by their contribution to the goal he has postulated. Thus, even if his acratic action is rationally explainable, it is not rationally chosen; for rational choice is not (in general) a simple function of forces including strength of desire (as in certain conceptions of decision theory).

These consequences mark out the differences between Aristotle's conception of rational choice and that which appeared to make *acrasia* problematic. Aristotle's rational deliberator does not (in general) bring to bear all the attitudes, motives and beliefs which relate to the options before him, or seek to assess which course has the greater value in light of all these reasons, since he will consider, in reaching his comparative judgment, only those factors which are relevant to the goal he has set himself. Further, in arriving at his best judgment, he will not take each reason at its 'face value' in terms of the grounds that support it (e.g. pleasure, strength of desire) and then compare them by putting the values which favour x in one pile and those for y in another and thus weighing them; rather, he will compare them in the light (only) of their contribution to his favoured goal. This affects Aristotle's account of the acratic case and its rational explanation.

(b) *Rational explanation.* If the *acratês'* better judgment is of the type sketched above, his acratic action will not be explained by means of a valuational argument that culminates in the conclusion that the acratic intentional action is the best available. Hence either it is not rationally explainable, or it is not a condition of rational explanation that a best judgment of this type results. The *acratês'* decisive acceptance of the conclusion: doing y is good, is not explained by the antecedent stages of the syllogism whose conclusion is that doing y is good. For while they may entail this conclusion, his decisive acceptance of it is not thus explained. Rather, his mode of accepting the acratic conclusion is to be explained by means (for example) of the motivational power of his acratic desires and not their valuational impact. As such Aristotle's conception of the role of rational explanation seems restricted even in cases of conflict of reasons, since why the agent acted is not rationally explained.

However, the *acratês'* action may be rationally explained in these cases in a weaker sense as:

(a) he acts on a proposition which is a conclusion of a practical syllogism;

(b) the proposition on which he acts is of a form appropriate to be a conclusion and is marked off from interim stages of practical reasoning (see Section C), and

(c) no factor need be used to explain the *acratês'* decisive acceptance of his acratic conclusion which is not itself a reason. A strong desire or image may constitute an appropriate reason, although the efficacy of the desire is not represented by its rational or valuational impact.

This agent's acratic conclusion and his decisive acceptance of it may be explained by reasons, although it is not only by their rational power that they explain. Since I will reserve the title 'failure of rational explanation' for cases which fail to fulfil (a)–(c), Aristotle's account of this type of *acrasia* will be (in this terminology) that the action is rationally explainable but not rationally choosen, and hence not rational. In the next chapter, we will examine more fully the achievement of becoming rational; but it appears that one precondition is that one avoids the split between the motivational and valuational impact of reasons that is the *acratês'* undoing. And this has consequences for the efficacy of rational explanation (in general). For if an action can be rationally explained by means of an argument of the appropriate type, this is because the agent accepts the relevant conclusion in such a way as to avoid the split between motivation and valuation which leads to *acrasia*. Since such actions can only be rationally explained because the agent's motivational and valuational states do not conflict radically, there must be an underlying and (partially) distinct form of explanation to account for its success in the case of reasoned encratic and wise actions (see Chapter 5, Section A).

It is a consequence of Aristotle's account that there can be within it no one uniform propositional expression of an intention, as the *acratês'* acratic intention is his acceptance of a different judgment from the *encratês'*. It does not follow, however, either that intention does not involve a valuational judgment or that there is no state common to all intentions. For intention might be characterised as the acceptance, in a decisive way, of a proposition which is unrelativised in the form '*x* seems best, *y* is good, etc.'; and decisive acceptance might also be characterised dispositionally as a state which leads to action, given opportunity and no external prevention (1048a12–15). Aristotle's account, therefore, does not preclude the possibility of defining one psychological or dispositional type which is intending.[40] But he

---

[40] Anscombe (1965, 59) (in effect) moves from saying that there is (for Aristotle) no one type of valuational conclusion that precedes all intentional action to the conclusion that there can be no one state: intending, in all such cases. But this conclusion only follows if one also holds that there is no common non-valuational state (e.g. a belief of a given type) and no common physical or dispositional state common to all intentions.

does not himself exploit this possibility, but prefers to characterise actions as resulting either from preferential choice or sensual desire. It is, therefore, no objection to Aristotle's account that he has no account of intention; for he could have defined such a state using his own machinery. The interesting question is, rather, why he preferred to use preferential choice and sensual desire in characterising the antecedents of intentional action (see Chapter 5, Section A).

(c) *Further aspects of rational choice.* The account of rational choice has assumed that Aristotle's deliberator postulates one goal as the best, and then assesses alternatives in the light of this goal. Nothing has been said of the conditions under which he postulates a goal, or whether he will always postulate the same goal in a similar situation, or whether his goals should be consistent with each other, or form a coherent framework. Indeed rational choice seems to require no more than weak commensurability of the two alternatives in the light of a shared goal (however momentarily espoused). If this is correct, Aristotle's theory of rational choice embraces much less than is commonly supposed; for it is generally held that:[41]

(a) all preferential choice (rational choice) is based on the agent's conception of well-being;

(b) all preferential choice is reached by moral and technical deliberation from the agent's most general premises about well-being;

(c) the agent's conception of well-being encapsulates those thoughts which habitually inspire his actions – and so express his fixed idea of the good life.

If (a)–(c) are correct, one cannot preferentially choose to do x without a conception of the good life, and one cannot have a conception of the good life without a stable moral character. Hence the *acratês* does not have a preferential choice to do the acratic action because his acratic conclusion is not based on his settled conception of the good life (1226b21–31; 1144b6–14), and nobody can choose preferentially to do x atypically in an uncharacteristic moment of moral virtue when in the grip of a fleeting but virtuous conception of the good life.

It is not clear, however, that Aristotle held either that one cannot choose preferentially to do x without a (more or less coherent) conception of the good life or that one cannot have a conception of the good life without a stable moral character. While the practically wise agent's choices may fulfil (a)–(c), none of these theses appears to be true of all rational (preferential) choices on Aristotle's account.

It appears (contra (a)) that there may be preferential choices not based on the agent's conception of well-being. In 1113a4–5, what is chosen preferentially is what is judged best from deliberation.

[41] In outline by Anscombe, Cooper, Wiggins, Nussbaum and Kenny.

Deliberation, however, may have goals other than and much more specific than well-being: persuasion (1112b13), good government (1112b14), strength (1140a28), good condition (1227b26), the acquisition of some goods (1226b28), victory, wealth (1094a9), peace (1177b5) or safety (1110a10). Such cases are subsequently distinguished from deliberation involving the most general goal (1139b3) of well-being, since they have partial goals (1140a27, 1142b29) which are the goals of a man *qua* doctor, trainer, politician, rhetorician, or soldier (1139b1–3). In these examples, the doctor, for instance, may ask himself 'What is best to do from the point of view of curing the agent?' and hence exclude certain considerations altogether. If successful, he will exemplify good deliberation in a limited sphere (1142b30) and have a preferential judgment. Since there can be limited deliberation, and preferential choice is what is chosen from deliberation, there must also be preferential choices in such cases. This is why the agent who has a limited goal of health has preferential choice (1140a27).

It is no part of Aristotle's terminology – goal, target (*skopos*), wish (*boulêsis*) or setting (assuming) a goal – that what is set as a goal (and hence wished) must be the most general goal of all in every case (contra (b)). Thus there is no good reason to insist that all rational choice is based on the agent's conception of well-being, although certain rational choices of the rational (and moral) agent will be (1142b30, 1139b3). Certain agents may assume that a given goal is best, and deliberate towards it without basing that goal on their conception of well-being. Their assumption that a given goal is best is their rational wish and this, together with their deliberation about means to achieve it, yields a preferential judgment.

Nor is it a requirement (contra (c)) of this terminology that the agent regularly assumes the same type of rational wish because it is a stable part of his settled disposition. The desire for a particular goal (as the best: 1113a12; 1136b8–9; 1136a2–4) need not be permanent: an athlete may wish for victory in a given competition (1111b22), but once the race is over (or even before) the wish may have faded completely. Nor does the notion of a goal itself require that a man's goals express his stable character, given that goals may be as specific as building a ship, or victory, or acquiring a given item (1226b28–31) – a man may find that two weeks trying to build a ship or fighting for Generalissimo Markos are enough, and immediately renounce that goal. Further, a man may assume a different picture of well-being (e.g. as an ascetic) for a very brief period (five minutes in the new year), act once on it, and then reject it and return to his normal conception. Of course, certain goals may depend on a man's stable character (1113a31; 1114a31–32), but not all need do.

Thus it appears that not all of an agent's preferential choices are based on his conception of well-being or encapsulate his stable picture of the good life. The latter may be true of the preferential choices of the practically wise; but they need not apply to all such choices.

There is, however, a conflict of evidence. Certain other passages appear to support the opposed conclusion that there is no preferential choice which is not based on the agent's conception of the good life. Thus, in 1097b1–5, Aristotle argues that well-being is the complete goal and (1097b9ff.) cannot be improved by the addition of other goals. Honour, pleasure, virtue are pursued for their own sake (for we would choose them even if they had no further result), and also for the sake of well-being. Well-being itself is never chosen for the sake of any other goal. However, this passage does not say that whenever (e.g.) virtue is pursued, it is pursued as a means to well-being; it only asserts that while virtue can be chosen (sometimes: 1097a31–34) for the sake of well-being, well-being can never be chosen for the sake of virtue. As such, it is not a requirement that here well-being is always the goal (although it may be always the final goal of the practically wise agent: 1139b1–3), only that it is never a means. And this does not support (a) at all.

Children will lack preferential choice in this account because although they may deliberate about means to a goal and have wishes (1334b24f.),[42] they lack the appropriate type of reasoning required to judge that a given goal is best (in conflict cases). That is, they live in accordance with their emotions (memories, desire, etc.) which say only that given goals are good – but not that they are better than other goals; they lack the calculative imagination which involves valuational comparison of the relevant alternatives on a given scale, and act only on perceptual imagination (434a6–10). Their progress to maturity involves first the development of the ability for valuational comparison – even in specific and unconnected cases (1226b26ff.; 1389a30–b6; 1144b9–14) and (perhaps) finally the integration of all goals achieved by the moral/rational agent (1144a29–32). If so, there is a stage in their development when they possess rational judgments of preference, but lack a picture of well-being.

There remains an exegetical argument designed to show that there is no preferential choice which is not based on the agent's stable character – his fixed idea of the good life. In 1139a31–b5, Aristotle accepts the following propositions:

(i) The origin, i.e. the efficient cause, of *praxeis* is preferential choice.

(ii) The origin of preferential choice is desire and reasoning for a goal.

---

[42] In this passage, children have wishes before they possess rational calculation and intellectual perception. However, elsewhere Aristotle appears to confine wishes to rational wishes (126a13; 432b5ff.; 433a23ff.). In such cases, wish – which involves calculation – will be (or involve) the assumption of a given good as *the* goal (i.e. as best) in (at least) the present.

(iii) This is why the preferential choice cannot occur without reason (*nous*) or the inquiring intellect or character.

(iv) (iii) is because good *praxis* and its opposite cannot occur without the inquiring intellect and character.

He then analyses the components of preferential choice:

(v) Intellect itself moves nothing: only the intellect which aims at a goal which is practical does so.

(vi) Practical intellect rules over the productive intellect – since its aim is an unqualified goal: the *praxis* done.

For good *praxis* is the goal, and the desire is for that. And he concludes from (v) and (vi): 'This is why the preferential choice is desiderative intellect or (alternatively) intellectual desire.'

Premisses (i) and (ii) fit the account of preferential choice sketched above; the difficulty is to see how (iii) follows from (ii) and (iv).

It is important to note that *praxeis* in this passage do not include either all intentional actions (as animals do not commit *praxeis*, but may act intentionally 1139a18–20; 1111b6–10), or productions (1139b1–3). Since some preferential judgments may be for productions (cf. above on 1140a26–29), not all preferential choices are considered in (i), (iii) and (iv), but only those that lead to *praxeis*.[43] Hence there are two possible explanations of why the preferential choice in (iii) cannot occur without a stable character: either because its presence is a condition for *any* preferential choice, or for the more limited case of *praxis*-producing preferential choice. But which is to be preferred?

The next stage in the argument (iv) suggests that the latter is correct; for Aristotle notes that (ii) explains (iii) because 'good *praxis* cannot occur without . . . character'. This thought may be developed independently of any general conditions on preferential choice as follows:

(a) *Praxis* of this type is a life of certain activities (1098a17–19); one good *praxis* does not make *eupraxia*. If so *eupraxia* requires stable desires to persist lifelong; one good preferential choice is not enough.

(b) Any *praxis* of this type is one which the agent desires to do for its own sake as a good in itself where the desire arises from deliberation (1139a34–35; 1226b22).

---

[43] Thus 'the preferential choice' in 1139a34 limits the relevant cases to those directed at *praxis* in the preceding sentence. Since *praxeis* are only a sub-class of actions, Aristotle could not generalise from these to all actions (or all preferential choices) by using 'and that is why' in 1139a33 without *either* committing a fallacy *or* holding the premiss that an agent never does intentional actions unless he does some *praxis* (contra 1139a19–21; 1111a26). If so, 'the preferential choice' in 1139a34 must refer only to those that are for *praxeis*.

That is, it cannot just be chance that the agent desires for its own sake what he judges best; it must rather be the case *both* that had he not judged the *praxis* best, he would not have desired to do it, *and* also that he would have desired to do the *praxis* even if he had thought that there was no further gain to be achieved. These counterfactuals rest on the presence of a set of desires which make it true that he would not have desired to do the *praxis* had he not judged it best and would not have ceased to desire the *praxis* if any ulterior goal had been removed. But support for these counterfactuals requires a stable set of desires which excludes these possibilities: in short, a settled character (see Chapter 4, Section D).

Both (a) and (b) explain why it is a condition on the preferential judgment which leads to *praxis* that there be a stable character and fixed desires, without requiring that it is a condition on any preferential judgment that it expresses a fixed character.[44] If so, nothing in this passage precludes the (restricted) analysis of preferential judgment given above: indeed the explanation of (iii) by means of (iv) in 1139a31ff. appears to support it. Hence I conclude that there may be, for Aristotle, preferential judgment without fixed character. Indeed this is why elsewhere fixed and steady character is added to preferential choice as a further condition for moral action (1105a30–33).

These (mainly negative) remarks leave open two major issues. (a) How does the rational deliberator postulate one goal as the best in Aristotle's account? Does the practically wise always or ever deduce the correct goal from his conception of well-being? (b) Why is the *acratês'* acratic action atypical of him? Nothing has so far been said to preclude the possibility of permanent *acrasia*; for there could, it appears, be a complete split between the agent's valuations and his motivational states. If so, *acrasia* (so far from being impossible) is all too clearly possible. The theory needs to explain why *acrasia* is atypical of the agent.

Solutions to both are required to complete the Aristotelian account of the rational choice of the acratic and practically wise; both are integral to the explanation of *acrasia* and practical wisdom which Aristotle offers, and not to his account of preferential choice and practical reasoning. For present purposes, it is sufficient to note that these two projects are distinct, and to show how Aristotle allows for the possibility of *acrasia* through his integrated account of preferential choice and practical reasoning, which together constitute his ground for rejecting both the Uniqueness and Rationality theses. Within his theory, at least one *acratês* reaches the judgment that doing x is best while intentionally doing y, which he considers as good but not best.

---

[44] Kenny seeks to explain this passage differently (1979, 100): 'Since wanting to be a certain type of person is a morally significant character trait, purpose involves character also'. But if one can want to be a certain type of person infrequently or very rarely indeed ('out of character'), it is not clear in what sense purpose need involve character.

E. **Aristotle on the possibility of acrasia**

Aristotle allows for at least two types of *acratês*: one fails to use the
minor premiss to draw an entailed conclusion, the other draws the
conclusion but grasps it only in an 'off-colour' way (which remains to
be explained). Hence the first failure is a failure of reasoning, while
the second is not: for the latter reaches the good conclusion, but fails
to act on it (Sections B, C, D). Thus, even if his failure is an intellectual
one, it is not to be represented as a failure of reasoning.

The first case might be challenged as follows: if the *acratês* fails to
draw an entailed conclusion, is this degree of irrationality too great
to be characteristic of the acratic man? Gross intellectual failure under
the influence of passion might appear to be a form of understandable
stupidity, rather than *acrasia*. At the very least it is too major an
intellectual failure to characterise the typical case of *acrasia*. (Similar
remarks apply to the impetuous *acratês* (1150b19–21), who may fail
to possess the minor premiss that 'This is sweet' under the influence
of passion.)

The second case is more central: for here the *acratês* reaches the
good conclusion but does not act accordingly. As such, there is nothing
in his reasoning which explains why he acts as he does; his failure –
whatever its source – is to grasp fully the conclusion he has drawn
from his reasoning. Hence his acratic action is not rationally explained
by the presence of one conclusion of all his practical reasoning which
favours the acratic course, although it is rationally explained in the
weaker sense indicated in Section D. Thus his action is not susceptible
to full rational explanation in the sense indicated in Section A.

The existence of the second *acratês* compels Aristotle to reject the
Uniqueness thesis since he is represented as holding two compatible
but conflicting valuational conclusions. Since this *acratês* can reach
the good conclusion and act acratically, Aristotle can hold neither the
Identity nor Sufficiency theses in a form which excludes this possibility. Thus his rejection of these three theses, together with the Rationality thesis, shows that he seeks to allow for the possibility of *acrasia*
by rejecting the picture of rational explanation outlined in Section A.

The weak *acratês* rationally chooses the better course, and hence is
not confronted by incommensurable values. However, although his
acratic action is action on a reason of a type which may be weighed
against his other options, since this reason is non-comparative (as
explained above) it is of a different type from the comparative reasons
on which the *encratês* acts.

The *acratês'* two conclusions are both unqualified valuational judgments, but only one is decisively accepted. Hence, although Aristotle
does not reject the view that the relevant conclusion is valuational,
he does not accept that the explanation of why only one conclusion
leads to action is to be given in terms of this type of judgment. That
depends rather on whether an agent fully grasps or decisively accepts

the conclusion. Hence, although Aristotle does not represent the agent's intention as non-valuational, his full account of the agent's intentional action does not depend entirely on his valuational judgment, but also requires reference to his motivational states.

Aristotle's second *acratês* rationally chooses the better course, but does not desire appropriately to do it since the valuational and motivational impact of his reasons differ. However, we still require an explanation of how his failure occurs, and how the self-controlled avoids it. If Aristotle has shown how *acrasia* is possible, he still needs to explain how it occurs. For it seems one requirement on the adequacy of any theory of the possibility of *acrasia* that it be part of some plausible explanatory theory of its occurrence (see Section A).

There are two further requirements that Aristotle's account (as any account of *acrasia*) needs to fulfil. The first is that it show in what the irrationality or failure of the *acratês* consists. Thus far the results have been negative: the failure of Aristotle's weak *acratês* need not be a failure to take a step in an argument, for he reaches the relevant good conclusion. In particular, his failure cannot be diagnosed (as suggested by Davidson) as that of not moving from an All Things Considered (ATC) judgment to a non-relativised conclusion in violation of a principle of reasoning analogous to the requirement of total inductive support: draw the non-relativised conclusion in favour of the action judged best in the light of all available reasons.[45] The irrationality of the Davidsonian *acratês'* consists in his not drawing an appropriate conclusion from antecedent premisses – although the conclusion is not (in Davidson's account) *entailed* by the antecedent premisses. For Aristotle, by contrast, the *acratês* does not violate a principle of reasoning through failing to draw an appropriate conclusion from his antecedent premisses; for there is no step in argument to a further propositional conclusion (for Aristotle) after the *acratês* has judged 'doing x seems best' at the point where the acratic failure occurs. His *acratês* fails only to *accept* a judgment of this type appropriately.

This appears to be an advantage of Aristotle's account: for in two central cases it allows for *acrasia* (without gross intellectual failure) and in a third it allows for the appropriate irrationality of the *acratês*. By contrast, if the final (non-relativised) evaluation is represented as

xBTy, given the rest of what I believe about the immediate future,[46]

then the relation between it and the All Things Considered judgment (ATC) seems to be either deductive or not of the appropriate kind for a case of *acrasia*. There are three relevant cases: two of well-considered judgments, and a third of ill-considered judgments.

[45] Davidson, 1980, 40ff.
[46] See Davidson, 1980, 99. I discuss these issues in more detail in Charles, 1982/83.

(1)   Well-considered cases

In one case the *acratês* judges:

(a) xBTy ($R_1 \ldots R_n$ and $R_1 \ldots R_n$ and these exhaust the reasons I
have assessed) and NOT ($\exists R_q$) (yBTx, R_q and R_q)
where R_q includes or is equal to R_n, to reach his ATC judgment. But
this seems to entail that: xBTy, given the rest of what I believe about
the immediate future.

In the second, the *acratês* judges:

(b) xBTy ($R_1 \ldots R_n$ and $R_1 \ldots R_n$ and these exhaust the reasons I
have assessed) and ($\exists R_q$) (yBTx, R_q and R_q)
where R_q includes or is equal to R_n, to reach the ATC judgment. But
this appears also to entail that: yBTx, given the rest of what I believe
about the immediate future.

If so, in neither case can the agent act acratically without either
failing to draw an entailed conclusion or holding (possibly self-consciously) inconsistent Non-Relativised Evaluations. But, intuitively,
there can be cases of *acrasia* against well-considered judgments in
which the intellectual failure is not so severe as that of failing to draw
an entailed conclusion. It seems a merit of Aristotle's account that it
can allow for them; for one of his acratic agents does not fail to draw
an entailed conclusion, but rather does not accept decisively that xBTy.

(2)   The ill-considered case

In these cases, the *acratês* has no view at all about whether he has
considered all his relevant reasons or about how the reasons he has
not considered would affect the overall assessment. His final judgment
should rationally reflect his limited set of reasons considered:

'xBTy, given the rest of what I *now* believe . . .'

and be entailed by the relevant (equally limited) ATC judgment. If
the final judgment is less limited in its range of considerations:

'xBTy, given what I now believe and a conservative extension of
what I believe'

and S has no view about the relevant conservative extension, it is
somewhat irrational for him to conclude either 'xBTy' or 'yBTx'. For
in this case S has no grounds for a view about which option will be
better in the light of reasons he has not assessed; this is what makes
the case an ill-considered one. But it is then irrational (to an extent)
for S to hold a proposition of the form '– BT – given what I now believe
and a conservative extension of what I believe' in favour of doing

either x or y; for this proposition is not properly grounded, but goes beyond what S is entitled to believe. Yet the central acratic cases seem to be ones in which it is clearly rational to reach a conclusion in favour of doing x, and clearly irrational to reach a conclusion (of the same form and generality) favouring y. Hence, while ill-considered cases allow for the formation of irrational beliefs (without failure to draw an entailed conclusion), they are not of the appropriate kind to characterise the central case of *acrasia*.

The cases allowed for by Davidson's theory at this point appear to involve either too severe an irrationality (the well-considered cases) or the wrong type of irrationality (ill-considered cases) to characterise the acratic man. Thus far, then, Aristotle's account appears preferable; for it involves neither.

Aristotle's theory is, in a certain sense, a mid-position between that adopted by Davidson and that advocated by the new-wave theorists: Bratman, Peacocke and Pears. For Aristotle (like Davidson) accepts that the conclusions of both *acratès* and *encratès* are valuational, while – for the new-wave theorists – the failure of the *acratès* is that of not moving from an ATC judgment in favour of x to 'I'll do x' or (perhaps) to a non-propositional intention to do x, since in their approach the relevant conclusion is never valuational. While both Aristotle's and Bratman's *acratès* may infer that $xBTy$, neither acts on this as his acratic conclusion. Aristotle's *acratès* differs as his conclusion is valuational and of a different form from the *encratès'*, while Bratman's *acratès* arrives at a non-valuational conclusion which is of the same form as the *encratès'*.

The new-wave theorist represents the irrationality of the *acratès* as a failure to form an intention in line with his best judgment, and this is taken to constitute a partial definition of irrationality. The difficulty is to see what the relevant *principle* of rationality itself is founded upon: why should we *aim* to be rational in such cases, and in what way does the relevant premiss *support* the conclusion? Bratman, in effect, defines what it is to be rational as applying a principle which takes one from (e.g.) an ATC judgment to 'I shall do x'. But this definition requires a foundation which connects it with, for example, our relevant psychological states, or shows how the premiss gives evidence for the truth of the conclusion. It remains to be seen whether Aristotle's account fares better in this respect (see also Chapter 4, Section D).

There is a further requirement for an adequate theory of the possibility of *acrasia*: that it possess the necessary generality. Aristotle's account focuses principally on acratic cases induced by the activity of sensual desire or anger, in which the *acratès* fails to act on a preferential judgment he then holds. In such cases, the *acratès* acts on a non-comparative judgment that (e.g.) y has a good feature against his comparative judgment that x is better than y. Can this account be extended to cases when one acts against one's better judgment through excessive love of honour or filial piety (1148a28–32, b6–8)?

The distinction between comparative and non-comparative desires seems to admit of a natural extension to these cases. The man who acts acratically through excessive love of honour cannot judge that this goal is best, and hence cannot infer that his action is the best (or the better one). His acratic goal may be good for him, but cannot support an unqualified comparative judgment in its favour. If so, he will act on a non-comparative desire against a comparative judgment in the way the man under sensual desire does. The structure of practical reasoning which allows for the case of *acrasia* in Aristotle's central examples will allow for its occurrence in any case in which there can be an unqualified comparative judgment favouring one option as best (given the agent's postulated goal), and another non-comparative judgment favouring an alternative. Which cases these are will depend on the psychological factors involved in postulating a goal and in acting on a non-comparative judgment against one's better judgment; but this depends on the nature of the appropriate explanatory theory in which *acrasia* is to be located.[47] Aristotle's structure of practical reasoning allows for the widest variety of irrational action against one's better judgment; it remains to be seen whether his favoured psychological theory is as liberal.

The specific unfulfilled requirements then are:

(a) to show in what the failure or irrationality of the *acratês* consists: whether his failure is one of intellect or of desire;

(b) to explain why *acrasia* is an atypical occurrence for a given agent;

(c) to account for the postulation of goals by the practically wise;

(d) to see in what range of cases *acrasia* can actually occur: whether it is limited to cases involving sensual desire or anger, or may extend to a wider variety.

Aristotle's attempt to resolve these issues forms the basis of his favoured explanatory psychological theory; to this we must now turn.

---

[47] Aristotle excludes certain cases from his paradigm set because they are not criticised as morally base (1148b4–6). Thus it appears that his principal focus is on that subset of irrational actions which are morally weak – because of their significance in his general moral theory. But the present issue is different: does his psychological theory permit cases of irrational action only in certain limited areas (e.g. involving sensual desire)?

CHAPTER FOUR

The Explanation of Acrasia: Rationality and Desire

A. Desire-based and Belief-based theories

Any account of the possibility of *acrasia* requires supplementation by a psychological theory of the factors which lead to its occurrence. The key concept in Aristotle's theory is *practical knowledge*, which embraces his analysis of the relevant emotions, desires, valued goals and better judgments of the fully virtuous agent.

Aristotle's weak *acratês* reaches the good conclusion, but does not 'fully know' it (1147b10–12). Is this an intellectual failure, or one of practical knowledge (1146a4–8)?[1] If the latter, is it fundamentally a failure of desire and motivation? What is the relation between the *acratês'* rebellious sensual desire (1147a34) and his failure to 'grasp fully' the good conclusion?

Aristotle's answers to these questions serve to determine part of his more general psychological theory by showing whether his theory of actions and moral character in the *Ethics* is Intellectualist or Desire-based. An Intellectualist account maintains the following general pattern of explanation:

Differences between the actions and relevant psychological states of the virtuous, self-controlled, acratic and self-indulgent are to be explained fundamentally by differences in their beliefs, thoughts and intellectual perceptions.

There are both Extreme and Moderate versions of this account; for the Extremist, thoughts, beliefs and intellectual perceptions by themselves explain differences in thoughts and actions (without the

---

[1] In *NE/EE* VII 2 practical knowledge is a candidate for the relevant type of knowledge (loc. cit.) overruled in the case of *acrasia* (1145b22–26). Aristotle rejects this possibility by saying that a man could not be practically wise and acratic. If practical knowledge is intellectual knowledge plus acting on it (1152a8–10), the *acratês* could fail to have practical knowledge precisely because he fails to act on his (unclouded) intellectual knowledge that doing x is best.

presence of other motivational states); for the Moderate, thoughts, beliefs and intellectual perceptions require desires to explain differences in actions or affections, but the presence and nature of these desires is to be explained by antecedent and more fundamental differences between beliefs.

The Intellectualist account of the weak *acratês* regards his basic failure as that of not fully understanding the good conclusion – or not fully seeing that it is the better course. The self-controlled man, by contrast, does fully understand the good conclusion, and his judgment is not clouded when he acts, although he is aware of the power of the attraction of the opposed course. (At least his judgment is not so clouded as to prevent him appreciating that x is best.) The virtuous agent differs from both because he does not even see – or allow himself to be rationally affected in any way by – the appeal of the option opposed to what he sees as best.

The Desire-based account represents the fundamental difference between the virtuous, self-controlled and acratic as one involving desiderative and other motivational states. The *acratês* (in one version) can fully understand (intellectually) that he is acting wrongly but still act thus because of the motivational strength of his sensual desire; the self-controlled man differs from the virtuous in having stronger internal opponents to the good course (sensual desire, anger, etc.) and from the acratic in avoiding the sudden onset of a decisive internal opponent (e.g. sensual desire).

Within the Desire-based account one may detect an Extreme and a Moderate position, but within both:

Differences in motivational states (and not beliefs) explain differences in valuational thoughts, beliefs and intellectual perceptions and differences in action between the *acratês*, *encratês* and virtuous agent.

For the Extremist, beliefs play no role in the production of any action except in means/ends reasoning as to how to achieve a desired goal; the desired goals themselves are determined by the agent's emotional response to particular situations or the state of his general desires; the value of each goal (or course of action) is – provided subjective probabilities are equal – a function of the strength of his desire for it at the time of action.

The Moderate Desire-based theory may allow that beliefs play a role in the formation of the agent's goals and his judgment as to which course is good or best, but will take differences in belief to be explained by differences in motivational states; the value of each course for an agent is a function of its contribution to the goals he has set himself, but what he does and the goals he has will be determined by his motivational states.

The distinct forms of Desire-based theory yield different treatments of *acrasia*. If the value of each course is a function of strength of desire at the time of action, the acratic action, if desired more strongly, will be judged better than the alternative. However, this action will not be acratic; for the agent will not see that – at the time – he is acting wrongly. Hence, if the framework of best judgment and practical reasoning proposed in Chapter 3 to allow for the possibility of *acrasia* is correct, Aristotle cannot have held this version of the Extreme Desire-based theory. The Moderate Desire-based account, by contrast, allows for a split between value and motivational impact, and hence may explain the occurrence of *acrasia* in (one of) two ways: either the *acratês'* desires run contrary to his better judgment, and he acts acratically (without intellectual failure) knowing throughout that he is doing the worst option; or, alternatively, his judgment may be affected by the presence of desires which cloud his judgment, or prevent him from seeing its implications. Only within a Moderate Desire-based theory can the *acratês* know fully that he is acting against his best judgment, but this theory does not demand that any or all acratic agents do (in fact) know fully that they are acting wrongly.

Both Moderate Intellectualist and Desire-based theorists, therefore, might accept two distinct forms of Sufficiency thesis:[2]

(a) *Intellectual sufficiency*: $(\exists J)$ $(pJ$ & p is the conclusion of S's good syllogism & Accords $(p,$ S's doing $x)$ & S undergoes no intellectual fault with respect to $p \rightarrow$ S does x, if he acts intentionally)

(b) *Desiderative sufficiency*: $(\exists J)$ $(pJ$ & p is the conclusion of S's good syllogism & Accords $(p,$ S's doing $x)$ & S desires decisively to act on $p \rightarrow$ S does x, if he acts intentionally),

although they would disagree on which was the fundamental explanation of encratic and acratic action. But only one version of the Moderate Desire-based theory can reject Intellectual sufficiency, and allow the *acratês* to act intentionally against an unclouded intellectual perception of the good.

Aristotle's treatment of *acrasia* (I will argue) is that of a Moderate Desire-based theorist: the difficulty is to see which type of Moderate Desire-based theorist he is, and (hence) what explanation he gives of the failure of the *acratês* and the general determinants of valuational judgments.

The Moderate Desire-based theorist holds that if the *acratês* fails to grasp fully the good conclusion, this is because his motivational states prevent him from having complete knowledge of it. By contrast, the Moderate Intellectualist theorist reverses the direction of explanation: the *acratês'* failure of knowledge explains, and is not itself explained by, failure of motivation.

Aristotle often writes as if the case of *acrasia* involved only, and

---

[2] See Chapter 2, Section B. Both these Sufficiency theses are amplified in what follows.

was fundamentally explained by, a conflict of desires (433b5ff.; 434a13–18; 1223b4–12; 1224a32–34; 1102b16–18, 26ff.). But in *NE/ EE* VII 2–3 Aristotle introduces the notion of a failure of knowledge on the part of the *acratês* into his account of the explanation of *acrasia*. Hence, it might appear as if in VII 2–3 he adopted a Moderate Intellectualist theory of *acrasia* ('clouded judgment') as the basic explanatory constituent, while elsewhere he accepted some form of desire-based theory.

The appearance of tension, however, is misleading: in VII 2–3, failure of knowledge on the part of the *acratês* is explained by his motivational states (1147a14–18):

> People in passion are in a state in which they possess but cannot use knowledge; for anger and sensual desire and things of that kind clearly produce a change in the body, and for some induce even madness. And this is the condition of the *acratês*.

Anger or sensual desire produce a physical change in the body which renders the agent's knowledge inert in the case of *acrasia*. The physical state produced by the *acratês'* sensual desire is not itself a reason for his action; it serves rather to prevent a line of reasoning leading to action. In this way, the *acratês'* motivational states cause his ignorance of the good conclusion as is required within the Desire-based theory, but do so by means of producing a physical change in the agent's body. How this change is produced, and how the resulting state is dissipated is the subject of physiology (1147b6–9); but the essential point on which Aristotle insists is that this change is explained initially at the psychological level by a distinct type of motivational state (sensual desire) which leads to the acratic action (1147a34–b3) and prevents the *acratês* from fully knowing the conclusion. Thus, if the *acratês* undergoes an intellectual failure, this is a consequence and not the explanation of his deviant motivational states.

The account so far is neutral as to which version of Moderate Desire-based theory is advanced in VII 3, as it has not analysed the *acratês'* failure to 'know' the good conclusion which he says but does not act on. Does this failure indicate one of intellect (e.g. insincerity, clouded judgment, failure to see a consequence) or one of desire which is compatible with the *acratês'* knowing full well (intellectually) that what he is doing is wrong? Elsewhere (1152a8–9, 13–14) Aristotle notes that:

> A man is practically wise not only by knowing but by acting; but the *acratês* does not act . . . for although he is near to the practically wise in reasoning, he differs in preferential desire.

Here, the failure of the *acratês* consists in his not properly desiring to do what he judges as best (1151a6–7); for if he did, he would do it

(1048a10–13). If so, his failure is one of practical knowledge which arises because he does not desire to do the good action decisively.

In VII 3 Aristotle cites three cases of those who speak words from knowledge, but do not themselves know (1147a18–24):

> (a) those in passion who repeat poems and proofs of Empedocles (cf. 1147b10–13);
> (b) young students who put together arguments, but do not know them; for that requires the arguments to become part of themselves – which takes time;
> (c) actors who speak on the stage.

To these are compared those types of acratic agents who say the conclusion (1147b10–13; a23–24). But wherein does the comparison consist? Are the three cases cited precise examples of the specific kind of ignorance which afflicts the *acratês*, or comparable cases of the same general type of ignorance, or cases of intellectual failure analogous to the failure of practical knowledge which besets the *acratês*?

The examples are different from one another: (c) may indicate insincerity – the actor does not believe that the lines he says are true, and hence does not act on them appropriately but only pretends to do so – but neither (a) nor (b) need do so. Students may believe the arguments they have encountered (perhaps on the basis of authority, but perhaps because they find them immediately convincing), and sincerely assert them because they believe them to be true even though they have not made the arguments 'a part of themselves'. Drunken singers of nationalistic songs may – for a time – sincerely believe that (e.g.) England is the land of hope and glory, as passionate reciters of T. S. Eliot may – for a while – accept that all will be well in the ground of their beseeching.

'Clouded judgment' may characterise the drunken singer; but it is not clear that young students suffer (or are thought by Aristotle to suffer) from this. They seem to see full well what they assert. One failure they sustain (in Aristotle's view) arises because they have not established certain of their intellectual beliefs in the appropriate way on the basis of their experience. Aristotle notes:

> The young may be good geometers and mathematicians . . . but it seems that they are not practically wise. The cause is that such wisdom is concerned not only with universals but with particulars which become familiar from experience, and a young man has no experience; for it is length of time that gives experience. Indeed one may ask why a boy may become a mathematician, but not a philosopher or a physicist. It is because the objects of mathematics exist by abstraction, while the first principles of other subjects come by experience, and young men have no conviction about the latter but merely speak properly, while the essence of mathematics is clear to them. (1142a13–20)

In physics or philosophy, the young merely speak properly without

conviction about the first principles because they have not themselves
the previous experience on which these beliefs rest, and hence have
not established them for themselves. If they have not properly made
the relevant beliefs their own (1147a22), it is because they lack the
necessary time and experience. But this is compatible with their
seeing clearly and sincerely believing what they assert, and wishing
to make it 'part of themselves'; for their failure resides only in having
inadequate grounds of the appropriate type for their beliefs.

While the *acratês* may exemplify either the clouded judgment of
the drunken singer or the insincerity of the actor, he cannot instan-
tiate precisely the lack of conviction of the young students. For he,
unlike them, must have had both time and experience to arrive at his
own moral convictions; indeed it is because he has done so that he can
now be acratic. Hence, while the knowledge failure of the actor and
drunken singer may be exactly that of the *acratês*, the young students
offer an *analogy* to the case of the *acratês*.

In what does the comparison consist? Aristotle says that the young
students lack knowledge because 'they had not made what they say a
part of themselves' (1147a21–2). But what type of lack of integration
is this? One suggestion might be that the students fail to integrate
their intellectual views properly; they do not see that it is a consequence of their newly acquired beliefs that certain of their other
opinions are rendered untenable. They fail to see the implications of
their beliefs, and do not make their belief set as a whole coherent.
This suggests an analogy with the *acratês* who judges (433b8–10) '*y*
is good' (an unqualified judgment about the value of *y* taken as a
whole in isolation from other alternatives), and fails to appreciate that
it is a consequence of accepting that '*x* is best' on his grounds that he
has no good grounds for accepting that *y* (taken as a bundle of properties in isolation) is good without qualification. This *acratês* does not
bring to bear against doing *y* the evidence which strongly supports not
doing it, and which he has used in judging that '*x* is best'. Under the
influence of desire, he reaches an unqualified judgment which runs
contrary to the valuational evidence which he accepts; he fails to see
a consequence of what he judges best, and hence has not integrated
his valuational beliefs fully.

In the second case (distinguished in Chapter 3, Section C) the *acratês* judges only '*y* has a good feature' and acts on that judgment. This
need involve no intellectual error, as he may see all the consequences
of his best judgment, and have made his belief-set consistent. His
failure to make the right rule 'a part of himself' does not betoken this
type of intellectual failure.

What is sought, then, is what is common to the young students and
the two acratic agents thus characterised. It is neither clouded judgment, insincerity, nor failure to integrate their intellectual beliefs.
Each *acratês* has, however, failed to make his best judgments 'part of
himself' in one clear sense, as both have a sensual desire which opposes

directly their best judgment and revolts against it (1147a33ff). Neither
acratês has succeeded in modifying or curbing the opposed desire so
as to make it obedient to his better judgment (1119b11ff.) They have
failed to render coherent their valuational judgments and their desires
so that their value judgments and motivational states fail to form one
unified whole. Had they made their value judgments fully their own
they would have ensured that there was no internal deviant desire of
sufficient power to lead them to be acratic. They – like the young
students – have failed to make certain beliefs their own; but the
nature of their failure, although analogous, is not identical. The young
students have failed to integrate their newly acquired beliefs with
their experience (or their other beliefs); the *acratês* fail to integrate
their value judgments with their motivational states (1095a8–11).

If this is correct, the *acratês'* failure 'fully to understand' the good
conclusion (through the presence of an opposed, recalcitrant, desire)
is compatible with his knowing (intellectually) full well that x is the
better course, and his realising that he has strong reasons against y.
While Aristotle may have thought that in certain cases of *acrasia*
there was intellectually blinkered vision of the best judgment (e.g.
insincerity: clouded judgment), he also held that version of the Moderate Desire-based theory which allows that the *acratês* may know
intellectually that what he is doing is wrong while acting intentionally. This failure of knowledge is a failure of practical rather than
theoretical knowledge; it is the *acratês'* preferential desire that is
flawed, because of the presence of an opposed sensual desire, and so
he does not want appropriately to do what he judges best.[3]

The argument, however, is inconclusive: for it relies on taking 'failure of integration' as the relevant point of analogy between the *acratês* and Aristotle's young students, and noting that this does not
consist in at least one acratic case in an intellectual failure, but is
rather a failure to modify sensual appetites (see 1095a7–11). And this
might be challenged: perhaps the point of analogy is less precise, or
perhaps Aristotle intended a further intellectual failure to characterise both young students and acratic agents apart from those (thus far)
discussed. Hence, to secure this argument, one needs to examine directly Aristotle's account of the achievement of the practically wise
and the failure of the *acratês* (and *encratês*), and his general theory
of *practical knowledge*; for this (see Sections B, D) will show whether
the crucial weakness of the *acratês* is a failure of integration of the
type suggested, which requires no attendant intellectual failure. The
remainder of the chapter is thus in part an attempt to locate the point

---

[3] In this reading of 1147a20–35 (and b9–12) the *acratês* need undergo no intellectual
failure. When he is described as saying the conclusion (a34, b11–12), this is to be
contrasted with his knowing practically what to do, and not with his asserting the
conclusion (1147a27–8). As such, he fulfils one of the disjuncts specified in 1139a25–26
as his reasoning is correct, and he asserts its conclusion, but since his desires are not
correct (see Sections D, E), he lacks practical knowledge.

of the analogy noted in this section as an element of a more general Moderate Desire-based theory.

Aristotle (it appears) held some version of the Moderate Desire-based theory, but it is not as yet completely clear which one he favoured. There are, however, outstanding difficulties for either version of the Moderate Desire-based theory. Each needs to explain why *acrasia* is atypical: why shouldn't an agent's desires regularly be 'out of joint' with his value judgments so that he was regularly acratic? Further, each needs to explain in what range of cases *acrasia* can occur: can the account which applies to sensual desire apply to other emotional (and non-emotional) states? Also, both are required to characterise more fully the notion of 'decisive desire' used in their formulation. Finally, both need an account of the distinctive irrationality of the *acratês* and the special status of his goals (see Sections C, D).

An attempt to elucidate Aristotle's version of the Moderate Desire-based theory must test whether he possesses answers to these problems. In the next section, we will consider his account of the differences between the virtuous and the self-controlled agents. Both these agents avoid, while acting in accordance with their definition, the several distinct types of *acrasia* which Aristotle considers:

(a) not drawing the entailed conclusion of the good syllogism: (failure of reasoning, and perhaps not possessing the minor premiss; see Chapter 3, Section B);

(b) not sincerely accepting the good conclusion (like actors);

(c) sincerely accepting the good conclusion, but not making one's other judgment cohere with it through a failure to integrate one's relevant psychological states (like the young students);

(d) undergoing clouded judgment (like the drunkard repeating 'Land of Hope and Glory');

(e) failing to see the consequences of one's better judgment (akin to a case of self-deception);

where (a)–(e) are distinct types of failure occasioned in different ways by the presence of opposed acratic desires. This investigation will enable us to examine further whether (c) is a failure of practical knowledge which parallels, but is distinct from, the purely intellectual failure of the young students. For if Aristotle's account of practical knowledge is desire-based, failures of practical knowledge should also be desire-based.

B.   Desire-based account of some differences between the virtuous, self-controlled and acratic

Within one version of the Moderate Desire-based theory, the virtuous, self-controlled and acratic agents may be alike in their valuation of the situation and differ only in their motivational response. However, within any version of Intellectualist theory, these agents must differ in their beliefs and valuational judgments. In this section, my method will be to sketch a simple version of the Desire-Based theory and then to argue that Aristotle held a variant of this in his discussion of courage, temperance and their attendant vices.

The simple picture runs as follows: the properly virtuous agent is practically wise and always acts on his best judgment because – in the case of conflict virtues – courage and temperance – he lacks an internal opponent (fear or sensual desire) whose motivational power is such that (within the range of permissible desires) (i) he acts reluctantly on his best judgment, or (ii) he would enjoy following another course against his best judgment. If the motivational power of the internal opponent is such that he acts reluctantly on his best judgment, he is either a coward or a self-indulgent man (1104b6–8). If the strength of his sensual desire is such that he would enjoy acting against his best judgment, he is encratic (1152a1–3). In either case, if the agent is subject to desires for a countergoal (within the permissible range)[4] which produce (i) or (ii), this is because his relevant desires are motivationally too strong (1146a10–12 of an *encratês*; 1118b27ff. of the self-indulgent). The practically wise agent, by contrast, has the correct motivational structure because he fulfils the following conditions:

(i) his desires for the counter-goal are not excessive but moderate (1146a12; 1152a2; 1119a14–20) and hence never lead him to act reluctantly on his best judgment, nor allow him to enjoy (overall) his following another course against his best judgment;[5]

(ii) his commitment to the goal of courage or temperance is such that he enjoys (overall) acting temperately and either enjoys or does not regret acting courageously (1104b6–8).

The correct motivational structure of the practically wise is shown (within the range of permissible desires) by his enjoyment (or absence of pain) when acting virtuously, and his hypothetical lack of pleasure if he were to act on his sensual desire against his best judgment. In this way, attendant and hypothetical pleasures and pains serve to distinguish the motivational structure of the practically wise, encratic and self-indulgent agents even when they perform the same action.

One consequence of this simple picture is that the achievement of the practically wise man resides in his success in controlling and

---

[4] The practically wise will lack certain sensual desires (1119a11–13) and fears (1149a5–12) which are such that the mere possession of them makes a man cowardly or self-indulgent.

[5] That is, to enjoy *overall* acting against his better judgment. As argued below, the virtuous agent would have the sensual pleasure of acting against his better judgment, but this would be out-weighed by his pain in not pursuing (e.g.) health arising from (i) the frustration of his desire for health, (ii) regret at not acting on his best judgment, (iii) the frustration of his preferential desire.

guiding his internal opponent so as to deprive it of the excessive motivational power required to lead him to act acratically against his best judgment. Since his motivational structure is such that he would not enjoy acting against his best judgment, he is not even a potential acratic. The *acratês*, by contrast, although he may share the valuational goals of the practically wise has not succeeded in controlling or modifying his internal opponent in a way which removes the temptation it affords to act against his best judgment. His failure lies in his long-term attitudes to his internal opponent, (e.g.) sensual desire, and is shown, even when he acts encratically, by the fact that he would have enjoyed overall acting acratically against his better judgment. Unlike the practically wise, he has not fully integrated his motivational structure and his valuational assessment of what is best to do (1115b19–20; 1119a18–20, b15–18).

The second consequence of the simple picture is reflected in the similarity between courage and temperance in Aristotle's account: both involve a certain type of counter-goal, and hence are essentially conflict virtues.[6] In both cases, the practically wise man assesses what is best in the light of his goals and – guided by them – decides against giving way to fear or indulging his sensual desire. In both cases, the motivational strength of his internal opponent is not so excessive as to make him regret acting on his best judgment or (hypothetically) enjoy acting against it (although Aristotle requires that the temperate man enjoys acting temperately, but that the courageous man faces danger only without pain (1104b4–6).[7]

---

[6] The courageous man will have fear when confronted with danger (1115b12–14; 1117b8–13), and this distinguishes him from those who are fearless – either through madness, lack of sensibility or racial origin (1115b26–28). Fear, for Aristotle, is defined as the expectation of evil accompanied by pain (1382a21–22), and is an emotion which in the *Ethics* involves pain or pleasure (1105b22). Given Aristotle's characterisation of fear as painful, the courageous man will not only be aware of the risks he runs, but also desire (to an extent) to avoid them. There seems no mechanism in Aristotle's theory to prevent fear from engaging the inclinations even of the courageous man (see below: contrast McDowell: 1978, 27–28). For Aristotle, training of the emotions to avoid excess takes the place of the 'silencing mechanism' (see Section C). The temperate man possesses moderate desires for pleasures which are not base or too expensive (1119a16–20); if so, he will have a range of internal opponents in the case of permissible desires which aim at certain sensual pleasures. If he never possessed any such desires he would be insensible (1119a4–6); if he had succeeded completely in getting rid of such desires as are common to men because of their physical needs (1118b8–11; 1370a20–22) he would no longer be temperate but possess heroic virtue (1145a19–21, 24–27) as he would then lack the emotions or virtues of mortal men (1178a19–22) (contrast David Pears's account: 1978).

[7] The courageous man is fearless in the face of a noble death (1115a32–34; 1104b7–8) because his identification with the goal for which he acts is such that the pleasure of so acting overcomes the pain of fear. Hence, although he feels pain at the prospect of death, his identification with his goal (acting courageously or saving his friends) produces an overall balance in favour of pleasure over pain (or at least an equal measure of each) with respect to the particular course of action he pursues. He will fear death, but not be pained overall at the prospect of a heroic death in a noble cause (1115b11–13; 1117b9, 15–16; 1169a22ff.).

This degree of similarity masks a difference between the two cases: Aristotle appears to restrict 'self-control' to resistance in the range of sensual pleasures, while characterising the man who resists fear with overall regret (1104b4–6) as cowardly. Thus, Aristotle seeks to avoid the dilemma: 'Either courage involves no fear or else it is not a true virtue – but self-control' by allowing the courageous agent to feel fear, but not sufficient fear to disturb his best judgment. But he also makes a further move: he does not regard the man who acts on his best judgment against excessive fear as *encratic*, but as cowardly (1104b4–6), while counting the man who acts on his best judgment against excessive sensual desire as self-controlled and not self-indulgent. This might seem paradoxical; if Aristotle possesses the additional category of self-control in the case of sensual pleasures, why does he not apply it to the case of resistance to fear (especially since courage is frequently conceived as an encratic virtue)?[8] The basis for a reply lies in his perception of the distinct nature of the two internal opponents: fear and pleasure, which exemplifies his Non-Intellectual theory.

The self-controlled man has excessive desires for permissible pleasures (1146a10f.), and hence, in contrast with the temperate, would (hypothetically) enjoy overall acting against his best judgment by indulging his sensual appetite (1152a1–3), because his sensual desire is sufficiently strong to override his distaste at acting intemperately and acratically. But the self-controlled agent cannot feel pain in acting temperately, for if he did so he would be indistinguishable from one type of self-indulgent agent (1104b5–8; e.g. 1166b18ff.). However, if he has excessive sensual desire, how can he avoid feeling pained overall while acting temperately? It appears that Aristotle's treatment of self-control in the case of sensual desires falls prey to a dilemma: the self-controlled *both* must *and* cannot feel pain overall when acting temperately.

This dilemma arises if the self-controlled's pain in acting temperately is as strong as the pleasure he would get in acting intemperately (as is the case for the self-indulgent). But Aristotle envisages cases in which this connection can be broken: in 1150a25ff. he separates (among agents who do not act from choice) one who acts from the pleasure of φ'ing and another who does so to avoid the pain arising from (frustration of) appetite. But this distinction is only possible if the degree of pleasure and pain involved do not vary together; if the pain of frustrating a desire were always as great as the degree of pleasure in satisfying it, there would be no grounds for this distinction.

---

[8] Similarly, why is there no *acratês* with respect to fear in Aristotle's discussion? (1149a24ff; 1148b1–14). Self-control and *acrasia* are defined with reference to sensual pleasures (1149a21–24; 1150a9–12), and the other cases discussed are taken as peripheral: anger (1149a25–b20), bestiality (1149a1–20), desires and pleasures other than sensual ones (1148a23–b14). Softness and hardness are also defined by reference to sensual or bodily pains (1150a22ff.). There is no extension of these cases to fear or emotions other than those which are the internal opponents of temperance.

In the immediate context, Aristotle applies this apparatus to distinguish the self-indulgent and the acratic; the *acratês* acts against his best judgment because he sees the pleasure of another course, not because he finds it painful (overall) to act temperately; the self-indulgent man with a temperate best judgment would act against it (if he did) because he felt pain (overall) in acting temperately. Since the *acratês* is the failed *encratês*, the *acratês* cannot find acting on his best judgment painful (overall) either, and in this resembles the temperate and differs from the self-indulgent.

Self-control in the case of sensual desires is possible, therefore, because such an agent focuses on the pleasure of the acratic act, and is drawn to the judgment that this act is good. The *encratês* does not feel, as a consequence, excessive pain in doing the temperate act, because the effect of the attack by pleasure is to render the opposed course pleasant and not to make the temperate action itself painful.

The self-controlled, unlike the *acratês*, in acting according to his definition succeeds either in disciplining his internal opponent so that it does not attack his best judgment so forcefully that it leads to acratic action or in ensuring that his settled disposition to act encratically is resistant to all attacks from sensual desire. The *acratês*' sensual desire, by contrast, either weakens his grasp on the consequences and grounds of his better judgment (as described in one case in the previous section) or is (simply) more forceful than his desire and settled disposition which favour the encratic course. Hence they differ in motivational states, although they resemble each other more closely than either resembles the self-indulgent or the virtuous.

When the internal opponent is fear, the attack on the best judgment is direct; the effect of fear is to make the course of action chosen as best seem painful overall, rather than (directly) making another option seem pleasant.[9] Hence, the degree of pain in acting courageously must be directly dependent on the degree of fear involved. If so there can be no case where the agent fears excessively but does not feel pain (overall) in acting courageously. By contrast with the indirect attack by sensual desire, which makes self-control possible when this is the internal opponent, the direct attack by fear on the best judgement[10] means that there can be no analogue for self-control in the case of courage (1104b5–8). In the case of physical danger, Aristotle sees only two alternatives: courage and cowardice (although there are different ways of expressing the latter). He offers the following classification of characters:

---

[9] Fear may indirectly make flight appear attractive (*Rhet.* 1385a24–26: see 1383a5–8) but this is a consequence of fear and not part of its essential specification. It also makes (e.g.) resistance painful: see below.

[10] Aristotle draws this contrast explicitly in *NE* III 12: fear 'upsets and destroys the nature of one who experiences it' (1119a23–24) with the result that he disgraces himself (a30). Pleasure, by contrast, does not upset the man's nature and does not involve pain (a23–29), and so need not represent following the best judgment as painful.

Courage	Temperance
(a) *Courageous man*: he resists because it is noble without pain overall, having successfully overcome his fear.	(a) *Temperate man*: he abstains because it is noble with pleasure overall, having successfully overcome his sensual desire.
(b) *First failure*: he resists because it is noble, but does so with pain overall, because he has not successfully overcome his fear (1104b7–8).	(b) *First failure*: (self-control) he abstains because it is noble without pain overall, but would enjoy overall acting against his best judgment – and hence has not completely overcome his sensual desire.
(c) *Second failure*: the man who does not resist although he judges this the noble course, but flees because he is overcome by fear.	(c) *Second failure*: (*acrasia*): He judges it best to abstain but indulges in sensual pleasure against his better judgment under the influence of excessive desire.
(d) *Third failure*: the man who judges it best to flee because he has excessive fear.	(d) *Third failure*: (self-indulgent 1): He abstains because he judges it noble but does so with pain overall because he has not successfully overcome his sensual desire (1104b6–7).
	(e) *Fourth failure*: (self-indulgent 2): He judges it best to indulge his appetite, and does so without qualms.

In considering courage, (b)–(d) are cowardly, while (a) alone is courageous. Since (b) is cowardly, and (c) is worse than (b), (c) cannot be acratic, as *acrasia* is less to be condemned than vice, but must be cowardly if (b) is.[11]

Aristotle thus detects a striking degree of similarity between courage and temperance. Both have an internal opponent which the practically wise has guided or modified so that it does not produce pain overall while acting virtuously. The corresponding vices arise (for example) when an agent does what is virtuous with pain overall. However there is one difference: one may fail to be temperate also

---

[11] In the case of sensual pleasures, since (b) is not self-indulgent, his case and (as a consequence) (c)'s can be classified as neither proper virtue nor full vice but as one of self-control and *acrasia*.

because one would hypothetically enjoy (overall) acting against one's best judgment, but there is no analogue for this failure in the case of courage; if one would enjoy fleeing against one's best judgment this is because one finds staying and resisting painful overall and hence is cowardly. Thus, because of the different focus of the attack of the two internal opponents, there is one way of failing to be temperate (i.e. being self-controlled) which is not a possible way of failing to be courageous, for the nearest analogue to self-control in the case of courage – resisting for a noble goal with overall pain – is, for Aristotle, a form of cowardice (1104b5–8).

Aristotle's description of courage and temperance serves to illumine two distinct, and independent, features of his Desire-based theory. One is attractive, but the other more paradoxical.

It appears that the temperate, self-controlled, acratic, and one type of self-indulgent agent (1104b6–7) may share a common valuation of the options before them, and differ only in the motivational factors which explain their differences in action. The temperate and self-controlled may both share a common goal (e.g. well-being) conceived in the same terms, and hence put the same valuational weight (in reaching their best judgment) on both options. Both will have a paradigmatic internal opponent (1118b27–33; 1119a29–31) which (in the range of permissible desires) represents an alternative option as pleasant and hence good, and both will act on their best judgment. But here the similarities end: the self-controlled man has excessive desires, and hence *desires* to do y more than he *values* doing it as, unlike the temperate man, he would enjoy (overall) doing y against his best judgment. The temperate, by contrast, desires the pleasant, but not so much that the motivational force of his desires fails to accord with his valuation of the options (1119b13–16; 1102b26–28; 1119a19–20). What distinguishes them, therefore, is the gap (in the case of the self-controlled man) between the motivational and valuational aspects of his sensual desire. The presence of this gap in his case explains how *acrasia* occurs: its absence in the case of the temperate man explains why he is never acratic. The self-controlled resists his internal opponent because he has an established disposition of acting on his best judgment (1145b10–14; 1150b23–25; 1152a24–26); it is this which allows him to resist the temptation to act on his acratic desire.

This account of the conflict virtues stands in marked contrast to any form of Intellectualist account: for in the latter the practically wise differ from the encratic solely in the reasons they have, and not in their motivational efficacy. For the Intellectualist, the courageous man does not allow his lively awareness of risk, normal valuation of life and health to become a reason to flee at all; within the Desire-based theory, by contrast, the courageous man typically will have a reason to flee, but never one so powerful as to make him reluctant to stay and resist. Aristotle's courageous man feels fear in moderation, and this is defined as pain or disturbance which arises from the imagination of future destructive or painful evil (1382a21–22), and leads to action because what is painful and evil is to be avoided (701b35–36), as each man in pain aims at something (1379a10ff.). If pain is an essential ingredient of fear, it is not possible (within Aristotle's account) for the courageous man to feel fear without his inclinations being engaged or his having thereby cause to flee. His fearlessness at the prospect of a noble death must arise because his fear is overcome by his commitment to the noble, and not because he has no inclination to flee. Hence the reasons which affect the self-controlled will be the same as those which affect the courageous; the difference between them must lie in their differing motivational states.

While the *encratês* lacks practical knowledge, this need only be because he differs in motivational states from the courageous or temperate. If so, practical knowledge has as an essential ingredient the control and modification of the internal opponents which the self-controlled has failed to achieve. The *acratês* is typically regarded by Aristotle as a man of the same type as the *encratês* (1145b10–14; 1146a13–15);[12] he regularly resists temptation (1150a32ff.) through his established disposition (although he always would enjoy acting acratically), but on occasion (1151a2–6) he succumbs because of violent and excessive pleasures and pains (1150b5ff.) or the quickness or violence of his passions (1150b25ff.). But if the difference between self-control and *acrasia* consists in the violence of passion, this need not affect their valuation of the situation; both may conclude that 'x seems best' while holding that y has a good feature (see Chapter 2, Section C). The lack of integration of desire and value judgment which prevents the *encratês* from being practically wise is precisely what accounts for the failure of the *acratês*: his desire for the counter-goal is excessive and uncontrolled, and leads him to be acratic. No further intellectual failure is needed.

This account of the motivational features of the *encratês* and *acratês* shows that it is not strength of desire alone that controls what action is done: permanent dispositions (character) which may involve commitment to certain goals (e.g. health) will also play a role. The *encratês* does not require a stronger desire for his goal than the temperate needs if he is to resist successfully; for the bulk of his defence against the onslaught of sensual desire may result from his settled disposition to pursue the healthy.[13] In Aristotle's theory not all motivational states are desires.

The self-controlled and the agent who abstains reluctantly (1104b6–

[12] But see 1152a24–26. The latter passage suggests that *acrasia* could also be a disposition distinct from that of the *encratês*. If so, this *acratês* would not be a temporally malfunctioning *encratês*, but rather one who has developed a permanently weakened state or character.

[13] Aristotle recognises distinct types of motivational state: desires of various types, habit (or character), commitment to various views (1151b4–6). See Section D below; also Rorty, 1970.

8) may also share the same valuational appreciation of the situation. But the latter's deviant desires are more formidable than those of the self-controlled, and hence make abstinence painful (overall) for him. His case differs from the temperate and self-controlled just in respect of his different motivational states, and the consequential pleasure or pain (or regret) they experience in acting as they do. Since not all self-indulgent agents in Aristotle's account suffer a complete breakdown in their perception of the good, there need be no intellectual failure which characterises the self-indulgent as would be required within the Intellectualist theory.

Thus, as within the Moderate Desire-based theory, Aristotle's differing moral characters may agree in their valuation and intellectual appreciation of the situation and differ only in their motivational states. Hence *the* crucial step towards acquiring practical wisdom is to modify one's motivational structure and not to improve the clarity of one's vision of the good. Since Aristotle's account of these distinctions is incompatible with any form of Intellectualist account, in which difference in beliefs, thoughts and intellectual perceptions alone explain the differences between self-controlled and practically wise, acratic and self-indulgent (etc.), his must be a Moderate Desire-based theory.

Aristotle's account of the conflict-virtues makes demands on his psychological theory of the relevant emotions, and requires support from his general theory of practical knowledge (see Sections C, D). However, it also contains a paradoxical description of courage, as it classifies the agent who resists the enemy with pain overall as cowardly – even though he may on occasion stay and fight in just the same way as the courageous man. On some views of courage, such a man is the more courageous because he overcomes the most fear in acting as he does; but for Aristotle he is not even self-controlled (or enduring: 1150a25–27; 1151a10–12) but cowardly and, as such, not different in fundamental classification from the man who actually flees (and judges it best to do so). And this seems to be mistaken.

So why did Aristotle place such a high premium on the absence of pain overall while acting courageously as to classify the agent who fails this stringent test as cowardly, even when he does the same actions as the courageous man with the same best judgment? An initial answer is that since this man's emotions are such as to generate pain overall, his emotions will be similar to (perhaps identical with) those of the man who flees. Since virtue is concerned with both emotions and actions, failure in either must be for Aristotle sufficient to produce a fall from virtue; perhaps he also thought that having the same emotional structure as the coward is sufficient by itself to make one a coward. But why? Shouldn't the paradoxical nature of Aristotle's conclusion make one doubt whether he is correct to place so much emphasis in his classification on the agent's emotional structure?

Aristotle's reply is (in part) that if the agent does not pass this

stringent test on emotional structure, he will not regularly act courageously because his perception of his goals and his situation will
change, as his ability to grasp the correct goal and make the correct
discriminations depends on the balance of his emotions and other
desires. This latter feature of the Desire-based approach will be considered further in the next section, when we consider more fully the
distinctive motivational states of the practically wise agent; it suggests an empirical theory about the acquisition and destruction of
valuational goals within a Desire-based account of the type Aristotle
employed to distinguish between the acratic, encratic and practically
wise. Taken together with this section, it shows that Aristotle's relevant psychological theory was Desire-Based and not Intellectualist.

C.   The achievement of the practically wise (1): the education of the sentiments and the formation of valued goals

Aristotle's account of temperance and courage depends on a theory of
the sentiments of fear and sensual desire which shows how their
valuational and motivational impact may come apart, and how the
practically wise can succeed in integrating them (1102b30ff.; 1119b10–
19). Aristotle also needs an account of the acquisition of goals. In
Chapter 3 the agent was taken as postulating a goal in practical
reasoning, and assessing what was best in its light. But no account
was given of the conditions under which an agent sets himself a goal
or group of goals. Aristotle's attempts to meet these two requirements
reveal his answers to three further questions crucial for any account
of *acrasia*: (a) In what range of cases can *acrasia* occur? (b) Why is
acrasia not a regular state for the agent? (c) Why is the *acratês'*
sensual desire mistaken and not his better judgment? These answers
indicate the special status given to the agent's goals in Aristotle's
theory. Aristotle's psychological theory forms a unified Desire-based
account which relates his ethical theory to his fundamental conception
of desire as a motivational state.

Sentiments are characterised (in their most extended treatment) as
physically enmattered psychological features which change men so as
to affect their judgments and are attended by pleasure or pain (*Rhet.*
1378a19–21). In the *Ethics* also they are said to be attended by
pleasure and pain (1105b21–23), and to be what move us. Examples
are sensual desires, anger, fear, confidence, kindness, pity, envy,
friendliness, hate, longing and competitiveness. This general characterisation allows for considerable difference in internal structure between sentiments, and hence between their appropriate mode of
education.

Fear (as noted above) is defined as pain or disturbance which arises
from the imagination of future destructive or painful evil (1382a21–
22). It leads to action because what is painful and evil is avoided

(701b35–36; e.g. 1379a11–12), but the desire to avoid what is painful is a necessary consequence of fear and not part of fear itself.

Anger, by contrast, does involve (in its definition) a desire for revenge, brought on by pain attendant on the appearance of an unjustified slight towards oneself or one of one's own (1378a30ff.; cf. 1379a10ff.). Unlike fear, anger involves essentially 'a particular kind of goal': revenge.[14] However, if it is to lead to action, there will be need for (e.g.) deliberation as to how to take revenge. 'Goal-directed behaviour' (action on the emotion) will be a consequence of anger, and not part of anger itself – as it would also be in the case of fear and sensual desire (701a32ff.).[15]

Anger and fear share two ingredients: an evaluation ('That slight was unjustified', 'That conflict will be painful') which causes pain or disturbance (1380a1; 1382a21–2) which the agent will desire to avoid. S's pain arises (in part) from S's valuational assessment of what has occurred (or will occur), and the relation between these will be causal. This account of anger and fear allows for a distinction between the motivational impact of the sentiments and the agent's valuation. In the case of fear, the former is determined by the degree of pain the agent suffers at the prospect of future evil, and the consequent strength of his desire to avoid it.

If the pain he feels is such as to make it overall painful to resist, the agent is not courageous in Aristotle's account. Excessive pain can arise within Aristotle's account in two ways: either the agent overestimates the amount of future evil, or he feels excessive fear at the prospect of a correctly assessed future evil. These are distinct phenomena. One may feel irrational fear, i.e. excessive pain at the prospect of a future event whose danger one evaluates normally and correctly, or excessive pain because one exaggerates the future danger. Thus one may realise that landing in an aircraft is as safe as take-off, but still be more apprehensive about the former than the latter. In such cases the degree of pain or disturbance one feels is not responsive solely to one's valuational appreciation of the dangers involved, but has other (psychological or physiological) antecedents. The gap between motivation and valuation opens between the assessment of future evil and the pain induced by this and other factors. This can affect the agent's action; for while his valuation determines the con-

---

[14] Fortenbaugh, 1975, 80; 1969, 167.

[15] Only friendliness (in Aristotle's list of sentiments) is defined to include appropriate actions ('helping someone . . . for the advantage of the person helped and not the helper': 1385a17–19: cf. 1380b36ff.). There is a wide variety of internal structures for different sentiments: some involve antecedent imagination (anger and hatred), but others (e.g. sensual desire) need not. Some involve (as part of their definition) a desire to act (e.g. anger) but others do not (e.g. fear). In general, Aristotle distinguishes action on an emotion from the sentiment itself. It is to blur these distinctions to force all Aristotle's sentiments into one uniform schema: antecedent imagination, an appropriate desire, consequential goal directed behaviour (cf. Fortenbaugh, 1975, p. 80).

tent of the premisses and conclusion of practical reasoning, his motivational states may be controlled by the degree of pain he feels. Thus
one may judge that a given evil (e.g. landing in an aircraft) is not too
bad (valuationally) compared with the benefits of flying, while at the
same time desiring very much to avoid it because of the excessive pain
one feels, and so not fly. In this way the non-rational impact of the
fear will explain why he accepts decisively the conclusion 'Flying has
a bad quality', and so does not fly, while also thinking that it is best
to fly.

In the case of anger, a similar distinction between valuation and
motivation may arise. The appearance of an unjustified slight may
lead both to a reasoned desire to avenge oneself and to excessive pain
which precipitates a desire of excessive motivational force to gain
revenge, and forces one to leap into action without considering either
how best to obtain revenge (like waiters who hear one's order (e.g.)
for steak, but rush away before hearing how one wants to have it
prepared: cf. 1149a26–28) or whether there are good reasons not to
take revenge at present (like dogs who howl before they know whether
the man approaching is a friend: 1149a28–29). In this way the motivational impact of the pain and subsequent desire is not dependent
on, or controlled by, the reasoned desire to take revenge; for the
presence of other psychological or physiological features leads the
agent to a more heated response than he thinks correct (or would
think correct if he reflected). Thus he may act acratically if the degree
of pain he feels causes him to act in a way which is not controlled by
his valuational assessment of what is best to do.

Sensual desire differs in its internal structure from both fear and
anger in Aristotle's account; in the simplest cases it need involve no
antecedent opinion, but be based on antecedent physical states (e.g.:
hunger, thirst, certain desires concerned with sex, taste and touch:
1370a19–25). In the case of hunger, one may be moved by the absence
of food (see 930a28–29; 1118b18–19). Such desires may be represented
as the acceptance of a proposition of the form[16] 'y is good to eat', but
the degree of desire will depend on the degree of pleasure or pain
involved, and this need not correspond to the value placed on satisfying
the desire or meeting the need. Thus two agents may disagree as to
how pleasurable the drink is but desire it equally strongly, as one
desires it irrationally (e.g.: the self-controlled man), while the other
(e.g. the self-indulgent) desires it rationally.

The distinction in the case of desire between the mode of accepting
a judgment (desiring) and the judgment thus accepted allows for a

---

[16] Aristotle need not hold that all sensual desires involve an agent in judging that
(e.g.) a drink would be pleasant; all that he requires is that desire may be represented
as the acceptance of this proposition. In this account, lowest level animals may be
represented as desiring even though they lack the capacity to form judgments of this
type.

distinction between motivational efficacy (outlined in Chapter 2, Section C) and valuational content. Thus the agent may judge that 'y has a good feature' but desire to do y overridingly because his decisive acceptance of this proposition is dependent on other conditions (e.g. physical states) which 'happen' to be present in his case (1147a33–34). In the case of the *acratês*, the motivational power of the desire may outstrip its valuational impact because the desire has different (non-cognitive) sources which cause him to act as he does. The latter, which depend on the degree of pleasure or pain he experiences, may have a source (1002b30–34; 1168b20; cf. *de Sensu* 444a32ff.) in the agent's constitution and physical states, and thus be only partially responsive to his perception of the good (1119b14–16); for even though the mode of acceptance characteristic of desire aims at the good, he can be prevented from accepting appropriately what is seen as good by non-rational features of the desire. Indeed it is this account of desire which shows how the relevant split between valuation and motivational efficacy can arise (for the acratic and self-controlled) in both this case and that of action based on fear and anger. Thus Aristotle's account of desire is the basis for his explanation of *acrasia* (see also Chapter 5, Section C).

The practically wise, by contrast, is required to achieve two distinct successes: (a) to ensure that the internal opponent is valued appropriately: (e.g.) only what is really fearful is judged to be so and to the appropriate degree, and (b) to ensure that the desiderative impact of each internal opponent does not so far exceed the relevant valuation as to make the virtuous action painful (overall) or the acratic action pleasant (overall). It is because he achieves both (a) and (b) that practical wisdom is 'prescriptive', and always leads to action (1143a8–9; 1146a7–9).

Aristotle points to a number of routes to achieve the second success: early training and habituation to feel pleasure and pain as one should (1104b12–13; 1105a4f.), and punishment when one fails (1104b16–18; 1179b24–29; 1180a5; 1105a5ff.), reproach, exhortation (1102b34f.) and the efficacy of shame (1128b15–18; 1179b8ff.) in regarding certain desires as ignoble (either because excessive within the permissible range or because outside the permissible range). In this way the practically wise seek to guide their desires by reference to what is noble (1119b16–18) and to ensure that their motivational structure is as it should be. Since certain sensual desires have a physical or non-rational basis, they will not be subject to rational persuasion (1113b27–29) but require that the agent's physical state be such as to prevent them becoming excessive (cf. 1148b19–30: see also 1150b15–18; 1104b16–18). In this way the practically wise (unlike the self-controlled) make their desires obedient to their reasoned valuations (1119b11–12; 1102b32ff.). Non-intellectual training of this general type seems a precondition for the fruitful study of ethics (1095a2ff., b4–8; 1179b29–31).

Obedience and punishment point to non-rational features of control over non-cognitive aspects of desire (see 1102b30–32; 1119b11–12). *Acrasia*, characteristically, occurs where the sentiments have motivational aspects and bases of this type which are distinguishable from the agent's relevant evaluation, and where the pleasure/pain involved is sensitive to, and dependent on, factors independent of his valuation. But Aristotle's theory has a wider application; for it can serve to explain the occurrence of *acrasia* in any case where there are sources of motivation (e.g. upbringing) which are not determined and controlled by the agent's valuational structure in the way achieved by the rational agent.

Aristotle's account of the sentiments gives an explanation of the occurrence of *acrasia* within a Desire-based theory. The *encratês/acratês* fails to be practically wise because his desires have excessive motivational power which he has not checked or controlled in the partially non-rational manner characteristic of the fully rational agent. Thus Aristotle's psychological theory provides a way in which this failure may be diagnosed within his more general Desire-based account of the education and corruption of the sentiments.

There remains one further major issue: how does an agent postulate his goals or arrive at judgments of value in Aristotle's theory? He could have used the Moderate Desire-based theory to differentiate between the practically wise and *encratês/acratês* but have given a Belief-based account of an agent's ability to assess what is best to do. In such an account the desires of the practically wise would play no determining role in the formation of the relevant valuational judgments;[17] that would depend (for example) on intellectual perception which sees what is good in new and complex cases, or on reasoning to a conclusion about what is best to do. If the *acratês*' valuational perception or reasoning is independent of his desires in this way, there is no difficulty in his having goals or judgments which do not cohere well with his desires; for the two are quite separate in nature and origin. But can the Moderate Desire-based theory also account for the needed division between motivation and evaluation? If strongest desires determine valued goals, the agent when he acts on his strongest desire may have to see what he does as most valuable. But if so, his action could not be acratic (contrary to Aristotle's account of the possibility of *acrasia*).

The Moderate Desire-based theory faces two challenges: (a) Can it explain how *acrasia* occurs if desire determines valuational assessment? (b) Can it explain the agent's ability to discriminate what is good in new situations? While Aristotle seeks to meet both of these within a unified Desire-based account, I will sketch an outline of his

---

[17] This account is adopted by theorists influenced by Aristotle, Ross 1939, 168; Irwin, 1975, 576/7; McDowell, 1978, 21.

response to the second question only in so far as this is required to provide an explanation for the onset of *acrasia*.

Aristotle emphasises the role of intellectual perception in grasping which action is to be done (the last term: 1143b1–5; 1142a25ff.; see Chapter 3, Section B) and notes that the acquisition of this marks one fundamental transition in moral development (1144b9–13). However, he also stresses the importance, as an essential first step in moral education, of training the young to enjoy certain types of activity – acting courageously, generously, temperately (etc.) – and to dislike others (1103b16–22; 1104b5–8; 1105b3–12; 1170b25–30).

> It makes not a little difference in what manner children are trained, but a great difference, indeed all the difference. (1103b23–25)

There is, however, no conflict between these two distinct themes; indeed they are essentially connected. Aristotle held that in general people get better at the intellectual discrimination required by those activities they enjoy doing (1175a30–36). Thus, if one enjoys acting courageously, one will get better at seeing what is the courageous action in particular situations. The acquisition of the discriminating ability in the moral case is explained by the presence of antecedently understood moral desires and emotions induced by training, which enable the agent to grasp what is (e.g.) courageous in new and complex situations, although the desires themselves do not already contain reference in their content to such cases.

This general theory also reconciles Aristotle's insistence in 1143b1–5 that induction from particular instances leads to principles and goals with his emphasis elsewhere that trained or natural virtue is the teacher of correct opinion about goals (1151a15–19). For the general desires constitutive of trained or natural virtue will enable the moral agent to discriminate what is courageous in a particular case, and hence to infer correct principles about what types of actions are valuable.

Nor is the role of trained desires as the origin of correct perception limited to particulars: elsewhere Aristotle holds both that virtue makes the particular goal correct (1144a6–8) and that the practically wise man will have the ability to see what is best on a given occasion (1144a32–36) only if he is virtuous. Here his (trained) morally good desires enable him to see what is the best course (1228a1–4; 1227a35–40), because the presence of the relevant discriminating ability is a consequence of the agent's possession of the relevant general desire.[18]

---

[18] For a different account, see Wiggins, 1976, 347–8. His view is based on 1072a29: 'we desire because something seems good, rather than it seems good because we desire it; for thought is the starting point.' But this seems compatible with the account of the origin of such thought given in 1175a12–15 and 30ff. (on which my account depends). The correct goal will appear to no one, if it does not appear to the good (1144a34) because of his goodness. This is compatible with the *encratês* also having a perception of the good; for it is only wickedness that destroys this perception (1144a34–36).

Just as correct enjoyment produces discrimination of what is really valuable, overall pain (see Section B) in acting thus destroys that discrimination (1140b11–16; 1144a35–36). If a man does what is courageous with pain overall, his condition is not stable (in Aristotle's account), as in time he will be prevented from seeing what is courageous, because fear will distort his assessment of the situation. This is why the agent characterised in 1104b7–8 as one who does what is courageous with pain overall is classified as cowardly; for he will eventually lose his power of moral discrimination (in Aristotle's theory). The *encratês*, by contrast, may enjoy (overall) acting temperately, and hence will preserve his discriminating ability, although he would also enjoy acting acratically. His hypothetical pleasure at acting non-temperately does not make his temperate action unpleasant overall – even if he would enjoy the intemperate action more. (see Section B). However, if he were regularly acratic, and enjoyed doing acratic actions overall, this would (in time) prevent him from seeing what was noble, and render him self-indulgent. Thus the *acratês*' state cannot endure for long without collapsing into self-indulgence; his condition cannot become permanent without changing his perception of his goals. This is why *acrasia* is an atypical occurrence for an agent.

Thus within Aristotle's Desire-Based general theory the acquisition and destruction of specific goals depends on the balance of the agents' motivational states; and this accounts for both why the agent has and why he loses his moral goals at a given time. But can this theory leave room for *acrasia*?

The practically wise agent not only makes the correct preferential choice, but also possesses the architectonic ability to form his goals into a coherent account of living well over a period of time (1144a29–36; 1140a25–28).[19] So he needs to see which of his goals are, in fact, constituents of well-being and desirable in themselves without further addition, and which are central and which peripheral.

But what guides this selection? The same mechanism as has already been responsible for the initial acquisition of his goals: his general desires. When confronted with unforseen conflicts between valued activities, they will (as before) lead him to discriminate which specific or general type is to be preferred (1143b1–5, 1144b30ff.) as the best among the competitors. These preferences will form the basis of his detailed view of the constituents of the best life.

While strength or obduracy of particular desires may play some role in determining the agent's preferences in these cases, this will not be the only factor. Since his concern is with well-being, he aims to isolate those desires which cohere best to form a co-satisfiable set which constitutes a worthwhile life. Thus he must determine (a) which of his

---

[19] Aristotle allows that there is a non-deliberative desire for this goal (1095a18ff.; 1097b1ff., b22ff.). The subject of reason is *which* activities should fit into our more detailed picture of what such a life is, and what part each plays in that structure.

general desires will, over time, prove most easily co-satisfiable, and (if this is a separate issue) (b) which co-satisfiable set of general desires will, over time, satisfy his desire for well-being. While his answer to (a) may be a belief, its content is constrained by his trained or natural desires; for it is these which determine what is, for him, the maximal co-satisfiable set of desires. Further, even if there are further structural or substantial constraints implicit in 'well-being',[20] the agent's view of which co-satisfiable set of desires satisfies these will be based on his past experience of activities he has enjoyed and found consistently satisfying. Thus acting generously would be taken as a constituent in well-being only by one who has consistently enjoyed acting thus (see 1105a5–7). In resolving these two questions, natural and trained virtue proves the correct teacher of goals (1151a17–19). While there may be reasoning (or discussion) as to what goals an agent should take as components in well-being, the conclusion of his reasoning will be constrained (and in large measure determined) by the set of general desires he already possesses.

One exegetical advantage of the Moderate Desire-based account of the origin of general goals and moral perception is that it points to a mid-position in a debate which has long been central in this area of Aristotelian scholarship. Loening (1903) suggested (and in this he was followed by Allan (1953)) that practical reason posited the end while desire promoted it; earlier scholars held that desire formed the ends without deliberation, and concluded that the role of reason was only to find means to ends. Loening's view gains support from those passages (1144a29–36; 1140a25–8, b4–7; 1142b31ff.) in which the rational planner is said to have a grasp on the correct goals, but fails to account so well for those (1144a6–9; 1151a15–19; 1228a1–4, etc.) in which virtue is said to make the goal right. The earlier view explains the second set of passages well, but fails in those in which it appears that reason plays some role in the formation of the goal. This debate arises because one party takes any mention of reason to show that Aristotle rejected a Desire-based account in favour of some form of Intellectualist theory (Loening, Allan, Ross, Irwin 1975), while the other party (Walter and Zeller) feels compelled to confine the role of reason to fixing means to ends in order to sustain their Desire-based account. The Moderate Desire-based strategy offers a way of solving this apparent dilemma, which does justice to the evidence cited by both parties; Loening was correct to note that practical reason forms the goal, and Zeller was correct to insist that trained desires fix the goal. This is possible because, in the sense explained, the structure of desires de-

---

[20] It lies outside the present project to investigate these structural or substantial conditions, as they are the proper object of a study of Aristotle's moral theory. If in general they favour simple over complex plans, or individual over social activities, *which* social activities form part of an agent's complex plan will be determined by his acquired or natural desires.

termines which goals are seen as good (and best) and are selected by the wise as elements of well-being. There is no inconsistency in Aristotle's account of the acquisition of goals provided that one does not add the (non-Aristotelian) premiss that reason's possessing any role in forming the goal proves that the goal-selection is not itself explained by antecedent desires which determine what reason selects. The exegetical debate appears to arise precisely because the two parties involved see no alternative other than an Extreme Desire-based theory (Humeanism) in which reason plays no role at all in arriving at the goal, or Intellectualism, in which the fundamental explanation of the selection of one's goal is given in terms of belief.

What is central for present purposes is that the Moderate Desire-based theory of the acquisition of goals (even in this outline form) is able to pinpoint the failure of the *encratês* and *acratês*. Their motivational structure yields as its most coherent set of values ones which do not include (or do not make central) all of their strong desires; for some (e.g. for sensual pleasure) may not be included because they cannot be (or have not been) integrated with their desire for a life of temperate or virtuous activity. Even though the *acratês* has a strong desire for sensual pleasures, this will not be one of the favoured set of goals which together will (in his view) result in well-being. One strong desire will be valuationally overruled if it is confronted with a coherent set of other desires which together are the basis for his perception of the best life overall.[21]

The motivational impact of the *encratês'/acratês'* sensual desire and its valuational impact differ, because the latter is a function of its contribution to his picture of well-being, while the former may be a consequence only of (e.g.) its strength. While his perception of well-being will lead him to favour abstention and assess a given sensual desire as weak valuationally, this ranking will not reflect the latter's motivational strength; for there is no general reason to suppose that the desire which is strongest at any given time will be valuationally preferred in the light of his conception of well-being. *Acrasia* occurs when the tension which results from his failure to integrate the motivational power of his desires with his valuation of them becomes intolerable; what seems best in the light of his structured conception

---

[21] The idea of well-being (good life for a human) may allow one to compare the distinct conflicting goals of virtue, creativity, pleasure and intellectual activity on a single scale: their contribution to well-being. As such, it provides a basis for a consistent and transitive set of preferences. If the agent's conception of well-being arises from his motivational states and attendant discriminatory capacity, it will not be a consequence of philosophical speculation about the goals of man based on a general theory of the species (1139b30–34). There is no requirement that the practically wise be his own philosopher. (I leave open whether Aristotle thought that the philosopher could defend a particular conception of well-being from general premisses of an anthropological or political kind, and whether his favoured view of well-being is 'dominant' or 'inclusive', etc. These issues belong to a study of Aristotle's ethical and political theory for which his philosophy of action is a prolegomenon.)

of well-being is not desired most strongly, even though that conception is itself dependent on desires which the agent has. The attempt to unify and order one's desires allows for the possibility of a gap between value and motivational strength which characterises the Moderate Desire-based account of the failure of the *acratês*.

The *acratês* had the capacity to control and integrate his motivational states with his picture of well-being but has failed to exercise this capacity. He could have disciplined his desires and made them obedient to his valuational perspective (in the ways indicated above), and would have done so if he had chosen to do so. If he had lacked this capacity through natural failing or disease, his subsequent actions would not be free (cf. 1148b31ff.).[22] The basis for an explanation of why the acratic agent is 'free' rests on Aristotle's thesis that goals are typically formed and destroyed over a period of time (and not at an instant) on the basis of motivational states that can be controlled by the agent himself.

If people find a given activity painful overall throughout a period of time, they will not continue to see it as good (1104b5–8; 1140b11–14). Thus a conception of well-being is built up (typically) over a period of time, and is not (typically) created or destroyed by one isolated action or passing emotional state (when one desires most strongly to do the acratic action and does so). If the latter were the case, *acrasia* would be impossible, as the acratic's state would immediately alter his perception of value and best judgment. So Aristotle's view rests on an empirical thesis about the creation and destruction of valued goals to allow for the possibility of *acrasia*, and can distinguish the *acratês'* case from that of the compulsive agent because the former alone possesses the ability to integrate his motivations with his goals and has failed to do so.

Aristotle's account of the formation of goals allows for the possibility of *acrasia* in a manner consistent with his Desire-based theory; for although desires determine which goals an agent has, there is sufficient slack to allow for the onslaught of *acrasia* (in certain cases) where the sentiments rebel against the goals he has set himself. But it also explains why *acrasia* cannot occur permanently; for if someone were regularly acratic, he would lose his perception of his valued goals. Unlike the Belief-based theory, it offers an empirical account of the rarity of *acrasia*, of the types of factor that precipitate its occurrence and of the success of the practically wise; for all depend on the interconnexion and mutual coherence (or lack of it) of the agent's

---

[22] The free agent has the ability (at some stage) to modify deviant desires in the light of his appropriately acquired goals (e.g. 1102b32ff.; 1119b12ff.; 1179b25ff.), and will do so, if he desires to do so. The formation of goals and the nature of his desires, thus rests, to an extent, with the agent, even though once formed they are difficult to alter (1114a12–21). (This is a sketch of an account. It faces major difficulties which lie outside the scope of the present discussion; Loening's (1903) systematic study of these issues tackles some successfully, but others still remain. See also Sorabji, 1980, Part V.)

desires. By contrast, if the agent's valuational perception was independent in origin of his motivational states it would remain empirically unexplained why *acrasia* was a rarity or why there is a general connexion between the agent's valuational and motivational response (see also Chapter 5, Section A).

Aristotle's Desire-based theory of the acquisition, maintenance and destruction of practical wisdom rests on two independent claims: (a) the more people enjoy an activity, the better they become at discriminating what is good within it, and (b) if they find a given activity painful, they will not continue to see it as good for a protracted period. The first thesis is exemplified by the courageous who can act correctly in sudden danger because they have the appropriate response (no excessive fear) and see what is best to do. Of these Aristotle writes (1117a19–22):

> Their actions spring more from character because less from preparation. They choose[23] to act courageously in line with their character in sudden danger and not from calculation, i.e. general reasoning.

What is significant about these men is that they arrive at a correct preferential choice on the basis of their immediate perception of what is best, which is derived from their courageous disposition constituted (in part) by their motivational states, without the need for more general consideration of (e.g.) the chances of success or all the beneficial consequences of doing the courageous action. They can trust their immediate valuational discrimination because it springs from their trained motivational structure (see also 1109b21–26; 1126b2–9). The second thesis is instanced by Aristotle's insistence that even if a man does the same act as the courageous, he is actually a coward if he acts with pain overall (see Section B) because he will in the end cease to be courageous (and, presumably for Aristotle, the properly courageous man will never lose his courage or begin to act uncourageously). Together they form a basis for his Theory of the Mean.

Both claims may be too simple in their present form (even if put forward as 'in general' claims), as valuational assessment may have a variety of motivational sources apart from enjoyment/pain, and not be determined just by these. But supplementation of these claims by other motivational features (see Section B) will not overthrow the general form of Aristotle's empirical theory of the acquisition and destruction of valuational goals and virtuous character. Indeed they would support it, if an empirical theory of this type is possible (see Chapter 5).

---

[23] I translate 'choose' in 1117a22 as (i) it is the verb of the original clause and hence gives sharpest contrast in the grammatical construction; (ii) virtuous action requires choice (1105a29–34).

D. Rationality, practical and theoretical wisdom: the achievement of the practically wise (2)

The discussion of Sections A–C allows us to analyse more directly Aristotle's account of practical truth and practical knowledge, and to see more clearly in what the irrationality of the *acratês* consists.

Practical truth is introduced in *NE/EE* VI 1 as follows (1139a21–31):

> What affirmation and negation are in thought, pursuit and avoidance are in desire. So, since moral virtue is a state concerned with preferential desire, and preferential desire is a desire which arises from deliberation, the reasoning must be true and the desire correct if the preferential desire is to be excellent, and the latter must pursue what the former asserts. This type of intellect and truth is practical: while the good and bad condition of theoretical (i.e. not practical or productive) intellect is truth and falsity respectively (for this is the appropriate goal of all types of intellect), the good state of practical intellect is truth in agreement with right desire.

Here Aristotle introduces the analogy between practical and theoretical reasoning which he employs elsewhere with added detail:

	Theoretical	*Practical*
(1)	Assertion and denial	Pursuit and aversion (desires) (see Chapter 2, Section C)
(2)	The aim of theoretical reasoning is to assert what is true.	The aim of practical reasoning is to assert what is true (e.g. to make the correct best judgment) *and* to desire appropriately to do it (i.e. to act on it).

Since in both the theoretical and practical case the aim is to ensure that one hits the target non-accidentally, Aristotle imposes a condition on reasoning in both cases:

(3)	What is asserted as true must be based on correct reasoning (i.e. from true premises by valid rules of inference).	What is asserted as good must be based on correct reasoning (i.e. true premises and valid rules of inference) (1142b22–25) *and* it must be non-accidental that it is desired appropriately (1139a32–b5: cf. Chapter 3, Section D).

Failure in theoretical reasoning may result either from false reasoning or (possibly) failure to assert the conclusion; in practical reasoning it arises either from false reasoning, or failure to assert the conclusion, or failure to desire it appropriately. Hence there is a further achievement required if one is to grasp practical truth: that the agent's desires be so ordered that he desires appropriately to do what is judged best, and does not desire most to do an action which is contrary to his better judgment. Fulfilment of this added condition characterises one part of practical wisdom and distinguishes it from the state of the *acratês* and the *encratês*; for the former may desire to do what is best somewhat but not appropriately, and hence fail to act accordingly, while the latter will desire to do what is best appropriately, but desire most to do another action (which he does not do, because of the presence of motivational states other than desires; see Section B.) The practically wise fulfil the goal of practical reasoning because they do what is best (non-accidentally), as they see what is best, desire it appropriately and desire no other action more than it.

Aristotle adds a further condition on knowledge in the two cases:

(4) The higher order premisses must be asserted in the light of one's own experience (1142a19–20).

What is asserted must not be simply taken from someone else (1147a18–21), but made part of oneself (1147a21–22).

In both cases, Aristotle imposes a condition on the route one must follow to reach the goal: if the goal is truth, the premisses must be ones which the theoretician has good reason to accept himself, i.e. not ones he has merely 'taken over' from someone else, but ones which he has arrived at himself or tested in the light of his experience (Section A). In the practical case the wise has made what is asserted 'part of himself' by modifying the remainder of his relevant psychological states in its light (Sections B, C), and has acquired the relevant higher-order premisses and particular perceptions on the basis of his trained motivational states. This is what makes it non-accidental that the wise man desires his correct best judgment appropriately.

The focus of this analogy may be sharpened in the light of Aristotle's account of desire as (in part) a mode of accepting a given type of proposition with the aim of doing what is good (see Chapter 2, Section C). If both assertion and desire are modes of acceptance, one may ask: what general features need to be satisfied if the proposition accepted is to be known? Aristotle imposes analogous conditions in the two cases:

(i) *Truth condition*. What is accepted must be true (in the practical case: about the good).

(ii) *Acceptance condition*. What is accepted must be appropriately accepted: (in the theoretical case, accepted as true: cf. 1147a22–24; in the practical case, appropriately desired: 1139a25–27, 31–33).

(iii) *Reasoning condition.* What is accepted (if based on reasoning) must be based on correct reasoning and true premises.

(iv) *Acquisition condition.* What is accepted must be accepted in the light of one's own experience and (at least, in the practical case) integrated with the rest of what one accepts to form one coherent theory.

Thus both practical and theoretical knowledge may be true justified acceptance, although the mode of acceptance and the acquisition condition may differ in the two cases. If knowledge is a form of true justified belief, practical knowledge will be appropriate and justified desire to do what is truly good (within Aristotle's account of desire). (Paul Grice developed a similar analogy differently in lectures in 1978/ 9.)

Conditions (ii)–(iv) are Aristotelian conditions on full rationality which outstrip his requirements on rational choice (see Chapter 2, Section D). Condition (i) is – apparently – a separate requirement on practical wisdom: the agent gets the correct answer, and hence possesses practical knowledge. The Aristotelian *encratês* and *acratês* fail to fulfil (iv); the self-indulgent, however, may (it appears) fulfil (ii)–(iv), i.e. promote his own conception of well-being in a structured way, discriminate what is most pleasant in its light and succeed in integrating his desires accordingly.[24] Hence the self-indulgent and practically wise need differ only in their goals and the desires that have led to them.

Condition (i) and the account given of its acquisition in a Desire-based theory suggest that there is no incompatibility between moral objectivism and a Non-Belief-based theory. The discriminating capacity of the practically wise sees what is best because of the agent's virtuous desires, and he will accept appropriately what he sees as best because he has integrated his desires accordingly. If desire is represented as a mode of accepting propositions about the good parallel to assertion, just as what is asserted is either true or false, so what is desired may be truly good or bad independently of the mode in which the relevant proposition is entertained. With the Desire-based theory, to represent an agent as seeing that φ'ing is good is, in general, a way of registering his acceptance (in the desiderative mode) that φ'ing is good. His moral perceptions either are or record his acceptances in the desire-based mode. Moral objectivism does not require either a Belief-based account of the acquisition of moral principles or perceptions, or a Belief-based theory of how they lead to action.[25]

---

[24] Aristotle does sometimes represent the self-indulgent as failing to fulfil clause (iv) and hence being at war with himself (1104b5–8; 1166b18–25); but elsewhere he is represented as enjoying sensual excess (1119a11–12). If so, while internal conflict may characterise some self-indulgent people, it does not appear to apply to all.

[25] Although one may (of course) be both a belief-based theorist and a moral objectivist (see McDowell, 1978).

A further consequence bears more directly on the failure of the *acratês*. Within Aristotle's account of desire (see Chapter 2, Section C), the weak *acratês* is irrational because he has set himself a goal, sees the way to achieve it and then fails to desire it in the way which fulfils the aim of desire (to do what is good). The parallel with belief is close; if belief is a mode of acceptance appropriate if one is aiming at the truth, then failure to believe *p*, given that one detects truth in *p*, would be irrational; for then one would have a goal, see how to achieve it and yet fail to do so. A similar pattern obtains in the case of desire (taking *p* as the proposition that '*x* is best'). If the agent fails to desire to do *x* appropriately, he fails to achieve the goal he has set himself *qua* desirer (of the good), even though he can see a way to achieve that goal. As failure to believe that *p* in the conditions speci-fied reduces S to merely saying *p*, so the *acratês* who fails to decisively desire to do *x* is in a situation analogous to that of merely saying *p*. This is why Aristotle emphasises in 1147b10ff. that the *acratês* is like the man saying *p* without knowledge. His Desire-based account gives clear point to this analogy in his central discussion of *acrasia*.

The irrationality of the weak *acratês* constitutes a failure distinc-tive of desire and practical reasoning, which is separate from the irrationality (self-deception, temporary blindness, gross intellectual failure) which affects belief within theoretical reasoning (see Chapter 3, Section E). In this way Aristotle's theory of practical wisdom, desire and practical reasoning is an attempt to show that weak *acrasia* is a type of irrationality (and failure of knowledge) without misrepresent-ing it as a Socratic failure in belief-based or theoretical reasoning. It lies outside the scope of the present project to test whether there are failures parallel to that of the *acratês* within that type of theoretical reasoning which involves doxastic states weaker than belief (e.g. conjecture).[26]

We may now formulate an approximation to an Aristotelian Prin-ciple of Continence as follows:

(1) If one possesses an unqualified comparative value judgment based on one's assessment of the options in the light of one's valued goals, accept it appropriately.

(2) If one possesses no unqualified comparative judgment of the type specified in (1), but one (and only one) unqualified non-compar-ative value judgment based on one's assessment of an option in the light of one's valued goals, accept it appropriately.[27]

---

[26] Stephen Williams has investigated this possibility in an (as yet) unpublished paper. The issues involved are complex and deserve extended treatment.

[27] Within the class of unqualified non-comparative judgments '*y* is good' should override (in the formulation of the Principle of Continence) '*y* has a good quality' (see Chapter 3, Section C). The salient feature of this Aristotelian principle for present purposes is not its formulation but its grounding in his account of desire and practical reasoning. (Compare the new-wave theorists' difficulty in grounding their Principle of Continence in this way: Chapter 3, Section E.)

From this it follows that one cannot appropriately accept a judgment in favour of an option judged less good than the other options before one. Hence, the *acratês* inappropriately accepts 'y is good', while also judging 'x seems best', which he fails to accept appropriately.

The basis of this principle is deeply rooted for Aristotle, and follows from his account of desire. Because this aims at doing what is good, it should (while true to its aim) do what seems to be the good in a given situation; this is why the *acratês*' desire is irrational in not desiring appropriately to do what is best. Further, because desire is focused on to the good, and two desires cannot both be appropriate acceptances and be inconsistent, the *acratês*' acratic desire is inappropriate because its satisfaction is inconsistent with the satisfaction of desires which he himself sees as good to satisfy. In both cases, his desires are incorrect because they turn their back on what seems to be good even though their aim is to do what is good. This is why the weak *acratês* violates a principle special to practical reasoning which itself aims at finding out what is good so as to do it.

Aristotle's *acratês* fails to transfer his desire from his goal to the means to achieve it. His failure (brought on, in the paradigm case, by the onslaught of sensual desire) is more than a purely causal one because desire is focused on to his picture of the good (which it has helped to form) and hence is irrational. Thus Aristotle aims at a position intermediate between those who see *acrasia* as a failure of theoretical reasoning involving belief and those who represent it as a purely causal failure between the agent's best judgment and his motivational states unconnected with reasoning. Like the former, he sees *acrasia* as a failure of reasoning, but in common with the latter he does not view it as a failure of theoretical reasoning in the mode of belief. The phenomenon of clear-eyed *acrasia*, in which (as Dostoyevsky remarks)[28] 'A man can wish upon himself, in full awareness, something harmful, stupid, even idiotic . . . Desire stubbornly disagrees with reason', shows that beliefs are not the only relevant motivational features; for if they were, clear-eyed *acrasia* would be impossible, and all acratic cases would exemplify some species of belief-based intellectual failure. (Self-deception, failure to draw a strongly supported conclusion, etc.) Desire appears to be the distinctive explanatory phenomenon required to allow for such cases.

Although desire has non-cognitive sources, Aristotle treats it as a mode of accepting a proposition, and not as a non-cognitive state completely separate from those which play a role in thinking or reasoning. This is why he says that sensual desires may have as their goal the good (1119b15–17) and be capable of listening in a way to (and of being persuaded by) the rational part (1102b30ff.). If desires of this type were blind (non-cognitive) motivational states, they could not pay attention to the rational soul or play a distinctive role in

---

[28] Dostoyevsky, 1864, section 8.

practical reasoning (see Appendix 3). Thus Aristotle is seeking to separate desire and belief without reducing desire to a purely non-cognitive motivational state cut off from practical reasoning, and only causally connected with it (as within the Humean picture). In his theory it is because desire may have non-cognitive sources (e.g. when directly connected with the sentiments: see Section C) that clear-eyed *acrasia* can occur, and because it is a mode of accepting a proposition when one's aim is to do what is good that the *acratês* is irrational in accepting decisively a proposition which is not justified by his reasoning.

Since for Aristotle desire has non-cognitive sources which determine its motivational efficacy, he would reject at least one of Davidson's principles which serve to render *acrasia* problematical:

P2. If an agent judges that it is better to do x rather than y, then he wants to do x more than he wants to do y.

For both *acratês* and *encratês* judge that it is better to do x rather than y, but want to do y more than x. Aristotle would replace this with a Principle of Virtue:

PV. If an agent judges that it would be better to do x rather than y, then, if the agent is virtuous, he wants to do x more than y.

But this leaves unclear the connexion between value and desire within Aristotle's account. Aristotle's theory of desire suggests a more general Principle of Continence:

PC. If an agent judges that it would be better to do x rather than y, then if the agent is continent he will accept appropriately a practical conclusion favouring x over y

(where acceptance is appropriate if it fulfils the aim of desire in doing what is good). Both virtuous and encratic agents will accept appropriately a conclusion in favour of doing x, even though the latter might want more to do y. Appropriate acceptance will be decisive, and lead to the agent doing x intentionally if he does either x or y intentionally.

Since Aristotle allows for a variety of motivational factors (e.g. character and strength of belief) in addition to strength of desire, he would not accept Davidson's other principle:

P1. If an agent wants to do x more than he wants to do y and he believes himself free to do either x or y, then he will intentionally do x if he does either x or y intentionally.

For the self-controlled man's actions may result from his character, as it is this (and not desire-strength) that ensures that his desire to abstain wins out (see Section B). Hence reference to strength of desire in P1 is misleading, as it picks out a subset of the relevant motivational states. An Aristotelian principle might run:

> PA. If an agent accepts appropriately a judgment favouring doing x over y, he will do x if he does either x or y intentionally.

Since the determinants of appropriate acceptance may outrun desires, Aristotle's account is neither 'hydraulic' (explaining action in terms solely of strength of desire) nor one which uses 'desire' as a 'catch all' for all motivational states.

PA, PC and PV articulate the outline of Aristotle's theory of the interconnexions between value, desire and the other motivational states he discusses. Taken together they offer a powerful theory of the possibility and explanation of *acrasia* and of its distinctive irrationality. But is it defensible?

E.   Aristotle on acrasia: problems and possibilities

Aristotle's account of the possibility and explanation of *acrasia* has several major strands:

(a) His account of the limited form of the rational explanation required for intentional action (Chapter 3, Section D: also Chapter 2, Section C).

(b) His view of practical reasoning directed to a best judgment as relative to the goal the agent has set himself (Chapter 3, Section B).

(c) His account of desire as a mode of accepting a proposition if one's aim is to do the good (Chapter 2, Section C).

(d) His use of the split between the valuational and motivational factors to account for the occurrence of *acrasia*, and his parallel theory of the achievement of the practically wise in integrating them successfully (Chapter 4, Sections A–C).

Of these, (c) and (d) raise immediate problems.

Within Aristotle's account of desire, the propositions accepted must be valuational (involving judgments about what is good). However, his own examples suggest that certain desires (e.g. a craving for drink) are better expressed gerundively than valuationally (701a31–33), since in such cases the object desired may not be one considered as good (even if one recognises that it will satisfy one's desires); for one may regret overall having this desire at all, or regret overall having to satisfy it with this object. But if there is a wider variety of premises than in Aristotle's theory, then the mode of acceptance characteristic of desire must be sufficiently flexible to accept gerundive as well as valuational propositions.

Further, within Aristotle's theory the *acratês* must act on a conclusion that a given course of action is good: 'y has a good quality' or 'y

is good' (see Chapter 3, Section C). But these examples appear only to be a subset of genuine acratic conclusions: in others the agent may be fully aware of the bad consequences of *y*'ing or (more radically) that *y*'ing (in this case) lacks any good quality, and judge in effect 'I'll do *y* – to hell with it!' and thus accept a non-valuational conclusion (contrary to Aristotle's account).

These difficulties arise because of Aristotle's (partial) characterisation of desire as:

AR. The mode of acceptance appropriate if one's aim is to do what is good.

Although this explains the irrationality of the *acratês*, it places too severe a restriction on the content of the propositions accepted; for not all desires are best represented as acceptances of a value judgment.

One alternative would be to characterise desire rather as:

AN. The mode of acceptance appropriate if one's aim is to make it true that there is an action of the type specified in the proposition.

Within this model of acceptance, there will be a distinction between conditional and decisive acceptance: S will accept a proposition conditionally if his aim is to make it true that there is an action of the type specified in *p*, *unless* this making it true is incompatible with anything else he makes true. S will accept *p* decisively, if S accepts it in the mode appropriate if S's aim is to make it true that there is an action of the type specified in *p* (without conditions). Decisive acceptance in this latter mode would be appropriate for the final stage pre-action.

There are difficulties, however, for this alternative proposal; for although the mode of acceptance it characterises may widen the range of propositions accepted to include both valuational and gerundive propositions, it snaps the direct connexion between value and desire and so leaves unexplained the irrationality of the *acratês*. While the *acratês* may violate a preferred Principle of Continence, there is no basis for such a principle in this account of desire. If desires were always for the good, this could be given (as in Aristotle's account) by strict analogy with belief. Once this link is severed, the ground of the *acratês*' irrationality is left underexplained.

The alternative proposal therefore requires supplementation. One suggestion runs as follows: if the aim of practical reasoning is characterised as finding out what is best to do so as to do it, the *acratês* would accept this aim, find out how to achieve it and then fail to do so. If so, the analogy with belief would be less direct. It would be between saying *p*, finding out that *p* is true and believing *p*, and for *desire in the context of practical reasoning*:

conditionally accepting *p*,	finding out that *x* is best and accepting the aim of practical reasoning, and	*decisively* accepting *p*.

If decisive acceptance is defined in this way, the *acratês* will violate the aim of practical reasoning in failing to accept *p* decisively, although he may still hold that *x* is best and conditionally accept that *p*.

The irrationality of the *acratês* now consists in his violating a principle of continence which follows, not from the nature of desire (as on Aristotle's account), but rather from the nature of practical reasoning itself. The analogy between desire and belief is less tight within this alternative than within Aristotle's account; for mention of the aim of practical reasoning is now required to legitimise the transition from conditional to decisive acceptance, while in the case of belief (as also for desire in Aristotle's account) the analogous transition follows from the nature of the propositional attitude itself. However, this weakening of the analogy does indeed seem forced on us by the variety of cases of *acrasia* and species of desire involved.

If this is so, rejection of Aristotle's account of desire would not render valueless his general explanation of the occurrence of *acrasia*. But it would lead to a somewhat different theory: for the achievement of the practically wise man would now consist in a process of integration of value and desire with a further stage: (a) ensuring that only what is valuable is desired; in addition to (b) ensuring that its valuation is as it should be, and (c) ensuring that the motivational efficacy of each option matches its valuational impact. It remains to be seen whether this modification of Aristotle's account of practical reasoning can be carried through successfully.[29]

Our present purpose is, however, different. Certain elements of Aristotle's theory of practical reasoning and wisdom suggest that it is conceived as a causal explanatory account of the acquisition, preservation and destruction of valued goals, and more generally of the antecedents of intentional, continent and virtuous action. It remains to be seen whether his theory as a whole, with its key concepts of acceptance, appropriate acceptance and preferential choice, rests on an explanatory theory of this type. In the final chapter, Aristotle's interconnected explanatory theories are examined within the context of his theory of mental states and their relation to physical processes. This will enable us to test whether a causal explanatory theory of the type Aristotle envisaged is possible, and to seek to integrate his theory with the ontological foundations laid in Chapters 1 and 2.

---

[29] For further discussion of parts of this theory, see Charles, 1982/3.

CHAPTER FIVE

Rationality, Practical Knowledge and the Explanation of Action

A. Teleological, rational and causal explanation of action

Aristotle's account of intentional action has distinctive causal elements (Chapter 2), and his ontology of actions rests on a causal explanatory basis. His theory of rationality presupposes an explanatory theory which accounted for the acquisition and destruction of value judgments in a causal way. Thus aspects of Chapters 2–4 favour the attribution to Aristotle of a causal explanation of intentional and rational actions.

However, this is not the whole story. Aristotle also offers a teleological explanation of intentional action which he sees as compatible with the causal explanation of the same phenomenon (195a3–8; 94b27ff.). So one major issue is to see whether these are in fact compatible, and if so, how. (See Chapter 2, Section E.)

Aristotle's theory also contains certain other elements which suggest an *a priori* connexion between desire, belief and intentional action. For example, in the Aristotelian Principle of Continence:

PC. If an agent judges that xBTy, then if the agent is continent, he will accept appropriately a practical conclusion favouring x over y;

the continent agent 'appropriately accepts' a practical conclusion when (and only when) the balance of his motivational states favours x over y, and he decisively opts (motivationally) for x. However, if 'appropriate acceptance' were to be analysed in terms of 'decisive acceptance', and that defined as the state which leads to the matching action in appropriate circumstances, then the connexion at the psychological (and psycho-physical) level between appropriate acceptance and action would be *a priori*. Since within a causal explanation the relevant states must be connected *a posteriori*, 'decisive' and 'appropriate acceptance' could not be elements in such an explanation at this level. More generally, can rationality and the other mental states in Aristotle's theory be elements in a causal explanatory story involving psychological terms? In this section, we will focus on Aristotle's account of teleological explanation and rationality; and in Section C on desire.

(1)   *The interconnexion of causal and teleological explanation*

Teleological explanation, for Aristotle, is explanation by what is good (or better) for the object/organism in question: 'The fourth cause is the goal: i.e. the good' (983a31–32). Thus we explain by showing 'that it was better thus – not simply but with respect to the essence of each' (198b8–9; cf. 195a23–25; 194a28–32; *G.A.* 789bff.; *Post An.* 95a8).

In some cases, this goal may be an organised structure,[1] but this is not so in all cases. For intentional action may be teleologically explained even when the goal is simple (e.g. obtaining money: *EE* 1226b26ff.) or atypical of one's general goals (e.g. *acrasia*). Similarly, while in some cases teleological explanation will have as its relevant goal 'constitutive activity of the organism',[2] this need not apply in all. What is distinctive of teleological explanation is that it is explanation by a *telos*: a goal (or an apparent goal) for S at *t*.

A first approximation to Aristotle's account of teleological explanation might run as follows:

S does *x* for the sake of *g* iff *g* is a good for S, and S's doing *x* tends to ensure that (he obtains) *g* (cf. 199a8–10).

But if *g*'s being good is to *explain* S's doing *x*, it must, for Aristotle, necessitate S's doing *x* (in given circumstances). That is, on the assumption that explanation for Aristotle involves necessitation, it must be possible to represent what occurs by a series of propositions which jointly entail S's doing *x* (see Chapter 1, Section D). This might be represented initially as follows:

g's being good for S at *t* and doing *x* being the best way to achieve *g* necessitate S's doing *x*,

where this mode of explanation has as its conclusion a proposition describing S's action and as its antecedents propositions stating that it is good to do *g* etc. That is, it is of the form 'P and Q and R necessitate S' where P . . . S are propositions of a given form.

In the present context, Aristotle's use of teleological explanation to account for intentional action is our prime concern. In *de Motu*, he considers cases which approximate to this form: 'A good is to be made (by S)', 'A house is a good', where the conclusion is a statement describing the resultant action 'S makes the house' (701a15–16) where the action occurs if there are no circumstances which prevent the

---

[1] Gotthelf cites several such cases: 1976.
[2] Martha Nussbaum favours this view: 1978, 83–5 (see her reservations, p. 88).

conclusion 'A house is to be made' from leading to action. If the conclusion of the practical syllogism is a proposition which represents a given type of action as good, the action will result only if there are no further features present which prevent the occurrence of the action. Thus, if the conclusion were 'φ'ing seems good', the teleological schema would run:

φ'ing seeming good to S at t and O(C*) necessitate S's φ'ing.

Using the premises of the practical syllogism (and ignoring its conclusion) the schema would run:

(A) ψ'ing seeming good to S and φ'ing being the best way to ψ and O (C*) necessitate S's φ'ing,

or

(A)' ψ'ing seeming good to S and φ'ing being the best way to ψ necessitate S's φ'ing (on the assumption that C* obtain).

In such cases, the necessitation is hypothetical in that the conclusion follows if C* obtain; it does not follow just from the explanans ('x'ing seems good'). In contradistinction to causal necessitation, (A) introduces features other than the explanans as necessitating the conclusion. This gives clear sense to the distinction between teleological and causal necessitation without treating the former as merely being a necessary condition.[3]

Aristotle believed that this schema of explanation was compatible with efficient causal explanation (195a5–15). S's building a house can be explained teleologically and also causally by citing S's desires, imagination, perception and thought. The latter account would yield a causal schema of explanation as follows:

(B) S's desiring to ψ and S's believing that φ'ing is the best way to ψ and O (C*) necessitate S's φ'ing.

How then are (A) and (B) compatible? Let us represent (A) by the

---

[3] In *Post An.* 94b10ff. Aristotle emphasises that teleological explanation necessitates in his favoured syllogistic form. Elsewhere (*Physics* II. 9; *P.A.* 639b21ff.; 642a1ff.) he suggests that this necessitation is hypothetical and requires the presence of (e.g.) the appropriate building materials (200a26ff.; 639b25ff.). There can be no house (shelter) if these are absent. These distinct passages might be reconciled (taking R as the proposition that there are appropriate building materials, P as expressing the goal and Q as stating that a house exists) as 'P necessitates Q (if R)' or, 'P and R necessitates Q' in line with the teleological schema for intentional action explanation. However, these issues are complex and require separate analysis which lies outside the scope of the present project; I intend to consider elsewhere whether teleological explanation exemplifies necessitation of this type (see Charles: forthcoming (b)). For a contrasting view see Balme, note on 639b21ff.; Sorabji, 1980, 148ff.).

propositional schema 'P and S necessitate Q', and (B) by the schema 'R and S necessitate Q' (as in Chapter 1, Section D). (A) and (B) are both explanatory accounts which necessitate one proposition describing the action. If so, either Q is necessitated by two independent sets of propositions, or there is a degree of dependence between the two explanations. Let Q be a proposition describing the action: Q is necessitated by R (causal explanation), and also by P (an aim or good). Assume that it is not the case that P necessitates R. If so, it is hard to see how P can explain Q. For if P explains Q, if P were not so, Q would not be so. But if Q is not so, R is not so – if R necessitates Q. Hence, if P is not the case, R is not the case. But this contradicts the assumption that P is not necessary for R. If so, *either* P and R cannot both necessitate Q, *or* either P is necessary for R or R is necessary for P. Thus *either* Aristotle cannot have held that causal and teleological explanations both necessitate their effect *or* he must have held that (at least) one proposition which figures in (e.g.) the causal explanation necessitates the truth of a proposition that figures in the teleological explanation.[4]

Aristotle's account of desire as a mode of accepting a proposition if one's aim is to do the good requires that the propositions thus accepted are valuational and state that a given course is good or best (see Chapter 2, Section C). Thus it is necessary that if S desires to ψ, then ψ seems good to S. Hence, in schemata (A) and (B), R necessitates the truth of P: if S desires to ψ, ψ must seem good to S within Aristotle's account. Thus he can represent the action as both causally and teleologically explained without incompatibility.

This mode of representing action as both causally and teleologically explained construes 'ψ'ing seems good to S' as the proposition which S accepts in desiring to ψ. In the explanation of intentional action, the propositions which constitute the teleological explanans are those which give the propositional content of S's relevant desires. In giving this teleological explanation Aristotle uses as explanans solely the propositional content of S's relevant psychological states (S φ'ed because it seemed good to him) and seeks to account for S's φ'ing by showing the content of the desire which led him to φ.[5]

This general abstract of the relation between causal and teleological

[4] This argument is derived from Barnes, 1975, 221–2. But I do not accept his conclusion; hypothetical necessity (construed as giving a necessary condition only) is not required to resolve the present difficulty. In this argument, 'P necessitates Q' ('P is necessary for Q') is true if for some S, it is necessary that *if* P, *then* if S, then Q. For Aristotle's relevant condition on explanation, see *Post An.* 98a35ff. and Barnes, 1975, 241–3.

[5] In this Aristotle's scheme of teleological explanation differs from those (adopted by Anscombe, 1957, and Von Wright, 1971) in which the premises are expressions of the agent's acceptance: (e.g.) S desires to φ, and not the content of the proposition accepted when S desires to φ.

explanation can be supplemented from Aristotle's treatment of acratic and virtuous action, discussed in Chapters 3 and 4.

The *acratês*' action may be rationally explained, but is not rational. The teleological pattern appropriate in this case will thus be:

(C) χ'ing seeming good to S at t_1 and ψ'ing seeming the way to χ and C* necessitate S's ψ'ing,

where the premisses state that ψ seems good and not best. His irrationality is explained within the Moderate Desire-based theory in terms of his distinctive motivational states. He violates the Principle of Continence by not drawing the entailed conclusion, or by not sincerely accepting the good conclusion or by failing to integrate his relevant psychological states. These distinct types of failure arise because of the presence of an opposed desire which causes him to act acratically (1147a34; 433b5–10ff.). The mode of explanation of why the *acratês* fails to act encratically and acts acratically is in terms of the impact of his motivational states and not (fundamentally) of the valuational impact of his reasons. Since it is the strength of his desire which explains his acratic action and not his reasoning (1147b1–4; 433b5ff.), his acting in this way rather than encratically is to be explained in terms of efficient and not teleological causality. This is why Aristotle employs his favoured efficient causal terms (433b10–13; 1147a34–35; 1147b16; cf. *Physics* 243b16–19) in describing the effect of the *acratês*' acratic desire. Thus, among the conditions relevant for the teleological schema (C*) will be those motivational states whose presence is sufficient in the circumstances to explain the *acratês*' action. The applicability of the teleological schema rests on the presence of those causal factors which lead the *acratês* to act as he does.

This account of the *acratês*' failure and of the successes of the *encratês* and practically wise shows the limitations of explanation through attributing to S (valuational) reasons on which he acts. The *acratês* who acts on the conclusion 'φ has a good quality' or 'φ is good' accepts the same propositions as the *encratês*, and differs from him in his (other) motivational states. His action, therefore, is not to be explained wholly by the valuational propositions he accepts. Had Aristotle adopted the Identity, Strong Sufficiency or Uniqueness thesis, rational explanation of this type would have sufficed for an understanding of intentional action. His rejection of these theses not only allows for clear-eyed *acrasia*, but points to the motivational conditions required if reasons are to explain action in the cases of the *encratês* and practically wise; for they have to avoid the types of failure that characterise the *acratês* by ensuring that their other motivational states are appropriately ordered (see Chapter 3, Section E).

In the case of the *acratês*, there is compatibility between rational, causal and teleological explanation precisely because among conditions C* will be those causal factors which explain why the agent acts as he does. Nor is this surprising: the first two propositions in Schema (C) represent the agent's desire and belief. If Schema (C) is to suffice to explain S's ψ'ing, there must be added information about the agent's other motivational states, and the efficacy of the desire and belief in question, and this information will yield the specific conditions to be placed amidst C*. Thus a detailed specification of the antecedents in this scheme of teleological explanation will contain information which is drawn from the efficient (non-rational) causal explanation of the actions. There must be interdependence and not incompatibility between the causal and teleological explanatory accounts; for the teleological explanation (in its specific form) incorporates *a posteriori* causally relevant material which is required to show a way in which the premisses may necessitate the conclusion.[6]

(2)   Can there be psychological causal explanation in Aristotle's theory?

The *encratês* and the practically wise appropriately accept the good conclusion, and act on it. If 'appropriate acceptance' is defined as the type of acceptance which leads the agent to do what he sees as good, it will be *a priori* connected with action and hence cannot explain it in an *a posteriori* fashion. Similarly if the weak acratic 'decisively' accepts his acratic conclusion. Thus we might conclude that the explanation of the actions of acratics, encratics and practically wise are not a species of *a posteriori* psychological causal explanation.

Aristotle operates in this context with sensual desire and preferential choice and does not introduce into his account a unified state – intention or decisive desire – to stand as the psychological cause of action (Chapter 3, Section C). This is significant in the present context as it shows that preferential choice is not defined by being decisive but by its content: the best judgment it accepts, which is the conclusion of practical reasoning. But of preferential desire (thus defined) it may be *a posteriori* true that it leads to action (on a particular occasion). Sensual desire is also defined by its objects (the pleasant: cf. 1370a18) and its causal antecedents (Chapter 4, Section C), and not by its role as being decisive for action. Similarly it seems an empirical question whether sensual desire (thus defined) leads to an action. Two agents might share preferential desires to do x and sensual desires to do y and yet act differently (although both able to do x and y in C*) because of the presence of other psychological or physiological conditions. (See also Section C.)

---

[6] There may be less specific forms of teleological explanation which do not give detailed *a posteriori* information derived from the causally explanatory account (cf. *de Motu* 701a16–18). In this case, the necessitation would arise because the conditions are whatever need to be present to lead to S doing y, given that z seems good to S and y seems the way to z (see Chapter 2, Section C). Contrast the account offered by Anscombe, 1957, 35ff.; Von Wright, 1971, 96ff.

Even if appropriate acceptance and decisive desire are *a priori* connected with action, explanation by desire and acceptance can be *a
posteriori* provided that (i) it is possible to state (*a posteriori*) the
conditions under which a desire is decisive (i.e. under what physical
or psychological conditions a given desire overpowers); and (ii) the
mode of acceptance (desire) can itself be characterised without showing
it to be *a priori* connected with action.

Aristotle's discussion of the practically wise, the encratic and the
acratic introduces several features which bear directly on the first
requirement; the second is examined in Section C.

(a) *Motivational impact showed by pleasure/pain balance.* The excessive power of the deviant desires of the *encratês* and *acratês* is shown
by their overall enjoyment of acting against their best judgment. The
practically wise man lacks an excessive internal opponent because he
enjoys (overall) acting virtuously, and would not enjoy (overall) acting
against his better judgment. Hence Aristotle attempts to locate the
failure of the *acratês* within a general explanatory psychological theory. However, while this test indicates the excessive power of the
internal opponent, it does not explain why, on occasion, the *acratês*
differs in action from the *encratês*; for both have – by this test – an
excessive internal opponent.

(b) *Physical impact of deviant desires.* Aristotle introduces physiological data to explain the effect of the *acratês'* deviant desire on his
best judgment and his subsequent acratic action. His sensual desire
produces a physical condition in which he does not 'fully know' the
good conclusion; when that physical condition is dispelled, he 'knows'
it again fully and will again act on it (1147a15–17; b6–9; 1150b34). If
he had 'fully known' the good conclusion, he would not have acted
acratically. Hence the presence of this physical state explains why the
acratês does not act encratically but acratically. That is, his condition
before acting is distinguished from that of the *encratês* by a difference
in physical state produced by the presence of sensual desire. Even if
both *encratês* and *acratês* shared desires of the same motivational
force, the latter's physical states would be altered by it in a way which
the *encratês'* state of character would resist. If so, the fundamental
explanation of the occurrence of *acrasia* introduces physical states
whose absence is required if the agent is to act rationally and which
are present when the acratic action occurs.

Elsewhere Aristotle introduces similar considerations: in *de Motu*
703b34ff. he writes:

Movement, however, contrary to reason sometimes takes place and sometimes does not in the organs as a result of the same thoughts: the cause
is that the matter which is likely to be affected is sometimes present in
proper quantity and quality and sometimes not.

The reference to the matter which is likely to be affected points back to the state of the central organ (703b25ff.; 703a14ff.) and the internal condition of its changing states (702a5–16). If the agent's sensual desire (702a3, 17–18) is such as to affect his central organ adversely, it will prevent the presence of the appropriate physical condition required for encratic action. Revolt on the part of the passions occurs when they adjust the agent's physical state (1147a35) so that the states needed if he is to act on his best judgment are absent. That is, the *acratês*' sensual desire prevents (702a16–18; 701a15–16; 1147a26ff.) the good syllogism from resulting in action by inducing a physical state which makes encratic action impossible, and produces rather the acratic result.

The introduction of physiological information here indicates the conditions under which a given acratic desire is decisive. The appropriate explanation of the occurrence of *acrasia* is *a posteriori* because it introduces physiological data whose presence and intervention explains why the *acratês* acts as he does – and whose presence is induced by the split between motivational and valuational factors of the type analysed above. Thus, in the case of *acrasia*, the favoured mode of explanation would be as follows:

(IA)   S's desiring to χ and S's believing that ψ'ing is the best way to χ and $P_1 \ldots P_n$ obtaining necessitate S's ψ'ing intentionally,

where $P_1 \ldots P_n$ will include (a) those physical states of the organism which obtain when *acrasia* occurs, and (b) those psychological states (motivational states) which obtain when the agent's valuational assessment of the situation and his motivational states come apart (as shown by the agent's enjoyment or lack of it in acting as he does). That is, $P_1 \ldots P_n$ will state those conditions under which the *acratês*' desire to ψ is in fact decisive by giving those conditions under which his acceptance of a non-comparative valuation leads to action contrary to his best judgment. $P_1 \ldots P_n$ will also be precisely the conditions required to complete the teleological schema.

Hence, although there may be *a priori* connexions statable using overpowering or decisive desire, there is no reason to rule out the possibility of *a posteriori* causal explanations using desires and beliefs. (IA) is not a purely psychological explanation as among $P_1 \ldots P_n$ there will be physical states of the organism in question, and S's ψ'ing will be a member of one equivalence class with (e.g.) a bodily movement of S's.[7] Thus Aristotle's explanation of *acrasia* is an *a posteriori*

---

[7] Chapter 2, Sections B and D. This point requires careful statement: basic acts are movements of the body or 'detached limbs' (S's moving his body) and distinct from his body being moved by S. The relation between these is reciprocal so that whatever is sufficient for one is sufficient for the other. If so, if the psychological state is sufficient in the circumstances for S's moving his body, it will also be sufficient for S's body being moved. See Appendix 1 and Section B below.

psycho-physical causal explanation which states the conditions under which S's desire for the acratic course is overwhelming. Appeal to physical data follows the pattern of 'in general' explanations which require supplementation from a lower level while retaining certain psychological terms (S's desires, beliefs etc.) (see Section E).

If (IA) is the fundamental mode of explaining the occurrence of *acrasia*, it is clear that some (or all) of $P_1 \ldots P_n$ must be absent if the agent acts rationally. Thus the *encratês* and the practically wise man must lack that physical state in which *acrasia* occurs; the practically wise (unlike the *encratês*) lacks those psychological states in which there is a split between the agent's valuational and motivational states. If so, one may begin to formulate a causal explanatory generalisation which will obtain in the case of rational action:

(RA) S's desiring to ψ as the best option and S's believing that φ'ing is the best way to ψ and $P_1 \ldots P_n$ not obtaining necessitate S's φ'ing intentionally.

This generalisation common to both the *encratês* and the *practically wise* is not as yet complete; for one will wish to specify under what physical conditions of the organism $P_1 \ldots P_n$ do not obtain: that is, under what physical conditions of the organism 'the appropriate matter is present with the proper properties' (703b35ff.) for rational action. Further, one is required to investigate those physical properties whose presence and intervention prevent the agent from drawing the appropriate conclusion and acting on it, and thereby uncover the physical conditions required if the agent is to draw the appropriate conclusion and act on it. In both cases (as with (IA)) there may be difficulties in completing the relevant generalisations, but this does not prevent them from being causally explanatory. (See Section E.)

Schemata such as (RA) and (IA) give those conditions under which rational and teleological explanation obtains. If the conditions in the antecedent of (IA) are realised, then it will not be the case that the agent will act rationally. If he does act rationally, certain of the antecedents of (RA) must be present.

Consider the putative *a priori* schemata for rational action:

(1) φ seeming best to S at t_1 and ψ'ing being the way to φ and C* obtaining necessitate S's ψ'ing.

This schema will apply only if S is rational; hence among C* will be those conditions under which S is rational as well as the relevant ability and opportunity conditions. Such a schema might be represented differently:

(1)′ φ seeming best to S at t_1 and ψ'ing being the best way for S to φ and S being rational and C obtaining necessitate S's ψ'ing, if he acts intentionally, where C state just the ability and opportunity conditions. This schema might plausibly be taken to be *a priori*, and called the Schema of Full Rational Explanation. (1)´ cannot explain all actions as it fails to explain the irrational action of the *acratês*. When it does apply, the psycho-physical features which account for irrational action cannot be present; their absence or non-interference is a pre-condition for the application of the schema of rational explanation. When an agent is rational he must be uninfluenced – in being rational – by those features which explain the irrational action of the *acratês*, and possess those features necessary for him to act in line with his best judgment.

If so, the schema of full rational explanation is not only compatible (195a9–11) with the causal explanatory schema (RA); in the sense given, it rests on it. There can be both psycho-physical causal explanation and teleological (rational) explanation of rational action in Aristotle's account as the latter is only possible when certain causal explanatory features obtain. At this point there is dependency and not incompatibility between causal and rational psycho-physical explanation of action.

The second schema runs as follows:

(2) φ'ing being best and S appropriately accepting that φ is best and C* obtaining necessitate S's φ'ing, if he acts intentionally.

This might also be classed as *a priori*, as 'appropriate acceptance' is defined as acceptance in such a way as to fulfil this aim of doing what is good. However, the agent will only accept the conclusion appropriately if his motivational states are sufficiently integrated with his valuational assessment as to exclude the possibility of *acrasia*. But these will be just the conditions under which (RA) holds true, and thus will require the presence of the psycho-physical causal material embedded in (RA); for it is these which prevent sensual desire from impeding the agent's desire to act on his best judgment.

In both these cases, the *a priori* schemata (1) and (2) involving rationality rest on the truth of *a posteriori* psycho-physical causal explanation of the type indicated above. There is dependency and not incompatibility between causal and *a priori* explanation of action, because *a priori* explanation rests on (and requires) the presence of an *a posteriori* causal explanatory story. *Acrasia* shows the door to be open for an explanatory story of this type precisely because it draws one's attention to those causally relevant features which lead to a breakdown in full rational explanation, and hence to those factors which must be involved (and taken for granted) when full rational explanation is successful (see also Chapter 2, Section C; Chapter 3, Section D).

Thus investigation of the conditions under which these *a priori* schemes apply leads one to develop an *a posteriori* causal explanation of intentional action. In this way empirical generalisations may arise (indirectly) out of *a priori* (or analytical) considerations. (See Chapter 2, Section E.)

Aristotle's account, however, is open to a more general objection: it assumes that one can isolate certain actions as acratic, and then spell out the physical and psychological conditions under which such cases occur and hence form the relevant psycho-physical generalisations. But precisely this assumption might be challenged if one held that *acrasia* (failure of execution) occurred only in cases in which an action could not be made to fit together into the rational pattern of the agent's preferences, in which one is required to make him overall as rational[8] as possible and hence to seek to interpret all his preferences as forming one rational system of desires and beliefs. In such a scheme of interpretation, there is no independent or atomistic access to cases of *acrasia* apart from a holistic mode of interpreting all the agent's preferences. But if we can have no access to his preferences apart from his behaviour, we will always choose to interpret them so as to be as rational overall as possible (since we aim at rational explanation) and hence be prepared to modify past attributions of preference to make them cohere optimally with subsequent preference. Thus, *acrasia* will occur in cases where the agent's action does not fit into the optimally rational pattern of real preferences. For we cannot grasp the agent's justificatory schema except by attributing to him the structure which makes his overall pattern of choices as consistent as possible. If so, future evidence of further preferences may lead us to change the pattern of attribution and hence to count as encratic cases formerly considered as acratic. Thus we cannot take the physical evidence from cases labelled as acratic above as the basis for psycho-physical causal generalisations; for such cases may themselves appear not to be acratic at all when further evidence becomes available which leads us to reinterpret the agent's preferences. Further, if we produced such psycho-physical causal generalisations, we would be able to characterise other cases as acratic or rational on their basis, and thus might find that the agent's overall pattern of preferences was not optimally rational, but that he was (e.g.) acratic more often than would be allowed within the schema of rational explanation. That is, the presence of such causal generalisations would be potentially incompatible with the pattern of rational explanation, which aims at detecting maximal rationality in the agent's preferences. Hence, while above it appeared that psycho-physical causal and rational explanation were compatible (indeed interdependent), this appearance is illusory.

This line of objection contains several elements; but for present purposes, three are central: (a) that the pattern of rational explanation requires a maximally rational pattern of real preferences to be

---

[8] This account is favoured by one interpretation of decision theory; it constitutes one ground for denying the possibility of *a posteriori* psycho-physical causal explanation. Other grounds for the same conclusion are given in Sections C and D.

attributed to an agent; (b) that there is no independent (or piecemeal) access to the agent's values apart from the pattern of preferences required to make his actions overall as rational as possible; (c) hence, that there can be no independent (or piecemeal) point of access to the agent's values or motivational structure as would be possible if there were psycho-physical causal generalisations.

These appear to support the conclusion that rational and causal psycho-physical explanation are incompatible; for they purport to establish that our concepts of desire and belief are connected *a priori* with a pattern of holistic rational explanation, and hence cannot be used in any psycho-physical causal explanation which might (in principle) dislodge desires and beliefs from their place in that *a priori* scheme.

Aristotle's theory of rationality, however, as outlined in the previous chapter, contains sections which reply directly to this type of objection and argue for the fundamental compatibility and interdependence of causal and rational explanation.

The practically wise have a structured (architectonic) goal which is (or is sufficient for) well-being, and have integrated their motivational states (as explained) with their picture of well-being. Hence, in their case, one will find a maximally rational pattern of preferences and actions because of their achievement of integrating and modifying their valued goals and motivational states.

Practical wisdom, however, is a high-grade achievement, and not the common birthright of all at each stage of their development. For Aristotle rational choice requires only weak commensurability: taking one value as the best goal on that occasion and deliberating in its light; it does not demand that all one's values form an integrated whole (see Chapter 3, Sections C, D). Hence there is no obstacle to attributing rational choice to agents who have not (as yet) integrated their distinct values into one coherent framework, and who would not be expected (thus) to possess a consistent set of preferences. Thus one may attribute desires and beliefs to them without the *a priori* constraint of fitting them into an optimally rational pattern.

The achievement of strong commensurability, however, does not by itself guarantee that the agent's actual preferences and actions fall into an optimally rational pattern; for he may fail to act rationally through failure to integrate his motivational states with his structured picture of well-being. The practically wise will act consistently rationally because they would not enjoy (overall) acting against their better judgment. Hence in their case one can predict that in general they will act on their best judgment, and so not be acratic or reveal inconsistent preferences. However, if the agent would enjoy overall acting against his better judgment, there is less ground to expect to find totally consistent preferences and no ground to discount relevant cases of inconsistent preferences as failure in correct attribution. Given his hedonic balance in such cases (shown by his putative overall pleasure in acting acratically), there is the possibility of his acting acratically in a larger range of cases than would be allowed if one's concern was to achieve the maximally consistent rational pattern. Since it appears to be an empirical possibility that one agent may act acratically more often than another consistently rational agent, desires and beliefs must be capable of being attributed without fitting into an optimally rational pattern. If (as we appear to believe) it is an empirical question how often a person succumbs to the pleasure of (e.g.) sweets of a given kind, attribution of desires and beliefs to them cannot be so closely tied to the overall ideal of rationality as to make this impossible.

The acratic's action may itself be rationally explainable (see Chapter 3, Section D), but is not rational. It may result from the acratic's decisive acceptance of the conclusion of a practical syllogism stating that 'y has a good quality', although S's doing y requires also the presence of other relevant motivational factors (see Chapter 4, Sections B, C). Since Aristotle holds that not all rationally explainable action is rational (as not all action results from an agent's acceptance of his best judgment), it cannot be an *a priori* truth (in his theory) that desires and beliefs have to be attributed so as to make the agent optimally rational. It may be an *a priori* truth that desires and beliefs need to fit into a scheme of rational explanation, and that attribution of desires and beliefs should make sense in the context of the agent's whole performance over time; but it does not follow that the attribution must aim to make him optimally rational. Indeed the attribution of desires and beliefs may be overall explanatory precisely because they explain why a given agent is so frequently acratic in a given range of cases. Desires and beliefs have their role in explaining (in Aristotle's theory) both rational and irrational action; and in this he seems both to recognise the flexibility of desires and beliefs and their lack of an *a priori* connexion with the optimally rational overall pattern of attribution.

But is Aristotle entitled to this theory? Can it be given empirical application? Can we grasp what an agent's values are apart from the pattern of preferences required to make his actions overall rational? If we cannot, even if there is no *a priori* connexion with overall rationality, we would have no clear (empirical) idea of what it would be to discover an agent as less than optimally rational.[9] If we have no access to the agent's values and motivational states apart from his actions, we can always choose to interpret him as always (or maximally) conforming to the axioms of our favoured theory of rationality. Given that there are no further points of access to his view of the consequences and preferences between alternatives, it is not clear how we would establish that an agent was other than maximally rational; for since we have a 'free hand' with the values and motivational states

---

[9] For this more cautious claim, see Davidson, 1980, 273. Contrast Peacocke, 1979, 11ff.

we attribute – guided only by a principle of rationality – there is nothing to prevent us attributing to him precisely those propositional attitudes which make his actions maximally rational. But, so construed, the attribution of rationality does not appear to be an empirical theory; for it is not clear that there could be any evidence which could challenge or confirm the attribution of attitudes thus made, as there is no further evidence to call upon. Hence this conception of rationality appears incompatible with the existence of psycho-physical causal explanation, or any genuinely empirical method for attributing values and motivational states.

The content of preferential desires in Aristotle's theory is fixed by their role in a *justificatory scheme* tied ultimately to the agent's view of well-being, and not primarily by their role in *explaining* action; and justification is tied empirically to the explanatory scheme by the theory of the acquisition and distribution of values in the light of the agent's hedonic balances and other motivational states (see Chapter 4, Section C). But can the justificatory scheme be grasped independently of the explanatory role of desires and beliefs?

Aristotle's theory has three ingredients (at the psychological level) which are addressed to this question:

(a) An agent's justificatory scheme depends on how he sees well-being (or the good), and what can be validly derived from his conception. The constraints that govern this attribution rest on a need to fit together his sayings about well-being and practical reasoning into a coherent framework of sincere utterances rather than (initially) seeing them as *a priori* connected with the overall pattern of his actions. Since the agent's conception of well-being is self-formed and expressed by the agent's beliefs about the good, he has special authority about its content; for even if he made errors in deriving those beliefs from the initial desires, the erroneous picture would still constitute his view of *his* well-being (provided that he is sincere: see (b)). If there are holistic constraints governing our attribution of an agent's view of well-being, they are linked to the pattern of his assertions about well-being (and practical reasoning) and not (primarily) to his actions. When these distinct sets of constraints pull in different directions, there is ground (provided sincerity is assured) for concluding that the agent imperfectly realises his picture of well-being in his actions, rather than that his picture of well-being is changed or incomplete. The agent's regret at not realising his view of well-being will typically be relevant evidence (see (c) below); but even if there were no regret, the agent's picture of well-being would be (in measure) independent of how he acts.

(b) An agent's justificatory scheme arises from the activities he has been trained to do, enjoys doing and will persist as long as this is so. When an agent claims that certain values are ingredients in his account of well-being and we can explain in this way how they arose we have good reason to believe him. It is not that he has privileged access or the last word on what his values are; it is rather that when what he says his values are matches what they should be, given the account of the acquisition of his values and earlier states, we have extremely good reason to believe him to be sincere. (See Chapter 4, Section C.)

Aristotle's general theory of the acquisition and maintenance of values is stated mainly in terms of hedonic balances and trained desires. This may make matters too simple, and other factors may be required to supplement and extend the account; but his general perception seems correct: we can have access to the agent's values by means of a theory which explains how he acquires them (an analogue of learning theory in the case of belief),[10] which does not require that his values be that maximally consistent pattern of preferences needed to render all his actions rational. That is, a theory of the acquisition and destruction of values allows independent access to the agent's real preferences apart from what is required for rational explanation of action, and hence gives ground for us to believe his assertion that he judges doing x best even when he fails to act encratically. If so, there is no conceptual difficulty in allowing that the agent's actions are not maximally rational in the light of genuine preferences; for his preferences are not to be determined just by what he does, nor are his claims about his preferences falsified exclusively by actions which fail to conform with his values. Assertions about well-being, backed by a learning theory of value acquisition, provide the basis for the attribution of value to the agent.

(c) Aristotle also held that the agent's motivational states were determined (in some measure) by a set of hedonic balances (see Chapter 4, Sections B, C) which can vary independently of, and be assessed separately from, the valuation of the options before him. Access to these balances (which determine the permanence of character-traits) provides an account of motivational states apart from the agent's valuation of the situation. In Aristotle's theory, these balances distinguish the practically wise and encratic even when they act in the same way, as regret in acting distinguishes the self-indulgent and the acratic.

(a)–(c) yield evidence about the agent's valuations and motivations apart from considering how he acts. If there are such points of access to the agent's values and motivations apart from his behaviour, then it is an open and empirical question whether or not the agent acts rationally in all or most cases; we no longer have a 'free hand' in the

---

[10] An empirical learning theory would show what agents learned in undergoing decision theory tests. If such a theory can be constructed and empirically tested, it would challenge Davidson's pessimistic conclusion that decision theory is not an empirical theory (1980, 237ff., 272ff.).

attribution of values and motives to the agent. Rather, through our independent grasp of his values and motivational states, we gain a 'clear idea' of what it is for him to fail to be maximally rational: to fail to integrate his values and motivational states in all cases (*acrasia*, impetuosity), or to fail to grasp in a particular situation what is the best because of an inadequacy in his discriminating capacity brought on by a deficiency in his motivational states (intellectual failure, failure of perception, self-deception). If we can grasp the agent's values and motivational states it is possible to establish when what he does matches or fails to match his picture of well-being. Aristotle did not, of course, attempt to devise experimental tests for determining empirically an agent's values and desires. His concern was rather to emphasise that there is a wider range of relevant evidence than the agent's behaviour alone ((b) and (c)), and that (given (b)) there is no general (non-empirical) reason for expecting the agent's preference to be maximally rational given the picture of well-being (see (a)). It remains to be seen whether his conception of rationality can be empirically validated.

If an Aristotelian agent is rational, we will be able to predict his actions accurately because he has integrated his motivational states and values, and ensured that his values are stable and his discriminating capacity in good condition. Thus, given his best judgment (based on his values and supported by his honest assertion), we will be able to say how he will act (given appropriately specified physical conditions); and also, given his values, we will in general be able to predict what his best judgment will be. Aristotle's conception of rationality (and the rational agent), so far from being incompatible with psycho-physical causal explanation, actually rests on it. If the agent is rational, certain connexions obtain between his values and actions whose explanation forms part of a psycho-physical causal explanation of his behaviour.[11] In particular, such connexions ground conditionals and counterfactuals such as:

(1) if S had not judged it best to φ – given that $P_1 \ldots P_3$ obtained – he would not have φ'ed, and

(2) given the fact that S judges it best to φ and that he is able to φ and $P_1 \ldots P_3$ obtain, then S will φ,

by giving those psychological and physical conditions under which an agent of a specified type acts rationally and is rational (in terms of the theory sketched in Chapter 4). This empirical theory will ground those holistic constraints (rationality, etc.) which apply perfectly for the rational agent and imperfectly for the encratic/acratic, and will explain why it is an empirical question whether a given agent succumbs to a specific type of *acrasia* once or more than once a day! This

---

[11] Contrast Davidson, 1980, 222ff.

is because Aristotle's empirical theory of the origin and destruction of valued goals and character explains why justificatory scheme and motivational states are in general in close tandem, and how they may come apart in certain types of case.

Aristotle's position suggests a more general moral: that while the conception of rationality advanced by Davidson and his followers may be incompatible with the possibility of psycho-physical causal explanation, this shows not that there can be no psycho-physical explanation but rather that they err in their view of rationality. Given Aristotle's conception of the rational agent, which depends on a wider range of empirical connexions related to the acquisition and maintenance of values and the integration of value, justification and motivational states, rationality is compatible with – indeed dependent on – the existence of psycho-physical causal explanation. His theory is holistic in the sense that (if successful) it must cover all the relevant evidence; but the attribution of individual elements (the scheme of justification, motivational efficacy) may be piecemeal (or molecular) and need not be governed at every stage by the ideal of a maximally rational scheme of interpretation.

However, even if psycho-physical causal explanation is compatible in the ways indicated with the teleological and rational explanation of action, there remain principled objections to its possibility. Some hold that desires and beliefs themselves are connected *a priori* with intentional action (independently of the governing ideal of rationality); others claim that the explanations offered at the psycho-physical level are not sufficiently rigorous or complete to count as genuine explanations. To these problems we will return in Sections C and E. Before that we should examine one consequence of Aristotle's treatment of desires as causes: ontological materialism.

B. Aristotle's non-reductionist ontological materialism (1)

Aristotle's treatment of ontology and causal explanation, and of rationality and intentional action as elements in a causally explanatory theory, places firm constraints on his account of the relation of the mental and the physical components in the explanation of action.

If Aristotle accepted that rationality is part of a causal explanatory psycho-physical theory, two consequences immediately follow: (i) since rationality involves the properties of processes of desiring (i.e. what is desired; how much; for what good) mental processes and mental properties play a role in a causally explanatory theory. But if they have such a role, it is necessary that mental terms and predicates denote psychological processes and properties, and not merely be construed as a mode of description of physical entities or properties. (ii) Since Aristotle's basic acts are movements of the body, they (if taken together with the resultant bodily movement) will possess (within his account) both a psychological efficient cause and a physical efficient cause, where both efficient causes are elements in distinct causal explanatory stories: the one psycho-physical and the second purely physical. But if the two causally explanatory theories cannot be independent of each other (for, if they were, there would be chance over-determination by independent causes), it seems that at least some of the mental processes and properties must be dependent on some of the physical processes and properties.

Both consequences make demands on Aristotle's ontological theory: for the first requires that his ontological theory contain mental processes and properties, while the second demands that mental processes and properties be dependent (in some way) on the relevant physical processes and properties. In these ways, the requirement of a satisfactory explanatory theory constrains the ontological account to be given of the relation of the mind and the body. In this section, we will investigate the second consequence, in the following the first.

In this section we shall consider how far his account of efficient causation committed him to a version of ontological materialism: the doctrine that

> For any true psychological description of the world (*either* a description of the psychological phenomena *or* a description making use of psychological vocabulary) there is some state of affairs characterisable employing only physical vocabulary such that: the obtaining of the physical state of affairs is sufficient (but not causally sufficient) for the truth of the psychological description.[12]

Causal sufficiency is excluded as its presence in this formulation would involve mental events, states or properties being (efficient) causally dependent on physical entities. In such a case, there would be mental events, states or properties 'over and above' the physical states of affairs. Ontological materialism is thus the doctrine that the occurrence of physical states 'makes true' psychological descriptions without (efficiently) causing the psychological events, states or properties, thus described, to exist.

Materialists, who are classified as ontological in this formulation, often hold that mental events are identical with physical events either in the sense that all mental types are identical with (or reducible to) given physical or functional types *or* in the weaker sense that each mental event (or property) is identical with some physical event (or property) (token-identity). Aristotle, while an ontological materialist (I will argue), was neither a type nor token identity theorist. He has a distinctive theory of the relation of the mental and the physical; but one which creates its own difficulties.

Ontological materialism is to be distinguished from a different version of materialism which will become important in the concluding

---

[12] By causal sufficiency is meant *efficient* causal sufficiency.

sections of this chapter: explanatory materialism. This doctrine states that

> For any state of affairs/true description of the world which can be explained, the only or best explanation of that state of affairs will employ only physical vocabulary.

That is, our only or best explanation (*the* explanation) of a given phenomenon is couched in purely physical vocabulary; thus, for instance, *the* (or *the* fundamental) explanation of a bodily movement which is an action will be given in terms of its physical antecedents and specify the effect in purely physical terms. At present, our concern is ontological materialism: did Aristotle accept it?

(1) *Aristotle's arguments for ontological materialism*

Aristotle held that the agent's desires were efficient causes of his actions (1111a22–23; 433a31ff.). His basic action is his movement of his body (or detached limb), which stands in one equivalence class with the body being moved (see Chapter 2, Sections A, B, D).

Aristotle also held that there was an efficient causal story to be told at the physical level in terms of antecedent physical states and processes causing those physical movements which were sufficient in the circumstances for the movement of the body. In the equivalence class consisting of the action and movement of the body, the occurrence of the latter is non-causally sufficient in the circumstances for the occurrence of the action (see Chapter 2, Section B; Appendix 1). That is

(0) O (*b.m.*) in C* necessitates O (*a*).

The physical antecedents in the circumstances causally explain the occurrence of the bodily movement. Thus, given Aristotle's account of causal explanation, there will be a set of physical processes (*ph*) which necessitate the occurrence of the bodily movement (*b.m.*). That is:

(1) O (*ph* in C) necessitates, in C*, O (*b.m.*),

where *b.m.* is the token bodily movement occurring in these particular circumstances. Thus one may write:

(2) O (*ph* in C) necessitates, in C*, O (*b.m.*).

Taking (0) and (2) together, we obtain:

(3) O (*ph* in C) necessitates, in C*, O (*a*).

Aristotle insisted that there being an action of this type necessitates the presence of an antecedent desire (see Chapter 2, Section D). Thus he adds:

(4) O (*a*) necessitates O (*p.s.*),

where '*p.s.*' denotes that psychological state of desire. Taking (3) and (4) together we obtain:

(5) O (*ph* in C) necessitates, in C*, O (*p.s.*).

The occurrence of these physical states in these circumstances necessitates the occurrence of this desire.

Aristotle also holds that the desire is an efficient cause of the bodily movement (*b.m.*) by means of a physical mechanism (433b21–22). Desire for revenge has a physical realisation in terms of the surging of the blood and heat around the heart (e.g. 403b1–2). In *de Motu* (703a10ff.) the heart (and the physical innate spirit there situated) plays a crucial role in the function of producing bodily movement by pushing and pulling – as this contains the requisite degree of heat and heaviness. The bodily substance (703a7) which stands to desire as potentiality to actuality, is capable of increasing and decreasing in size, since such increases and decreases cause the movement of an animal's limbs. Similarly in 701b13–16, certain physical quality and quantity changes are said to be produced by heat and cold which co-occur with the operation of desire (701b33–55) and to play a role in producing the bodily movement.

Leaving on one side the (occasionally bizarre) details of Aristotle's physical theory, the picture he presents is of psychological conditions (desire) and physical conditions both being causes (efficient) of the bodily movements which constitute actions. He now has to explain what relation obtains between the physical and psychological phenomena if both are to play such a role.

His style of argument also appears to lead to some version of ontological materialism in the following way: the movement of the body which is sufficient for the action has both physical and psychological efficient causes. But the bodily movement is not overdetermined by two independent causes; for, if the desire is necessary and the physical antecedents sufficient for its occurrence, the occurrence of desire and physical antecedents cannot (plausibly) constitute two separate causes which (by chance) happen to co-occur and produce the same result. Hence the desire and physical antecedents cannot be independent of one another.

Neither of these sets of considerations, however, forces ontological materialism on us. Take the second set first: the psychological might interact causally with the physical so that while both were necessary for the occurrence of the bodily movement, the bodily movement would not be overdetermined by two independent causes. For example:

(a) the psychological event might cause the physical event, which in turn causes the bodily movement;

(b) the physical event might cause the psychological event, which in turn causes the bodily movement;

(c) the physical and psychological events might stand in two-way immediate causal relations, and the physical event also cause the bodily movement;

(d) the physical and psychological events might have an immediate common cause (x) such that the only way in which they would not have occurred would have been if x had not occurred. If so, psychological states might be 'over and above' the physical states in a way inimical to ontological materialism.

Further, (b)–(d) would be compatible with the occurrence of the physiological event necessitating in C* the occurrence of the psychological event. So Aristotle requires further premisses for an argument for ontological materialism.

Desire is something which is in motion and causes movement (433b16–18): desire is a process of a given type. Either desire is a cause in which the soul moves itself or it is one in which it is moved by something else. But in 408a31–34 Aristotle writes:

> It is possible that the soul may be moved, and even move itself, *incidentally* (e.g. that which contains it may be moved – and that be moved by the soul); but in no other sense can it move in space.

The soul is moved or moves itself incidentally when what contains it is moved or moves essentially. The soul, like passengers at sea, is in motion incidentally only because what it belongs to (the physiological analogue of the ship: 406a2–12) is in motion essentially. The soul which is in motion in space is, like the passengers at sea, only in motion incidentally. If so, whether desire is a cause in which the soul moves itself or one in which it is moved by something else, it is in motion only incidentally, while that which contains it is moved essentially.[13]

The process of desire moves only incidentally in space, while that which contains it moves essentially in space. Therefore, if the process which moves the body (essentially) is one which itself occurs essentially in space, this cannot be desire but must be the process which contains it. Further, if the process which moves the body (essentially) is the one which is essentially in motion in space, this must be the process which 'contains' desire and cannot be desire itself.

---

[13] Aristotle notes in 408a31–34 that what contains the soul may itself be moved by the soul. In such a case, however, the part of the soul which moves it (if it is itself in movement) will either move itself or be moved by something else. Yet – if one applies the principle of 408a31–34, this part too can only be in motion incidentally – as that which contains it moves essentially.

Spatial movement has four species: being dragged, pushed, spun or pulled (243b14–18). In the case of bodily spatial movement (433b26–27; 703a7–10), the relevant types of movement are being pushed and being pulled. Hence the mover must have power and strength (703a7–10) and this is supplied by the 'connate pneuma'. Of this Aristotle writes:

> It is obviously well disposed by nature to impart movement and supply strength. The functions of movement are pushing and pulling, so the relevant mechanism has to be capable of expanding and contracting. This is just the nature of the pneuma: it expands and contracts without constraint, and is able to push and pull for the same reason; and it has weight by comparison with the fiery, and lightness by comparison with its opposite. Whatever is going to impart motion without itself undergoing a quantity change *must* be of this type ... We have said what the part is in virtue of whose motion the soul imparts motion and what the reason is. (703a18–29 – with one gap)

The mover which pushes and pulls does so by expanding and contracting. What expands and contracts moves in space (essentially), and is in motion in space (essentially). Desire only expands and contracts in the way in which it moves in space: incidentally, in virtue of that part which contains it and itself expands and contracts essentially – the connate pneuma. If so, Aristotle is correct to conclude that the soul moves the body in virtue of a physiological part which is fitted by nature for its task: the pneuma which has spatial extension and itself contracts and expands.

What imparts movement in this case has weight (703a23) as well as extension. What has weight and extension has spatial magnitude and thus is (essentially) in space.[14] What has extension and spatial magnitude is essentially divisible into smaller parts (702b30ff.: cf. Nussbaum 1978, ad loc.; 433b20–27); but the soul, and psychological phenomena in general, are distinct from spatial magnitudes of this type, though located in them (703a1–3). The soul, that is, is a formal unity, which is a 'ratio and potentiality' of the extended subject, but is not itself extended (compare 424a28–30) essentially. If so, the soul (desire) cannot be the essential mover, since that is something which (essentially) has bulk and extension.

---

[14] Aristotle appears to construe being a body as equivalent to having spatial extension (cf. 268a14). 'Physical' is sometimes characterised as 'having in it the source of movement' (1059b18; 1064a15; 304b14). This may be explained as follows in the light of Aristotle's treatment of what (essentially) imparts motion: it must have weight and extension itself (non-derivatively), and be essentially physical. This account of the physical puts into clearer focus some of Aristotle's remarks on the relation of the soul and the body in his general definition: 412b16–18; 'the soul is the essence of ... a certain kind of physical object which has in itself a principle of ... movement.' In this sense the connate *pneuma* is physical, even though its physical nature is distinctive (703a25–27; cf. 700b30ff.).

Thus the physical movement of the body is caused by desire incidentally only because desire is located in a physical state which is in motion in space essentially and has the attributes required (expansion and magnitude) to cause the body to move. That is, desire is in movement only incidentally as the physical base in which it is located expands and contracts; but it is *qua* expanding and contracting that desire causes (incidentally) physical movement by pushing and pulling. It is because desire is only in motion incidentally that it causes movement incidentally; for the essential mover is that which is essentially moved, since it is *qua* expanding and contracting that the mover brings about the requisite physical changes (pushing/pulling).

Two consequences follow. If physical effects (such as bodily movements) require essential physical causes, then: (1) Desire cannot be a cause of bodily movement unless it is enmattered in some physical state which necessitates the bodily movement as its essential cause. Thus any psychological state which causes a bodily movement must be enmattered in some physical state. Such psychological states then have to be enmattered.[15] (2) The four cases (a)–(d) envisaged above as ones which avoid over-determination without commitment to ontological materialism all require that a psychological event be an essential cause of a physical event. If physical effects require essential physical causes, then none of these cases is possible within Aristotle's theory. If so, Aristotle cannot avoid overdetermination or allow for the physical events to necessitate the occurrence of the desire by any of the causal structures (a)–(d), since each would run contrary to his thesis that physical effects must have essential physical causes. Hence the physical events must non-causally necessitate the occurrence of the desire; for if this necessitation were causal, Aristotle would also need to avail himself of one of the causal structures (b)–(d), contrary to his thesis.

It seems that the only way in which desire can be a causally necessary condition for the occurrence of the bodily movement and be necessitated by the occurrence of a set of physical states compatible with (a) the relevant physical event necessitating the bodily movement, (b) there being no over-determination, and (c) physical effects having essential physical causes, is for the physical state to be non-causally sufficient for the occurrence of the psychological state. Aristotle,

---

[15] Any psychological state which does not itself cause a physical/bodily movement need not be necessarily enmattered; for only states with these causal powers need be. However, this does not imply that ontological materialism is false in the case of any state which is not necessarily enmattered; for it is possible that physical states in any given situation are non-causally sufficient for the presence of the relevant psychological state in question, even though that state itself is not *in essence* enmattered as it does not itself play a physical causal role. Thus, that it is not *in essence* enmattered does not entail that Aristotle rejects ontological materialism.

therefore, must (it appears) be an ontological materialist in his treatment of desire.

(2) *Aristotle's version of ontological materialism*

What version of ontological materialism did Aristotle hold? In our own day arguments of the type given above have usually been held to favour some version of the identity theory: Dennett (once) took it to establish a variety of type/type identity while (more recently) Peacocke construed it as establishing a version of token/token identity.[16]

Desire itself is a process (433b16–17) *qua* actualisation of a given disposition. So clearly is the surging of the blood around the heart (403a29ff.; 702b13–32). Hence the relation between desire and the surging of the blood depends on Aristotle's account of process (and state) identity given in the *Physics* (III 1–3; V 1–4). In order to grasp Aristotle's version of ontological materialism, we need to use as a premiss his account of the identity of processes.

This account[17] yielded the following identity conditions:

$x = y$ iff
(1) x's and y's species of process are identical (i.e. same in analytic or scientific definition);

(2) $(\forall t)$ (x is at t iff y is at t);

(3) $(\forall s)$ (s is x's essential subject of change iff s is y's essential subject of change).

So, applying this to the case at point, is the process of desire identical with the process of blood surging round the heart (a physiological specification), i.e. is it either type or token identical with a physically specified process?

Two species of process cannot be the same in analytic or scientific definition if one occurs without the other. Thus, if there is a case of desiring without the surging of blood, the two relevant species of process cannot be identical. If so, since particular processes are only identical if they share identical species, no particular process of desiring can be identical with any particular process of the surging blood.

Aristotle's investigation (empirical) of varying kinds of animals led him to conclude that psychological processes such as desire could have varying kinds of physical realisations. Animals with and without blood

---

[16] Dennett 1969, 1ff. Peacocke, 1979, 134ff.

[17] Chapter 1, Section B; see Appendix 1. The argument here rests on the identity conditions for processes given above, together with the premiss that desire is a process (433b18–19) as the realisation of a disposition (433b1–3 etc.) of the appropriate type.

have different physical structures which enmatter sensation (681b15–17, 33, 647a25–34; 455b29–34, 456a10ff.). Fear affects the physical bases of different animals differently (679a25ff.), the perception of pleasure is realised in different physical types of animals (661a8–10). Desire, in warm-blooded animals, involves heating and cooling of the heart (702a2ff.; 647a26), while in *bloodless* animals it involves contraction and expansion in the part of their physical structure which corresponds to the heart (456a10ff.; 703a14ff.). Hence, given that these psychological states are common to different types of animal with different physical bases, it is not possible to identify the psychological type with any individual physico-chemical type.

Thus, while for the reasons given *being physically realised* is part of the definition of *desire*, this is not a 'natural kind term' if these always denote something with one underlying physico-chemical state. Further, since within Aristotle's account of process-identity, difference in species of process spells difference in particular process, no particular process of desiring can be identical with any particular process of the surging blood (physico-chemical state). Hence Aristotle held neither type nor token identity of mental and physical processes.[18]

So what is the relation of these mental and physical events in Aristotle's theory?

Aristotle uses the following relations to explicate the connection of physical process and relevant mental state:

matter: form (403a29–b2);
potentiality: actuality (433b16–17; 703a15–22).

In *Physics* III 3 Aristotle characterises the relation of 'the same . . . but different in essence' between processes in these terms (202b9–10, 20–22, 25–27: see Chapter 1, Section B: Appendix 1). This we interpreted as follows: two processes (z and y) stand in this relation iff

(1) z and y occur at the same time and in the same substance;
(2) z and y begin and end at the same extensionally specified point;
(3) z and y share the same underlying process,

where w is an underlying process relative to z iff

(1) and (2) as above, and
(3)' the occurrence of w (in C*) necessitates the occurrence of z.

This relation is transitive, reflexive and symmetrical, but is not identity. Since it is an equivalence relation, Aristotle's ontological

---

[18] This leaves open the possibility that desire might be identical with a functional state of the organism: a state identified by reference to its causal role in the organism. Desire (like breathing: see Chapter 1, Section B) might be a functional natural kind (see Section C and D).

materialism might be characterised as *'equivalence class materialism'*.[19]

In this account the occurrence of the underlying process (in C* – or with that physical specification) necessitates the occurrence of the psychological process. But – as in the case of premisses and conclusion – the relation is one-way; that is, just as a given conclusion can follow from more than one set of premisses, so a given whole could (it might be argued) actually have been constituted by different parts – and, in the case of psychological states, a given psychological state could actually have been constituted by different physical processes. Thus, in the case of blooded and bloodless animals, a particular psychological process (*that* very token) could have had different physical constituents depending on whether it occurred in cold- or warm-blooded animals. While the physical events in the circumstances necessitate the occurrence of that psychological event, the psychological event does not itself necessitate the occurrence of that physical event.

The significant features of this account are twofold:

(a) While Aristotle held that the mental process had to be physically enmattered, he did not identify the relevant mental and physical process. In this way his version of ontological materialism is independent of the truth or falsity of token or type identity. Hence, it is no part of his account of their relation that there is one process which has both mental and physical properties. He requires only that the occurrence of the physical state in those conditions makes it the case that there is a mental event of a given kind.[20]

(b) The equivalence class is distinguished from a set of merely chance co-occurring events by the relation of necessitation between the underlying process and the other process (or processes). The necessitation in question is distinguished by Aristotle from efficient causation, since it occurs in the same objects at the same time and does not involve the transfer of energy (pushing/pulling) which characterises efficient causation. However, as yet, no positive character-

---

[19] See Chapter 1, Sections B and C. This relation plays a general role in Aristotle's account of processes which mirrors that of the 'is' of constitution in discussing substances. Aristotle draws this parallel explicitly in 412b6–9, where he notes that this yields a basic sense of 'oneness' (which explains why it is senseless to ask if the body and soul are one). See for a contrasting view, Putnam, 1980, vol. 2, 302–3.

[20] This liberates Aristotle from the need to show how (e.g.) a particular thought can be identical with a particular physical state when (it appears plausible that) it is an essential property of the former, but not the latter, that it has a given content. That is, difficulties for either version of the identity theory do not undermine ontological materialism provided that it is possible to account for the non-causal dependence between physical and psychological states. See Section E. If so, arguments from the difference in essential property between mental and physical states can only undermine Aristotelian materialism if they are shown to challenge the *possibility* of an explanatory connection between physical and mental states.

isation of this relation has been given; indeed, on occasion, Aristotle appears to regard it as a basic relation (see Section E).

Aristotle uses the terminology of 'the same but different in essence' to explicate the relation of a psychological process and attendant physiological state. Thus in 424a25–28 'perceiving', which is characterised as a potential activity of the extended sentient organ,[21] is represented as standing to the extended physical state in this relation, since predicates true of the physical state (e.g. having extension) are not true of perceiving (which lacks extension). Therefore these two cannot be numerically identical; rather they exemplify the equivalence relation.

Since the relation expressed in 424a25–28 is the Aristotelian matter/form relation, one may detect the relation:

matter   :   form
potentiality   :   actuality, activity

obtaining between processes which are 'the same but different in essence': for example, in the case of

the surging of the blood   :   desire (*de Motu* 703a15–22;
around the heart   701b13–16; 33–35)
change in physical state   :   perception (424a25–26)

Thus, if this account were to be generalised to all psychological processes which were antecedents of action for Aristotle, we could derive the following picture of their ontological relation:

Model I

Psychological token events:

Physiological token events:

$$\begin{pmatrix} a \\ z \end{pmatrix} \rightarrow \begin{pmatrix} b \\ y \end{pmatrix} \rightarrow \begin{pmatrix} c \\ x \end{pmatrix} \rightarrow \begin{pmatrix} d \\ w \end{pmatrix}$$

where a is this perceiving, b the operation of imagination, c this desiring, and d the resultant action; at the physiological level z would represent the movement in the 'sentient organ', y would be a change in 'the imagining organ', x would be the surging of blood round the heart which attends 'desiring' and w the resultant movement of the body. In Model I a and z would be members of one equivalence class as defined above but would not be numerically identical. (The arrows represent causal connexions: see below.)

Model I, however, does not utilise the full expressive power of 'equivalence class' materialism. Elsewhere Aristotle's account suggests a more complex model. In 427a14–16 there is one faculty which is potentially that of judging but which, in activity, may judge of two different objects at the same time. Hence a physical state (or

---

[21] As interpreted by Rodier and Ross ad loc.

movement) which is one in potentiality may be several in entelechy, and hence several in essence if the entelechies are differentiated by the distinct objects of judgment. Thus there is one underlying physical state which is related to two distinct psychological states (427a4–5). As such, the three related states may be specified as 'the same but different in essence'; for although numerically distinct they are based in one underlying physical state and occur at the same time. If so, in this passage there is a one-many relation (as allowed by the equivalence relation) between physical and psychological processes.

Aristotle appears to use the same structure in discussing the interconnection of imagination and desire. In *de Anima* and *de Motu*, Aristotle holds three theses about their interconnexion:

(1) It is not possible that there is intentional action and not both imagination and desire;
(2) It is not possible that there is intentional action and imagination and not desire;
(3) It is not possible that there is intentional action and desire and not imagination.[22]

In *de Motu*, imagination 'prepares' desire, which stands to it as 'patient' to 'agent' (702a18–21); but, as above, the agent/patient relation obtains – as in the case of teaching and learning – between processes which are 'the same but different in essence': members of one equivalence class. The product of imagination is the object of desire (433b12ff.; 701b34–35) which is itself unmoved but causes movement when desired: the object of desire is what is accepted by desire when movement results. Hence there are two processes: imagining that a given state is desirable and desiring it, which are inseparable and occur at the same time and place in the organism. That is, there is one physical magnitude (702b29–35) which stands to the distinct processes as potential to actualisation. Thus the two processes are different in definition, but inseparable in that they are realised in the same physical state (a given quality state: 701b13–26). If so, they share one underlying physiological process, to which they stand in the equivalence relation. Hence they are to be construed as 'the same but different in essence', and thus as members of one equivalence class together with the underlying quality change.

If this is correct, Aristotle's picture of the ontological relation of the antecedents of action is as follows:

Model II

Psychological token events $\begin{pmatrix} a \\ z \end{pmatrix} \rightarrow \begin{pmatrix} b,c \\ y \end{pmatrix} \rightarrow \begin{pmatrix} d \\ w \end{pmatrix}$

Physiological token events

---

[22] The relevant evidence for (1) and (3) is 433a10–11, b29–31; *de Motu* 702a16–17. The evidence for (2) is 433a11–25, b29.

where *b* and *c* are the processes of imagination and desire which are caused by perception *a* and result in the basic action *d* (*poiêsis*), and *y* is the physiological process which underlies *b* and *c* and *w* the body's being moved (*pathêsis*). Hence there is a one-many relation between the relevant physiological process and the psychological events which constitute imagining and desiring. If so, since imagining and desiring are distinct psychological processes, and since there is no psychological process which is represented by Aristotle as including desiring and imagining as parts,[23] Aristotle cannot hold any version of the identity thesis between physical and psychological events. Rather he is employing his favoured ontological structures to develop a less rigid form of ontological materialism than is favoured by the identity theorist. All that Aristotle requires is that the relevant physical states *make it the case* that the organism is in the psychological states thus characterised; either form of identity theory is a more ambitious version of ontological materialism than the one which Aristotle embraces.

The flexibility of his account emerges elsewhere when he allows that several physical processes may enmatter one psychological process: the relevant internal organs may both heat and expand when (e.g.) S desires to φ (701b10–18: 702a4–8). Since becoming hot and expanding are different species (as the former is a quality change, the latter an increase), the processes must be distinct. If both enmatter a given psychological state, there is a many-to-one relation between the physical and the psychological in such cases which corresponds to the one-to-many relation discerned above. In such cases the equivalence relation will be defined by the set of physical processes sufficient for the relevant psychological process. Hence in two contrasting ways Aristotle's version of ontological materialism is more flexible than contemporary accounts which rely on an identity claim. Since the cases he specifies seem at least conceivable, the flexibility of his theory appears a definite advantage. Contrary to one current in contemporary theory, he shows that denial of either form of the identity thesis does not by itself spell the falsity of ontological materialism. The ontological elements marked out at the different levels need not match one another either by being token identical or parts of a whole which are token identical; for since they are parts of distinct explanatory accounts, there is no general necessity that the units thus selected

---

[23] He represents them as standing in external relations to one another: see *Meta.* 1072a29ff.; 433b15–17; 702a16–19. In such a case the relevant relation would be dependent on the presence of a given physical state, and would not require a difference in underlying physical states. Compare Wittgenstein's remark: 1967, 610ff: 'Why should there not be a psychological regularity to which no physiological regularity corresponds? If this upsets our concept of causality, it is high time it was upset . . . The prejudice in favour of psycho-physical parallelism is a fruit of primitive interpretations of our concepts. For if one allows a causality between psychological phenomena, which is not mediated physiologically, one thinks one is professing a belief in a gaseous mental entity.'

should coincide in these ways. More positively, Aristotle's version of ontological materialism suggests that materialism requires in the case of desire only (a) that desire is necessarily enmattered in some physical state, and (b) the occurrence of given physical states necessitates (non-causally) the occurrence of certain specific psychological states. Materialism appears to require no more than this. Indeed for those psychological states which do not cause (and are not caused by) physical movements only (b) is required.

Aristotle's espousal of the equivalence relation to articulate the relation of mental and physical processes allows him to accept many of the premises of two arguments which are taken to lead to some version of the identity theory without accepting the conclusion. Thus Aristotle could accept both:[24]

(a) Mental events cannot be the causes of bodily movements unless they are (in some sense) physical events, and

(b) At least one of the psychological events (a, b, c) is related to at least one of the physical events (z, y) in such a way that (e.g.) had z not occurred, a would not have occurred,

without holding that any psychological process is token identical with any physical process. In his theory, the sense of oneness characterised in (a), and the dependence specified in (b), would both be captured by the equivalence relation, which represents (e.g.) particular desires and physical processes as distinct members of an equivalence class. If this is acceptable, his ontology will account for the relation of mental and physical processes and states in a systematic and attractive way (in Chapter 1, Section C, this was the third *desideratum* for an adequate ontological theory).

The central issue raised by Aristotle's version of ontological materialism is clear: is the form of non-causal sufficiency he advocates defensible? To this we will return in Section E after considering in more detail Aristotle's positive characterisation of desire and its role in a psychological (or psycho-physical) causal explanatory story. In Section A it was assumed (on the basis of Chapter 4) that Aristotle employed psychological states in causal explanation. This section supports that assumption. Aristotle's argument for ontological materialism required only that desire be a cause, and that the action could not occur without desire; it did not demand that desire be causally explanatory (an essential cause) of the action. However, if Aristotle held that desire is non-identical with any (particular) physical state and that a process can only be a cause if there are descriptions of it which may be placed in an explanatory scheme (see Chapter 1, Section D), desire can only be a cause if it (appropriately described) is part of an explanatory schema. Hence Aristotle must have held that psychologi-

---

[24] See, for example, Dennett, 1969, 3; Peacocke, 1979, 134ff.

cal states (under some psychological description) are causally explanatory (the essential causes) of actions, while physical states (under physical descriptions) causally explain bodily movements. This places severe demands on his account of desire; to these we must now turn.

C.   Aristotle's non-reductionist materialism (2): functionalism and psycho-physical causal explanation

Aristotle's theory treats desires and preferential choice as elements in a causal explanatory theory, together with the practical reasoning on which the latter rests. This explanatory pattern rests on the agent's acceptance in the relevant mode of the propositions which appear in his practical reasoning. Aristotle's use of the practical syllogism reflects this phenomenon: it is because of the content of the propositions which constitute it that the agent acts as he does, when he accepts them appropriately. What is distinctive of psychological explanation in his account is that it essentially involves the content of the propositions the agent accepts and his attitude towards them.[25]

Aristotle's theory commits him to several distinctive consequences: (a) to a realism about the psychological features which play a role in his causal explanatory account – desires and their propositional content; and (b), since desires play a role in Aristotle's psychological theory in virtue of their content, to a content-based psychological theory in which the semantical features of propositions play an ineliminable role. The rational agent acts as he does because his action is justified (in his eyes) by reasoning from his valued goals which comprise (e.g.) his picture of well-being.

Can Aristotle's theory of the relevant mental states be developed in detail? (a) and (b) place considerable constraints on a theory of mental states; they require nothing less than an account of the relevant mental states and their content, which shows how it is possible for them to play a role in a causally explanatory theory. For present purposes, it will be more than enough to consider only Aristotle's account of desire and its role; but a full examination would demand elucidation of his theory of imagination, thought and perception as well.

Had Aristotle defined desire to φ as being in a state which causes φ'ing if nothing intervenes (or in a more complex way by reference to its input/output conditions),[26] then he could not have held consistently

---

[25] See Chapter 2, Section C: Chapter 4, Sections A–E. Fodor (1978) adopts a similar view of psychological explanation. He correctly describes the relevant condition as 'Aristotelian'.

[26] See Lewis, 1966 and 1972. For present purposes, it is sufficient to characterise functionalism as the view that the constitutive properties of a given mental state can be defined by reference to its causal role in the explanation of the organism's behaviour. The characterisation is independent of whether mental states are realised by physical states, or whether the causal role is specified in non-mental terms.

that desires themselves play a role in a (psychological or psycho-physical) causal explanatory theory. If it is a condition that elements in such a theory are connected *a posteriori*, then if (e.g.) desires are implicitly defined by their explanatory connexion to action, they cannot (it appears) themselves play a role in a causal explanatory theory, as, thus characterised, they are not connected with their explanandum in a causal explanatory way. Nor is the position fundamentally altered if Aristotle had held that the essence of desire was its causal explanatory role; for since the connexion between the fundamental specification of desire and the explanandum would be *a priori*, it would be difficult to hold that desires themselves play a causal explanatory role.[27]

This difficulty points to a watershed in current discussions of the explanatory role of psychological states. On one side, some are drawn to the idea that desires and beliefs are themselves part of a causal explanatory theory, and thus require an account of desire which allows it to play such a role. However, rarely (if at all) does one find a detailed spelling out of the required concept.[28] On the other side, some accept mental states as implicitly defined by their role in an explanatory theory, and conclude from this that the (psychological) explanatory theory cannot itself be a causal one since it is not *a posteriori*. Hence they are constrained to discern and develop a distinctive conception of explanation which holds at the psychological level and which can be integrated with the conception of desire they adopt.[29]

Aristotle developed through his theory of teleological explanation an account of the way in which mental states (via their content) can play an explanatory role which is *a priori*; but this rested on an *a posteriori* causal explanatory theory of desire and rationality (see Section A). Hence his account presupposes an account of desire which is such that it can stand in a causal explanatory theory of this type. If he failed to articulate such an account, his theory is without basis; if desire is in his account *a priori* connected with the explanandum, his theory is inconsistent. Aristotle was represented as holding in Chapter 2 the following account of desire;

S desires to φ iff

---

[27] Putnam construes functionalism as a scientific (and presumably *a posteriori*) hypothesis about the nature of mental states (1980, vol. 2, xiii) and attributes this view to Aristotle (ibid., xiv). See also Kathleen Wilkes, 1978, ch. 7.

[28] David Pears appears to be an exception. He notes that for certain mental states (e.g. desires) there are two 'criteria' for their presence: the agent's sincere statement and his doing the appropriate action (1971, 148ff.). His account, however, is concerned only with the criteria for ascribing a mental state and not with the nature of the state itself.

[29] Peacocke (1979, 179ff.) attempts to do this by employing holistic constraints on the psychological, but it is not clear that this account satisfactorily articulates the explanatory role of the psychological. On this, see Lennon, 1982 and forthcoming.

(1) S accepts the proposition that φ'ing is good in the way appropriate if one's aim is doing what is good; and
(2) S is in a state which causes φ'ing if nothing intervenes.

Subsequently clause (1) has been employed to show how causal and
teleological explanation are compatible, and to give an account of the
analogy between practical and theoretical reasoning. (Chapter 4, Sections D, E.)

This account of desire contains one element which allows for an *a
posteriori* connexion with action (clause (1)) and one element (clause
2)) which suggests the functionalist account which renders an explanatory link of this type problematical. Clause (1) allows for *a posteriori*
connexions with action if the mode of acceptance appropriate if one's
aim is doing what is good can be explained without reference to its
role as causally explanatory of behaviour. Thus what is required is an
account of the ingredients of clause (1) which does not tie them directly
with action. Also, one needs an account of how the two clauses cohere,
and which (if either) is essential.

Within clause (1) Aristotle emphasises the goal-directedness of desire; this suggests that desire may be (at least partially) defined by
reference to its goal (the good) and not by its role in a causally explanatory theory (see also 403a31ff.; 414a14–16, where final causes
give the essence of psychological phenomena). Value is also introduced
by Aristotle into his theory of the rational agent, as this employs
valuational goals as final causes in its account of his relevant discriminating capacity, his grasp on his well-being and his integration of the
relevant motivational states with that picture of well-being. This introduction of valuational terms into the account of psychological states
affects Aristotle's theory of the role they play in causal explanation
and his view of their nature (and reducibility). Let us take the question
of their nature first, as this makes possible their explanatory role.

If the valuational goals cannot be reduced, the psychological states
defined by means of them also resist reduction. Thus Aristotle would
hold an irreducible concept of rationality dependent on the goals and
distinctive capacities of the rational agent (e.g. to discriminate what
contributes to well-being). The irreducibility of psychological concepts
(thus construed) would depend on the irreducibility of the valued
teleological goals of those states. For Aristotle, desire and belief would
not be irreducible because they fit into a certain distinctive rational
pattern of explanation,[30] but because, *qua* members of a teleological

---

[30] Put in a slogan: Aristotelian irreducibility depends on the concepts in terms of
which desire is defined (goodness/well-being), and not on the absence of psycho-physical
causal explanation. Certain psychological processes are defined in terms of their role in
a teleological (and perhaps causal) pattern (the *form*), where the former is not reducible
to *matter*. This view stands in sharp contrast to modern anti-reducers for whom the
failure of reduction springs from the impossibility of psycho-physical causal explanation
(see Davidson, 1980).

system, they are defined (in part) by their role in promoting the valued goals of the organism, and hence possess a feature (the consequential value which this bestows on them) which is lacked by any state which is not thus defined. Since physical states are not defined in this way in Aristotle's account (although the states thus specified are appropriate for the mental states, they are not defined directly in terms of the teleological goal),[31] they lack the value which constitutes the psychological teleological system. Therefore psychological states could only be fully explained in physical terms if the value system which defines the former could be shown to be reducible.

Aristotle seeks to resist the possibility of this type of reduction. Thus he rejects the attempt to reduce well-being to a certain description of man's distinctive psychological functioning, since he defines psychological states (such as perception of varying types: 435b19ff.; 434b25; 434a30ff.) as involving the well-being of the organism. If the psychological capacities necessary for life are thus defined (in part) by their role in the teleological system which has *well-being* as its goal, one could not hope to specify neutrally the relevant psychological states and then to define well-being in terms of their characteristic or successful functioning; for within Aristotle's account, their characteristic functioning is itself defined by reference to well-being.

Nor is he prepared to reduce the concept of well-being to a certain mode of accepting propositions about well-being: (e.g.) to deeply entrenched desires which one would never surrender (easily) *or* to desires towards which one has a further relevant desire (e.g. if one desires to desire it). For Aristotle, our desiring to ϕ rests on finding ϕ good (1072a29ff.); hence what is distinctive about our concern with well-being arises from the content of our thought, and not directly from the mode of desire itself. Since one may have second-order desires for reasons other than their contribution to well-being, there is good ground not to reduce the concept of well-being to that of second-order desiring.

His type of irreducibility argument appears to be an instance of a more general claim: that the specification of what it is to be in a given psychological state depends on concepts (e.g. value, truth, reference) which are distinctive of systems of a given kind, and not applicable to physical organisms. Desire cannot be reduced if it is defined as a mode

---

[31] The surging of the blood may be fitting for – i.e. sufficient for – the presence of desire in an organism of given type k, but it does not follow from this that it is defined in terms of the teleological goals which define desire (i.e. the good: well-being). This exemplifies the Aristotelian hierarchy of mode of specification: at higher levels (e.g., the psychological) there are entities whose essential properties reflect the teleological goals of the organism; at lower levels there are entities whose essential properties reflect their role in ensuring the presence of higher order entities (e.g. desire), but not the teleological goals by which these are defined. If concepts should be defined by their role in a teleological system only if they are always necessary for its presence, Aristotle had good ground for defining only desire (and not the surging blood) in this way because he accepted the empirical argument for variable realisation.

of accepting a proposition with well-being (or doing good) as its aim. The irreducibility of value within a teleological system is a general feature of Aristotle's biological writings: the underlying physical structure may determine what higher-order states are present in the organism, but the nature of these states is clarified by reference to their teleological goals (703a34–36; 658b4–10; 663b22ff.; 673a32ff.). Thus the state of man having the most hairy head of all animals is due to the underlying physical structure of the brain and skull, but is also explained by its role in protecting the head and securing the survival and well-being of the organism (656a5ff.): in promoting a good. In such cases,[32] there is a mode of explaining the phenomenon which is distinct from upwards necessitation by the physical base. However, what is distinctive of Aristotle's treatment of psychological states such as desire and rationality is that they are essentially *defined* as aiming at *the good* or *well-being*.[33] It is not just that their presence is explained teleologically, but that their essence (*qua* processes of a given kind) is connected in definition with teleological concepts of this type. In the case of desire, this encapsulates two intrinsic features which distinguish his account from one which defines it only by its causal role in the organism: (a) its interconnexion with value; (b) its essential directedness on to that value. Since desire is defined as a mode of accepting a proposition if one's aim is to do what is good, Aristotle resists a purely functionalist account because his account of desire possesses these two value-directed elements which are not captured (in this theory) by the causal role of desire (see Section D).

But what of the notion of 'acceptance' itself? Can this be characterised without reference to action-production? Consider the practical syllogism:

ψ'ing is good
φ'ing is a way to ψ
———————————
φ'ing is good

This inference (see Appendix 3) is not deductively valid (within Aristotle's logical system), and rests on a principle particular to desire: *if* one desires to ψ, and believes φ'ing is a way to ψ, *then*, other things

---

[32] Other examples would be 642a31b4; 642a14–17; 776b32–4; 640b23–30; 687a5ff; 755a18; 663a27–33, b22–24; 640a35ff.

[33] Through their connection with *well-being* these psychological concepts are irreducible in a manner distinct from that which characterises other functionally defined organisms: e.g. thermostats. Psychological states may differ from their biological counterparts in that in their case the good and the apparent good may play a similar role, while the actual good is required for teleological explanation in biology. For sceptical doubts about the latter, see Woodfield, 1976. This is not (of course) an attempt to give an Aristotelian criterion of the mental or the psychological, but to differentiate various types of teleological explanation and kinds of irreducibility argument.

being equal, one desires to φ. The connexion between the content of the relevant propositions is mediated by a special feature of desire, which explains why the conclusion is validly inferred from the premises, and why it represents φ'ing as good. The former point is central for our present purposes, since the inferential connexions special to the practical syllogism may be used to mark out one distinctive feature of desire. It is this which focuses on to the goodness of the proposed course, and transmits the relevant value from premisses to conclusion in a way separate from that of belief. Thus the mode of acceptance characteristic of desire has as special features (not *a priori* connected with action) the distinctive inferential patterns involving the good/well-being which it articulates. These Aristotelian connexions tie desire *a priori* with goodness and the pattern of justification based on that concept, and not it with action. In this way the presence of states defined by their role (or potential role) in practical reasoning (of the type outlined in Chapter 4, Sections D and E) allows for the possibility of an *a posteriori* explanation of action.

The second clause in the definition of desire requires that S desires to φ only if S is in a state which causes φ'ing if nothing intervenes, and thus ties desire *a priori* with action. Thus the two clauses (as they stand) locate desire within two distinct types of theory. Clause (1) situates desire within a *justificatory (teleological) schema* involving S's aim to do what is good; and analyses it as accepting a judgment which, if justified, is justified by its connexions with S's final goals (well-being) within a system of practical reasoning of the distinctive type discussed in Chapters 3 and 4. Clause (2), by contrast, locates desire within an *explanatory schema* in which desire is defined as a factor that leads to action if nothing intervenes. In modern terminology, the account of desire brings together two distinct senses of being a *reason for action*; in the first, reason is tied to the *justification* of action, in the second, to the *explanation* of action. Justification shows desire to be conceptually connected with well-being and practical reasoning; explanation suggests a conceptual connexion with action. It is because for Aristotle the first sense is basic that he does not represent the rational explanation of action as a full account of its antecedents (Chapter 3, Section D; Chapter 5, Section A).

The presence of the justificatory connexions for a central class of desires suggests how they may play a role in the causal explanation of behaviour. There is no incoherence in representing the *acratês* as accepting that 'φ seems best' relative to this justificatory schema, and not acting on it, since the mode of acceptance is not (thus construed) connected *a priori* with *action*, but with S's practical reasoning and valued goods. The *acratês* accepts the conclusion of practical reasoning but does not act upon it. Because desire is conceptually connected with practical reasoning and S's valued goods, there is slack in the connection between desire and action which allows for the case of *acrasia* in which what is justified by practical reasoning is not what is done.

Thus the distinctive form of reasoning discussed in Chapter 3, Section C and Chapter 4, Sections D and E, provides the basis for an account of desire which can be used in giving an *a posteriori* causal explanation of action.

What then is the connexion between the explanatory and justificatory roles of desire? Why do they cohere as they do? Is the account of desire with these two distinct elements itself coherent?

One cannot, in Aristotle's theory, be in a state which leads to the intentional action of φ'ing and not think that φ'ing is good. Nor can we accept that φ'ing is good without being in a state which leads to intentional φ'ing (in appropriate conditions) because this acceptance is based on the agent's goals which are determined by his antecedent desires and express his desire for well-being. Aristotle holds that the two separate aspects of desire always co-occur: desire is the process which begins when we grasp that a given object is good and is what sets the body in motion to obtain it (if one acts intentionally). But how are they related? One suggestion is that desire just is a cluster-concept: clause (2) is required if the acceptance in the relevant mode is to be appropriate and lead to intentional action, but clause (1), by itself, is sufficient to specify desire when desire is used to explain (*a posteriori*) action. This account would have the advantage both of showing how desire can play a role in a genuinely *a posteriori* causal explanation, and of noting its *a priori* connexions with action. Aristotle, however, appears to take clause (1) as essential, and clause (2) as accidental, since clause (1) expresses the final cause which gives the essence of psychological phenomena and those that are (like desire) in motion because moved. In 1048a11ff. Aristotle does not claim that the causal role of desire is essential to it. His emphasis on the good-directedness of desire (clause (1)) allows him to locate desire (primarily) within a justificatory scheme and thus to treat it as *a posteriori* that desire (thus defined) is explanatory of action. If so, his definition of desire is given by clause (1) (cf. 431a8ff.), while clause (2) states a universally co-occurring but non-essential feature of desire. What is central, however, for an *a posteriori* account of the explanation of action is that *acceptance* as characterised in clause (1) is not itself defined by its role in causally explaining action but by its connexions with well-being and the content and inferential connexions between the propositions it accepts. It is because acceptance is specified in this way that it can causally explain intentional action.

Aristotle's definition of desire (clause (1)) in effect challenges the functionalist to show how these features of desire can be accommodated within his theory (see Section D); it also represents his attempt to develop a form of ontological materialism that allows for desire, value and goal-directedness to be irreducible and at the same time to play a role in an *a posteriori* causally explanatory account.

Aristotle's acceptance of these irreducibility claims places limitations on the extent to which the presence of given physical states can explain the relevant properties of psychological states; for while the relevant physical states may make it true that the organism is in a given psychological state, it does not explain what it is to be in a psychological state of that type, as that depends on its role in a teleological system of explanation.[34]

What is required, then, is an Aristotelian explanation of how it is that given physical states in the circumstances are sufficient for the relevant psychological states: desire and belief. Aristotle also needs to give an account of the content of the propositions thus accepted, and to explain how this can be determined by a set of physical states in given circumstances; for, thus far, we have considered only his account of what it is to accept a given proposition, and have not investigated his picture of what is thus accepted. Without an account of propositional content his theory is incomplete. But it would be undermined only if this account was itself determined by the role of content in explaining the agent's actions. Thus it appears a condition of adequacy for an Aristotelian theory of the content of the propositions that the latter be determined by semantical or referential features independent of their role in explaining the agent's behaviour. At very least it could not be a demand on the adequacy of such an account that it makes the agent optimally rational; for Aristotle's psychological theory allows for an explanatory account of how an agent may fail to achieve this (see Section A). However, the full development of this account calls on features which are central to Aristotle's semantical theory and lie outside the present study.

In the next section we will focus only on the way in which physical states may determine the agent's desire to φ and not on the proposition which he accepts *qua* desirer (see Chapter 2, Section C).

D. Preferred levels of explanation: the interconnexion of the distinct levels

Aristotle's account of psychological and physical processes integrates three levels of explanation with two distinct levels of entity (Sections A, B, C).

The particular physical and psychological processes are non-identical, but both are efficient causes of the bodily movement which is sufficient for the action, and the psychological processes are causes of

---

[34] Aristotle's irreducibility claims match in their emphasis on the *value-saturated* nature of mental states, Dennett's characterisation of the 'intentional stance of explanation'. (Dennett, 1975, 11–14). They differ, however, in two respects: (a) Aristotle does not view mental states, thus characterised, as being incompatible with causal explanation of intentional action; Dennett appears to conclude that the introduction of causal explanation compels one to surrender the intentional stance and with it the psychological states (desire, belief) which – together with rationality – constitute it; (b) Aristotle's teleological theory is not an idealisation, for it contains reference to the conditions under which the goal will not be achieved (see Section A).

actions which are necessitated by physical processes. These distinct causal stories are possible without overdetermination precisely because the particular psychological process is causally efficacious only *qua* enmattered in a given physical state which necessitates (upwards determination) the presence of that psychological state. In this account, this desiring and this surging blood are *both* causes, and this is permitted only because they stand in the matter/form relation (Section B).

Thus, there are two interconnected causal explanatory stories:

(A) *Psycho-physical causal schema.* S's desiring to ψ *qua* best and S's believing that ϕ'ing is the best way to ψ and S's having psychological/physical states $C_1 \ldots C_n$ and C* obtaining necessitate S's ϕ'ing.

where C* refer to the ability conditions, and states $C_1 \ldots C_n$ to these states of S in which S is rational and ϕ is the action.

(B) *Physical causal schema.* An organism of type k being in physical state W and C$m \ldots$ Cq obtaining necessitate that a bodily movement of type S results.

At the psychological level, there is also a teleological explanation which necessitates the action:

(C) *Teleological schema.* ψ'ing seeming best to S at t_1 and ϕ'ing being the best way to ψ and C* obtaining necessitate S's ϕ'ing.

But this schema rests on the presence of causal explanatory features of desire (Section A). Since desire is only causally efficacious if there is a causal explanatory story at the physical level (Section B), the teleological explanation of an action rests upon the *causal* explanation at the physical level. The three explanatory accounts tightly cohere; for since (for Aristotle) it is a necessary condition for the application of a teleological scheme of explanation that there is a psycho-physical causal account, and a necessary condition for that (see Section B) that there is a physical account, the occurrence in certain conditions of the relevant physical states necessitates the presence of these given mental states. That is, if what is essential for desire is its role in a teleological scheme, and this depends ultimately on a causal account involving physical states, those physical states in given conditions are sufficient for the presence of a state with that teleological role – even though they do not serve to explain the teleological role itself (see Section C).

Within Aristotle's ontological theory one may detect the following general type of account of the explanation of action:

Model III

$$\begin{array}{lll} \textit{Psychological Level (I)} & \begin{pmatrix} a \\ z,\, y \end{pmatrix} \rightarrow \begin{pmatrix} b \rightarrow c \\ x \end{pmatrix} \rightarrow \begin{pmatrix} d \\ w \end{pmatrix} & \text{action} \\ \textit{Physical Level (II)} & & \text{movement of the body} \end{array}$$

in which Level II processes are non-causally sufficient for the Level I processes in their equivalence class, and there is a physical causal explanation as well as a psycho-physical causal and teleological explanation. The interdependence of the distinct explanatory accounts requires that the psychological is determined by the underlying physical states.

Aristotle's theory raises several issues. Two are pressing:

(a) Which of the distinct explanatory accounts did Aristotle regard as preferable and why? This will show whether Aristotle was an explanatory materialist as well as an ontological materialist: one who believes that the only or best explanation for any state of affairs that can be explained will employ only physical vocabulary (see Section B). In Aristotle's favoured ontology, he would be an explanatory materialist only if he held that the only or best explanation was phrased with reference to the physical processes in the equivalence classes and used with the physical events as explananda and explanantia.

(b) How can the physical states of the organism be sufficient for psychological states with the properties of goal-directedness, intentionality and value connectedness specified in the previous section?

Aristotle shows a preference for psycho-physical causal and teleological explanation over physical explanation even though he cedes that causal generalisations at this level hold only 'for the most part' and do not issue in exceptionless generalisations. Thus he holds that desire is the 'essential cause' of intentional action (433b19–20, 28–29), and that the teleological explanation of phenomena given by (C) is preferable to physical explanation of the same data.[35] Hence, in contrast to modern materialist doctrine, Aristotle holds that the preferred mode of explanation is psycho-physical and not purely physicalist.

Preference for psycho-physical causal explanation does not follow from the irreducibility of the psychological. One might accept this, but maintain that the best explanatory schema was physicalist on independent grounds: because physicalist terms are non-dispositional or because they fall within one unified picture of all physical change or because they alone admit of universal exceptionless generalisations. A functionalist might accept, on the basis of Aristotle's claim that psychological states were goal-directed or had intentional content, that such states were irreducible, but argue that the preferred level of explanation involves (reducible) psychological states defined exclu-

---

[35] Examples of this preference fall within Aristotle's biological works: cf. 639b13ff.; 640b25ff.; 641a15f.; 642a16ff.; 646b24–30; 674a10ff.; 679a10ff.; 741b25; 776b30ff.

sively by their causal properties (see, for example, Dennett, 1979). Aristotle, therefore, required independent grounds for preferring (A) and (C) to (B) apart from his insistence on the irreducibility of the mental.

Aristotle suggests three lines of consideration to meet this challenge. The first is that Schemata (A) and (C) are couched in terms of the theory of rationality and well-being in terms of which we understand ourselves. It is these explanatory schemata that we must employ as long as we regard ourselves and man as rational.

This pragmatic ground for preferring (A) and (C) over (B) understates Aristotle's grounds: since he held that man was *essentially* rational, it is not a matter of choice for us to employ certain generalisations to explain human behaviour. It is these generalisations that we must employ as long as we are explaining *man's* behaviour, since he is essentially rational and aims at his well-being. Preferred Aristotelian explanations involve the essence of the objects under discussion, and are (thus) closer to the subject matter itself (87a31ff.). Proximity to the essence points to one type of superiority of psychological explanation which is compatible with the physical explanation being the more complete.

But how strong is Aristotle's ground for this preference? Rationality and well-being are essential to his account of practical knowledge (see Chapter 4, Section D), as a type of knowledge specific to (and incomprehensible without) these concepts. For Aristotle, the importance of practical knowledge is that it is an exception to the contention that all knowledge is part of a theory which comprehends (in principle) all phenomena (a *total* explanatory theory), because the terms which constitute it are inapplicable to physical phenomena. There can be no *one* type of knowledge which applies to both domains, as the concepts which define the domains are distinct. Practical knowledge is distinct from theoretical knowledge, and the information it gives us of ourselves and of others constitutes a ground for refusing to accept that all knowledge must be theoretical, and couched in purely physical terms.

But the argument is only permissive. What is required is ground for employing terms such as practical knowledge, desire and rationality within the preferred scheme of explanation. For some might be happy to give them up (and the interconnected account of the essence of man) in the hope of finding a more enlightening form of explanation at a different level. That we do use this schema of terms in our everyday understanding of ourselves would seem to them to be no more decisive than our everyday preference of talking of tables rather than of molecular structure or quarks (see Dennett, 1979).

Aristotle's account of the practical syllogism and his ontological theory provide two deeper motivations for his preference for psychophysical explanation.

The practical syllogism represents rationalising connexions

between propositions which are essential for the psycho-physical causal explanation of reasoned action. It is because the agent accepts the premisses that he accepts the conclusion and φ's (in appropriate circumstances) (see previous section). Thus, the relevant causal inter-connexions make ineliminable reference to the links between the prop-ositions (and their content) in the syllogism. The issue (for present purposes) is whether these connexions between the propositions, their content and the relevant mode of acceptance can be captured within (extensional) causal terms.

Aristotle's position is that they cannot be. The difficulty of the implicit challenge he offers to the reductionist can be illustrated by considering one recent attempt to account for desire and its proposi-tional content in the way suggested. Harty Field (1978) seeks to analyse desire as follows:

X desires that *p* iff there is some sentence (or sentence analogue) S, such that (a) X desires* S, and (b) S means that *p*,

where S consists of some set of items internal to the desirer which have functional properties sufficiently complex to be assigned se-mantical content, and desiring* is an extensionally characterisable relation to such items. Within this account the aim is to give an account of desiring* (regardless of the meaning of S) and to assign content to S independently of considering the function of desiring*; for (a) and (b) point to two distinct sub-problems which (it is claimed) once separated individually yield to extensional treatment.

Aristotle's account of desire and the syllogism gives ground for unease with this type of approach for two major reasons. Field char-acterises desiring* (in effect) as follows: 'I desire* a sentence of any language iff I am disposed to use that sentence in a certain way in reasoning, deliberating and so.' Aristotle is firmly set against this type of proposal by his insistence that to desire something is to accept a given proposition in the mode appropriate if one's aim is to do the good. For this requires that desire be characterised by its goal-direct-edness towards doing the good, and also that the propositions accepted by desire represent the given object as good. These internal connexions explain why only certain propositions are thus accepted by desire (e.g. as conclusions of practical reasoning, *x* is best, good) and why desire is directed towards good actions. To delete them might yield a concept extensionally equivalent with desire, but not one which has the ex-planatory value characteristic of desire.

There is a second difficulty: can content be assigned to S indepen-dently of the concept of desire? In the syllogism,

ψ'ing is good
φ'ing is a way to ψ
———————
φ'ing is good

a principle of desire is required to explain why φ'ing is good given the premisses. This explains why the conclusion is validly drawn, and represents φ as good (see Section C). Desire and propositional content are thus doubly interconnected within Aristotle's account of practical reasoning. It may be that one could devise a syntactical (non-intentional) characterisation of the items thus accepted, and state laws by which beliefs and desires (thus characterised) lead to other desires, but these generalisations would not capture *desire* precisely because (as Aristotle insisted) they would leave out of the picture what it is about desire which explains why the propositions accepted are as they are (containing reference to the good) and why the generalisations governing the items used in practical reasoning are as they are (because of the features of desire and the good noted within the syllogism). While the Field-style generalisations may be those on which desire and belief (as we use them) depend, they could not be sufficient to characterise the explanatory work done by desire, belief and their propositional contents, because they omit the interconnexions which the latter illuminate. What would be required to capture their explanatory work would be an account which succeeds not only in (a) stating the conditions under which (at a given time) an agent is in a set of psychological states – desire that p, belief that q etc. – and (b) stating law-like connexions between the functionally characterised states which the agent is in when he desires that p, etc., but also in giving (c) a characterisation of the property of the functionally characterised states (compatible with a broadly functionalist approach) which explains why S moves from the desire to ψ, and the belief that φ'ing is the way to ψ, to the S desire to φ (when S reasons). In giving (c) one would require an account of a property analogous to goodness (or truth) which articulates the interconnexions between the relevant functional states. Direction on to this value would account for the transitions found at the functional level, and allow for projection to the set of relevantly similar cases. Aristotle's challenge to the functionalist is to find a way of fulfilling (c) compatible with his causal extensionalist framework. His claim – that (c) cannot be given, although (a) and (b) may be – represents a powerful and central challenge to functionalist theory which still requires a complete (or even the beginning of an) answer. It amounts to the claim that we possess an irreducible idea of what it is to be a rational agent which depends not on the purported openness of the mental but on the concepts and *a priori* connexions in terms of which desire and belief are defined. To delete these connexions is to cease to consider desire and belief[36] and to surrender the kind of intelligibility implicit in our

---

[36] If this is correct, the idea of what it is to be a rational agent with desires and beliefs cannot be captured without specifying well-being and goal-directedness in a way that is non-neutral as to the nature of the concepts of desire and belief. This would still apply even if the psychological system were a closed deterministic one. Compare Peacocke, 1979, 54, 173–4.

understanding of rational agency, which (he claims) cannot be captured using only lawlike connexions between functionally characterised states.

Aristotle's ontological schema supplies a second motivation for preferring psycho-physical explanatory theories: in the equivalence class
consisting of imagination, desire and the relevant psychological process, desire is the cause of intentional action (*de Anima* 433b19–20,
28–29), while imagination is taken as a necessary condition of intentional action, but not its cause. If this is so, the underlying physiological process cannot be construed as the essential cause if one is
seeking the most specific and precise characterisation of the cause
(195b20–25; 1044b1–3).[37] For since the physiological change is corre-
lated equally with both imagining and desiring, to cite it as the essential cause would be to fail to distinguish between it *qua* underlying
a necessary condition for action (imagination) and *qua* underlying a
cause of action (desire). Hence, if one is seeking the most specific cause
of the agent's behaviour within this model, one must use the psychological theory, as this draws more fine-grained distinctions than are
required in the underlying physiological theory.

Nor is this conclusion surprising within Aristotle's general account
of the relation of imagining and desiring. The latter either accepts or
rejects the proposition entertained by imagination or perception (see
Chapter 2, Section C). But if one rejects the conclusion (by not desiring
at all that which the imagination takes as e.g. 'pleasant'), one must
also reject the proposition. Thus, if one thinks that the object is pleasant, one must desire it at least somewhat, as not desiring it at all is
tantamount to rejecting the proposition. If so, the judgment that 'a is
pleasant' is logically sufficient for a to be desired; absence of desire
constitutes a denial of the judgment. The two psychological events are
so connected that if this type of imagining is present, desiring must
be as well. There need be no physical correlate of the *logical* connexion
between the two psychological states; for there seems to be no general
ground for insisting that there must be distinct psychological events
to capture relations which do not obtain at the physical level. Hence
there is no absurdity in Aristotle's proposal that the judgment that 'a
is good *qua* pleasant' and the desire to do a are two distinct psychological processes enmattered in one physical state, or that the determinate relation between imagination and desire is important for the
explanation of action, but is not mirrored at the physical level. Therefore, if one is seeking the most specific explanation of what occurs,
Aristotle's essential cause will be desire (psychologically described)
and not a physical-quality change (physically described). Aristotle
thus allows that there are psychological regularities and connexions
with which no physiological regularity or connexion coincides.

[37] I follow Ross (Commentary, 514) in taking *akrotaton* as meaning 'precise' (i.e.
specific to the production of this effect).

Although the relevant psychological states are determined by physiological states there is no physiological connexion which matches that between thinking φ good and desiring it (1072a29) in the case of intentional agents. If so, the relevant connexion can only be understood psychologically within his account because it casts no shadow at the physical level.[38]

Aristotle thus had two arguments which favour taking the preferred level of explanation to be psycho-physical provided that what is to be explained are the actions of rational agents. If the teleological scheme (C) rests on the psycho-physical causal explanation (A) (see Section A), his arguments in fact favour (A) over (C) as the preferred mode of explanation of action. If so, the preferred Aristotelian mode of explanation is psycho-physical causal explanation.

There remains one major difficulty: Aristotle needs to explain how it is that these physical states in a given organism are sufficient for the relevant psychological states of desire.

Aristotle's replies to this question are tentative: for while he speaks of the underlying physical states as 'suited' to realise the psychological states (703a34–36; 407b14ff.), and notes that it is 'with good reason' that they are as they are (702a7ff.) in order to play their role in the organism, he does not explain what it is about such underlying states in the circumstances that makes them suited to realising particular psychological states. Reference to 'fittingness' and 'suitability' appears to cover absence of a theory to explain in what way physical states (in C*) do determine particular psychological states; what is required is an account of how the specified physical state is fitting for psychological states with intentional content. Perhaps Aristotle thought this was a question for the special sciences and would have welcomed support from evolutionary theory to show how a given physical state with given causal powers determines certain psychological states (such as desire) with a related causal role; for if they did not do so, the organism would not survive.

Aristotle's confidence that the results of the special sciences would support his account followed from his view that there *must be* upwards determination because of the related causal roles. Thus he was not concerned himself with the detailed empirical investigation of how this actually occurred. However, Field's own proposal suggests one way in which the relevant underlying states could be characterised so as to show the required dependency of the intentional states of desire and belief on certain extensionally characterised states of desiring* and other physical states of a given kind with certain causal antecedents. The states Field describes may be extensionally equivalent with, and hence the base for, the relevant psychological states, even though they do not themselves capture the explanatory connexions which characterise desire or belief and their role in the practical

---

[38] See Wittgenstein's remarks (1967, 608–11), cited in part in n. 23 above.

syllogism. But this is only one type of proposal; there may be other comparable ways of showing how complex informational states may determine the occurrence of psychological states with given content.[39] From Aristotle's perspective, the problems of how extensional physical states are non-causally sufficient for the occurrence of a psychological state awaits an empirical resolution.[40] The philosophical enterprise (as he conceived it) is to show that the physical states must be (non-causally) sufficient for such psychological states, and to point to those irreducible and explanatory features of the psychological (e.g. propositional content) which would not be captured even if one had established the requisite non-causal dependency on the physical. Failure to fulfil the empirical requirement of establishing which types of physical states make true the psychological descriptions is not a failure within the enterprise he set himself.

E. Problems and puzzles in Aristotle's materialism

In Aristotle's discussion of the relation of the mind and the body several basic features of his account of processes (and states), and of the causal and teleological explanation of intentional action interact to yield a distinctive form of materialism which occupies a mid-position in several major debates on these topics.

Aristotle saw that the psychological and the physical antecedents of action constituted different levels of explanation and of ontology. His ontological theory of processes precluded him from holding either version of the identity theory of mental and physical processes, but led him to view the physical as determining the psychological. This seems sufficient to commit him to ontological materialism.

Aristotle's causally-based analysis of intentional action and his causal explanatory theory of the occurrence of *acrasia* led him to embrace a version of ontological materialism (Section B). But he also saw that there could be a teleologically-based mode of explanation at the psychological level which was compatible with (indeed rested on) the psycho-physical causal explanatory story (Section A). Further, since his teleological theory introduced concepts to define mental states which outrun those at the physical level, Aristotle had grounds for resisting the reduction of psychological to physical states (Section C). Indeed the teleological concepts thus introduced allow an account

---

[39] Recent work on Artificial Intelligence suggests other alternatives; see Winograd and Hinton and Anderson, essays in Schank and Colby chapter 1. I am indebted to Adrian Cussins for bringing them to my attention.

[40] Aristotle is able to regard the issue as empirical because his view of mental states (see Sections A, C) does not show them *a priori* to be non-determinable by physical states. His conception of the problem distinguishes his answer fundamentally from those offered by Quine or Davidson, whose view of mental states as essentially indeterminate and not part of causal explanatory theory, renders this problem *a priori* non-solvable.

of mental processes which shows how they can be elements of a causally explanatory scheme. Thus Aristotle accepts both the causally and teleologically based accounts of the psychological explanation of action which are sometimes treated as competitors in modern discussions, and argues for the priority of these two types of explanation of action over physical explanation, provided that man is regarded as rational.

This account has four basic constituents: (a) that identity is not necessary for ontological materialism, but that a weaker relation is all that is required, (b) that there may be both psycho-physical causal and teleological explanation of action, and purely physical explanation of the bodily movement, (c) that psychological states are irreducible to physical states, and (d) that teleological and psycho-physical causal explanation are to be preferred to the explanation offered at the physical level.

(c) and (d) have been discussed in the previous section. (a) and (b) both raise major difficulties.

(a) Aristotle's ontological materialism

Since Aristotle did not require the identity (type or token) of psychological and physical processes, he had no need to show how mental properties could be properties of physical states, or to resort to intensional contexts (events under description) to account for the difficulties involved in doing this. Within his account it is enough that the physical states are non-causally sufficient for the psychological states. If he is correct, it is a historical accident that in recent years the majority of ontological materialists have been identity theorists, and employed an ontological framework in which mental and physical events have identity conditions such that they can be construed as identical. Aristotle, in effect, argues that the truth of materialism does not depend on preference for one account of the identity conditions for processes rather than another, and hence seeks to give a more general characterisation of ontological materialism which is not committed to token identity.

Aristotle's ontological theory has a second feature. Although it is realist about mental states and their propositional content, it does not assume that they are 'intervening distinguishable states of an internal-behaviour causing system' (Dennett 1979, 13), if this means that each (core) desire is 'stored separately as . . . a separate concrete item in the agent's physiology' (Dennett 1979, 17). For Aristotle need not assume that the beliefs or desires in question are separately stored (e.g.) as explicit representational items in the physiological structure (see Section D). There is no paradox (within Aristotle's theory) in being a realist about beliefs and desires, without these being identical with one separate physiological item (discrete item or a physiological whole consisting of parts), provided that the underlying physiological items are such as to necessitate the presence of the psychological states. While the physiological states have the potentiality to produce the relevant psychological states in C*, there is no requirement either that (i) they possess the same internal complexity as the propositions that are actualised, or that (ii) they are individuated at the physiological level in a way which matches the individuation at the psychological level (in either of the two ways suggested: token identity/ part-whole). Aristotle argues that the presence of physiological states of this type is not required for realism about mental states. Thus he avoids the (seemingly misleading) set of alternatives posed as exclusive and exhaustive in some current theorising: *either* there must be a 'clean-cut' downwards if mental realism is true, so that physiological states are identical with (or parts of a whole identical with) psychological states,[41] *or*, since it is implausible that there is such a 'clean-cut' downwards, mental realism is false.[42] Aristotle rejects both of these alternatives by seeking to show that mental realism may be true without there being a 'clean-cut' downwards, provided that the relevant physiological states (non-causally) necessitate the occurrence of the psychological states.

These two respects illustrate Aristotle's view as a mid-position. While dualism is sometimes construed as the denial of token-identity, and anti-realism about the mental taken as the denial that there is a 'clean-cut' downwards of this type, Aristotle shows that one can accept both these denials and yet be both a materialist and a realist about psychological states. If his position is defensible, ontological materialism and mental realism involve far less strong doctrines than is commonly supposed.[43]

But how defensible is his position? Consider two major objections:

(i) It is sometimes said that the matter/form relation is actually incoherent in Aristotle's theory because the matter is so specified that it necessitates the psychological processes, and cannot be picked out without being thereby conceived as having that form.[44] If the matter in question cannot be specified except as 'potentially F' *or* as the material of a living animal, it cannot be conceived except as a matter of that form, i.e. being ensouled.

It is not clear, however, that this objection – thus phrased – applies straightforwardly in the case of desire and the flowing of the blood

[41] See for instance Fodor, 1976 and 1978; he also claims that the underlying states have the same complexity as desire and belief and that they may be represented as 'syntactic'.

[42] Dennett, 1979.

[43] It is not surprising that anti-materialists (e.g. Robinson, 1978) move directly from the claim that there are distinct mental events non-identical with physical events to the conclusion that Aristotle was not a materialist. The characterisation of ontological materialism offered suggests that the move is over-hasty, as (within it) materialism requires neither identity nor reduction. Hence Aristotle is not an anti-materialist simply because he rejects the identity thesis (see, for a contrasting view, Barnes, 1971/2).

[44] See Ackrill, 1973/4.

around the heart. For while the latter may be impossible except in a living creature, it does not follow *a priori* from this that the psychological process it enmatters is *desire*. That is, the flowing of blood around the heart could (epistemically) have enmattered imagination, *or* practical reasoning *or* a distinct psychological faculty, *and* need not (epistemically) have enmattered desire. If so, it appears to be an *a posteriori* discovery that this type of physico-chemical state enmatters desire in blooded animals.

Similar considerations apply equally in the case of particular desires: even if the flowing of blood of type k enmatters a desire to eat sweets in animals (of a certain type), this will prove to be an *a posteriori* discovery – as it does not follow from the conception of this very physico-chemical state that it enmatters that desire. Aristotle may need to provide a general theory of this relation and appear to sidestep that requirement with his talk of physical states 'being fitted' for certain psychological states; but that is a different matter.[45]

(ii) Within this account, Aristotle characterises the relation between desire and the surging blood as a type of necessitation which is distinguished from efficient causation but is not clarified except by analogy. But, while it may *seem* clear to say that the occurrence of the physical process materially necessitates the occurrence of the psychological process, it remains obscure what type of necessitation this is. The identity theorist, by contrast, says that the (token) mental and physical event are identical, and hence avoids this difficulty; and this may seem an advantage for the Davidsonian account of events.

A full reply to this would require a specification either of the truth conditions for material necessitation or a reduction of it to other better-understood categories. Aristotle notoriously does neither, and might be taken to treat material necessitation here as a type of primitive. This problem, however, is also shared by Aristotle's discussion of the 'is' of constitution in discussing substances.[46] So his account is at least incomplete; but is it worse than incomplete?

There is an Aristotelian reply to an objector who insists on the token-identity of events, allows that there are mental descriptions of these events which are irreducible to physical descriptions and pick out real mental properties (i.e. are more than *façons de parler* for describing the physical) and also holds that these mental properties supervene on physical properties. The reply is *ad hominem*: 'What account do you give of the relation between the mental and physical

---

[45] See Section D. The basis for a further reply to Ackrill's criticism is implicit in the discussion of the analogue for processes of the 'is' of constitution in Appendix 1.

[46] See Wiggins, 1981, 30, 33, 66n. 12 (and passim). It seems paradoxical that many are prepared to allow the 'is' of constitution to play a central role in their account of substances, but insist that in the case of events an apparently comparable relation must be token-identity. Aristotle's concern was to give a general account of substances and processes within his favoured matter/form analysis: see *Physics* 202b7–9 (discussed in Chapter 1, Section B, and Appendix 1).

properties in question which is compatible with materialism? If the relation is causal (efficient), then it appears that – in the harmful sense – you are admitting mental properties into your ontology *over and above* physical properties. If one wishes to remain an ontological materialist, the characterisation of this relation must be a form of necessitation distinct from causality and *a priori* (logical) entailment. If so, you too need a necessitation relation which obtains between the occurrence of the physical property and the occurrence of the psychological property which is similar to what Aristotle himself requires.'

This mode of argument is effective (if at all) only against those who are *neither* dualists about mental properties *nor* (alternatively) prepared to treat mental descriptions as merely *façons de parler* without commitment to mental properties. Thus (in particular) it applies to those who treat desires and beliefs as causally explanatory in virtue of their content and do not wish to treat the content of belief dualistically. If one is attracted to this position, one faces, with respect to mental properties, the difficulties which Aristotle's account encounters with respect to processes. Nor is this unexpected: for Aristotle's theory of processes introduces at least certain properties into the identity conditions for processes, and hence the difficulties it encounters in the case of *processes* are the same as those which arise for mental *properties*, when events are differently individuated. If so, the problem which Aristotle needs to resolve appears a general one, not confined to his own ontological theory. Since under plausible assumptions it arises also for the rival Davidsonian scheme, it cannot (by itself) be used as a ground for rejecting Aristotle's account.

Aristotle appears to have taken the notion of the material cause as a brute modality to be explained only by analogy (matter/form). A given piece of bronze being in a certain state is non-causally sufficient for there being a statue of a given kind. Two telephone wires being in contact are non-causally sufficient for there being an open-line between two speakers. In modern terminology this relation is sometimes called *supervenience*; but the issue is to determine the type of necessitation (assuming that it is not causal) which obtains between a named mental state and a named physical state when the supervenience conditional states that the occurrence of the latter necessitates the occurrence of the former.[47] Aristotle's contribution is to force us to focus on the significance of this relation; but his major failure is to have advanced no further to clarify the fundamental ontological relation on which his account rests.

---

[47] In contrast to the functionalist relation between a named physical state and a definite description describing a mental state.

(b) *Psycho-physical causal and teleological explanation*

In the account given both causal and teleological necessitation were treated as distinct (but related) *brute modalities*. In earlier chapters, we saw their interconnexion in discussing practical reasoning, rational choice and *acrasia* (see also Section A). The suggestion has been that teleological necessitation articulates a type of necessity which is ir- reducible to causal necessitation and which is applicable in cases where there is a coherent account of the good of an organism in irreducibly valuational terms. This account also requires supplemen- tation. As in the case of material causality, one needs either a full specification of the truth conditions for 'teleologically necessitates' or a reduction of it to better understood categories. Such an account should also specify in general terms the conditions under which 'te- leologically necessitates' can be applied to organisms. Must they, for example, be of a given kind (at a certain stage of development) or with certain intentional states?

Aristotle's account of levels of explanation allows that there can be psycho-physical as well as purely physical causal explanation; for while he develops an account of teleological explanation at the psycho- logical level, this rests on psycho-physical causal explanation. Purely physical explanation may possess certain advantages over psycho- physical explanation: it may issue in exceptionless generalisations (and not ones that hold 'for the most part') which require no supple- mentation from a lower level (cf. 1094b11–26; 1112b1–9), and may (in the sense discussed above) explain why the organism has certain psychological states (cf. 87a31ff.: for Aristotelian criteria for the best explanation). However, psychological elements may causally explain within Aristotle's schema; for the connexions involved meet his re- quirements on explanation: necessitation or generality, appropriate connexion with the substances involved. The relevant generalisations will hold 'for the most part' (see Chapter 1, Section D), and may not be such as we ourselves can complete. Further, they will contain among their antecedents 'A's which are B's and C's and D's are Z', information which is physical (D) as well as psychological (A's which are B's and C's), without changing the subject matter (A's) (see Chap- ter 4, Section A); for this mode of explanation allows the addition of physical conditions which limit the cases of A's under discussion with- out the necessity of giving a purely physical specification of A. Thus Aristotle can accept that such generalisations will require supplemen- tation from the physical level without being compelled to phrase them in exclusively physical vocabulary.

Aristotle's 'for the most part' psychological generalisations are con- nected *a posteriori* with the actions they explain. They appear (in an appropriately modified form) to meet Hempel's requirements for

explanatory and lawlike generalisations.[48] They fail, however, to meet
several tougher constraints which might be suggested as necessary for
explanation or lawlike generalisation. In particular, it is sometimes
held (a) that the predicates which the generalisations or explanations
contain must fall within the same conceptual domain, and be such
that we can know *a priori* that they are made for each other,[49] or (b)
that the predicates which the generalisations or explanations contain
must be true of objects with a physico-chemical essence which determines that the relevant properties always co-occur.[50] Both (a) and (b)
require that the predicates involved be necessarily connected in virtue
of either their semantic properties or the relevant underlying essence;
if predicates are not so connected, it is claimed, the generalisations
(even if with restricted antecedents) involved cannot be lawlike. We
have seen above (Section B) that Aristotle does not regard mental
terms as denoting natural kinds with one physico-chemical essence;
nor are psychological and physical domains semantically connected in
his account. Hence, if either (a) or (b) are well-motivated, Aristotelian
psycho-physical causal generalisations could not be lawlike. His purported explanations at this level would not be genuine explanations.

Both (a) and (b), however, seem extremely strong conditions to require of the lawlike. If a given generalisation is part of the simplest
general theory adequate for a given subject matter, sustains counterfactuals and subjunctive conditionals, and is predictive, it is not clear
why it cannot be lawlike. Such an account at least explains why (H_1)
'All emeralds are green' and (H_2) 'All emerires are grue'[51] are lawlike,
while (H_3) 'All emeralds are grue' is not. For in the simplest overall
theory of emeralds (as it now stands) there is no place for an unexplained colour change observed at t_1. If on the other hand, our simplest
theory of emeralds made them like chameleons, H_3 would be lawlike,
and H_1 not. Some connexions which appear in the simplest theory are
prefigured in *a priori* connexions between predicates (as in H_1); but
not all, if H_3 could be lawlike under the conditions specified. Generally
it seems optimistic to expect that all future explanations and laws yet

[48] Hempel's requirements run as follows (as I understand them): P (a generalisation
with no singular terms) is lawlike iff (1) it supports subjunctive and counterfactual
claims, (2) its predicates (and antecedent conditions) are sufficiently precise and explicit
to allow us to determine in advance whether the conditions of its application are
satisfied: (it must be testable and projectible). See 1965, 341–3, 292–3. To this might be
added (in the light of remarks about 'grue' below), (3) it is part of a simple general
theory of the subject matter (see Goodman, 1970, 605–8).

[49] Davidson, 1980, 217ff. I take this argument separately from Davidson's other worry
about psycho-physical causal explanation: that it cannot be *a posteriori* because of the
analysis of mental terms or the content of propositional acts (see Section C).

[50] McGinn, 1977/8, and 1980/1.

[51] x is an emerire if x is observed pre t_1 and an emerald, otherwise a sapphire. x is
grue if x is observed pre t_1 and green, otherwise blue. The treatment suggested here
follows (in outline) Goodman, 1970, 605–8. Compare Davidson, 1980, 225–7.

to be discovered will be implicit in *a priori* connexions between our present predicates within our present theory.

Moreover (b) also seems to be an over-stringent requirement to place on the lawlike. Some of our most basic laws are formulated in terms such as shape, mass, energy and weight which cut across natural kinds and appear independent of them; similarly with laws governing motion in space or (on one construal) colour transitions. Hence, if such laws are metaphysically necessary, their status does not follow from the predicates involved denoting natural kinds, but either from the inconceivability of their falsity or from their being part of the best theory of the subject matter. But either consideration could apply to the restricted generalisations linking specific psychological states of a given organism and its resultant bodily movements. If so, the Aristotelian generalisations may be lawlike, and psycho-physical causal explanation of the type he canvassed possible.[52]

Aristotle's explanations require that a disposition or state be described in such a way that another property follows necessarily or in general, and that the relevant disposition or state be described in such a way that it belongs to the substance *per se*. (He construes necessity as a basic notion, and does not seek to locate that within a framework of Humean generalisations and laws: see Chapter 1, Section D).

This view of explanation allows Aristotle to resist the temptation to find only one (or *the*) explanation at the fundamental physical level expressed solely in non-dispositional terms. There may be different levels of explanation in ascending order – physics: biology: psychology: sociology – in which the former is more complete and its generalisations exceptionless, but the latter remain explanatory even though their 'in general' statements cannot be completed at their own level but require information from a lower level to be exceptionless. Indeed Aristotle (see Section D) actually preferred psycho-physical causal explanations of human behaviour (as long as man is regarded as rational) to purely physical causal explanation: for although the latter may approximate to the perfect generalisations of a completed science, the former (although less complete) reveal our essence as rational animals and our favoured means of understanding ourselves and one another. At this point Aristotle's defence of psycho-physical causal explanation seems secure: it is needed to supplement teleological explanation and to account for the explanatory work of the psychological;

---

[52] These sceptical doubts about (a) and (b) as conditions of the lawlike require a more detailed defence than is possible here. Even if (a) and (b) were justified, Aristotelian causal generalisations would be very much like laws – even if laws had to meet a higher requirement. Hence it is not clear what would have been achieved if either (a) or (b) (contrary to the sceptical doubts raised here) were vindicated. See also Lennon, forthcoming. In this discussion of (b), I assume (*argumenti causa*) that all natural kinds possess a unique physical essence. However, I suspect that, in reality, natural kinds are precisely the kinds described in genuine laws, and that there are therefore psychological natural kinds if there are Hempelian laws involving the psychological.

it relates desires, defined without reference to action, to intentional actions (appropriately described) and meets plausible conditions on explanation (generality, or necessity; being *a posteriori*). Thus he seeks to avoid the set of alternatives posed as exclusive in some current debates: *either* there must be exceptionless generalisations stated using terms drawn from the same domain or denoting objects with one physico-chemical essence if desires and beliefs causally explain action; *or*, since there are *not*, there can be no causal explanation involving desires and beliefs, and hence psychological phenomena explain action in a non-causal way (e.g. teleological, holistic) which is incompatible with a psycho-physical causal explanatory account.

Aristotle rejects both these alternatives by showing that there can be genuine psycho-physical causal explanation which meets less stringent conditions than these on what is to count as explanation. If his use of 'for the most part' generalisations is acceptable, the defence of psycho-physical causal explanation which he provides shows that this task is less demanding than frequently it is assumed to be in modern discussion. Indeed his account of intentional action, action-ontology, *acrasia* and rationality together constitute a unified general theory in which the psycho-physical causal explanation of behaviour can be partially vindicated.

Aristotle's views on materialism and explanation constitute an unoccupied mid-position in contemporary discussion on these topics; for while he accepts premises that lead some to reject materialism, or realism about psychological states or psycho-physical causal explanation, he does so while defending a version of ontological materialism and a form of psycho-physical causal explanation. Together they represent the width of his perspective within the philosophy of mind, the ingenuity of his approach to particular ontological and analytical issues, and his conception of how these should cohere within an explanatory theory of the antecedents of action. In these ways Aristotle's approach to the philosophy of mind reflects both his specific insight into individual topics and his conception of how these cohere to form a general explanatory theory.

Aristotle's ontology of processes, activities and actions

In Chapters 1, 2 and 5 an interpretation of Aristotle's ontology of processes and activities is developed. It contains four main features:

(1) If processes have different goals, they are distinct.
(2) If processes have different subjects of change, they are distinct.
(3) If processes stand in the relation 'the same . . . but different in being (essence)' they are distinct members of one equivalence class.
(4) Productions are located in the same place as their effects.

The first three features are argued for in Chapter 1 on the basis of:

(a) several arguments based on the analysis of *Physics* III 1–3 and V 4: (Section B)
  (i) the *ousia*/the *logos* of what it is to be that thing argument;
  (ii) the analysis of III 3 showing teaching and learning as distinct because they have different goals *and* different subjects;
(b) an account of different processes as essentially the realisations of different capacities of different subjects of change: (*the natural kind theory of processes*);
(c) an analysis of processes which are 'the same . . . but different in essence' in *Physics* III 3 (Section B);
(d) an account of the activity/process/state distinction as involving distinct classes of phenomena with different goals (Section C);
(e) an account of efficient causation as involving processes and states of this type (Section D).

Further support for (1)–(3) was given in Chapter 2, Section B by

(f) Aristotle's separation of basic and non-basic acts as distinct acts, and
(g) Aristotle's account of productions and *praxeis* as distinct classes of actions.

In this presentation (a)–(c) depended on the analysis given of certain *Physics* passages. This was partly an exegetical device as *Physics* III 1–3 and V 4 contain Aristotle's most extended treatment of the nature and identity of processes. However, there is evidence outside *Physics* III 1–3 and V 4 which strongly supports the interpretation offered. Indeed, it would have been possible to proceed less directly by beginning with evidence outside *Physics* III 1–

3 and V 1–4, and then working towards an interpretation of the passages discussed in Chapter 1. Even if one were unconvinced by the arguments given under (a) and (c), the separate arguments (b), (d)–(g) would show that Aristotle's account of processes etc. was distinct from the extensional event theory of the Davidsonian type. In this Appendix, I wish to consider further exegetical evidence for the first three ontological claims made in Chapters 1 and 2. This will be divided into two main sections: *Section A*: Difference in processes because of different goals and subjects of change. *Section B*: Processes which are 'the same but different in essence'.

Section A: Processes, activities individuated by their goals and/or subjects of change (= claims (1) and (2))

Claim (1): *different subjects of change*: Aristotle defines processes as in the class of relations (200b28–31). But '*aRb*' (in '*a* moves *b*') is a different relation from '*bRa*'; for if they were the same, in the latter case, *b* would move *a*, rather than vice versa. That is, relations depend on the *order* of the objects thus related; the relation of the agent to the patient (1020b28–30; 1056b35) is different from that of patient to agent. Difference in subject (in this case) means difference in relation (see 324a25ff.).

Claim (2): *if different goal, then different process*:
  (i) See: 639b12f.; 641b24, 31; 641a31: goal determines essence; therefore different goal gives different essence. See also: 1115b21–24; 1140b6–7; 1174a23–25; 227b32f. (affection not place as goal); 194a28–32.
  (ii) This principle explains why quality, quantity and spatial changes are distinct genera; for they possess different kinds of end point (e.g. 226a24–b1).

Section B: 'Processes which are the same . . . but different in essence' are distinct members of one equivalence class

Claim (3): *the processes are distinct . . . but related:*

(i) *Perception*: 425b27–426a2, a8–24. The external cause produces the hearing and the sonance which occur simultaneously in the hearer: one of them is called hearing, the other sonance (a1–3). They are exercises of different capacities (a2–6, 11–13, 16–18), and are destroyed simultaneously or continue to exist for the same time. Aristotle writes of such cases: 'For some of them, we have names: e.g. hearing and sonance, but for others, one of the two is without a name: e.g. the activity of colour' (426a12–14). Since the thing without a name must be an activity (which could be named), there must be two distinct occurrences in such cases which both exist at the same time (a15–17). (Contrast Ross and Hamlyn: ad loc., who depend on a different analysis of *Physics* III 3).

(ii) *Thinking*: 430a10–25 (cf. 417b16–27; partial analogy with perception). The actual thinking is the production of the active *nous* (a15–17), is compared with the activity of light and contrasted with the distinct nameless activity of colour (cf. 426a13–15), which is the activity of the passive *nous*. That the active thinking and the activity of the passive *nous* are distinct is confirmed by the difference in faculties (the immortal superior to the mortal: a18–24), where the immortal faculty is essentially an activity while the passive faculty is essentially a potentiality which becomes (*genesis*) specific objects of thought (a14–15, 17–20); in this, the relevant subjects of change and the changes themselves are different. Further, the active faculty *makes* an object of thought while the passive *becomes* one. Since making and becoming are distinct genera of changes (cf. 225a35ff.), the activities must be distinct. (This interpretation is influenced by Brentano 1867, 110ff.).

(iii) *Reciprocal change*: acting and undergoing both occur in one substance (that which is affected) (322b18–21), but are activities of specifically distinct capacities for change (324a5ff.) which are opposites. The passive object (e.g. cold water) is assimilated to the active (a10–12) when heated, while the hot assimilates the cold to it (a9–10). Thus the subjects of the changes, and hence the changes themselves, are distinct. This is confirmed when Aristotle describes the hot as assimilating the cold to it (when heating occurs), while the cold does not assimilate the hot to it (to the same extent: cf. 328a18ff.). Since, in this way, the relations in which agent and patient stand are distinct (see claim 1), Aristotle treats first and last agent as distinct from the patient (323a17–32; 324a8ff., b15ff.; 328a18ff.). See Joachim ad loc. pp. 147, 152, 185f. If so, they must be subjects of distinct processes: acting and undergoing.

In (i)–(iii) the acting 'results in' the undergoing, and is distinct from it. The production is the cause which brings about the distinct effect: e.g. 195b16–21: this man healing brings it about that another man is cured. The two activities occur simultaneously (b17, 21), and (we later learn: III 3) are located in the patient. But in II 3 and *de G.C.* I 6 and 7 the activities are distinct, and this throws light on the relation of agency and patiency in III 3. (For a contrasting but less detailed view, see M. L. Gill, 1980, 129ff). It lies outside the scope of the present Appendix to analyse further 'results in'. But it should be noted that while the undergoing occurs by means of the acting, the 'by' need not (itself) be causal (see, e.g. Goldman, 1970, 24–28).

(iv) *Simultaneous activities*: (426b21–427a16; 449a17–20; 431a21–24). There are distinct judgings (427a9ff.): 'The soul judges two distinct and separate objects as with a divided faculty' (cf. 431a28–29). Different qualities perceived determine different genera of judging (449a17–20), and hence different individual processes. In such cases, therefore, there is one physical effect and two distinct judgings, which are specified as the same but different in essence (see Brentano, 1867, 59ff.). Simultaneity is also guaranteed by 426a16–17 ('same time saved and destroyed') and 195b17 (see b21).

Claim (3)': *The distinct processes are related as 'matter to form'*:

(i) *Physics* 202b9–11: Aristotle distinguishes that which is potentially F and that which is actually F, and treats them as apparently distinct entities (although one in some sense). Potentiality and activity are elsewhere Aristotle's favoured relata for his account of the relation of matter/form: in *Meta.* VII, VIII this appears as the central analogy around which his account of matter/form is based (cf. 1048b8–9; 1045b35–1046a2). 'Some are as movement to potentiality, others as substance to matter'. That is, Aristotle is employing the potentiality/actuality distinction as it obtains in the case of movement to illuminate his account of matter/form relation. In the case of movement, what is potentially buildable is distinct from the activity of building, although an object will have the potentiality for φ'ing at the same time as the potentiality is being exercised (201a11ff.: cf. footnote 11 to Chapter 1). If the potentiality is distinct from the actualisation in this case, it must also be distinct in the case of matter/form (1048a36–b4: cf. b3). If so, the two processes characterised in this way in 202b9–11 must be distinct.

(ii) Aristotle is, therefore, developing an analogy between matter/form and movement which favours the two-entity account. The point of the analogy appears to be that in both cases a given potentiality to φ in C* (together with the occurrence of C*) necessitates φ'ing where C* are the conditions in which the potentiality is exercised (no external prevention etc.) But the analogy is only partial: for in the matter/form case, the given potentiality to φ in C* and the φ'ing occur in the same substance at the same time, and do not operate by dragging, pulling (etc.) which characterise causal relations between distinct entities. Hence the modality is different in the two cases.

(iii) In this formulation, several features are significant:
    (a) The conditions C*, *may* refer to the final cause achieved by φ'ing: the aim of the potentiality: (e.g.) bricks arranged for a given purpose yield a house, but they *need* not do so as (e.g.) a piece of wood in a given place yields a threshold (1042b26–27; 1043a7–8), or ice is made up of water frozen in a given way (1042b26–28, 30; 1043a9–10). Aristotle lists a series of possible conditions (1042b29–31) which do not include goal-directed features (mixed, frozen, etc.). These are not identified with the form but are in some way analogous with it (1043a5).
    (b) This proposal is *not* equivalent to the claim that syllables = letters + organisation of those letters (1043b5–6; 1041b11); for if letters and organisation were the matter, they could not be identical with the form, which must be beyond these (1043b7–8). The form is dependent rather on the (e.g.) use to which these letters, thus organised, are put (1043b8–10; cf. a7–10). This is based on the letters thus organised but is not reducible to it.
    (c) The matter always has the potential to be this form, but 'becomes' it only when C* obtain. There need be no change in the matter when C* obtain: the same process may continue identically before C* obtain, while they obtain, and thereafter. The difference consists only in whether its potentiality to become the form is realised. Since this depends on whether C* obtain or not, it is possible to describe the underlying matter in a given way: 'blood boiling' (understood as 'red liquid of a material kind boiling') without building into this whether or not C* obtain. The test would be: can this 'matter', without change in its material composition, be placed in C* and generate the relevant form? This test is independent of whether there is some (perhaps favoured) contingent description of the 'matter' (placed in C*) whose terms are analytically connected (by the homonymy principle) with its form. (Compare Ackrill, 1972/3, 126–7, 128, 132–3). This interpretation offers a way in which the matter can be conceived as existing without the form (if C* do not obtain), and conditional powers can belong to a material base without being exercised. I aim to develop this line of interpretation in more detail elsewhere.

(d) Aristotle's account has, therefore, the following salient features: (i) the matter in C* is non-causally sufficient for the form; (ii) this relation although not identity is that of 'oneness in a certain sense'; (iii) both matter and C* may be described in such a way as to leave out reference to the form. The equivalence class formulation is an attempt to capture (ii) in a way which shows the relation to be distinct from, but analogous to, identity. (i) expresses Aristotle's relation of 'material causation', (iii) allows for his form of material-ism (see Chapter 5, Sections A, B). The asymmetry of material causation, and the absence of reference to efficient causation, distinguish his account from certain accounts of 'realization' (Compare Peacocke, 1979, 118ff.).

Caveat (for Section B): The equivalence class formulation is not presented as a full account of all of Aristotle's uses of the matter/form relation. That would require a detailed analysis of his discussion of substances as well as processes. I cite evidence from his treatment of substances only to show that his appli-cation of this structure in *Physics* III 3 to numerically distinct but closely related processes fits *one* aspect of his theory of substances. There may be *other* features of the matter/form relation to which this account fails to apply in the case of substance (e.g: if matter/form are treated as strictly identical and not as 'one in some sense').

(I am grateful to Dory Scaltsas for helpful discussion of these topics.)

Is Aristotle analysing intentional action in *NE* III 1–5 and *NE/EE* V 8?

In Chapter 2, Section A it was assumed, on the basis of *NE* 1111a22–24, that it is a necessary condition of an action being intentional that the agent knows while acting what he is doing.

One objection to this account runs as follows: Aristotle held that (a) actions are open to praise and blame if and only if they are 'intentional'[1] (1109b30–35), and (b) the drunkard who acts in ignorance of what he is doing, is open to blame. Hence, if one adds the assumption (c) that the drunkard's being blamed entails that he acts intentionally, it follows that the drunkard acts intentionally even if he does not know (and is not aware) of what he is doing.

This objection[2] challenges the claim that Aristotle is actually analysing intentional action in the *NE*; for if the drunkard acts in ignorance of what he is doing, he does not act intentionally. If correct, it shows *either* that Aristotle is concerned exclusively in these passages with acts for which a man may be held responsible (e.g. the drunkard's act done in ignorance), *or* partially with such acts and partially with intentional actions. And this would affect the translation of *hekousion* used in Chapter 2.

The third assumption (c) is both substantial and necessary for the objector's conclusion. However, it is not explicitly stated in Aristotle's discussion of drunkenness in III 5: 'They punish even in cases of ignorance, if the man appears responsible for the ignorance: e.g. double the punishment for a man who is drunk; for the cause is in him as he is responsible for not being drunk, and this is the cause of his ignorance' (1113b30–33). Rather, Aristotle emphasises that the man is responsible for being drunk, and this is the cause of his ignorance.[3] If the man causes himself knowingly to be ignorant, he can be

---

[1] The objector interprets rather than translates 11109b30–33. Literally translated it says 'Virtue and vice are concerned with passions and actions. Praise and blame apply to what is intentional, pardon to what is unintentional, and sometimes pity. Therefore it is perhaps necessary for those concerned with virtue and vice to define the intentional and the unintentional, and also it is useful for those who set laws about rewards and punishments'. In this, 'intentional' is not stated only to apply to acts (see below).

[2] See Allan, 1955, 333ff., Hardie 1968, 7–8. It derives originally from Leoning 1903, 130ff.

[3] The context of this passage supports the same conclusion: what is voluntary is what is in our power and where the starting point is in us (1113b21). This is confirmed by judicial practice (1113b22) where only what is in our power is punished and encouraged. This supported initially by considering bad acts (b22–30). A further example is the ignorance of the drunkard which is punished because the starting point of the ignorance

punished for being ignorant, as he is to blame for being in that state. For example, if a man drives his car while drunk and knocks down a pedestrian whom he does not see because of his drunkenness, he can be punished for being unaware of what he was doing while driving as he is 'voluntarily' in that state, even though he does not intentionally knock down the pedestrian. Hence, the drunkard can be blamed for *being ignorant* voluntarily even if he *acts* unintentionally.

That the focus of blame is the state of ignorance and not the acts done in ignorance is supported by Aristotle's treatment of ignorance of the law and culpable negligence. For he emphasises that in these cases men are punished for being ignorant, and does not mention any act which they do while ignorant (1113b34–1114a5). It is the *state* of ignorance which is 'up to them' and hence 'voluntary', and not any *act* which they do when ignorant.

The suggestion that while the drunkard's ignorance is voluntary his act in ignorance is involuntary or unintentional is further supported by Aristotle's discussion of similar cases in 1136a5–9: 'Of unintentional acts some are pardonable and some not. Acts that are done not only in ignorance but through ignorance are pardonable, but acts that are done not through ignorance but in ignorance because of a passion that is not natural nor common to all men are not pardonable.' If drunkenness is neither natural (compare growing old: 1135b2) nor common to all men (cf. *Rhet. ad. Alex.* 1427a35–40; 1444a10)[4] and hence not necessary, acts done in ignorance through drunkenness are not pardonable but unintentional. If this passage is consistent with the discussion in III 5, the drunkard's action done in ignorance must be unintentional, and if blameworthy only so because it is the product of ignorance for whose presence he is causally responsible. Hence it is the drunkard's *ignorance* which is 'voluntary' in III 5 and not his *action*.

This account of the drunkard is compatible with the first sentence of III 1:

---

is in him (b31–33) and hence not being ignorant was in his power (1114a2 – using Aristotle's second example) and so being ignorant was also up to him (cf. 1113b6–13). That is, Aristotle appears to argue: (a) ($\forall x$) (x has the starting point of the proper type in us iff x is in our power and voluntary) (1113b20–21); (b) ignorance of the drunkard has the starting point of the proper type in him (b31–33); therefore (c) his ignorance is in his power (b30); therefore (d) his ignorance is punishable (b30). He does not say that there was a starting point of the proper type of his *action* in him, but locates as the focal point of the punishment *his ignorance* and not his action (1113b32: 1114a2). Nor is this surprising; since his action is not intentional (by Aristotle's earlier definition: cf. 1111a22–23: see below) as there is no starting point of the proper type in him. A starting point is of the proper type only if the agent causes what occurs knowingly (cf. 1114a9–14).

   [4] *Anthrôpinon* may also have a weaker sense: 'what most men do or that to which men are prone' (1429a14, 18–20). In the latter case, drunkenness is given as a case of a human passion together with rage, sensual desire, anger and ambition. If drunkenness is taken in this way in 1136a6–8 the drunkard's act is (still) unintentional but would now be pardonable. Hence there would be a difference in the legal treatment of such cases between the demand for double punishment in III and the pardon given in V, although in both cases the action itself would be (as argued here) unintentional. However, I prefer the stronger reading of *anthrôpinon* (1427a36ff.: all men in 1429a14) in this context because (1) it matches the reference to necessary passions in 1135b21, and (2) it justifies pardon (and not merely the appeal for pardon cf. 1429a15–20), since if an emotion is one which a person cannot avoid experiencing (in a given context) it may excuse their consequential actions and errors.

for that notes that praise and blame may be attached to whatever is voluntary, including emotions, and is not confined to actions, while elsewhere states are designated as voluntary (1114b20; 1113b14). Thus, the drunkard could be punished either for 'not knowing what he is doing' or being 'in a drunken state'. Therefore, that the drunkard is punished does not entail that he acts intentionally when he acts in ignorance, contrary to the third assumption in the objector's argument.

In *NE* III 1 and 5 and *NE/EE* V 8 Aristotle's only consistent position appears to be that praise and blame are applicable if and only if there is something relevant to the production of an action that is 'voluntary' – whether the action itself, a passion or a state. If each of these is involuntary, pardon is appropriate. Further, the stage which is voluntary is the focal point of the blame (1113b30 etc.). However, although acts which result from a voluntary 'passion' (e.g. ignorance) are unintentional (1136a5–8), these may be blamed (cf. also 1113b31) as they are the consequence of a voluntary state. The blame which attaches to these *acts* is derivative from the voluntariness of the *state* which causes them, and goes no way towards showing that the *acts* themselves are intentional. Hence the objection considered at the outset does not establish that Aristotle is not analysing intentional *action* in III 1–5.

In III 5 the drunkard's ignorance is the focus of the punishment (1113b30), because he is the cause and appropriate starting point of his ignorance by getting drunk (b31–33). Thus, his ignorance rests with him, and is punished – as is the case also of those who do not know something in the laws which they should know (b35–a2) (see also footnote 3 for more detailed comment on this passage).

There is however further independent objection to the account of *NE* III 1 and 5 which I have offered. It runs: (1) In *NE* 1111a22, Aristotle classifies as 'unintentional' acts that are done through force or through ignorance, and does not classify as 'unintentional' acts that are done in ignorance through passion (1110b26–1111a2). (2) Actions done in ignorance through passion are not 'non-intentional' as this category is defined by reference to the absence of regret when the act is done through ignorance (1111a20–21). Therefore (3) since actions done in ignorance through passion are neither unintentional nor non-intentional, they are best classified as intentional. If so we can classify the drunkard's ignorant act in III 5 as intentional within the framework of III 1–5, even though Aristotle holds a different view in *NE/EE* V 8.

While it is difficult to determine Aristotle's classification of acts done in ignorance through passion in 1111a22, it is extremely paradoxical to describe them as intentional, because in the next line Aristotle insists that the latter are 'acts done knowingly when the cause is in the agent', and thus must be done knowingly. But if the drunkard's act done in ignorance is classified as intentional in this context, Aristotle contradicts himself within one sentence. Since it seems uncharitable to attribute so gross an intellectual failure to Aristotle, it is reasonable to conclude that whatever the correct location is in 1111a22–24 for acts done in ignorance through passion it cannot be within the category of the intentional.

Elsewhere, in III 1, Aristotle appears to classify actions as follows:

(a) *The intentional*

(b) *The unintentional*

(c) *The non-intentional*

Classification I

acts caused knowingly by the agent

(1) acts done through ignorance with regret

(2) acts done under compulsion

(3) acts done in ignorance with regret[5]

(1) acts done through ignorance without regret

(2) acts done in ignorance without regret.

Thus acts done in ignorance through passion seem to fall *either* into the class of the unintentional *or* the non-intentional depending on whether they co-occur with regret. Since in neither case are they intentional, there is no evidence in the remainder of III 1 or V 8 which favours classifying the drunkard's act as intentional; rather it should be construed in III 5 as not intentional (in one of the two ways specified) although blameworthy because it is produced by ignorance which was caused 'voluntarily' by him.

There remains a difficulty about the interpretation of the phrase 'acts done through ignorance' in 1111a22; for if 'through ignorance' has the same meaning as elsewhere in III 1 (i.e. 1110b18ff.),[6] and if 1111a22 gives necessary and sufficient conditions for 'the unintentional', acts done in ignorance through passion cannot be unintentional. However it should be noted that this problem arises for *any* account of this chapter which attempts to render it consistent with 1111a22–24 and is not a special difficulty for my account.

One suggestion to meet this difficulty is to construe acts done through passion in ignorance as *non-intentional* (rather than intentional or unintentional) in 1111a22 and give 'through ignorance' the meaning it carries before in III 1. However, this would be inconsistent with Aristotle's claim in the previous sentence (1111a19–21) that acts done in ignorance through passion

---

[5] In this, I take *NE* 1111a19–21 to give a necessary condition for unintentionality and this to be assumed by Aristotle in his discussion of 1111a1–18 (with Ramsauer, Gauthier/Jolif). However, if one takes 1111a19–21 as merely giving evidence for an act being unintentional and not as stating a necessary condition, all acts done in ignorance will be unintentional and 1111a1–5 will be taken to confirm this. I have preferred the first assumption as this maintains the parallel with the discussion of acts done 'through ignorance'. However, since both readings of 1111a19–21 classify all acts done in ignorance outside the category of the intentional, both readings support the conclusion that the intentional does not include acts done in ignorance through passion. Hence, for present purposes, it is not necessary to seek to argue conclusively for either interpretation of 1111a19–21.

[6] That is, 'with ignorance as the only relevant causal factor'. This means that in the explanation of the action there is no state or emotion for which the agent is responsible prior to his ignorance which explains the act. Hence it is compatible with an act being done '*through ignorance*' that the agent would have done it even if he had known what he was doing, and thus with his feeling no regret at what he does unawares (see 1110b19–24). Acts done *in ignorance*, by contrast, are acts where the state of ignorance is to be explained by a preceding state or emotion of the agent, which is relevant to the full account of the antecedents of the action. In this account, I follow Grant and Ramsauer ad loc.

Appendix 2

with regret are unintentional.[7] Nor is this inconsistency diminished by the absence of mention of regret in 1111a22; for if there all acts done *through* ignorance are unintentional (in contrast to non-intentional) irrespective of the agents' subsequent lack of regret, it is difficult to understand how actions which are unintentional, if done *in* ignorance with regret, become non-intentional when regret drops out of the picture.

A second suggestion might be to weaken the sense of 'through ignorance' in 1111a22 so that it means 'with ignorance as *a* relevant (causal) factor' and not 'with ignorance as the *only* relevant (causal) factor' (see 1113b18–25 where Aristotle seems to use this term to cover cases both where the man is responsible for his ignorance (e.g. by being in a passion) and those where he is not.) If he is using 'through ignorance' in this way in III 5, it would embrace acts classified elsewhere in III 1 as done *in* and *through* ignorance within the category of the unintentional.[8] However, since in the remainder of the chapter, acts done *through* and *in* ignorance are treated as falling into distinct categories, it would be a major inconsistency on Aristotle's part to construe acts done *in* ignorance as cases of acts done *through* ignorance in 1111a22–24. And this counts strongly against this proposal.

The previous suggestions have both taken 'through ignorance' as giving – together with 'by force' – necessary and sufficient conditions for an act being unintentional in 1111a22. An alternative is to take acts done through ignorance as *one paradigm case* of the unintentional and to treat acts done in ignorance as unintentional because they resemble this paradigm more closely than any case of intentional action since they involve ignorance as a relevant causal factor. If so, 1111a22–24 would yield the following classification:

	Classification II
(a) *The intentional*	acts caused knowingly by the agent:
(b) *The unintentional*	(1) Paradigm case: acts done through ignorance (with or without regret)
	(2) Approximation: acts done in ignorance through passion

where (b)(2) resemble (1) sufficiently to be causes of unintentional action.

This proposal has two advantages in the context of III 1: (a) it reduces the inconsistency between 1111a22–24 and the remainder of the chapter to the bare minimum: that in 1111a22–24, which has no reference to regret, there is no third category of the non-intentional actions defined by absence of regret (1110b22–24). Indeed, acts done through ignorance without regret are paradigm cases of the unintentional in 1111a22–24. This degree of inconsistency seems unavoidable on any account which takes regret as a criterion of the unintentional in the remainder of III; (b) the use of the paradigm case method appears to articulate the development of Aristotle's thought throughout III 1. He begins his account of 'the intentional' with acts done knowingly and wanted per se by the agent (1110a9–10; 15–21). Mixed acts present a difficulty,

---

[7] I assume that 1111a1–21 is concerned with actions done in ignorance as well as those done through ignorance since the actions are classified as those of an ignorant man (1110b25; 1111a2) in both contexts.

[8] See note 5 above.

and Aristotle asks: 'do they resemble intentional more than unintentional acts (1110a11–12)?' He concludes that they do (1110b6–7), and thus offers an altered account of intentional action which does not require that the act is wanted *per se* (1111a22–24). Similarly, he begins his account of the unintentional with one paradigm: acts done through ignorance with regret.[9] In considering acts done in ignorance, he concludes that regret is not necessary for unintentionality and that acts done in ignorance through passion may be classified as unintentional (1111a1–2). Thus in stating his conclusion in 1111a22–24, he omits 'regret' from the paradigm of unintentional action, but maintains 'through ignorance' as the central case – while at the same time giving a more complete account of the intentional which amounts to necessary and sufficient conditions.[10]

This third proposal seems preferable to the other two as it involves less inconsistency within III 1. However, since each of the three proposals avoids the degree of inconsistency involved in taking acts done in ignorance through passion as intentional in 1111a22–24, we may conclude that neither within III 1–5 nor V 8 is there any basis for taking acts of this type as intentional. Therefore, there is no ground for interpreting Aristotle's analysis of *hekousion* (in so far as it applies to actions) as other than of intentional actions in these passages.

[9] If Aristotle took the presence of regret to indicate that the agent wanted not to do acts of the type he actually performed through ignorance, this case might constitute an opposed paradigm to his introductory treatment:

The intentional:	*The unintentional:*
S does *x* and S wants to do *x*;	S does *x* and S wants not to do *x*

But since his treatment of the intentional had to be modified to include mixed acts which the agent did not want *per se* to do, his final account of the intentional excludes reference to wanting *per se* (1111a22–24). If so, he had reason to drop reference to wanting *per se* from his paradigm of the unintentional in 1111a21, and hence to leave out reference to regret in his final account of the unintentional. Thus the tension between 1110b18–111a21 and 1111a22 may be explained by the evolution of Aristotle's thought in III 1 on the importance of wanting *per se* in the definition of the intentional and the unintentional; in 1111a22 he realised that he should delete reference to regret from his account of the unintentional to match his earlier deletion of wanting *per se* from the definition of the intentional (1110a16ff., b5–8).

[10] Aristotle employs central cases in giving an account of 'good' in 1096b25–27 where other cases may be called good because they are derived from this central core of examples. Aristotle used this methodology elsewhere in the *Nicomachean Ethics*: see, for example, his discussion of the good of man (1098a16–18) and *theôria* (1178b29–32). This (together with the consistency of III 1–5 and V 8) has implications for the dating of *NE* and Common Books: see Owen, 1965.

Aristotle on practical reasoning: vocabulary and concepts

Part A: Practical syllogisms, truth, goodness and validity

1. *Practical syllogisms*

(a) *Examples*

(1) *Rule-case*		(2) *Means-ends*
434a16–21	1142a20–23	701a16–17
701a14–15	1144a29–34	701a17–21
701a15–16	1147a5–7	1032b6–9
701a32–3	1147a29–30	1032b15–21
	1147a31–34	1142b22–26

Rule – case reasoning
ψ'ing is in general good
φ'ing is a case of ψ'ing
_____
φ'ing is good (has good quality)

Means – ends reasoning
ψ'ing is good
φ'ing is a way to ψ
_____
φ'ing is good (has a good quality)

or (more schematically)

DES.p
AS.p→q
_____
DES.q

DES.p
AS.q→p
_____
DES.q

2. *Truth and goodness*

(i) The reasoning has to be true: 1139a24, 30; 1142a20–23; 1142b22–26.
(ii) The conclusion is an opinion: 1147b9 (1112a5–7)

For Aristotle, in the syllogism the conclusion necessarily follows from the premises, and holds true because each of the premises hold true (24b18–20: cf. Barnes: 1981)

(iii) The premises state that a given course is good: 701a22–24: one kind involves the good (i.e. major premiss)

(iv) Conclusions state that a given action (type) is good 1111b34 (1112a7–8); 1141b10–13.

If there are major premises which do not explicitly involve the good (e.g. 701a16–17, 17–18, 29–31; 434a16–21) they should be translated into sentences using the good or bad (1144a29–34; 1142a20–23) to be in the canonical form for the practical syllogism (701a22–24):

3. *Validity*

If the reasoning is truth-based and fulfils the conditions for being a syllogism (24b18–20) Aristotle has to explain for the validity of Means-ends reasoning:

DES.p
AS.q→p
———
DES.q

as this does not appear to be deductively valid (see Kenny, 1975, 70ff.). Desire seems to explain the relevant necessity: if one desires to ψ, and believes that φ'ing is a way to ψ (all else being equal), one desires to φ. If desire is a mode of accepting these propositions (which takes the place of thought: 701a31ff.) the propositions thus accepted stand connected in a way which explains how the conclusion is validly inferred from the premises. Without this principle of desire (and relying only on belief) the validity of Means-ends reasoning (within Aristotle's deductive account) remains obscure. That desire thus construed as a propositional attitude can play this role in explaining validity supports its attribution to Aristotle (see Chapter 2, Section C, Chapter 5, Section C, D).

Part B: Syllogistic vocabulary: terms, propositions, conclusions

1. *Terms and propositions in the syllogism*

In syllogisms of the form:

(1) B belongs to A	or	A's are B
(2) A belongs to C		C is an A
(3) B belongs to C		C is B

A is the middle term, B the first term and C the final term. (This is neutral as to the specificity of the final term).
References: First term: 26a2, 5, 10 etc.
        Middle Term: 25b33; 47a35–38; 71a22; 93a33ff., b11–13; 98b23 etc.
        Final Term: 25b33; 26a10; 71a23 etc.
Syllogistic vocabulary of this form is used in discussing practical syllogisms in the following contexts:
        First Term: 1143a36–b3 (cf. 1142a26).
        Middle Term: 1142b24.
        Final term: 1142a26–27; 1143a35–b4; 1147b14.
Sensitivity to Aristotle's quasi-technical usage of 'final term' for a given term

in a syllogism yields a clear reading of the role of *nous* in grasping the final term and minor premiss in 1143b2 (see Chapter 3, Section C).

(1) is described as the *general proposition* (Protasis): 1147a1–3; a25; 434a16–18; 1142a20–23 (see also 24a17; 25a4) and (2) as the *other proposition*: 1143b3; 701a26 (see also 41b28; 1201b25ff). Awareness of Aristotle's use of these terms affects one's understanding of 1147a25–26 and b9–11 (see Chapter 3, Section B, especially fn. 13.)

2. *Specificity of terms in the syllogism*

In 1143a32–33, Aristotle uses '*ta kath' hekasta*' as well as '*ta eschata*'. Both may mean (when *eschaton* is not joined to *horos* (e.g.) 1017b24, 1059b26)

| either | (a) individual | vs. | universal |
| or | (b) specific | vs. | general |

| *individual* | *specific* |
| 1017b24 | 1059b26 |

(See Barnes (*Post. An.* p. 91) and Zabarella, Commentary, 664a) It is not clear, therefore, whether Aristotle allows for actions to be designated as particulars (individuals) before the action has occurred or not. Thus, while he uses 'this' to designate actions within the process of practical reasoning (434a19; 701a23–24; 1032b19–21) pre-action, it is not clear that he had decided between the following two views: (a) all stages of deliberation are concerned with types: the most specific is the last stage, but this is not a particular; (b) certain stages of deliberation (e.g. the final stage) may refer to particular actions before acting, and these may figure as the final term. Neither (a) nor (b), however, is compatible with the view that Aristotle insisted on taking '*ta eschata*' as referring to act-types, and hence on their designating a stage prior to the final specification of what is to be done. For in the first account all stages pre-action concern specific act-types: in the second, '*ta eschata*' will denote particular acts. (For a contrasting view, see Cooper, 1975, 36ff.).

Part C: Specific form of practical syllogisms

1. *Aristotelian distinctions*

(a) *haplôs* vs. *pêi*: (e.g.) good vs. good in a way

49a8	75b8	1115b33
49a27, 38	116b23	1027a5
71a26	168b11–16	1030a23
		1077b16

(b) *haplôs* vs. *hôs epi to polu* : (e.g.) good vs. in general good

21a19, 31	198b6
1095a1	261b4
1148a4	

(c) *haplôs* vs. *dunamei, ex hupotheseôs*: (e.g.) good vs. potentially good, or good if

Potentially F vs. Actually F		*Ex hupotheseôs F vs. Actually F*		
208a6	305a21	30b33, 39	84a6	108b32
1002a23	100a10	72b14–16	1238b6–8	199b35
1048b5	1113a3	83b38	1293b4–6	1332a10–11

2. Application of these distinctions

If the first distinction separates 'φ is good' from 'φ has a good quality', and the second distinguishes 'φ is good' from 'φ is in general good', then it is possible that 'φ has a good quality' and that not merely 'φ is in general good' but that 'φ is not good'

Thus Aristotle could distinguish (1) 'φ is in general good', (2) 'φ has a good quality', and (3) 'φ is good'. (3) represents φ as good (taken as a whole bundle of properties, including consequential properties), and is distinct from (2). (3) does not represent φ as the best option as it is innocent of comparative judgments. Hence, two options (considered by themselves) may both be good although one is better than the other: e.g. two chocolates with desirable flavour and no ill effects, where one is better because (e.g.) larger. Similarly, the options may both be equally good (as in Buridan's Ass cases) but neither better. Aristotle distinguished also (4) 'φ seems best',[1] and thus operated with three possible specific conclusions: (2) 'φ has a good quality', (3) 'φ is good', (4) 'φ seems best'. What Aristotle needed was a route from (1) to (2) (cf. 1374a32–36), and from (2) and (3) to (4) (cf. 1139a32, b4–5; 434a5–12).

---

[1] 'φ seems best' is preferable as it emphasises the role of imagination (434a7) and the epistemic limitation implicit in some of the conclusions (*a* is to be done). Similar grounds should lead Aristotle to represent (3) as 'φ seems good'.

Bibliography

Commentaries

Analytics

Barnes, J. (1975) *Aristotle's Posterior Analytics*, Oxford
Ross, D. (1949) *Prior and Posterior Analytics*, Oxford
Zabarella, J. (1582) *In duos Aristotelis libros Post. An. commentaria*, Venice

de Anima, Parva Naturalia, de Motu Animalium

Hamlyn, D. W. (1968) *Aristotle's De Anima II, III*, Oxford
Hicks, R. D. (1907) *Aristotle. De Anima*, Cambridge
Nussbaum, M. (1978) *De Motu Animalium*, Princeton
Rodier, G. (1900) *Aristôte, Traité de l'Ame*, Paris
Ross, D. (1961) *De Anima*, Oxford
          (1955) *Parva Naturalia*, Oxford

Eudemian Ethics

Dirlmeier, F. (1962) *Eudemische Ethik*, Berlin

Nicomachean Ethics (including common books)

Burnet, J. (1900) *Ethics of Aristotle*, London
Gauthier, R. A. & Jolif, J. A. (1959) *L'Ethique à Nicomaque*, Louvain
Grant, A. (1858) *Ethics of Aristotle*, London
Greenwood, L. H. G. (1909) *Aristotle. Nicomachean Ethics VI* (reprinted by Arnos Press, New York, 1973)
Joachim, H. H. (1951) *The Nicomachean Ethics*, Oxford
Ramsauer, G. (1878) *Aristotelis Ethica Nicomachea*, Leipzig
Stewart, J. A. (1892) *Notes on the Nicomachean Ethics*, Oxford

Physics

Charlton, W. (1970) *Physics I, II*, Oxford
Hussey, E. (1983) *Physics III, IV*, Oxford
Pacius, J. (1596) *Aristotelis Naturalis Auscultationis*, Frankfurt
Ross, D. (1936) *Physics*, Oxford
Zabarella, J. (1590) *In tertium Aristotelis Physicorum librum commentaria*, Cologne

Articles, Books

Ackrill, J. L. (1965) 'Aristotle's distinction between *energeia* and *kinêsis*', *New Essays on Plato and Aristotle*, ed. R. Bamborough, London

— (1972/3) 'Aristotle's definition of *psuchê*', *Proceedings of the Aristotelian Society*

— (1973) 'Aristotle on "good" and the Categories', *Islamic Philosophy and the Classical Tradition: essays presented to R. Waltzer*, ed. Stern, Oxford

— (1974) 'Aristotle on *eudaimonia*', *Proceedings of the British Academy*

— (1978) 'Aristotle on action', *Mind*

Allan, D. J. (1953) 'Aristotle's account of the origin of moral principles', *Actes du XIeme Congres Internationale de Philosophie*, vol. XII

— (1955) 'The practical syllogism', *Autour d' Aristôte*, Louvain

Ando, T. (1958) *Aristotle's Theory of Practical Cognition*, Tokyo

Annas, J. E. (1977/8) 'Basic acts', *Proceedings of the Aristotelian Society*

— (1978) *Aristotle on Inefficient Causation*, Triennial Conference, Cambridge

— (1983) 'Aristotle on inefficient causes', *Philosophical Quarterly.*

Anscombe, G. E. M. (1957) *Intention*, Oxford

— (1965) 'Thought and action in Aristotle', *Essays on Plato and Aristotle*, ed. R. Bamborough, London

— (1969) 'Causality and extensionality', *Journal of Philosophy*

— (1971) *Causality and Determination*, Cambridge

Armstrong, D. (1973) 'Acting and trying', *Philosophical Papers*

Baier, A. (1971) 'The search for basic actions', *American Philosophical Quarterly*

Balme, D. M. (1962) '*Genos* and *eidos* in Aristotle's biology', *Classical Quarterly*

— (1965) *Aristotle's Use of Teleological Explanation*, London

Barnes, J. (1969) 'Aristotle's theory of demonstration', *Phronesis*

— (1971/2) 'Aristotle's concept of mind', *Proceedings of the Aristotelian Society*

— (1981) 'Proof and the syllogism', *Symposium Aristotelicum*, ed. Berti

Bogen, J. (1974) 'Comment on Moravcsik', *Synthèse*

Brand, M. (1976) 'Particulars, events and actions', *Action Theory*, ed. Brand & Walton, Amsterdam

Bratman, M. (1974) Acrasia, Rockerfeller University PhD thesis

— (1979) 'Practical reasoning and weakness of the will', *Nous*

Brentano, F. (1867) *The Psychology of Aristotle*, Mainz

Burnyeat, M. (1981) 'Aristotle on learning to be good', *Essays on Aristotle's Ethics*, ed. A. Rorty

Charles, D. (1979) Review of Kenny's *Aristotelian Ethics, Journal of Hellenic Studies*

— (1980) Review of Kenny's *Aristotle's Theory of the Will, Classical Review*

— (1981) Review of Lear's *Aristotle and Logical Theory, Classical Review*

— (1982/3) 'Rationality and irrationality', *Proceedings of the Aristotelian Society*

— (forthcoming a) 'Ontology and Moral Reasoning in Aristotle'

— (forthcoming b) 'Aristotle on the Form of Teleological Explanation'

Chisholm, R. M. (1966) 'Freedom and action', *Freedom and Determinism*, ed. K. Lehrer, New York

— (1970) 'Structure of intention', *Journal of Philosophy*

— (1976a) *Person and Object*, London

— (1976b) 'The agent as cause', *Action Theory*, ed. Brand & Walton, Amsterdam

Chomsky, N. (1970) 'Remarks on nominalisation', *Readings in English Transformational Grammar*, ed. Jacobs & Rosenbaum, Toronto.

Cooper, J. M. (1975) *Reason and Human Good in Aristotle*, Harvard
— (1981) Review of Kenny's *Aristotelian Ethics, Nous*.
de Ste Croix, G. E. M. (1975) 'Aristotle on history and poetry', *Ancient Historian and his Materials*, ed. B. Levick, Farnborough
Cummins, R. & Gottlieb, D. (1972) 'An argument for truth functionality', *American Philosophical Quarterly*
Danto, A. C. (1965) 'Basic actions', *American Philosophical Quarterly*
— (1976) 'Action, knowledge and representation', *Action Theory*, ed. Brand & Walton, Amsterdam
Davidson, D. (1980) *Actions and Events*, Oxford
— (1982) 'Paradoxes of irrationality', *Essays on Freud*, ed. Wollheim & Hopkins, Cambridge
Davies, M. K. (1983) 'Function in perception', *Australasian Journal of Philosophy*
Dennett, D. (1969) *Content and Consciousness*, London
— (1978) *Brainstorms*, London
— (1979) 'Three kinds of intentional psychology' *Thyssen Foundation Philosophy Group*, ed. Healey
Dostoyevsky, F. (1864) *Notes from the Underground*
Ebert, Th. (1976) '*Praxis* and *poiêsis*', *Zeitschrift für philosophische Forschung*
Evans, G. (1976) 'Logical form and semantic structure', *Truth and Meaning*, ed. Evans & McDowell, Oxford
Field, H. (1978) 'Mental representation', *Erkenntnis*
Fodor, J. A. (1976) *Language of Thought*, London
— (1978) 'Propositional attitudes', *Monist*
Fortenbaugh, W. (1969) 'Aristotle: emotion and moral virtue', *Arethusa*
— (1975) *Aristotle on Emotion*, London
Frankfurt, H. (1969) 'Alternate possibilities and moral responsibility', *Journal of Philosophy*
Furley, D. J. (1978) 'Self-movers', *Symposium Aristotelicum*, ed. Lloyd & Owen
Gill, M. L. (1980) 'Aristotle on causal action', *Phronesis*
Glover, J. (1970) *Responsibility*, London
Goldman, A. (1970) *A Theory of Human Action*, New Jersey.
— (1976) 'Discrimination and perceptual knowledge', *Journal of Philosophy*
Goodman, N. (1970) 'Comments', *Journal of Philosophy*
Gotthelf, A. (1976) 'Aristotle's conception of final causality', *Review of Metaphysics*
Grice, H. P. (1975) 'Method in philosophical psychology', *American Philosophical Association*
Hardie, W. F. R. (1968) *Aristotle's Ethical Theory*, Oxford
Hartman, E. (1977) *Substance, Body and Soul*, Princeton
Hempel, C. G. (1965) *Aspects of Scientific Explanation*, London
Hintikka, J. (1973a) 'Remarks on *praxis*, *poiêsis* and *ergon* in Plato and Aristotle', *Annales Universitatis Turkuensis Sarja*, Series B Osa-Tom, 126
— (1973b) *Time and Necessity*, Oxford
— (1974) 'Practical and theoretical reasoning', *Practical Reason*, ed. S. Korner, Oxford
Hinton, G. E. & Anderson, J. A. (1981) *Parallel Models of Associative Memory*, New Jersey
Hocutt, M. O. (1974) 'Aristotle's four becauses', *Philosophy*

Hornsby, J. (1980) *Actions*, London

Irwin, T. (1975) 'Aristotle on reason, desire and virtue', *Journal of Philosophy*
— (1978) 'First principles in Aristotle's Ethics', *Mid-West Studies in Philosophy* III

Kenny, A. (1963) *Action, Emotion and Will*, London
— (1966a) 'The practical syllogism and incontinence', *Phronesis*
— (1966b) 'Intention and purpose', *Journal of Philosophy*
— (1975) *Will, Freedom and Power*, Oxford
— (1978) *The Aristotelian Ethics*, Oxford
— (1979) *Aristotle's Theory of the Will*, London

Kim, J. (1970) 'Events and their descriptions', *Essays in Honor of C. G. Hempel*, ed. Rescher, Amsterdam
— (1971) 'Causes and events: Mackie on causation', *Journal of Philosophy*
— (1973) 'Causation, nomic subsumption and the concept of an event', *Journal of Philosophy*
— (1976) 'Events as property exemplifications', *Action Theory*, ed. Brand & Walton, Amsterdam

Kosman, L. A. (1969) 'Aristotle's definition of motion', *Phronesis*

Lear, J. (1980) *Aristotle and Logical Theory*, Cambridge

Lennon, K. (1982) Intentional Explanation, Oxford DPhil thesis
— (forthcoming) *Explaining Human Behaviour*, London

Lewis, D. (1966) 'An argument for the identity theory', *Journal of Philosophy*
— (1972) 'Psychophysical and theoretical identifications', *Australasian Journal of Philosophy*

Loar, B. (1981) *Mind and Meaning*, Cambridge

Loening, R. (1903) *Die Zurechnungslehre des Aristotelis*, Jena

Lukasiewicz, J. (1951) *Aristotle's Syllogistic from the Standpoint of Modern Formal Logic*, Oxford

Lycan, W. (1974) 'The extensionality of cause, space and time', *Mind*

Lyons, W. (1980) *Emotion*, Cambridge

Mackie, J. L. (1974) *The Cement of the Universe*, Oxford

Martin, R. M. (1971) *Language, Logic and Metaphysics*, New York

McCawley, J. (1968) 'Lexical insertion in a transformational grammar without deep structure', *Papers of the Chicago Linguistics Society*

McDowell, J. H. (1978) 'Are moral requirements hypothetical imperatives?', *Proceedings of Aristotelian Society*: Supplementary Volume
— (1979) 'Virtue and reason', *Monist*
— (1980) 'Role of *eudaimonia* in Aristotle's Ethics', *Proceedings of the African Classical Association*

McGinn, C. (1977/8) 'Mental states, natural kinds and psychophysical laws', *Proceedings of Aristotelian Society*: Supplementary Volume
— (1980/1) 'Philosophical materialism', *Synthese*

Mignucci, M. (1981) '*hôs epi to polu* et nécessaire dans la conception aristotélicienne de la science', *Symposium Aristotelicum*

Miller, F. Jr (1973) 'Did Aristotle have the concept of identity?', *Philosophical Review*
— (1975) 'Actions and Results', *Philosophical Quarterly*

Milo, R. D. (1966) *Aristotle on Practical Knowledge and Weakness of the Will*, The Hague

Monan, J. D. (1968) *Moral Knowledge and its Methodology in Aristotle*, Oxford

Moravcsik, J. M. E. (1974) 'Aristotle on adequate explanations', *Synthese*

— (1975) '*Aitia* as generative factor in Aristotle's philosophy', *Dialogue*
Nagel, T. (1965) 'Physicalism', *Philosophical Review*
— (1975) *Possibility of altruism*, Oxford
O'Shaughnessy, B. (1973) 'Trying', *Journal of Philosophy*
Owen, D. W. D. 'On Kim's theory of events' (unpublished paper)
Owen, G. E. L. (1961) '*Tithenai ta phainomena*', *Aristôte et les problèmes de la méthode*, ed. S. Mansion, Louvain
— (1965) 'The Platonism of Aristotle', *Proceedings of the British Academy*
— (1971/2) 'Aristotelian pleasures', *Proceedings of the Aristotelian Society*
Parry, R. (1974) 'Agent's knowledge of one's own actions', *Personalist*
Peacocke, C. A. B. (1979) *Holistic Explanation*, Oxford
— (1981) 'Intention and acrasia', *Essays in Honor of Donald Davidson*, ed. M. Hintikka & B. Vermazen, Los Angeles
Pears, D. F. (1971) 'Two problems for reasons for action', *Agent, Action and Reason*, ed. Binkley, Bronaugh & Marras, Toronto
— (1975a) *Questions in the Philosophy of Mind*, London
— (1975b) 'Internal deviant causal chains', *Critica*
— (1978) 'Aristotle on courage', *Mid-West Studies in Philosophy* III
— (1981) 'Intention and belief', *Essays in Honor of Donald Davidson*, ed. M. Hintikka & B. Vermazen, Los Angeles
Penner, T. (1971) 'Verbs and identity of actions: a philosophical exercise in the interpretation of Aristotle', *Ryle*, ed. O. P. Wood & G. Pitcher, London
Putnam, H. (1970) 'On properties', *Essays in Honor of C. G. Hempel*, ed. Rescher, Amsterdam
— (1980) *Mind, Language and Reality*, Collected papers I & II, Cambridge
Robinson, H. (1978) 'Mind and body in Aristotle', *Classical Review*
Robinson, R. (1969) 'Aristotle on acrasia', *Essays on Greek Philosophy*, Oxford
Rorty, A. (1970) 'Plato and Aristotle on belief, habit and akrasia', *American Philosophical Quarterly*
— (1974) 'Pleasure in Aristotle's Ethics', *Mind*
Ross, D. (1939) *Foundations of Ethics*, Oxford
Rowe, C. J. (1983) 'de Aristotelis in tribus libris Ethicorum dicendi ratione', *Liverpool Classical Monthly*
Santas, G. (1970) 'Aristotle on practical inference, the explanation of action and akrasia', *Phronesis*
Schank, R. C. & Colby, K. H. (1973) *Computer Models of Thought and Language*, London
Siegler, F. A. (1968) 'Voluntary and involuntary', *Monist*
Slote, M. (1975) *Metaphysics and Essence*, Oxford
Smith, M. (1983) 'Actions, attempts and internal events', *Analysis*
Sorabji, R. (1969) 'Aristotle and Oxford philosophy', *American Philosophical Quarterly*
— (1974) 'Body and soul in Aristotle', *Philosophy*
— (1980) *Necessity, Cause and Blame*, London
Stoutland, F. (1968) 'Basic actions and causality', *Journal of Philosophy*
— (1970) 'Logical connection argument', *American Philosophical Quarterly*
— (1976) 'Causation of behaviour', *Essays on Wittgenstein in Honour of G. H. Von Wright*, Amsterdam
— (1980) 'Oblique causation and reasons for action', *Synthese*, vol. 43
Strawson, P. F. (1959) *Individuals*, London
— (1974) *Freedom and Resentment*, London

Taylor, B. M. (1974) Facts and Adverbial Modification, Oxford DPhil thesis
— (1976) 'States of affairs', *Truth and Meaning*, ed. Evans & McDowell, Oxford
— (1977) 'Tense and continuity', *Linguistics and Philosophy*
Taylor, C. C. W. (1965/6) 'States, activities and performances', *Proceedings of the Aristotelian Society*
Teichmuller, G. (1879) *Die praktische Vernunft bei Aristoteles*, Gotha
Thalberg, I. (1972) *Enigmas of Agency*, London
— (1977a) *Perception, Emotion and Action*, Oxford
— (1977b) 'How does agent causality work?', *Action Theory*, ed. Brand & Walton, Amsterdam
— (1977/8) 'The irreducibility of events', *Analysis*
Thomson, J. J. (1977) *Acts and Other Events*, New York
Urmson, J. O. (1968) 'Aristotle on pleasure', *Aristotle*, ed. Moravcsik, London
— (1973) 'Aristotle's doctrine of the mean', *American Philosophical Quarterly*
Vendler, Z. (1967) *Linguistics in Philosophy*, New York
von Wright, G. H. (1963) *Norm and Action*, London
— (1971) *Explanation and Understanding*, London
— (1972) *Essay in Deontic Logic and the General Theory of Action*, Amsterdam
— (1979) 'On so-called practical inference', *Practical Reasoning*, ed. Raz, Oxford
Walsh, J. J. (1963) *Aristotle's Conception of Moral Weakness*, New York
Walter, J. (1876) *Die Lehre von der praktischen Vernunft in der griechischen Philosophie*, Jena.
Waterlow, S. (1982a) *Nature, Change and Agency in Aristotle's Physics*, Oxford
— (1982b) *Passage and Possibility*, Oxford
White, N. P. (1971) 'Aristotle on sameness and oneness', *Philosophical Review*
Wieland, W. (1970) *Die Aristotelische Physik*, Gottingen
— (1975) 'The problem of teleology', *Articles on Aristotle* I, ed. Barnes, Schofield & Sorabji, London
Wiggins, D. (1967) *Identity and Spatio-Temporal Continuity*, Oxford
— (1975/6) 'Deliberation and practical reason', *Proceedings of the Aristotelian Society*
— (1976) 'Truth, invention and the meaning of life', *Proceedings of the British Academy*
— (1978/9) 'Weakness of the will, commensurability and the objects of deliberation and desire', *Proceedings of the Aristotelian Society*
— (1981) *Sameness and Substance*, Oxford
Wilkes, K. (1978) *Physicalism*, London
Wilson, N. L. (1974) 'Facts, events and their identity conditions', *Philosophical Studies*
Winograd, T. (1972) *Understanding Natural Language*, New York
Wittgenstein, L. (1967) *Zettel*, Oxford
Woodfield, A. (1976) *Teleology*, Cambridge
Zeller, E. (1960) *Outlines of Greek Philosophy* (13th Ed.), New York

Indexes

Index locorum

Index of names

General index